HOMER'S ODYSSEY/IDIOCY
(World Famous in New Zealand)

THE BEST BITS

By John Dybvig

TO MANISH (AKA-RAY ROMANO)
MAN - I LOVE YOUR ENERGY
GREAT MEETING YOU AND TINA
AT LOMANI.... !!!
ALL THE BEST
John T. Dybvig
(JANUARY 20 23)

ISBN: 9798705687251

Also by John Dybvig:

Technical Foul (with Tom Hyde)

Fastbreak (with Joseph Romanos)

John Dybvig on Basketball (with Joseph Romanos)

Microphones Up My Nose (with Ray Lillis)

Gullible's Travels

The Two of Me

Cupertino High School
Fremont Union High School District
Sunnyvale-Cupertino, California

 his Certifies that **John Thomas Dybvig** has completed the Course of Study prescribed for this School and is therefore granted this Diploma of Graduation

Given in the month of June, one thousand nine hundred and sixty-seven.

Lawrence E. Didier
President Board of Trustees

Charles D. Pond
Vice-President Board of Trustees

Helene Madson
Clerk Board of Trustees

Howard G. Diesner MD
Member Board of Trustees

Earl A. Goodell
Acting Superintendent

George Finnning
Principal

Howard H Wyant
Member Board of Trustees

I never missed one day of high school in four years... not one not a single day... day in and day out I was there, and yet they couldn't even manage to spell my last name correctly on my Cupertino High School diploma - Dybvig came out Dyvbig.

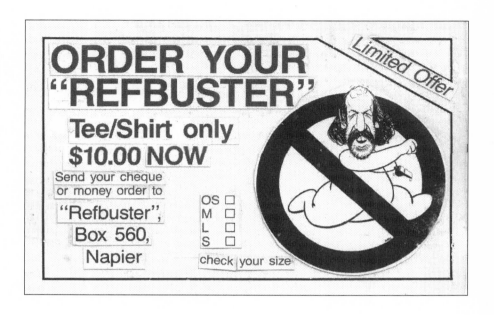

Do ya think I pissed off the referees of New Zealand!?!

A sign of the times.

'

Author's Note

Wow! Wow! Wow! I came to New Zealand to do one thing and one thing only - to coach some basketball... hoops, round ball, slammin' and jammin' and shooting the J - gawd I'm so American. That was it. That's all I wanted to do. I was to be the basketball director for the town of Napier for 18 months. After that I'd be back in the States sucking down chili dogs and drinking 40-ounce Big Gulp cokes. But it wasn't meant to be... fate had other ideas for the direction my life was about to take. I arrived full of enthusiasm and naivety on January 17, 1980... so on January 17, 2020 I celebrated living and working in New Zealand for 40 years. Like I said: Wow!

In honour of that I've put together this book of that time in the various areas (as it turned out it wasn't all about basketball - I ended up being a television sports commentator/radio sports show host/ radio contributor and radio talkback host/writer/actor/accent coach and a house husband) where I've floundered and sometimes succeeded. This book is written in the form of the 'best bits'. There's no filler material here about what a cute kid I was growing up - un huh - this immediately gets down to what Sergeant Joe Friday from that old television show 'Dragnet' would say in his totally deadpan expression every week:

"Just the facts, ma'am."

So, yeah, we're getting down to 'the nitty and the gritty' here... just the best bits. If it seems to you that I've concentrated more on my foibles and failings than successes, it's because that's what I find interesting. The obstacle course is much more fun than the primrose path. So, if books are supposed to be portentous, well, I've certainly kicked the shit out of that one.

This is me on a plate in a book. Warts and all.

Comments Note

Throughout the book after some stories I make a personal comment on that story about how I felt or the circumstances surrounding said story. These are just some additional personal thoughts about any given situation that appears in the book. These comments are me doing voice/overs in the best tradition of what Tom Selleck did in my favorite television series Magnum P.I. only my voice/overs are in print.

Grammar Note

Grammar is the study of words, how they are used in sentences, and how they change in different situations. I bring this up because in this book there's all kinds of grammar exploding throughout the following pages. I drift between two different cultures. I carry two passports - I'm a citizen of both New Zealand and America - colliding worlds. Sometimes I spell the American way and then at other times I'm spelling the English way, I do both unconsciously, it just happens. At times I'm talking to an American audience and at other times to a New Zealand audience. Then there are the times when I'm talking to no one in particular. And sometimes I'm just talking to myself. But, hey that's me that's who I am at times I'm neither here nor there. But, please don't get yourself into a flap because whatever shape the grammar takes you'll still get the message.

Comment: But more to the point here about getting the message no matter the circumstances or grammatical purity of the situation... back in the day for me television commentary... hell life itself was all about emotion and passion and just being involved and having some fun... being creative and definitely not about being dull and bland and technically correct in your presentation. When I was working at Sky television I would sometimes just make up words when doing my commentary describing the action. My director would immediately be in my ear piece yelling at me: "That's not a word, John." And I would always reply - "No big deal bucko... the audience will get the point that I'm conveying and the description behind my made-up words." Believe me there's more than one way to skin a cat... people aren't dumb... if you're passionately engaged in whatever you're doing people will one way or another get the message. You don't always have to go down the straight and narrow path. If you don't believe me then go back and re-read Dr. Seuss.

Swearing Note

This is a word of warning before you delve too deep into this book. I have a wee confession to make... an obvious one to anyone who knows me: I swear:

Big fucking deal... right!?!

Or as comedian Billy Connolly would sometimes say at the beginning of his comedy routines: "If you don't like it - then you can just fuck off!" I used to use that bit when I was on the rubber chicken circuit myself and it always got a few laughs. But seriously if you're easily offended please take Billy's advice... thanks...

Comment: When I was an assistant basketball coach at Gonzaga University, a Jesuit school, I use to play a lot of tennis with Father Carrol. I thought of myself as a pretty handy tennis player in those days but Father Carrol was a lot handier... he used to kick my butt every time and wow did I get frustrated. It must have showed because one day in between sets when Father Carrol was once again killing me on the court he called me up to the net and in that fatherly way Priests have of communicating told me that he could tell I was getting pretty frustrated and really wanted to swear and that it was okay... "Go ahead and let it out John." So there ya go I was given the go ahead by a man of the cloth to swear... so I rest my case.

CONTENTS

INTRODUCTION

Hi how ya doin'? My name is John Dybvig.

I'm from San Francisco.

Yeah, that's DYBVIG: D as in David... Y... B as in boy... V as in Victor... IG... DYBVIG.

How'd you like to be stuck with that moniker? I feel bad for my kids because I know I've sentenced them to a life-long spelling bee. If I had a dollar for every time I've spelled my name I'd be rolling in clover. I never missed a day of high school in four years, but my last name is misspelled (Dyvbig) on my high school diploma. They misspelled my son's last name on his very first day of school, everything's so much more instant today. They even got it wrong on my King Kong manuscript.

It's Norwegian. It means 'deep fiord' in Norway.

But, as for me I'm one hundred percent American and then some.

I'm loud, aggressive when I need to be and my Heroes are John Wayne and Buddy Holly.

I'm just your average Joe Blow who grew up in a California suburb - you know where it takes about a thirty-minute car ride to escape your neighbourhood.

I'm an ex-basketball coach who one day did what a lot of people dream about. I went down to the corner store for a pack of cigarettes and never came back.

I disappeared...

I vanished in a puff of smoke...

Only kidding ... about the cigarettes. I don't smoke. But I did leave. I left to start a new life, one of my many crazy lives, on a journey that's taken me around the world to work for everyone from the Mob to Oscar-winning film director Sir Peter Jackson.

It all started on a balmy late January afternoon - 1980. A day I will remember forever. A day an actor became President. Ronald Reagan was making his entrance and I was making my exit. I was living in Spokane, Washington, at the time and was heading for California. Along the way I fell down my own private rabbit hole much the way Alice did. My wonderland was at the ass end of the world. A place sitting in total isolation on the outer fringe of the South West Pacific. A country so quiet even Perry Como would have been considered loud there.

I landed in a place called New Zealand where I had a torrid affair with a gorgeous native girl and accidentally got caught up in one of those grand adventures that you read about in books. Only in this case it actually happened - to me!

Okay, so becoming an actor who would appear in films alongside such greats as Tom Selleck, Christopher Lloyd, John Hurt, Ron Silver, Lucy Lawless and Jack Black wasn't part of the initial plan. But my life didn't have a plan in those days. You certainly don't plan on stumbling across Salman Rushdie while walking down to your local bakery or breaking the O.J. Simpson murder-chase live to the nation. You don't plan on running off to the South Seas paradise of New Zealand. Remember this is the New Zealand before it entered the world stage as the home base of 'Lord of the Rings', 'The Last Samurai', 'Hercules', 'Xena' and 'King Kong', before it became world renown as "Middle Earth."

New Zealand is such a small place that it affords you the opportunity to do a multitude of things if you've got the gumption to go for the brass ring. I discovered that I possessed plenty of gumption. When I arrived, my once sane middle- class American life took an oblique left into another dimension and became a side circus freak show. I often felt like I was the lead character in a lost episode of Rod Serling's Twilight Zone forty years after it went off-air.

I actually became a living, breathing modern day Walter Mitty. I suddenly had the opportunity to do so many things I'd only dreamt of doing as a child. For instance, I used to fantasize about being John McKay on ABC's Wide World of Sport when I was in high school. Later I wanted to emulate John Madden and who wouldn't big John was having loads of fun. And I just loved reading witty opinionated newspaper sports columns that made you laugh out loud and thought what a 'neat' job that'd be, and how about this for a walloppuloser - like a lot of kids I used to dream about being a Big Time professional wrestling commentator.

But I was an American nobody floundering around at the bottom end of the world, in New Zealand of all places, so fat chance. As it turned out I was exactly in the right place at the right time to fulfill all those dreams. When I arrived I was an oddity. You wanna laugh, then introduce an American to the anal New Zealand culture. I bungled my way thru New Zealand with perseverance and a strong sense of self. Homer Simpson and I have a lot in common. Doh!

Technically I may be an ex-patriot. But I take extreme exception to the term ex-pat. I have never stopped being pat. I am very patriotic and very American. New Zealand has been great to me but that is largely because I have been so true to America. It creates friction. And friction is interesting.

Comment One: Ah ha... I just made up a word towards the end of my Introduction... and it's a beauty as far as I'm concerned and perfectly explains what I'm trying to say: 'Walloppuloser' is definitely not a word... but it fully describes what I'm trying to say about being a Big Time wrestling commentator... for those who still don't get it... in this instance when I say:

"and how about this for a walloppuloser - like a lot of kids I used to dream about being a Big Time professional wrestling commentator."

So when I say 'walloppuloser' I mean... there's no way I'm gonna get to be a Big Time wrestling commentator... I'm dreaming... fat chance... it's just not gonna happen... and you instantly get my drift... and besides 'walloppuloser' and 'wrestling' just go together.

Comment Two: Thank the Lord that you're holding this book... for a time I was convinced that this was going to be the 'never ending story'... I actually finished writing this book over a dozen times... but it never seemed to be completely done there always seemed to be one more story to tell... so then one day I just put my foot down and declared to no one in particular - that's it... it's done... finito... no more... so congratulations to me and congratulations to you... I've finished it and now you're reading it... so enjoy.

Part One

I'M LOUD, AGGRESSIVE WHEN I NEED TO BE AND MY HEROES ARE JOHN WAYNE AND BUDDY HOLLY

CHAPTER ONE

HOW TO SURVIVE TRAVEL AS A LOUD AMERICAN.
John Dybvig learns his booming voice and forthright views immediately set him apart as a world traveler.

World Famous

I became world famous in New Zealand for swearing. Television New Zealand poked one of their microphones into my huddle during a live televised basketball game just as I screamed:

"SHOOT THE FUCKING BALL!"

That statement made headlines and not in small type, but: "The Ugly American."

A friend of mine actually congratulated me on that story. He told me that it was the first-time basketball had made the main section of the paper. And even in this backwater that kind of publicity meant doing the chat show circuit. When I arrived at Television New Zealand's studios I was ushered down into the green room. All television stations have a green room. I don't know how they got their name because they're never green and there's never much room. They're a holding pen where guests and performers can all be nervous together.

There's always a TV going in these rooms and the five or six other guests already in there all had their eyes glued to the screen on this particular night. There I was in full flight doing my John McEnroe routine.

It was a clip from a Saturday game where I was taking my frustrations out on any inanimate object that came to hand: the wall, the floor, a metal beam. The commentator was comparing me unfavorably to the mad monk Rasputin.

When I walked through the door you could have heard a flea fart.

'Hi. How're you guys doing?'

Silence.

Finally, one of the guests, the lead singer in a heavy metal band, spoke.

'Hey, man, we were just catching your act. I like it. What else do you do?'

'Nothing. That's my whole repertoire. I'm the scream and shout guy. It's new to New Zealand.'

Comment One: So, I had this immediate reputation as the loud mouth American basketball coach who swore on television. It got to the point where kids would run up to me on the street and shout, "Hey, there's the American!" (like I was an endangered species) and then shout, "beep...beep...beep...beep...beep!" Ya gotta laugh.

Comment Two: The guests for that show were an all-stars line-up by New Zealand standards: That night they had the hottest Australian comic at the time George Smilovici, top Kiwi comedian and all round performer Ricky May, New Zealand Ambassador to Zimbabwe Chris Laidlaw, iconic New Zealand rock band 'Shane', and Real Estate magnate Bob Jones who had just punched out journalist Rod Vaughan for interrupting his fishing trip.

I have to note here that Jones had his own private Green Room with a couple of security guards standing guard on the door. Why? Who would possibly know... maybe he thought the New Zealand Journalists Association was gathering outside the television studios to launch an attack.

Looking at that line-up ya gotta ask the question: What the hell was I doing there?

Maybe they had me down as their 'Pet American'?

Nobody can be that Loud

One time in Hawaii I was louder than the shirt I was wearing. I have some very good friends who live on Pualani Way which is just a couple of streets back off Kalakaua, the main strip in Waikiki. One day I decided to take an early morning jog. I left my friend's apartment which sits on the 24th floor of a high rise with a stunning view of the entire Waikiki strip and Kapiolani Park running up to Diamond Head and was pounding the deserted neighborhood streets with rivers of sweat running down my body when I rounded a corner and nearly smashed through some porcelain dolls. The dolls turned out to be ten of the most elderly and delicate Japanese ladies I've ever seen. They were dressed to the nines in their Sunday best including beautiful pink parasols. Startled they looked up in unison at me in total confusion. The disparity between us couldn't have been greater than if a T-Rex had stumbled upon a group of chickens.

They were lost - they had a map. They didn't speak English. I wasn't lost - I didn't have a map and I certainly didn't speak Japanese. We were at an impasse; tentatively we eyed each other up. Now isn't it funny-peculiar how loudly we speak to foreigners, like volume is going to make them understand. Towering over them and weighing considerably more than their entire group combined I completely dominated their space. I kept inching forward while they kept inching backward. I opened my mouth and literally blew them right out of the neighborhood with the intensity of my volume.

"YOU DON'T SPEAK ENGLISH!?!"

A rush of hot hair engulfed them, rustling their transparently thin candy cotton blue rinse hair as they daintily shook their tiny heads, no.

"OH! OKAY WHERE ARE YOU GOING?"

Their eyelids were now fluttering from the shock waves bombarding them. I suddenly swooped down with a meaty hairy paw and grabbed their map and bent low so I was leering, dripping sweat only inches from their petrified faces and spoke exceedingly slowly like they were idiots.

"L-O-O-K...W-H-E-R-E...DO-O-O...Y-O-U...W-A-N-T.. ...TOOOOO...GO-O-O-OH!?!"

It was like I was verbally bashing them with each word: KAPOW! BANG! WHAM! BAM! They seemed rooted to the spot arching backwards like wilting flowers in a windstorm. And then the most amazing thing occurred, this extremely ancient Japanese lady in the front deliberately placed both of her delicate bony hands, whose skin was the texture of transparent rice paper allowing you to see all of her thin blue veins running underneath it, over both of her tiny wee ears and slowly shook her head from side to side, moaning.

I stood there intently watching her and as the realization of what she was silently telling me became abundantly clear, even to an idiot like me, I did something even dumber, inexplicably I pumped up the volume even more pointing out the blinking obvious.

"OH, I'M TALKING TOO LOUDLY."

Now I've got all of them moaning and clasping their heads in agony. One of the all-time strangest and funniest sights I've ever seen. Laughing, I put my hands up in surrender and did a Marcel Marceau number waving them to follow me and silently leading them to the Waikiki strip and a hotel where there was a concierge who spoke Japanese. I still can't believe I'm that loud. I can't be that loud. Nobody can be that loud. Fade to black. Maholo.

Working Voice
I've strained my vocal cords for McDonald's McBacon Deluxe hamburgers ('It's big, but not THTHTHTHHHHHAAAAAAAT thhhhhaaaaaat BIG.'?)

I've played a piece of toast named Troy in an advertisement for Tip Top Bread. And I've sneered down my nose at Hercules star Kevin Sorbo in a Jim Beam ad.

Having a booming voice that sounds like a clogged lawn mower choking on a dog bone had its advantages.

Super-Size
Most Americans have a weight problem - me, I've got a loudness problem like fast food I tend to super-size my noise.

When I say I'm loud. I mean I'm way up there. When I go for a hearing test, I gotta declare my mouth under the section 'Have you worked around heavy machinery?' That's no joke!

I've had recording engineers put their fingers in their ears to protect their own eardrums and I ain't even miked up yet!

When working as an actor on the set of Sir Peter Jackson's Hollywood blockbuster King Kong, I accidentally created mayhem during a sound check.

While waiting to record my scene, in front of a model of New York's Empire State building, an audio technician herded all the actors with speaking parts into a cramped space beside a row of video monitors.

The technician wanted to mike up the actors and test the volume levels for when we began recording.

Not far away, Sir Peter Jackson, his partner Fran Walsh and a few others huddled over the monitors, watching them in intense silence.

The technician worked his way through the sound checks and all was fine until he got to me.

He asked me to speak at my normal level of volume for my scene. No problem.

I bellowed full force.

My words hit the air and reverberated off the walls. Sir Peter Jackson was jolted out of his chair.

Comment: I am a naturally loud person. I put it down to three things: Number one I'm an optimist in every sense of the word... always have been even when I'm down and of course we all get down at times, but even then I'm optimistic that I'll get back up soon. Number two I have enormous enthusiasm. I just get excited about stuff... any kind of stuff from the insignificant to the life changing stuff. And number three and this is the big one - I have a tremendous endless amount of 'energy'. I don't know where it comes from but I've always had it and I never seem to run out of it. So, there you go throw optimism, enthusiasm and boundless energy into one person and you get - LOUD!

Minion

For my very first acting audition I hit Mach One, I was going for the role of a minion. Not an ordinary minion, but one from hell. "The Underworld," in Hercules-speak. When I first started acting, what I lacked in technique I made up for in enthusiasm. I had boundless energy. In fact I was so fired up I broke the sound barrier with my first line. I'm not kidding. I shut the camera down. I was completely red in the face with bulging neck veins and smoke pouring from my ears when there was a meltdown in the recording system. The camera automatically shut itself off in self-protection. The casting agent had that stunned look like she had just swallowed a hot chilli. Whole! She blinked several times in utter disbelief and muttered half to me and half to herself.

"You shut the camera down."

But, the director loved all my energy and solved the loudness problem by turning my minion into a Trappist monk (vow of silence). I had no lines.

Comment: I have to confess here that I was pretty pumped that I actually shut the camera down - holy shit that's loud man, I thought to myself. This has been one of my biggest hurdles to overcome in the acting world. I'm a big guy to begin with and that coupled with my loudness means it's just too much on film - being subtle has never been my forte. But I'm working on it.

For my very first dramatic role - a role I was a finalist for best supporting actor in a drama - for one scene my American character was threatening a New Zealand politician, when the scene was completed the director instructed me to lower my voice more.

We re-shot the scene, when it finished the director yelled, "cut!" And again he instructed me to lower my voice even more and yes he asked me to do it a third time even lower. I almost balked here because it seemed to me that I was talking so low that no one would be able to hear me. But, much to my amazement when the director showed me the completed scene... wow! I could hardly believe how much power and punch and how threatening my dialogue was delivered at that low sinister volume.

Hal Prieste

However not even my glass shattering vocal chords could crack Harry (Hal) Prieste (November 23, 1896 - April 19, 2001). Hal won the Bronze medal in the 10 metre platform diving event at the 1920 Antwerp, Belgium Olympic Games. The father of modern surfing Duke Paoa Kahanamoku just happened to be one of Prieste's teammates on that United States Olympic team and dared the young Prieste to steal the Olympic flag. Hal promptly shinnied up the fifteen-foot flagpole and nicked the first ever Olympic flag to display the now-famous five interlocking rings. Once back in the States Hal tossed the flag into a suitcase in his attic and promptly forgot about it, taking up a career as one of the original Keystone Kops appearing with Charlie Chaplin in 27 of Mack Sennett's silent comedies.

Hal never regarded the flag as valuable or worth returning until a reporter told him at a United States Olympic Committee banquet that the International Olympic Committee had been unable to find the missing historic Antwerp flag.

Hal blinked and declared: "I can help you with that, it's in my suitcase in my attic." So, at the age of 103 the United States Olympic committee flew him all the way from New Jersey to attend the 2000 Sydney Olympic Games and return that historic Olympic flag that he had nicked 80 years previously.

And that's where I first spotted Hal sitting, in my Sydney apartment overlooking possibly the most beautiful harbor in the world, watching the televised ceremony of the oldest living Olympic medal winner returning that historic 1920 Antwerp Olympic flag. I was in Sydney with a camera crew to cover the 2000 Olympics for the Sky Network back in New Zealand.

The next day Sydney's Darling Harbor was bathed in brilliant sunshine as I ran around with my camera crew doing some Olympic stories, when I spotted a swarm of photographers snapping away at somebody that I couldn't see, so we ambled on over and there he sat Harry (Hal) Prieste in his wheelchair. I immediately yelled at my producer, "Hey, this is the dude we saw on the tube last night with the flag, we've got to interview this guy, he's living Olympic history."

Thus, began the funniest non-interview I've ever done. Naturally Hal was being escorted around by the United States Olympic Committee so I went over to this official posse and asked if I could interview Hal. They all just looked at me like I was nuts and informed me that Hal was severely deaf and legally blind. I responded that that was cool and I'd still like to give it a shot. They had a quick huddle and then collectively they all nodded their heads up and down like those toy dogs in the back of cars giving me the green light, then one of the committee team walked up to me and smugly declared that I'd have to virtually scream into Hal's ear. He looked dubious that I would be successful but I merely smiled, cocky in the fact that this red, white and blue clown had no idea who he was talking too, after all, I possessed a thunderous voice that could make grown women moan (get your mind out of the gutter - I'm talking about those dear old Japanese ladies).

I approached Hal with my camera crew, bent down and boomed out an introduction.

'I'm John Dybvig. I wanna ask a few questions, Hal.'

Nothing. Just silence.

I cleared my throat and moved a bit closer.

'I'M JOHN DYBVIG. I WOULD LIKE TO INTERVIEW YOU.'

Still no response. It was as if I wasn't there.

I boomed louder which was followed by more silence. Now like that nasty wolf in Walt Disney's Three Little Pigs I huffed and I puffed and I gave him my all-time breaking the sound barrier blast and backed off. I was lightheaded from the effort, and stuck my microphone under his nose...after a very long silence Hal tilted his head slightly in my direction and grunted,

"Huh!"

The US Olympic committee guy yelled at me to get closer to his ear. So now I literally had my lips inside Hal's hairy old ear screaming at the top of my lungs making poor old Hal's head vibrate. Then I'd back off in eager anticipation and after a lengthy silence Hal would grunt,

"Huh!"

This was hilarious. I kept this routine up for a good fifteen minutes:

Scream, silence, huh? Scream, silence, huh?

Finally, old Hal got tired of this young whippersnapper (I was fifty, but when you're talking to a guy over a hundred that makes you a whippersnapper) hanging out in his ear so he suddenly declared to no one in particular that he was still fit enough to touch the ground. I stood back Hal stood up bent over with his legs locked straight and cleanly placed the palms of both of his hands flat on the ground. I was impressed.

The gathering mob of photographers and curious onlookers were all impressed too and cheered wildly while the United States of America Olympic committee all nodded their heads in collective approval, and that concluded my non-interview with the world's oldest living Olympic medal winner: My booming voice had finally met its' match, good on ya Hal!

Comment: Just might add here that those 2000 Olympic Games in Sydney, Australia were probably the last peaceful Games before the entire world became aware of the word 'terrorist' in 2001.

Have Bag Will Travel
My love for travel started when my parents put me on the San Francisco to Los Angeles train all by myself at the tender age of 7.

Try that today and see how fast you end up in jail. It was an all-day 600-mile journey where my grandparents collected me on the other end.

When the train stopped in Santa Barbara on impulse, I made a sudden bold move - I leaped off the train and ran into the depot wandered around a bit and then raced out again jumping back on the train with my 7-year old heart pounding so much I thought it was going to explode. I was so thrilled with myself.

What would have happened if the train pulled out before I got back I hadn't a clue.

Comment: From a young age I was bold and brassy... when I was 10 or 11 I talked my mother into letting me take a bus alone into downtown San Jose, California, to watch a movie (Jules Verne's - Twenty Thousand Leagues Under The Sea).

I distinctly remember three things about that trip:

Firstly the movie theatre was in a fairly seedy section of town and I had such a feeling of exhilaration as I walked to the theatre by myself with me imagining danger lurking at every alleyway.

Secondly I had to pass by a burlesque house with photographs of semi-naked women with huge hooters on their billboards outside. I gave those billboards a certain amount of careful study.

And thirdly I screwed up taking the bus back home. I was supposed to transfer at some stage but didn't know this so when the bus got to the end of the line and I was nowhere near my house I just marched up to some stranger's house and called home.

The only down side of this trip to prove my independence was the ribbing I got from my older brother and sister for getting lost.

Airports

Today it's all about airports. And I gotta say I've had more than my fair share of Homer Simpson moments collecting my-luggage.

I love emerging from the plane when everyone suddenly starts to scuddle (the pace in between a brisk walk and a slow jog) frantically for the baggage carousel. I've never understood this sudden urgency because you always get there way before your bags do.

The last time I was at LAX with my own family in tow I hadn't been home in a few years so I was just itching to do something 'American' in my-homeland and what better way to do that than to hit McDonald's. I broke out of my scuddle and ordered a large fries. I got my fries and handed over a buck fifty to the gal serving me whereupon she informed me with an attitude dripping with sarcasm that it was $1.75

I instantly stiffened and barked back pointing to the board that it said $1.50 slightly puffing out my chest! The young lady behind the counter (who looked about 3) curled her lip, rolled her eyes like I was the dumbest American in the world (which I was at that point) and snorted, "Sales tax... duh!"

Yikes, I'd been living in New Zealand so long I simply forgot about sales tax. Turning a deep crimson with everyone watching I mumbled, "Oh yeah, right." I was home two seconds and already I felt like a foreigner.

Arriving at the baggage area we needed a trolly so I made my way over to the trolly rack and what luck there was a lone trolly just sitting there so, I grabbed it and saved myself a couple of bucks. I wheeled it over to Jennifer and the kids.

While we were checking for our bags I noticed a sharply dressed man in a blue suit intently eyeing me up he kept checking me out and for a while I thought I might be under airport security surveillance. Our bags started arriving and by the time I had everything stacked on the trolly it felt like I was standing in a hole I couldn't see anything in front of me. I kid you not we had enough stuff to easily employ 12 Tanzanian porters on a safari on the plains of the Serengeti.

Eventually after a Titanic struggle to get that tricky first pulse of inertia (why are trolly wheels always pointing in the wrong direction?) going I had my-moving mountain out on the sidewalk. I had sent the kids and Jennifer on ahead to the bus station. I'm slowly pushing Mt. Kilimanjaro towards the shuttle bus totally blind when suddenly the sidewalk dips down rather sharply.

That's where I lost it - my trolly was screaming down the sidewalk with me trying in vain to pull it back when I felt a sickening thump closely followed by an avalanche of screaming and cursing. I tentatively peered around my tower of luggage to see a smartly dressed middle-aged woman hopping up and down gingerly holding her throbbing digit (big toe) hurling insults at me.

Ouch!

Double ouch!!

I actually had this nutty conversation with her: She's literally purple with rage calling me every name under the sun and I'm agreeing with her, "Yeow, you're right lady... I totally agree... I'm a dolt an idiot, I feel your pain... man that must hurt!"

Finally, I got to the shuttle, Jennifer and the kids were already seated on the bus when I plopped down next to them - looking up I was surprised to see the dapper CIA agent who'd been keeping close tabs on me in the airport sitting directly across from us.

Upon seeing me he immediately leaned over and whispered to his wife that I was the jackass who stole their trolly and his wife glaring at me immediately whispered back that I was the jerk who ran over her big toe.

I just sat there amazed and wondered - wow - what are the odds of that happening?

Comment: As you can imagine the atmosphere on the bus ride over to the car rental agency was pretty intense as we sat there across from each other trying to avoid looking directly at one another.

Dollar Notes
The shuttle bus took us to the car rental building and the driver who was maybe a fraction taller than my 10-year old son and as thin as any model walking down a runway strained every muscle in his body removing our tonnage of luggage. The man was sweating.

This is where Homer Simpson and I morph into one: I tell every New Zealander going to America that they must carry a wad of single dollar bills for tipping. America is the tipping capital of the world and like it or not Americans expect to be tipped. I'm standing there the dripping Hobbit is standing there (it's that awkward moment just before money exchanges hands) and I'm furiously digging in my pockets for some loose change a crumpled dollar bill... anything.

All I've got in my wallet is hundred-dollar bills and all I can muster from the depths of every pocket I own is one single Quarter (25 cents).

Sheepishly I handed it over and words here would fail utterly to describe the look of disdain on the man's face. I felt bad. I flunked another American test.

Comment: Yeah, I really felt bad about this - I hate under tipping or not tipping at all. After all I grew up in a household of restaurant workers so I understood the tipping world. I know these workers aren't getting paid much so they need those tips.

Smart Ass

One time when I flew into Perth, Australia to visit a Kiwi friend I actually was under airport security surveillance.

I was standing at the baggage carousel minding my own business waiting for my bag when I noticed several guys intermittently checking me out. These guys had cops written all over them: Short hair, short sleeve white shirts, dark slacks and they all looked like they worked out.

I'm standing there watching the bags circle around and I'm thinking to myself, "Are these guys for real? It's so obvious they're staking me out."

Finally, when I picked up my lone bag, the vultures pounced, big time. I felt the rush of air as they hurriedly scrambled over to surround me. The lead detective immediately started grilling me:

"Is that your bag?" I was totally bemused by this and couldn't help myself, "What, you mean this bag that I'm holding?"

Mr. Flathead quickly stepped in even closer giving me a close-up inspection of all the pock marks in his face and acidly shot back, "Don't get smart with us." Then he asked me how long I was staying and who I was visiting etc. I told him that I was staying for two weeks, he snapped, "That's a long time with only one small bag" (it was a sports bag).

"Is there a minimum bag requirement to come into Australia?" I queried.

That burst the bubble, he grabbed me and hustled me over to a side room with the goon squad in close pursuit and searched my bag.

They were on a drug bust and were expecting a courier. Luckily for me I didn't even have an aspirin on me.

Comment: The other weird thing about landing at that airport I remember was when I walked outside... the temperature in Perth that day was 48 degrees Celsius... it was just like walking into a gigantic oven... I suddenly felt light-headed. I was stunned because I just hadn't been expecting anything like that.

Holy Shit

I'm a sixties and fifties guy when it comes to music... I used to own a 1953 Wurlitzer Jukebox stacked with songs from the Beach Boys... The Temptations... Buddy Holly... Dion... Elvis... Pat Boone... etc. And Gene Pitney's soulful tune 'Twenty Four Hours from Tulsa'...

So I was pretty pumped up that when I was playing basketball for Stanislaus State which is in the San Joaquin Valley in central California which is in actual fact the fruit basket of the world. We took a road trip to Tulsa, Oklahoma to go up against The Golden Eagles of Oral Roberts University.

I don't really know what I was expecting... maybe to see Gene walking down the street who knows I was young and stupid in those days... now I'm just old and stupid... but in the end I had one of those unexpected weird moments that just stay with you forever.

Unbeknown to us this game was to be no ordinary experience... we were all about finding ourselves up close and personal with a miracle.

Oral Roberts was one of the original holy rollers in America. He was a Choctaw American Charismatic Christian televangelist, ordained in both the Pentecostal Holiness and United Methodist churches. He is considered the godfather of the charismatic movement or in lay man's terms - he was one helluva a smooth entertainer when it came to talking religion... he was also one of the most recognized preachers in the United States at the height of his fame.

He founded Oral Roberts University where we were about to witness this special and rare occurrence namely a close-up view of the nation's number one holy roller in action

Towards the end of the first half of the game one of our players sky rocketed up into the rafters in an attempt to block an Oral Roberts player from taking the ball to the hoop.

Both players met in mid-air and smashed into each other right above the rim (ten feet from the floor) with our guy (Stanislaus State Running Warrior) flipping over the Oral Roberts player's shoulder and landing heavily on his back with an enormous thump!

Our guy was lying motionless on the floor not moving a muscle.
The sell-out crowd fell silent as everyone rushed to his aid.

And then like a scene right out of a Hollywood block buster (Elmer Gantry) the man himself - Oral Roberts silently rose up and the crowd immediately went into a chorus of 'ooooooooooooooooohs' with their hands to their mouths... I'm standing there watching this scene play out a few feet from our guy knowing that he's alright... at this point he's just stunned.

When you crash land like that you just lie there and get in tune with your body making sure that nothing is seriously wrong.

Oral is now gliding over to our fallen hero with every set of eyes in the stadium fiercely following his every move... he gets down on bended knee and proceeds to place his hands on our guy... and let me tell you this is no ordinary placing of the hands because there's some kind of aura as to how these holy rollers do it... the feeling is almost like Moses standing before the Red Sea just before it parts... you can almost hear the Archangels blowing their trumpets in the background... by now our guy is starting to collect himself stirring just a bit which makes the crowd go absolutely nuts:

Crowd: Look... look Oral is getting the player to rise...

Crowd: It's a miracle... Oral's touch did it...

Crowd: Oral touched him and he's gonna be alright... thank the Lord...

Finally our player gets into a sitting position and Oral is talking to him and the crowd is absolutely enthralled... at this point you could have heard a pin drop in this immense stadium.

I'm standing there thinking that Oral is definitely gonna milk this as far as it will go... he helps our player get up and gently holding his elbow he guides our guy who is a bit shaky on his feet towards our bench.

The crowd is absolutely besides themselves at this point going bonkers... yelling and screaming and pointing and I'm sure some have even fainted.

Finally our guy gets to our bench and Oral helps him sit down and then he turns to his flock and puts both hands up in the air palms facing outward in this very serene and solemn moment and the crowd immediately becomes silent... reverent to Oral and they sit down fizzing within themselves for witnessing this amazing miracle.

I'm just cracking up inside thinking: "Well, I just witnessed my first miracle which really wasn't a miracle at all, but probably the closest I'll ever come to seeing a miracle real or not and, besides, the crowd thought it was a miracle so there ya go." I'm sure they're still talking about that night to this day.

Comment One: That was one hell of a trip... our next stop was Shreveport, Louisiana. Hmmmmmmmmmmm... Louisiana... this was back in 1971 and I don't know if it's changed or not but back then it was one helluva racist State.

We had a traveling party of ten players on our team with seven of them being black, so every time we went to a restaurant to eat only three menus came out for the white guys... it was so obvious they didn't even try to hide it. So in the end we just ordered take out food to avoid all the hassles.

But my lasting memory of Louisiana is when we dropped off one of our former classmates who had been drafted into the Army... remember the Vietnam War was still in full swing.

When he found out that we were playing Centenary College of Louisiana which is affiliated with the United Methodist Church, hence their nickname which I just love because it's so Southern - Gentlemen & Ladies he got leave to spend the weekend with us in Shreveport.

Well this guy had a blast drinking and partying with his old classmates and going to our game... believe me it was a full weekend. But, like I said, when it was over we had to drive him back to his base which was Fort Polk, Louisiana... and I'll never forget the surrounding area as we approached the fort.

It was nothing but swamps on all sides with the low overhanging trees dripping with moss and it just looks nasty and sweaty and dangerous... like alligator dangerous!

My lasting image is of our former classmate standing in front of the gates to Fort Polk in his Army fatigues surrounded by a swamp bawling like a son-of-a-bitch crying his eyes out as we drove away. Sad... sad sight.

Small World: Years later when I was an assistant basketball coach at Santa Clara University I ran into this same guy who was in the stands watching the game.

He survived the war and Fort Polk and the swamps and was an accountant working in San Jose, California. We had a beer and laughed our asses off about that time so... so... so long ago in Louisiana.

Comment Two: In America we may have holy rollers with magic hands... but in New Zealand you've got holy water with magical powers.

It used to crack me up when I first arrived in New Zealand watching some poor bastard playing rugby getting rucked to death with sprig dents in his head and strips of skin missing looking for all the world like he just survived the Bataan Death March and then out trots a St. John's guy with a bucket and sprinkles the guy with some water like the Pope and pats the back of his neck with a damp sponge and presto he's good to go... funny as a fight really.

Big Foot
One year when I was living in Hawaii I went to visit the garden island Kauai with a group of friends. When we arrived at the airport on our return journey we were told that one of us had to stay behind and catch the next plane out. No big deal... I volunteered and my friends took off leaving me the only passenger in the very small airport.

The next plane was only about ten minutes away so I'm standing in the middle of the floor at the boarding gate way when all of a sudden I'm surrounded by about 200 Japanese tourists who had just arrived on a couple of buses. Now this is weird because I'm the only white person period in this sea of Japanese people and we're packed into this small room like a can of sardines. I'm like a lighthouse towering above them. I'm looking around and laughing to myself because this is just too weird for words... when suddenly this diminutive little guy standing next to me looks down and excitedly points at my feet and screams something out to the surrounding crowd in Japanese and the entire room bursts into hilarious laughter and everyone is straining to get a look at my feet. Next this guy shouts out something else again pointing down then raising his hands into the air spread about three feet apart... and the room is just going nuts with laughter.

I mean I do have big feet... but they're not thaaaat bigggg!?! Whudaaaya gonna do - another one of those Homer Simpson moments for me... Doh!

The Language Barrier
My father-in-law had me worried. Ever since I had married his daughter, he would visit and everything seemed to go well. Then, when it was time to leave, he'd smile, head for the door and wave.

'Hooray!' he would shout.

Hooray? What did he mean 'hooray'? Was he so pleased to escape our company he felt the need to cheer on the way out?

My wife, Jennifer, explained. In her country, 'hooray' meant 'so long'. Her dad was being friendly.

Once again, I felt like the loneliest American in New Zealand.

Comment One: And here's another New Zealand custom that always had me scratching my head: Whenever I would meet a stranger walking down the street who knew who I was I'd stop and chat a bit which I'm always happy to do... but then when I would continue on my way the stranger would always say, "Good luck," and I would always wonder what the hell does that mean? Good luck with what?

Comment Two: And how about this for a wacky custom in New Zealand - when it's your birthday you have to shout (buy) the drinks. How ass backwards is that!?!

Comment Three: The funniest and most confusing of Kiwi slang expressions is: 'Yeah... nah... yeah... nah...yeah... nah'. That's it... when you ask a kiwi a question they just give you this succession of double talk in the affirmative and then the negative... of yeah and nah... it's really just a non-committal statement where you can keep the conversation going without agreeing with someone...kind of sorta but not really... yeah... nah... yeah... nah... yeah... nah... it's hilarious!

Comment Four: Their other slang term I love is: 'Sweet as'... which simply means awesome... sounds good... and can apply to any situation or question such as - how was your holiday and the response is likely to be - sweet as... or can you do me a favour: sweet as...

Comment Five: And then one day I had to do a reversal on the language front and explain myself to a local. Whenever I walked into my bank in St Heliers I would exclaim, "Hey big guy" to one of the tellers who I always had a good chat to about what books we were reading or politics when I was doing my banking business.

Then one day he pulled me aside and in a somewhat worried expression he explained to me that he had recently lost some weight and he really wasn't all that big.

I looked at him with a bemused expression and then just busted out laughing my ass off. I explained to him that, "Hey big guy" was just an American expression of endearment and it had nothing to do with weight whatsoever.

Comment Six: And this custom down here is really... really frustrating for me... in fact it's torture... food torture:

In America because we're sloths with no manners as soon as your dinner plate is set down before you... you simply dig in... like immediately.... eat it while it's hot... that's the American way!

But down in this neck of the woods... oh no... manners are all important... certainly way more important than hot food... you have to wait until every plate is ready for the table... and for some reason getting everything on the table seems like an exercise in glacial movement...

I'm not kidding... you can literally grow old before you get to tuck in... and it seems that I always get my plate of food first so you're sitting there and the steam is rising from the food in front of you and everyone is just flapping around in absolutely no hurry and by the time all the food is on the table and everyone is seated... well you can forget about any steam rising anywhere near your food... by this time the polar bears are out sniffing around because your food is stone cold...

In the name of manners I've eaten an awful lot of cold dinners in New Zealand... but sometimes when no one is looking I sneak in a mouthful of hot food... yum!

Cheeseburger

Even the simplest of activities Down Under can have their moments. For example, one day when I tried to order a simple cheeseburger and a beer. I discovered the gap between our two cultures was wider than the Grand Canyon.

The waiter informed me that they had a chicken burger, a beef burger and a steak burger.

Cool, buddy. I replied I'd like a cheeseburger and a beer.

The waiter was totally clueless, repeating again what was on their menu. Every time I mentioned 'hamburger' he repeated his line of chicken burger, beef burger and steak burger - we sounded like Abbot and Costello doing their 'Who's on first' routine.

Of course I knew that a beef burger was your classic 'American hamburger' but hey I wasn't about to order a beef burger with cheese - how Un-American sounding is that!?

A cheeseburger comes under your classic American saying: 'It is what it is' there's not a lot of explaining to do here that is unless you live in a strange... strange land.

Finally I called a timeout and explained the situation to him that when somebody wanted a hamburger or a cheeseburger those came under the heading of his 'beef burger' and the terms chicken burger and steak burger weren't even in the same conversation- he was delighted to learn this and at that point I was finally able to order a cheeseburger and a beer and his response was: "Of course sir." Hooray! I shouted! Only that means so long in New Zealand.

Egg

Every day I lived in New Zealand, I was reminded of the differences between the countries, and how different I felt.

I once ordered bacon and eggs at a café in Russell, on a trip to the Bay of Islands. When my order arrived, there was only one egg on my plate.

I looked at the waiter and bellowed, 'Hey, Mac, you've forgotten one of my eggs.'

The waiter merely pointed to the menu on the board which clearly stated: Bacon and egg. That is the only time in my life that I've been served one egg. A notable first.

Free Range

I had a short spell living in Australia where I worked in a small café as a waiter. And I discovered the language could be just as confusing there.

A young woman came into the cafe and asked me if we had 'free range eggs'.

I looked down at her and gave her one of my warmest disarming smiles. Behind my dimples was pure panic. I had never heard of 'free range eggs'.

All I could think of on the spot was that she was referring to the grill as a range.

So, I looked straight into her sparkling face and seriously explained to her that we normally cooked the eggs inside a metal ring on the grill so they kept their shape.

But for her I would instruct the chef to discard the rings and let the eggs run free on the range. Words here would fail to do justice in describing the look on her face. She ordered pancakes.

That's Random

Walk into any bakery in New Zealand and ask for a jelly donut and all you'll get is a blank stare or maybe a giggle or two. Jelly there is Jell-O, what you want is a 'jam' donut.

There's life down there, Jim, but certainly not as we know it. They have a little outhouse inside their house. The loo or the bog, otherwise known as the toilet, is a little eeny weeny room all by itself just big enough to squeeze in and do your business and nothing but your business.

Kiwi men go for a 'slash' (taking a pee) which always causes me to wince and instantly cross my legs. I don't want to hear the word 'slash' in any connection that involves my penis. And with no central heating in the winter when your butt hits the lid, you'll know what it's like when Jack Frost takes a crap.

And while we're considering basic body functions, New Zealanders use the term 'fanny' to describe a vagina. Hence there is no such thing as a 'fanny pack' in New Zealand unless of course you're looking to get a good slap to the face. They call a 'fanny pack' a 'bum bag' Down Under.

When they write the day's date, they put the day first instead of the month so 911 is 119, just doesn't have the same ring, does it? My birthday in America is (8/4/1949) in the middle of summer, down here it's (4/8/1949) in the middle of winter. And naturally they call a two-by-four a four-by-two and, yes, the water going down the drain in a bathtub does spin in the opposite direction.

And the light switch. Yeah, that's ass backwards too. You flip the switch DOWN to turn on the lights. I've never gotten used to that.

I've yet to meet anybody in New Zealand called 'Randy' because if you're 'randy' that means you're horny. In America we root for the 'home team.' In New Zealand they 'root' between the sheets. You can well imagine the excitement of the young men on visiting rugby teams to the States when the local cheerleaders bounce up to them in their itty-bitty little skirts and figure-hugging sweaters and squeal in that inane bubbly way that only cheerleaders have of expressing themselves: "Hey, guys, we're here to root for you." Oh, lucky day!

Comment One: After living here for forty years I'm serious when I say I still to this day haven't gotten used to flipping light switches or any switch for that matter 'down' to turn them on. It just goes to show how we really are ingrained in the habits of where we come from. In an American accent class one night I had the roles reversed when one young actress exclaimed, "What! You flip the light switch up to turn on the lights in America?" She just couldn't wrap her head around the fact that in America it was just the opposite to New Zealand.

Comment Two: And I have to comment on how exceptionally small their toilet rooms are: More than once instead of getting off the toilet standing straight up I have absent-mindedly leaned forward without thinking and bang I've head-butted the near wall facing the toilet (that's dinky folks) - hurts like a son-of-a-bitch!

Comment Three: I've saved the best for last here - they even eat with their fork upside down. Yeah, they pile their food on the back of the fork. Go figure?

Best Comeback Ever

And this is one of the best one liner's from a kiwi I've ever heard... it stopped an entire party along with my effervescent American buddy Michael Saccente stone cold...Mike is so involved as an actor and as an acting teacher that he has a million and one stories in his repertoire... he's one of those guys who are the life of the party in a pithy way... funny as hell and very quick with a sharp clever retort no matter the subject matter... he was always unstoppable hadn't met his match that is until he met the woman sitting next to him at Jennifer's 40th birthday party... As was his norm Mike the ever charming raconteur was entertaining the entire table with his amusing anecdotes and wise cracks... when suddenly he focused his attention on the beautiful woman sitting next to him and purringly demurred in a somewhat flirtatious manner that she had lovely hands... and without missing a beat this woman in that wonderful low key New Zealand matter of fact understatement just stopped Mike dead in his tracks... he had absolutely nothing... no comeback whatsoever when she replied: "That's what my husband says to me when I have them wrapped around his cock."

A Distant Land

When you live abroad it's the little things that will throw you off balance. And even after more than 40 years away from California, I still feel I'm a foreigner living in someone else's land. Rarely do I ever feel in synch Down Under.

I've lived here over half my life and I still "don't get it," whenever I say that to someone in New Zealand, they always query: "Get what?"

And I simply shrug my shoulders and lament: "Get whatever it is, you're supposed to get." Of course I'm talking about the pulse of life Down Under which is so radically different to the American way of life.

The life force between our two distant countries couldn't be any more diverse: The United States is a place where over 300 million people defend their individual freedoms at the expense of the community whereas New Zealand with a population of five million people insist on community at the expense of individual freedom. America shot at and symbolically killed British royalty over 200 years ago while New Zealand is a place where royalty is not only alive and well, it's honored and sometimes cherished.

Comment: It's kind of like our expression: "It is what it is," which can be pretty much applied to every situation in life. I can't ever imagine a New Zealander coming out with that expression - it's just so American it hurts. In fact that was the absolute funniest moment in the Roger Clemens investigation before Congress over steroid use in Major League baseball when one of the Congressmen (a guy who looked to be about a hundred and ten) seriously asked Clemens former trainer Brian McNamee to explain the expression: "It is what it is."

McNamee just sat there looking very confused while he tried desperately to come up with a suitable explanation, you could actually see his mind ticking over and finally he just shrugged his shoulders and mumbled: "It is what it is."

Ya gotta laugh.

Red White & Blue

Yes! I am the American. When you live abroad you always get the odd question about America - people who haven't been there are naturally curious... This question was one right-out-of-the box: One night Jennifer and I are at the Michael McIntyre show - and I gotta say here this dude is one funny Son-of-a-Bitch... I mean a really hilarious comic... so the show ends and as we stand up the couple in front of us stand and turn around and immediately the young lady looks straight at me and says - "Great - you'll know!"

And then she proceeds to tell me that she and her partner are going to the States and they only have time to pick one city - either Boston or New York... she wants to go to New York while her young man wants to go to Boston... so she asks me - "Which one would you go to if you had to choose?"

Man that's a tough question on the spot especially as they're both staring... boring into me with enough intensity to melt the polar ice-cap... and we're like only inches apart standing in the packed stands... so I told them... ok first ya got Boston with all its rich history of the American revolution and then there's Fenway Park and the Boston Red Sox... with Cambridge and Harvard University near by and a beautiful city with a great harbour... and then you've got New York with its famous skyline... great museums... Broadway... the Statue of Liberty... the Empire State building... the Chrysler building (my favorite building in New York)... the House that Ruth built, Yankee Stadium and the equally world famous New York Yankees... and of course the chance to eat the world famous New York hot dog... there's always more in New York... so at the end of the day it's a no contest... a no brainer... because it's New York! So there really isn't a choice - New York it is... and immediately she jumps for joy and screams out - "Yes!" Her partner took it on the chin... I think he knew all along even without me it was gonna be New York.

Comment: And I just have to comment here on the astronomical amount of money it takes just to sell you that $2 New York hot dog... we're talking about the half-million-dollar wiener! Just to set up that lone hot dog stand near New York's Metropolitan Museum of Art the license fee is going to cost you $53,558 bucks... smackaroos... greenbacks... a week... yeah you heard right - $53,558 a week... that's $642,696 a year... man you've gotta sell a shit load of hot dogs to make a profit.

Men In Black
Staying in America except now we're on the opposite coast - if you're ever in San Francisco you just have to take a ride on their Cable Cars through the city.

I guarantee you'll love it... especially at night... I've been on those cable cars a ton of times and yet every time I go back to the City I always catch a ride... but the most unusual cable car ride I've had occurred in the city of Christchurch in the South Island of New Zealand.

It happened right before the country's national basketball championship game... Anthony Ray Parker and I were calling the game so we decided it would be cool to catch the cable car into the stadium in the city centre... we're both in our exquisite black tuxedo's when we jumped on this cable car... instantly the entire cable car just went ballistic... unbeknown to us this particular cable car was jammed packed with IHC kids (intellectually handicapped children) who immediately upon spying us standing at the front of the cable car erupted in screams of - "It's the Men in Black... it's the Men in Black"... and I guess we kind of looked like the Men in Black... I'm white and Anthony Ray is black and we're standing there in our black tuxedoes and the movie had just been released... but the funniest thing to me was this kid in the front seat all of a sudden screamed at Anthony - "I'm gonna bite your dick!" And Anthony Ray looked down at this youngster with a terrific scowl and in his deep rumbling baritone voice told the kid in no uncertain terms - "That's not gonna happen little buddy... know what I mean." Of course the kid had no idea what Anthony meant – he was just 'Happy as Larry' as he sat there staring at the Men in Black... hilarious!

Aotearoa
New Zealand is a country made up of three islands: The North Island, the South Island and the patio they like to call Stewart Island. The latter is really too small to be considered anything notable. It's a wildlife reserve. A doorstep - a place to leave your gumboots/galoshes before stepping onto the mainland.

Except nobody lives on "The Mainland" - i.e. the South Island - despite it being the country's largest stretch of grass. No, the bulk of the population live on the North Island and most of them are centered in gridlocked Auckland near the island's upper half. Auckland now boasting a population of over 1.5 million and counting.

Aucklanders have long heard rumors regarding the existence of the former two islands but apart from skiing holidays and the like they don't let it overly concern them. From their point of view, Auckland is New Zealand.

You might not have gathered but Aucklanders are known - within their own country - for being uptight. They're cosmopolitan or so they imagine. Translation: They have traffic! And they have all the attitude that comes with negotiating traffic.

The Mainlanders or South Islanders are cow-cockies - translation, they're farmers. They work with cows and sheep. They're laid back. Will shoot the breeze with ya. They're in no big hurry. But under their gentle, droll humor the cold shoulder from their well-to-do brothers up north makes their blood boil, but when you're that laid back who can really tell?

Comment One: Aotearoa is the Maori name for New Zealand which means: "Long White Cloud".

Comment Two: It is almost like living in two different countries. Driving through the South Island is like taking a step back in time. I highly recommend it.

The attitude of indifference Aucklanders have toward their cousins on the South Island is kind of like most Americans' attitude to those moose lovers at the top end of our continent... The Canadians... Yeah, most of the time we barely notice they exist. Do they?

World Series
And talk about culture wars: Take our national pastime baseball: Every October Dantes Hell meets Groundhogs Day for me in New Zealand as I get swamped with the same question over and over again: "Why do they call it the World Series when the rest of the world can't compete?" Even my beautiful wife Jennifer can't help herself whenever I mention the World Series she quips: "Would that be the World Series that's only played in America?"

"Yes dear."

And English comedian/actor John Cleese also got in on the act when he pointed out the difference between the USA and the UK (United Kingdom) is that when the UK holds a world Championship they actually invite other countries. Puhleeeese. Cleese did qualify his broadside by pointing out that since only 2 per cent of Americans are aware that there is a world beyond their borders, their error was understandable. Ha. Ha.

I just turn the question back on them: "Why do you care what we call our sports?" It's an American thing, don't worry about it. A squillion things are miss-named, death for instance, according to the Dalai Lama only our bodies die.

It's called the World Series because baseball was invented in America. At the time nobody else in the world played the game. Therefore, we have a legitimate claim to the history, if not the modern reality. Major League Baseball considers the 1903 World Series to be the first. This modern first series was played in 1903 between the (AL) champion Boston Americans (today's Red Sox) and the (NL) champion Pittsburgh Pirates in a best-of-nine series, with Boston prevailing five games to three.

These early series were promoted as "The Championship of the United States," or the "World's Championship Series," but that kind of branding just doesn't work... there's no snap to it... no zing... so the marketing boys got involved and shortened it to the "World Series." Well now you're talkin' brother... if you're gonna go big - go huge... go for the whole enchilada... like in the whole entire world!

Let's put it this way: Guy walks into a bar and excitedly exclaims - "Hey guys I just got 'World Series' tickets!

Or...

Same guy walks into a bar and says - "Hey guys I just got 'The Championship of the United States' tickets.

You can see my point... the simple phrase 'World Series' is like a fire cracker going off - it instantly says it all!

And the name stuck. It's all about 'Tradition' so why would you debunk such a strong brand name with over a century of history behind it. You wouldn't. And besides Americans are just arrogant enough to pull it off!

Comment: Hopefully this will finally put an end to the urban legend that the World Series was named after a newspaper, the New York World, it wasn't.

The Wave
And take another pure slice of American pop culture: 'The Wave' New Zealanders call our 'Wave' the 'Mexican Wave' even though I've patiently explained to one and all that 'The Wave' was invented by a former Silicon Valley high school electronics teacher turned professional cheerleader by the name of Krazy George Henderson.

Of course there are others who claim credit for the Wave in its shaky chaotic beginnings but generally Krazy George is considered 'The Man' when it comes to the Wave.

I used to catch Krazy George's act in the San Francisco Bay Area at football games at Stanford University as he'd thunder into the stadium with his pounding drum and a booming set of vocal chords to rile up the fans like no other in the business.

I was an unintentional witness like everyone else to the humble beginnings of 'The Wave' when the seed was first planted, unbeknown then even by Krazy George. He'd start pounding his drum while he galloped across the stadium whipping the crowd into a frenzy. Suddenly he'd pop up in front of a section of the crowd and bellow at them to stand up and cheer and then just as suddenly he'd dash off to another part of the stadium for a repeat performance. Every section in the stadium would be on pins and needles waiting for Krazy George so when he came they'd eventually spring out of their seats in compliance. He ran around like a blue-ass fly for the entire game, criss-crossing throughout the vast crowds - exhausting work by anyone's standards. But what a show he put on.

Krazy George thinks his first Wave was originally inspired by accident at an Edmonton Oilers National Hockey League game at Northlands Coliseum in Edmonton, Alberta, Canada. But hey no one saw it.

Then on the night of October 15, 1981 at an Oakland A's and New York Yankees playoff game, in front of a national television audience Krazy George Henderson created something original that everyone saw and was talking about the next day at water coolers all across America: The Wave.

At one point during the game he stood huffing and puffing bent over sucking in oxygen like a wounded buffalo, he couldn't move, so when that section of fans were starting to sit down he merely pointed to the next section and thus with that simple move the tricky first connection from one section of the stands to another section in a split second created a ripple effect and thus The Wave was born.

It started slowly like a shaky newborn animal struggling to gain momentum - the first Wave was a small curler with just three sections involved, then it grew to a bigger swell with five or six sections down the line, finally George got one entire side of the stadium in unison standing and sitting in a perfect rippling motion. With that fifty thousand individual souls suddenly clicked as one as the Oakland Coliseum transformed itself into one monster of a human rippling Wave taking everybody in it along for the ride, clean around the entire stadium!

The game announcer, Joe Garagiola was up in the broadcast booth yelling at his cameramen to get that thing. Of course, no one knew what it was.

Comment: The Wave became known as the Mexican Wave in New Zealand and the English-speaking world outside of North America when five years later - yeah five whole years - at the 1986 Football (soccer) World Cup in Mexico it was broadcast to a mass audience including little old New Zealand. See I told you things were slow down this way - it took them half a decade to see their first Wave, wow.

And of course, New Zealanders have adopted it with their own unusual Down Under messy twist as kiwis insist on throwing their garbage (banana peels, cups, half-eaten meat pies, whatever) into the air as they stand up so when you sit down a ton of crap rains down on you.

McDonald's

But it wasn't only New Zealanders who kept me on my toes. Loopy Americans were still doing their bit. One hot humid summer's night we were having pizza and wine on St Heliers beach when this wacky American from Illinois proudly and cockily proclaimed that McDonald's was founded by Ray Kroc in Illinois, a double whammy. I just looked at him momentarily stunned that he could be serious, but he was, he honestly believed that Kroc created McDonald's. I calmly explained the McDonald's facts to him: Contrary to popular belief, Ray Kroc did not open the first McDonald's and neither is he the founder.

I mean come on they're called 'McDonald's' not 'Kroc's' that should be a massive clue as to who originally came up with the idea.

In a quick nutshell this is how McDonald's came to be and not surprisingly at the beginning it involves the McDonald brothers Dick and Mac - more formally known as Richard and Maurice, in 1948 in San Bernadino, California. Dick and Mac originally opened their drive-through barbecue restaurant in 1940 but it just wasn't making a profit so in 1948 Dick and Mac shut down their drive-through and totally redesigned their restaurant by concentrating on speed of service, low price, volume and turned it into a hamburger and milkshake joint.

They dropped their 25 item menu and came up with their "Speedee Service System" which meant eliminating their car hops (who were very slow and you had to pay them wages) and opened up a walk-up self-serve window (this meant they could drop their prices) basically serving just hamburgers, fries and shakes... inside the restaurant three grill men did nothing but flip burgers... two others made milkshakes and another two handled the French fries... like Henry Ford before them they developed an assembly line of food: 'Fast Food.' McDonald's Fast Food.

Ray Kroc came into the picture in 1954 when the McDonald boys ordered eight multi milkshake mixers from the company Ray worked for because they were selling about a squillion shakes a month from one little old joint. Kroc drove down to San Bernadino to find out why they were selling so many dang milkshakes. Eventually Kroc became their exclusive franchising agent for the entire country and opened his first ever McDonald's franchise restaurant in Illinois in 1955, and then in 1961 he bought all rights to the McDonald's concept from the McDonald's brothers, for 2.7 million. The fact is he didn't even open the first franchise, that honor went to Neil Fox of Phoenix, Arizona. The McDonald brothers, sold their first franchise to Neil in 1952 for a $1000 bucks and because his new store was to be the prototype for all future McDonald's stores in the process of designing it they "invented" the 'Golden Arches' which became the world-wide symbol of McDonald's. There were seven golden-arched stands already in operation in California and Arizona when Kroc opened his first franchised store in 1955 in Des Plains, Illinois. The original golden-arched store in Phoenix has been demolished, but the second one in Downey, California (Los Angeles area) which opened on August 18, 1953 remains today in virtually its original condition.

Those are just the facts but this American guy wanted to bet me his house that Ray Kroc started McDonald's. Go figure.

Comment: End of story or rather the beginning of Ray Kroc's McDonald's empire. I think what confuses people is the fact that Ray Kroc is the founder of 'McDonald's Corporation', which is an altogether different animal, it's his testament and vision to being an entrepreneurial genius in the fast-food franchising business. But, the original idea does, and will always, belong to the McDonald's brothers. Still, there's confusion as to when McDonald's actually started. I don't know why when once again the facts are pretty straight forward: The McDonald boys opened their restaurant in 1940 which was exactly like every other restaurant at the time.So, in 1948 they closed down their restaurant and completely re-modelled it with an assembly line of fast food inspired by America's great car maker Henry Ford.

That's it in a nutshell... that's when the idea of fast food germinated 1948 not 1940... pretty simple really, but I've even seen the answer to pop quizzes about when McDonald's started being 1940 (wrong).

Pluto

Ask the average American where New Zealand is and they usually put it somewhere near Finland or just this side of the Balkans. In other words, they haven't a clue.

I'll give you a tip: If you're looking for New Zealand on your world globe just flip it upside down.

On the other hand, my younger sister thought New Zealand might be a distant suburb of the planet Pluto (uh yeah, it's still a planet to me regardless of what some astronomy geeks say). She wanted to send our kids a present but she wasn't sure about sending a Sesame Street Big Bird talking alphabet toy - in case New Zealand didn't have the same alphabet as the United States. Hello, Earth calling New Zealand.

Comment: When my mother came to visit me in Napier in 1981 she honestly asked me if I had indoor plumbing.

Weekends

There were many things that had appealed to me as soon as I first arrived in New Zealand in 1980. Nobody worked on weekends, for instance. The shops were all shut. In fact, the whole country closed down every January. Television didn't start till midday and shut down at midnight. You had a choice of only two channels with no ads on a Sunday. The first time ads appeared on a Sunday was for the opening of the 1984 Los Angeles Olympics because Television New Zealand took their feed from ABC (American Broadcasting Corporation), and what an 'outcry'! You'd have thought the Americans had murdered the Queen. Televisions commercials on a Sunday, bloody (kiwi swear word) outrageous! I really did love it when Television New Zealand had only two channels because even though television had become my career, there's a point where too much television is not necessarily a good thing.

Milk

But, for me by far and away the coolest thing about New Zealand was they sold milk in bottles, glass bottles. I can remember drinking milk out of bottles in the States when I was a kid. Hell, I can recall the milkman just casually strolling into the kitchen (is that where all those milkman jokes came from?) and putting our milk bottles in the ice box. Can you imagine that happening in today's uptight society? The pleasure of taking a cold bottle of milk with its clean crisp taste and gulping it with gusto is a lost art form. And little old New Zealand still had it when I got here. I paid fourteen cents for my pint of milk with the silver foil cap top which was delivered to my door. But modern technology is a pernicious evil and while it took a while to snake its way down to the South Pacific it eventually did. Free weekends are a thing of the past, satellite dishes and cable have brought in a squillion TV channels here, but the most dastardly thing they did was to put milk in wax cartons and plastic bottles, then spent untold millions trying to convince the public that milk encased in wax tasted the same as when it came out of that cold-to-the-touch bottle.

They killed milk.

Wrong Side

Driving on the left side of the road really brought its own challenges and often a surge of adrenaline when I forgot why the steering wheel was on the side of the car usually reserved for the passenger. In fact everything is swapped around: the turn signals, windshield wipers and the gas and brake pedals. And it just feels wrong. I would signal to turn left and my windscreen wipers would whip into action, much to the amusement of my passengers. And by the way New Zealand drivers don't signal they indicate. Like I said even the gas and brake pedals seemed to be reversed. I discovered this one day when I drove right through my closed garage door. I had parked in front of the garage and hopped out of my car. I swear I had put it in park but apparently not as the car started rolling towards my garage door. In a panic I quickly jumped back into my car and slammed on the brakes, but, because I was in panic mode I reverted back to my American heritage and instead had slammed on the gas pedal where I thought the brake pedal was and smashed right through the door... oops.

And I had to force myself after a lifetime of training to look the other way... to look in the opposite direction for oncoming traffic when coming out of a driveway. I made the fatal mistake of asking my beautiful wife if the way was clear when we were in the States and I was coming out of a supermarket parking lot onto a four-lane expressway. She gave me the all clear and for whatever reason - i.e. divine intervention, stroke of luck, whatever - just as I was about to pull out I suddenly had the presence of mind to hit the brakes hard... just as I did an eighteen wheeler came screaming past in a blur. Oops, that would have been messy.

Fred Flintstone

When I first arrived in New Zealand as a passenger in a car taking a long sweeping bend - cruising on the left side of the road I would swear that we were about to collide with another oncoming car head on as both my feet were furiously pumping the floor a la Fred Flintstone in a sustained panic.

But the feature I feared most about New Zealand drivers was their side street game of chicken. It works like this: Whenever you're driving down a straightaway some mad bastard from every side street is going to approach every intersection at about the same speed as a jet-powered car blasting down the Bonneville Salt Flats in Utah. And at the last possible second they'll slam on their brakes barely screeching to a shuddering halt. You just never knew for certain if they were going to stop or not. Maybe that was the point! The bastards!

Wachyamacallits

In America I was a suburban kid born and raised with asphalt between my toes. I've got absolutely no idea of what to do with a trailer once it's hitched to your car, and if something's broken, forget it. I go out and buy another one.

That ain't the way it's done Down Under. My extended Kiwi family put me to shame as they're all home handymen. They've got tools and gadgets and wachyamacallits; everything you need to build it, fix it, knock it down and sweep it up. If it has a name and a purpose, it sits in their toolshed, awaiting to be called into action.

This DIY (Do It Yourself) state of mind is neatly summed up by the locals as 'Kiwi ingenuity and a piece of #8 fencing wire.'

Don't ask me what the fencing wire is actually used for, other than fencing. I've never actually seen it in action. I can only assume that it played a similar role to Moses' staff in the early days of the DIY religion, the first Testament of which was written somewhere in the dark recesses of New Zealand's rural background.

Tow bars get good usage in New Zealand -practically every second car has a trailer being dragged behind a car. And they whip in and out of the tightest spaces. Honestly you get the impression these black singlet blokes could happily reverse a trailer carrying the Queen Mary into the bedroom closet.

Me? I'm hopeless! Oh, occasionally I've tried to drive ass backwards with a trailer hooked up. Just reverse the damn thing down the drive and out onto the road. And every time it will jack-knife! Right into that pinched 'V.'

I mumble and cuss under my breath as I inch forward to straighten out the trailer. Then slowly - ever so slowly - I try to navigate down the driveway, inch by inch... and son of a bitch, two feet later it's back in the jack knife!

Finally, in total frustration, I unhook the trailer and push it out onto the road by hand. I then drive the trailer-less car onto the road and re-hitch the trailer.

It's a tedious process, to say the least, and I become acutely aware of the entertainment I provide to the neighbors who are watching from their windows and laughing at the idiot American.

Green Thumbs

Kiwis are also dab hands at gardening - they know all the secrets of Mother Earth. It's like they're all related. They lay their collective horny hands on her breast and make her spurt beautiful flowers and huge unblemished vegetables. They know her cycles and moods and all of her different soil types across New Zealand. Well, across their own backyards, at least. Any Kiwi can knock up three different kinds of compost bin, lay a begonia bed, cause daffodils to spring from the earth well before their appointed time and re-pot a Ficus Benjamina all in a single afternoon.

I guess my gardening efforts look rather pathetic with my one potted cactus.

The Modest People

New Zealand is a paradise, flat out beautiful and spectacular. It's a scenic wonderland of natural light and colors. But what distinguishes New Zealand is not its picture-perfect postcard scenery, but its people.

They are an absolute hoot! Five million quirky rugged souls who appear so stoic at times you'd swear that they've been pumped full of formaldehyde.

Half the time I didn't understand what the hell they were on about. New Zealand is a country which seems at first glance to be simple and straightforward. But underneath that polite reserved exterior there lies a stubborn, perverse, un-American little outpost. You're never quite sure if they're having you on or not. They call it - taking the mickey.

They are modest to the point of shrugging off their achievements. They hate show offs. And they suffer from terminal politeness.

I love watching the daily politeness of most New Zealanders. They're forever giving you a pre-apology and thanking you. If you step on their toes their immediate response is, "Sorry." And buying anything in a New Zealand dairy is an exercise in who can 'out thank' whom.

It goes something like this:

Customer: 'I'll have a dozen eggs, thanks.'
Store clerk: 'Thank you.'
Customer: 'And a loaf of bread too, thank you.'
Store clerk: 'Thank you.'
Customer: 'Thank you.'
Store clerk: 'That'll be $6.70, thank you.'
Customer (handing over money): '...Thank-you.'
Store clerk: 'Thank you.'
Customer: 'Thank you.'
Store clerk (handing back change): 'Thank you.'
Customer: 'Thanks.'
Store clerk: 'Thank you.'

Steak & Fries

I know where I got the reputation for being loud and vulgar, but the reputation for being weird just sort of developed. I dispute the whole thing. I'm not too loud; people are too quiet. I'm not weird; people are too straight. I think people are too quiet through excessive politeness. People spend too much time concealing their weirdness in the name of being civilized... for instance:

Kiwis are just so polite in so many ways in everyday life. When I was in Invercargill for a speaking assignment I had dinner in the hotel restaurant.

It had been a long day and I was enjoying a nice cold glass of beer when the young waiter came by for my order. I told the young man that with my beer I'd just like a nice big juicy steak rare with French fries. The kid looked down at me and gulped several times looking like someone had just murdered his cat when he timidly apologized and told me that the steak and fries came with vegetables.

I looked at him bemused... then told him: "That's ok... I'll tell ya what... when you pick up my plate of steak and fries and vegetables... grab a knife and walk over to the kitchen sink and carefully but slowly scrape those damn vegetables right off my plate into the sink and then presto you'll be left with my plate of steak and fries." Problem solved. The kid gulped and apologized a few more times and said, "Yes, sir... thank you." And I replied, "No, thank you!"

The guy that was eating with me said that's weird man... why couldn't you just eat the steak and fries and leave the vegetables?

I just looked at my friend and told him that he obviously had no appreciation for aesthetics... beer... steak and fries paint a beautiful picture... the addition of limp broccoli watered down mushy peas and scorched carrots would just ruin the effect.

And my friend exclaimed, "Yeah, Like I said - You're weird!" Maybe he had a point.

Comment: Tell me this isn't true - I think one of the most maligned foods in the world is the humble French fry. People just don't take pride in their work when it comes to preparing a quality French fry. I absolutely love French fries. They are so tasty when they are fried to perfection so they're crunchy and hot and salty yum! But how many times do they come out looking limp and under-cooked. You hold one up and it droops - that's a crime folks. In fact, a drooping fry is simply not a French fry it's just a limp piece of potato. Ordering French fries is like buying a lotto ticket - the odds are great that you're going to be disappointed.

General Custer

Though more polite, I found New Zealand's rhythm a lot stiffer than in the States, California's mood is casual and loose. Easy. New Zealand is more formal, definitely not jocular. They don't do 'grab ass' here.

Mmmmm ... grab ass.

Living abroad I was constantly marching to the beat of a different drummer and that got me a lot of party invites. Every one of my antipodean friends wanted to show off their pet American... There were "theme parties" where I was the theme.

On the other hand every time I went to any function I always felt like Custer at the Battle of Little Big Horn. I was always in the midst of strangers.

For instance: When I went to my first father and son outing at kindergarten - a fish and chips night - I watched all the other fathers casually chatting in groups of two or three about local politics and rugby. I talked to my three-year old son Sam.

Every day I know I'm not going to see an old high school classmate or a university classmate or any of my family ever. They say no man is an island, but on this island you can come pretty damn close.

Muhammad Ali

New Zealand's isolation from the rest of the developed world has forced its citizens to be inventive - they've had to find their own solutions to problems. Their ability to innovate borders on genius. But because they live so far away, the rest of the world doesn't always hear about their achievements, and that's a pity.

For instance, did you know that the jogging revolution began in New Zealand? Running gently for basic fitness and good health is a craze that Olympic track coach Arthur Lydiard inspired with the Auckland joggers club in 1962 as a keep fit group for obese businessmen. Lydiard coached the great Peter Snell who beat American miler Jim Ryan and then went on to Olympic Gold. Too bad Arthur didn't take out a patent on jogging.

One New Zealand entrepreneur who had the business sense to commercialise an ancient form of a daring stunt was kiwi A.J. Hackett, the man credited with inventing bungy jumping, has made a fortune as New Zealand positioned itself to the world as the home of extreme sports.

That would probably come as a surprise to the Melanesians of Pentecost Island, who have been practising the art for some centuries, long before Mr Hackett came along. Granted the Melanesians used a vine... and not always with the desired effects. Ouch!

A sore point in New Zealand is the issue of who became the first humans to make a powered flight. Of course, Americans accept it was the Wright Brothers who were pioneering their aircraft contraptions early in 1903 at Kitty Hawk, North Carolina. Round about the same time, New Zealander Richard Pearse (1877-1953) was gluing together his balsa wood creation on his father's farm at Waitohi, South Canterbury, in the South Island. New Zealanders argue that their man got off the ground first - and that the Wright brothers just had access to better press.

Of course, New Zealand also lays claim to having invented feminism. They were the first country in the world to give women the vote in 1893. Go figure.

Scientist Ernest Rutherford, another South Islander, was a Nobel Prize winner and is credited with being the father of nuclear power - he worked out how to split the atom, which is no mean feat.

But, for all their achievements, New Zealanders will do anything other than stand up in public and beat their chest with joy. That would be seen as showing off and, as they say here, that would be 'skiting'.

When New Zealand beekeeper Sir Edmund Hillary became the first man to climb to the summit of Earth's highest mountain, Mt Everest, in 1953, with Sherpa Tenzing Norgay, his response was short and simple:

'Well, we knocked the bastard off.'

And that was it as he crunched off in the snow.

A nation of Muhammad Ali's they ain't!

Comment: I had the rare pleasure of interviewing Hillary at Sydney's iconic Opera House during the 2000 Olympics and even at eighty he was an imposing figure.

I asked the world's most obvious question: 'What was it like on the top?' And got the world's most unexpected reply.

'I was not as excited as you might have expected. I was aware that we had to get down the mountain again.'

And that's it in a nutshell - the laconic under statement is the staple of their language.

American Billboard

Me. I'm loud. I'm full of energy. I'm a walking American Billboard. I wear my ego on the outside. My flamboyant style went totally against the grain. I was the only American in the country hosting national programs. I had my own national newspaper column, my own radio show and yes, even my own television show. I was in their living rooms in living color. I was right in their faces BIG TIME. I was an American billboard in a very, very strange land. They couldn't avoid me even if the wanted to. The main criticism I heard from the New Zealand public had to do with the size of my "huge ego." They thought this was a crime against nature and that I should be embarrassed about it:

'Listen, mate, I'm sorry, but you like yourself a bit, don't you?'

'No. Not a bit. A lot!'

'Well, it's just, you know, I'm sorry, I like your broadcasts, but I don't like you.'

'That's cool. I like myself enough for the both of us. And buddy, don't apologize. It's not your fault.'

'Are you having a go at me, mate? You want to step outside?'

'Nah, thanks anyway.'

"Stepping outside" is the most popular way of solving problems in New Zealand. This is a man's country, where men are men and the sheep are nervous.

Ego
When you've got an ego the size of Texas you don't bother with trivial things. Ego is, as they say in Latin, the sine qua non... or as we say in California, 'the nitty' and 'the gritty.'

In California, we understand ego. In California, we have movie stars and heavyweight boxers with egos so big they have to charter buses to carry them around. They call them entourages. The entourage is made up of a group of people each charged with carrying a bit of the ego. Whenever the champ or the current world's hottest actor is relaxing in his penthouse suite, he's got a built-in group of totally open and honest friends to say things like:

'You the champ, baby.'
'You the greatest.'
'Looking good, baby, looking good.'

And so forth.

In New Zealand, it's a lot lower key and they use the language of understatement.

'Hey, you weren't too bad, you old bastard.'
'You didn't stink.'
'I've seen worse.'

Comment: They really do like to underscore themselves. I was fronting a television show called 'Neighborhood" where they got local personalities to just basically talk about where you lived and the people who lived there.

When I was talking about all the cool kiwis I knew in my neighborhood I gave them a really good build-up with lots of energy and enthusiasm: These people are - Amazing... Talented... Kind and Generous to a fault... which they were but when I finished my New Zealand director told me that we'd re-shoot this segment and he asked me to tone it down on my over-the-top praise of the kiwis in my hood.

Honest, that's what he said... I just looked at him and thought - "Wow man... you guys really are wet."

Asshole of the World

Or else they simply ignore you. I once gave an after-dinner address at the world's last bus stop. It's a small rural windswept city situated at the end of the South Island. Go any further south and it's just you and the planet's biggest ice-box (penguins included), the South Pole. The desolation of Invercargill had such a devastating effect on Scottish comedian Billy Connolly, he immediately walked through the streets crying out, 'Bring out your dead. Bring out your dead.'

And when Mick Jagger of the Rolling Stones got stranded there in the 1960s, he called it the asshole of the world.

So, there I was, at Earth's very last War Memorial Hall, staring at an auditorium packed with people who looked like they had either just survived the Great Depression or were extras in a remake of the movie Invasion of the Body Snatchers. We're talking a serious looking crowd here. I didn't see a lot of jovial banter going on.

I talked. I shouted. I jumped up and down. I sweated. I did party tricks. Dead silence. I cajoled. I philosophized. I regaled. I pulled my pants down. Zip. Zilch. Zero. Nodda.

A big fat nothing. It was a room filled with intent stares.

Afterwards, this mob (who took Omerta to unheard of levels) conveyed to me how enthralled they were by my talk. Like I said, I had no clue as to what the hell they were on about.

Comment: Invercargill was the location for the filming of the movie: 'The World's Fastest Indian' starring Anthony Hopkins, based on the true story of local resident Burt Munro the New Zealand motorcycle racer famous for setting a world record of just over 183 mph at the Bonneville Salt Flats, Utah on August 26, 1967 on his 1920 Indian motorcycle. Check out the movie it's excellent I recommend it.

The Taliban
New Zealanders don't make a fuss. That probably makes it the ideal place to hide in.

Over the years, New Zealand has become the out-of-the-way destination for the rich and famous. It's somewhere they can wander along the street, knowing that even if New Zealanders recognise them, they won't have the nerve to let them realise it.

Everyone from singer Shania Twain to Titanic director James Cameron have built homes in this country while American presidents, rock stars and business moguls have found it the ideal place to have a private holiday.

Hell, just walking down the street one day in my neighbourhood I bumped into actor Laurence Fishburne sitting on the sidewalk sipping a coffee and nobody was paying him any attention.

Anyone can disappear in New Zealand... and I mean anyone.

After 911, when the world's media converged on Afghanistan, the lone New Zealand journalist there asked the Taliban if New Zealand was on their terror list for retribution?

The Taliban all looked at one another quizzically scratching their beards, and then eyed him up suspiciously and declared:

"Maybe... where is New Zealand?"

Comment: I know that you're thinking that that is a load of bullshit... go on admit it... I know you're thinking that... but it's not. I didn't make that up - it's true!

Comment Two: The other thing is being anonymous can work in reverse living in New Zealand. You too can hide from the world. One year I was home on a flight from San Francisco to New Orleans to watch the NCAA Final Four (University basketball) at the Superdome. I got up from my seat and walked to the back of the plane to stretch my legs... so I'm standing in the back where the stewardess's are making the coffee when one of them excitedly exclaims to me: "Isn't it exciting Howie Mandel is on our flight!?! I just look at her and replied: "Yeah, that's cool... who's Howie Mandel?" And man it was like in a cartoon when the character's lower jaw drops all the way to the floor... hers did exactly that and she screeched: "Howie Mandel... you don't know who Howie Mandel is?" Again I replied: "Nope."

Ok so for anybody who's reading this and like me at the time didn't know who big Howie is here's the lowdown: He's a Canadian comedian, television personality, screenwriter, actor, producer, director, entrepreneur, game show host and author. Wow... I got tired just writing all of that... at the time I was on the plane Mandel's current rise to fame came from playing rowdy ER intern Dr. Wayne Fiscus on the NBC (National Broadcasting Company in America) medical drama St. Elsewhere. And seeing as I had never seen the show I hadn't a clue as to who Howie Mandel was and that was very cool with me.

Salman Rushdie

I live in one of the nicest little seaside villages imaginable. It's the Auckland suburb of St Heliers. Think Mayberry R.F.D. by the sea with sweeping beaches, streets lined with huge palm and Pohutukawa trees (native New Zealand tree known as their Christmas tree from its beautiful red blossoms) lying in the shadow of Rangitoto, a massive volcano rising majestically out of the harbor.

Surely, there is no better place in the world to raise kids.

After school we all head down to one of a half dozen pristine beaches where the kids play in the surf or dig through the rock pools. It's beautiful, clean, not crowded and best of all, it's about a minute from our home.

Although even in this exceedingly quiet Norman Rockwell painting of a town some pretty amazing things take place. For instance I was cruising through the village one day when I spotted him. His presence screamed attention as if he were the only man on the planet. I turned abruptly and lumbered straight towards him. Two shadowy men wearing tiny earpieces were simultaneously reaching inside their double-breasted jackets.

I'm not a small guy either. I am 6' 3" and 245 pounds. I'm completely bald, and sport a full and wild-looking beard. I had also perfected a glare that matched my decidedly non-shrinking violet demeanor. Looking back, I was extremely lucky I wasn't mowed down in a hail of bullets. If this happened in America I'm certain I'd be dead now.

As I approached him I recognized some publishers I knew from Random House. They quickly shouted out a pre-emptive 'John!'

The shadowy hands reappeared empty from behind the double-breasted jackets.

Phew. A sudden and violent death appeared to have been averted.

And there he sat. The world's most wanted author on the lam:

Salman Rushdie.

I felt some kind of connection to him having just read his book 'The Satanic Verses' that earned him a fatwa calling for his assassination issued by Ayatollah Ruhollah Khomeini, the Supreme Leader of Iran, on 14 February 1989 (note that's Valentine's Day I guess no love lost there).

The British Government put Rushdie under police protection. Hence the men with tiny earpieces and double-breasted pin striped suits hiding weapons.

I looked down. Salman looked up. There was an uncomfortable awkward silence. It was the classic scene of I-knew-that-he-knew-that-I-knew and he-knew-that-I-knew-he-knew.
Know what I mean?

I was trying to be cool and not blurt out loudly and wildly, 'Hey, it's Salman Rushdie!' He looked sheepish. It was that all-time haunted look that actor Richard Janssen gave so convincingly every week as Dr Richard Kimble in the old television series The Fugitive.

And the really weird thing was all these grown men were standing surrounding the seated Rushdie easily being the most ill-at-ease group I've ever seen in my life and nobody introduced anybody.

Finally, I looked down and nodded. Rushdie looked up and sheepishly nodded back. I guess that makes us nodding acquaintances.

And that was it. I couldn't stand the uneasy tension a second longer so I nodded to everyone and left.

Richard Attenborough

And one day Mother Nature put on one helluva a show right on St. Heliers beach. A pod of fifty killer whales (Orca) sealed off the entrance to the bay. Why? Because they were on a hunting feeding frenzy for stingrays.

While the main pod sealed off the stingrays' escape route smaller groups of Orcas were chasing stingrays flipping them high into the air and then leaping spectacularly clean out of the ocean and swallowing these rays down in a single gulp. Absolutely amazing to watch only feet from where I was standing on the beach. And as I walked along the beach the shallows were teeming with hundreds and hundreds of frightened stingrays.

The most amazing thing to me was how quick the Orcas were as they ran down their prey. The speed of these giant monsters slicing through the water and then exploding from the ocean high into the air was in a word "awesome." The stingrays would probably have another word for it.

Maori

While most New Zealanders are retiring types, often afraid to show their emotions, the same can't be said of Maori.

I've experienced and relished many different aspects of Maori culture. Up north, I was on the receiving end of a full Maori challenge and thought the warrior was going to strike me with his taiaha (weapon). I've learned and performed the haka (a war chant) in front of a crowd of 20,000. I've slept on a marae (meeting house) and I've attended a tangi (funeral).

That came about when I was working on a television mini-series about the 1840's Maori Land Wars and in the middle of the production, the assistant director's wife suddenly died. The cast and crew were invited to a marae for the tangi.

A marae is a place where the culture can be celebrated, where intertribal obligations can be met and where important ceremonies such as welcoming visitors and farewelling the dead can be performed. Even though I wouldn't ordinarily rush to the funeral of someone I barely knew, this was a special invitation for us only so it was an honor to be there.

I didn't know it but I was about to witness a real life version of Frankie Goes To Hollywood's song 'When Two Tribes Go To War', our First AD and his wife came from two different tribes and each had their own ideas about the funeral protocol. Suddenly we had ringside seats to a fierce debate between the two elders of each tribe. They were distinguished white-haired older gentlemen who stood with walking sticks, the fire and brimstone erupting from them all in Maori was a sight to behold!

After they finished, guests and family came together. I found myself hugging and embracing each and every relative as we slowly proceeded to file past the open casket in the meeting house, and as we drew nearer my heart did one of those funny little pitty-pat things as I realised that everyone was kneeling down to do a Hongi (Maori greeting by pressing noses) with the deceased... Whoa! I'm not overly comfortable being around dead people full stop. I had a quick anxiety attack looking rapidly around for an escape route but didn't want to offend or be rude, so I got down on my knees and embraced this deceased stranger pressing my nose to hers.

Comment: The longer I lived in New Zealand, the more I tried to reconcile the differences between my culture, my language and my view of the world with those I needed to fit in with my adopted land. After more than 40 years, I still have much to learn.

Good Humor Ice-cream Man

Nowhere were the differences in my old and new comfort zones more obvious than when someone suggested I have a crack at cricket.

Cricket. There's a reason it's named after an insect. Long before I landed in New Zealand, the game had been explained to me. I had been sitting in a stuffy postgraduate classroom at San Jose State University, 45 miles south of San Francisco, listening to a visiting Australian professor unravel the mysteries of cricket for his young American audience. Part of the mystery was trying to understand the dude in the first place and to decipher his hilarious accent. I had barely heard of the game of cricket and casually wrote it off as some kind of English version of baseball.

I had my mind in Candlestick Park where the San Francisco Giants used to play when I was a kid, (the very first game I went to was won by Juan Marichal behind a Willie Mays homer) with score lines of 2 to 1 or 5 to 3 and after a couple of dogs, a bag of peanuts and a couple of hours it was all over.

Captain Kangaroo explained that cricket matches went on for five days (this drew a lot of snickers from the class - Hollywood marriages don't last that long) and that one player can stay at bat all day scoring in the vicinity of one hundred, two hundred and sometimes as much as 300 runs all by themselves and that teams can score five, six or 700 runs.

And to top it all off, much of the time nobody wins with the games ending in what he termed 'glorious draws.' I just couldn't get my head around those numbers - I leaned over to the guy sitting next to me and jokingly laughed: 'What's this guy been smoking?' We both laughed and I immediately forgot about that bullshit.

But, eight years down the track there I was standing in my all white playing strip (looking for all-the world like your neighbourhood Good Humor ice-cream man) in Napier, New Zealand. And that's where I discovered what my professor had been talking about; I played a summer season of third grade cricket. Third grade would be like playing 'Triple A' ball in the Florida Development League. There was a mix of raw talent, veteran talent, no talent and one American, and everybody was serious as hell. On opening day I'm fired up! Yeah, baby, let's play ball! They do it a little differently down there, it's all stiff upper lips and curt nods and a quiet "gidday, mate," each to his own.

We're fielding first so my skipper (captain) tells me to go out to "deep cover" (which sounds like a CIA gig) and be a sweeper. Right? I grimly nod to humor him, but as I'm walking past him, I realize that I'm short of a couple of fundamentals.

The Aussie professor never mentioned 'deep cover.' And I'm wondering... where's deep cover and what's a sweeper? Do I need a broom?

I soon discover that deep cover is like in Little League when they send the nerd into right field where he can't do too much damage. There's not much action and unlike baseball you're out there for hours baking in the hot sun.

I might be fired up, but I'm also starting to wilt. No ozone layer down that way equates to sizzling, crispy fried white heat. It's kind of like being the bug under the magnifying glass the little kid is frying to death. So, here's a health tip: "Wear sunscreen in New Zealand."

Eons later, I'm still beyond where anybody can see me sweeping my nose with my right index finger, when there's an almighty whack! The batter has smashed a towering drive in my direction. I know that everyone in the park will be watching intently to see what the big Yank will do with this monster hit. No sweat, I give it the casual half-circle trot and I position myself under the rapidly descending cricket ball.

I'm standing there with my feet firmly planted, waiting with nonchalance to tuck that baby away. I put both my hands up in position and remember they don't use gloves in cricket they play barehanded and a cricket ball is just as hard as a baseball. Suddenly the ball is upon me and it sails right through that little space that the thumb and forefinger make when stretched wide with the velocity of a small crashing moon rock smashing square in the middle of my chest. THuuuuunnnnnk! Cracking it I think. As I slowly sink to my knees, gasping for air, eyes watering and pain spreading quickly throughout my upper body I'm thinking, in one play I've become the Charlie Brown of cricket. I know this from the suppressed laughter and giggles I hear all around the park. My skipper trots over to see if I'm alright and in true Kiwi laconic understatement he consoles: "Aaahhhh, you just misjudged that one a fraction, mate."

I gasped in agreement. He then suggests in an off-hand manner that I might like to try another position. You bet! He wanted to know how I felt about playing Silly Mid-off.

"Silly Mid-off?" I repeated off-handedly.

"Yes. Silly Mid-off," he repeated back happily.

Of course, I didn't know what in the world he was talking about and he knew that I didn't know. It's like when guys start talking about car engines and all the doo-dads attached to them... all my life I've just nodded in agreement with whatever was being said without having a clue. But I could feel all of those British clones looking down their collective upturned noses at this intruder, this baseball person from the colonies. Well, a man's gotta do what a man's gotta do, this called for action we're talking ego here, manhood, cojones, big balls. Me, Silly Mid-off? Of course. No problem. Besides, it didn't sound very dangerous, it sounded like I might have to wear a court jester's hat or something?

A suit of armor would be more like it. Let me explain it this way: Take any Major League infielder, the first baseman, second baseman, shortstop, whomever, and put them about a foot and a half from home plate when Aaron Judge or Bryce Harper is at bat. Yeah, right. But, they do it in cricket.

I know it sounds silly and maybe that's where they got the name from... like I said it was all new to me? The skipper saw that I was giving all this some serious thought so he explained to me that he was bringing in his best spinner (junk ball pitcher). The theory is that a good spinner will put enough action on the ball to fool the batter into popping it up somewhere in the vicinity of my new position Silly Mid-off and I shouldn't have any trouble making a soft catch. Of course, this was in no way a slur upon my previous Deep-Cover catching abilities.

The game of cricket kills baseball in the weird name game for labelling pitches: instead of knuckle balls or sliders or curveballs... cricketers throw flippers or googlies or left arm Chinaman. So, I'm standing about what seems to me to be about a fraction of an inch from the batter (I can see all the zits on his face) who's clutching this huge slab of wood. The bowler is approaching and I'm gulping... he delivers the softest looking pitch I've ever seen... it's a floater for crying out loud and I'm trying desperately to control my sphincter, which is going into overload spasms. I feel certain that the batter is going to drive the fat part of his bat into the fat part of the ball which will then smash into the fat part of my forehead.

After an eternity of slow motion the ball finally arrives. It bounces on the dirt in front of the batter and goes into some kind of crazy spin. I can clearly see the batter's facial muscles tighten in anticipation.

The ball starts to rise.

The batter brings up his bat.

My heart is booming.

The cricket bat makes contact with the ball.

My heart has literally leaped into my throat.

WHHhhhoooooosh! All the air escapes from my body as I anticipated my last moments on earth.

He's bunted it. Or in cricket parlance he's blocked it.

I go limp. I'm drained. I'm like a deflated rag doll.

And that was only the first bowl (pitch). I've got to endure five more such deliveries before I can safely get me and my balls the heck out of there with my manhood intact.

Batter Up

Finally, it's our turn to bat and I discovered that on the sideline there's plenty of time to eat, especially when your team is batting. I was sitting by the cakes and sandwiches when the skipper ambled over and in the demurest tone imaginable whispered, "Mate, pad up." Padding up is the first step to discovering that under all this serene idleness there's a deep pool of raw adrenalin lurking away in cricket. It's what happens when it's your turn to bat. All the sloths sitting by the cakes and sandwiches heaved a sigh of relief and loaded up with another couple of pounds each of cake and a gallon or so of tea, to recover from the fright of possibly being picked to go out in the blistering sun and bat. "Me?" I exclaim. "Yeah, great, let me at'em!"

The skipper sombrely whispers, "Good on ya, mate."

I got handed about five hundred pounds of gear. Cricket pads are huge, bulky and take forever to strap on. Doing all that bending and twisting and pulling and whatever to get the pads in position is like a whole Yoga workout. By the time I finished encasing my body in pads I looked like a contestant on American Gladiator.

Next, I got handed a chunky slab of wood. This is not a Louisville slugger (baseball bat) but a cricket bat which looks like something a high school woodshop dropout let loose with a tree trunk and a lathe would produce - a baseball bat handle protruding from the end of a very thick piano leg.

My instructions are to proceed out to the middle and protect my wicket. I start to shuffle off when somebody yells out, "Hey, mate did you remember to put your cup on?" Yee gods, I haven't!

The protection of the family jewels is a universal language that men the world over intuitively understand. I quickly shuffled back and started fumbling through the equipment bag. Only I can't find one big enough. That's not a boast. It's just that boxes come in different sizes and the big ones are all gone. I suspect the other guys took them whether they needed a big one or not. It's like condoms only come in three sizes: Big, large and extra large. Nobody out there is a medium or small. I managed to squeeze into a box meant for a ten-year-old in place. Only now with my shuffle I've also got this exaggerated tilt - hello John Wayne.

Finally, I get out to the hard-mowed slab of grassless cracked dirt that to me looks like a Lilliputian airport runway on the Serengeti Plains. The wicket that I've been entrusted to protect is a set of three croquet sticks stuck into the runway at either end with a couple of small wooden looking barrels placed into slots cut into the top of the sticks.

I pounded the dirt and looked up to face the bowler, only I couldn't see the bastard as he was damn near out of the park. They run like a half mile before they deliver the ball, there are no pitcher mounds in cricket. I was always out of breath, before I had even taken a swing, just watching these clowns run in. Watching someone deliver a pitch in cricket is hysterically funny. They're all arms and legs ass over end.

There are two reasons for this: Firstly they aren't allowed to bend or break their elbow during the delivery action (stiff arm) and secondly they must throw the ball down into the cracked dirt so that it skips to the batter. The end result is they look like they're going to do a running cartwheel and at the very last second they've bailed out of it. I tried to bowl once and threw myself straight into the ground. Damn near broke my nose. This is where cricket can be dangerous. Nobody bothered to mention this when I solemnly marched out to protect my wicket. In baseball when the pitcher throws a bean ball (at the batter's head), all hell breaks loose. The batter throws down his bat in disgust and he along with both teams rush the pitcher's mound for a good old-fashioned donnybrook (fight).

I discovered that's not how it works in cricket where your head is a moving target for the bowler. He's going to fire that ball at your head at roughly the same speed as a major league pitcher. As the ball whizzes past your ear - or God forbid your nose - forget about your team sprinting out to tear the bowler to shreds. What I saw was my team muttering, "Gosh, that was nasty!" to each other while they were looking around for another sandwich. I learned that a good strong glare at your opponent is considered outrageous on the cricket pitch, which is just so English and so very wet.

At last the long distance runner roared in and fired a fast ball straight down the pike (middle of the stumps - croquet sticks). Now, seeing as I'm the new kid on the block and I haven't seen this guy's stuff before and I've spent all that time padding up I decided to take one, whomp! It smacks me square in my leg pad. Suddenly this numb nut goes into a standing epileptic fit scaring the bejesus out of me:

"Hooooowwwwwwwwwwwwwwwwwwwwzzzzzzzaaaaat!"

He's screaming at me? Gesticulating and thrusting his finger in my direction. He's all purple with rage and the veins in his neck are about to burst. I merely shrugged my shoulders, I don't know. Beats the hell out of me what he's on about! So I just bellowed right back that I was okay, let's go again, buddy!

Turns out his venom wasn't being directed at me at all, but at the umpire. The guy was pleading, begging for a strike. I can't imagine a Major League pitcher in the States grovelling before the umpire for a strike. How goofy is that? And they think we're 'strange.' I was standing there laughing until the parking lot attendant in the white lab coat (umpire) slowly raised his index finger like he's testing the wind direction and suddenly the other team was jumping for joy and hugging each other.

This is where cricket has a lot in common with soccer: In soccer 'scoring' is extremely tough so when the ball does find the back of the net suddenly it's a huge hug-a-thon amongst the players, likewise in cricket 'outs' are so difficult to come by (except when I'm batting) that when they do come there's much bonhomie among the players.

I'm looking around confused. What's new? The wicketkeeper (catcher) told me that I could go back to the sideline now for a few beers. Back on the sideline I'm told that the umpire's raised finger indicated an LBW, this stands for 'Leg Before Wicket' which simply means that in the umpire's mind if my leg hadn't been in the way, the ball would have hit my wicket and I would have been out. And we think calling balls and strikes is tough. I instantly segued, "What's that, a Down Under version of a BMW?" Nobody laughed. As I was sipping my beer on the sidelines, I thought, "I think I'll stick to baseball. At least when you go home at the end of the day you know who won."

Comment One: My goal as a batter was to get double figures... ten or more runs. But, I just couldn't get there...several times I got to nine runs and then every time I got out... bummmer!

Comment Two: So what did I discover to be the difference between baseball and cricket? I'll tell ya the major difference between baseball and cricket... the big difference... the HUGE difference... the major league difference... there's no hot dogs! They don't do hot dogs in cricket! I have never been to a major league baseball game in the States without having a hot dog that would be so un-American! Babe Ruth definitely wouldn't have been able to play cricket!

Comment Three: Napier is the art deco capital of the world. A massive earthquake destroyed Napier on February 3, 1931. The town was rebuilt in the architectural style of the day. Thus all of its buildings are beautiful monuments to the preservation of art deco. The Napier Art Deco Festival is held every February and attracts visitors from around the world.

Limited Stay

As a carrier of both American and New Zealand passports, it makes for an interesting choice when you arrive at US customs. When we went to the States I opted to use my New Zealand passport and enter through the line of foreign visitors along with my wife Jennifer.

The customs officer checked my papers and immediately stated: 'You're an American citizen. Why are you presenting a New Zealand passport?'
I explained to him that I was with my wife who was a New Zealander.

'But, you're an American citizen,' he repeated, as if my New Zealand citizenship didn't count for anything.

He kept looking at my passport and then up at me and then at the screen with that puzzling look that starts to fill your armpits with pools of sweat.

Finally, he called over his supervisor. This higher official gave me the same puzzling once-over and boldly declared: 'You're an American citizen.'

Once more I carefully explained to these idiots that I was being chivalrous and standing by my wife.

Both of them huddled and muddled over this, as if it was the most unheard of thing - a man wishing to be with his wife. It must be a plot of some kind.

Finally, and almost reluctantly, they stamped my passport but not before the senior official delivered one last judgment.

'Under this passport, you can only stay in America for six months,' he said with a smirk.

So much for 'Give me your tired, your poor/Your huddled masses yearning to breathe free...'

A Little Misunderstanding
When I flew to Fiji to get married, I learned that Fijian New Zealand All Black Walter Little was also in Fiji recuperating from a pulled hamstring.

Not one to miss an opportunity, one of my wedding guests was my director who just happened to have his camera with him so I decided to mix in a little business with a lot of pleasure by doing a story about Walter for a Sky sports show called Sports Cafe.

Since I didn't have a clue as to where Walter was I decided to do a spoof about trying to locate him. I marched up to unsuspecting hotel guests where we were staying on Denarau Island asking if they knew where Walter Little was. The reactions were hilarious; first they'd furrow their brow, repeating the name slowly to themselves while squinting their eyes.

'W-a-l-t-e-r L-i-t-t-l-e.' They would roll the words around their mouths as if inspiration might strike them at any moment. Finally, they would shrug their shoulders with palms up, exclaiming that, no, they didn't know where he was and in fact had never heard of him.

When I heard a group of Italians excitedly jabbering away in the hotel lobby I rounded on them with my question and they instantly began waving their arms in every direction like an Italian traffic cop on steroids screaming 'All Blacks... All Blacks.'

But, alas, when pressed for details about Walter Little's whereabouts, their down-turned faces said it all - they couldn't help me.

I had a half dozen great reactions and was about to wrap it up when I spied a young Japanese couple out by the pool. I sauntered over in their direction with my cameraman/director in tow and popped the question. The young Japanese lady barely spoke English so we played a game of verbal ping pong.

'Do you know where Walter Little is?'

She scrunched up her face. 'Walter Little?'

'Yes, Walter Little,' I repeated.

'Walter Little?' she queried back at me.

Uh huh... 'Walter Little,' I shot back at her.

By this time I was expecting her to shake her head and call a halt to this charade when her face lit up and offered me a glorious, beaming smile.

She confidently announced, 'Yes! Yes, I know where Walter Little is.'

I was absolutely gob-smacked. I couldn't believe it. I nearly dropped my microphone.

I quickly recovered, screaming at her, 'You know where Walter Little is?'

By way of confirmation she did that little Japanese bow thing. I was delirious now.

'Where is he?' I shouted, 'where?'

She took hold of my arm and motioned for me to follow. I was intrigued beyond imagination.

I yelled to my cameraman to keep rolling as we scurried between the deck chairs around the pool deck much to the amusement of the other hotel guests... through the expansive lobby with everybody's heads jerking up to watch this travelling circus - a hulking reporter running with microphone in hand chasing a young Japanese couple followed by a lumbering cameraman.

We ran out the lobby past the pitch and putt golf course, finally arriving in a beautiful garden where she pointed: 'There!'

She was pointing at a pond.

'There,' she said again. 'There is Water Lily.'

I stood there and beamed. I absolutely loved her enthusiasm for that Water Lily.

I looked at the water lily floating on the pond and then turned to the camera and exclaimed: Walter Little or Water Lily it's all a matter of interpretation."

Tale of Two Sandwiches
People are always travelling to the far ends of the planet in search of that rare gastronomic experience. These days, there are entire television channels devoted to plates of food.

But, what exactly makes for a great meal? Is it the finest meats... the absolute best wines... the company... the location... what? Really it's a combination of all those things and a bit more because 'context and memory' play powerful roles in all truly great meals in one's life.

On the road anything can be out of this world, even the simplest of ingredients can take on a special aura given the right 'context.'

Take the humble sandwich, for instance. For me, a simple ham sandwich on fresh fluffy white bread with mustard, washed down with a Coca-Cola, is a great combination. That's it, nothing more... nothing less. I've had my fair share of this singular American treat in my own kitchen, but one particular ham sandwich sticks out in my memory.

It took place in a remote Indian souvenir shop near Suva, Fiji. Jennifer was inspecting their goods (shopping) and knowing that that would take a while, I decided a quick bite to eat was in order. I spoke to the attentive Indian man behind the counter who was seemingly surrounded by a million and one trinkets.

'How ya going, brother? I'll have a ham sandwich on white bread with mustard and a Coke!'

The smiling man stood still and kept smiling.

So, I repeated my order and he kept smiling. We were at a standstill; finally, a young Indian woman appeared from nowhere and translated my American bellow into the language of India.

The man indicated that I should sit.

I responded, 'I'm cool,' upon which he scooted around and personally escorted me to a small table with a big grin on his face.

Who was I to argue with such a gesture? I sat down.

In short order in walked a tall thin waiter with a set of silverware which he elaborately laid out in front of me. By now, I was thinking this has gotta be one helluva big ham sandwich to require a knife and fork, especially one from their exquisite silver collection. My waiter shook out a freshly starched linen napkin with an authoritative snap and delicately placed it on my lap. Such formality.

But the best was yet to come; another waiter brought out my sandwich on a silver platter with the concentration, pomp and ceremony you'd have thought was worthy of the delivery of a Russian Faberge Egg. Behind him trotted another guy with my chilled Coke on a smaller silver platter.

And then they all stood to one side, intently watching me eat.

Wow! Best damn ham sandwich I've ever eaten. How could it not have been?

Sandwich Number Two

Contrast that with another sandwich caper; this one in a swank motel in the far north of New Zealand's North Island. I was staying at the Waitangi Copthorne Hotel which was newly refurbished and, according to the literature plastered everywhere, a fine four-star establishment with a picture of a beaming Mitt Romney look-a-like from Chicago assuring me that my every need would be their pleasure to deliver.

I checked into my room and immediately ordered room service. I fancied a light snack to tide me over until dinner; a cheese and onion toasted sandwich and a Coke.

No big deal right. Wrong.

Two hours later I finally heard a knock on my door.

I opened it and was handed a cold congealed cheese sandwich (it looked pathetic - it was green like it had gangrene). I took it and inquired, 'Where's my Coke?'
Without missing a beat, this young New Zealand Maori waiter instantly snarled at me, 'You're lucky you got the sandwich.'

He turned and he casually strolled away. Most people would be fuming, but I was busting up. I just loved the guy's attitude. It was like, 'yeah, sure some fancy American's spent a lot of money sprucing this joint up, but that certainly doesn't mean the locals are going to kiss your ass.'

Hilarious! Like I said: 'context and memory.'

Sky High

I have a food confession to make. I actually like airplane food for a reason you wouldn't normally think of. To me there's no better city in the world to fly into than Sydney on a sparkling clear sunny morning (except San Francisco, of course). From the aircraft, you look down to see the Sydney Harbor with its aqua green inlets and white sandy beaches spread out before you, like a cluster of fine emeralds. Then the Sydney Harbor Bridge comes into view, with the distinctive Opera House snuggled beside it. Magnificent!

But back to the food. In the good old days there were two basic airline tickets. If you had a fat wad of bills encased in a gold money clip you bought a ticket up at the front of the plane with Champagne and caviar included.

On the other hand, if moths flew out of your coin purse when you opened it, you found yourself in cattle class wolfing down hotdogs and boxed Chardonnay. Either way, everybody got fed. Today, it's all about choices and cost so on this particular trip we bought a no-frills ticket which meant that we didn't get a drop of grog nor even a slither of ham or grate of cheese. But lucky for me I could take one itty bitty 7kg carry-on bag aboard.

I figured it's only a three-hour flight from Auckland and I could tuck into something at the David Jones food court.

But this trip taught me the true meaning of airline meals - whether you like airplane food or not these little brightly colored tin foiled wrapped surprise packages are great time eaters.

First comes the anticipation as they wheel the food trolley down the aisle, then you have your little interchange with the stewardess; 'Will that be the yellow melted cheese on the chicken sausage (what's with airlines and chicken sausage?) Or the tuna casserole? Would you like wine with your meal?

The tray and your beverage of choice are placed in front of you.

You pick up the utensil package carefully spending the next five minutes attempting to rip it open without stabbing anyone with your wobbly plastic knife or spraying them with your pepper sachet.

Then you peel back the foil top on the water; doesn't it always kind of burp as you do this and spray a tablespoon of water on your crotch? Or maybe that's just me.

Anyway, by now you're thirsty so you have a small sip.

Next you check out the small bowl of fruit salad and then comes the big moment when you slowly peel back the foil top on the main dinner dish.

You commence to peck and probe your various food dishes... finish your water or juice... set up your coffee cup and then repack everything into neat little bundles and anticipate the next trolley that will pick up all your little eaten treasures.

This all takes time and concentration.

Without my meal on the Sydney flight I was left to twiddle my thumbs, craning my neck to see what the more fortunate travelers were receiving in their hot packages making the three-hour flight seem like three months.

The lesson in this is don't be Scrooge McDuck. Sit back, relax and order the meal, and time will fly.

You'll feel a lovely warm glow on arrival - thanks to your allocated booze allowance!

Fiji Bitter
And speaking of alcohol, I'll never forget my first trip to Fiji and my first taste of Fiji Bitter. It was the week before Christmas and it was stinking hot... I mean like taking a stroll in an oven of suffocating heat that you couldn't escape. We came upon this little dairy (a shack really) deep in the lush jungle - we walked in and I noticed that they served beer... ice cold beer. My throat was bone dry so I bought my very first quart bottle of Fiji Bitter.

I can distinctly recall how pleasing it felt in my grasp as my anticipation built... how the little beads of condensed water rolled down its sides and how thrilling it felt to raise that cold bottle up to my parched lips and feel it's pure chilled carbonated pleasure gurgling down my throat.

Best damn bottle of beer I've ever drank.

Bula.

Aloha

People watching and 'kibitzing' is one of my favorite past times with my wife Jennifer. Airports are great for this but even better is the beach wall that runs along Kalakaua Avenue in Waikiki, drinking bottled Margaritas (another ritual) that we've purchased from one of the many ABC stores that dot the strip. From there, Jennifer and I watch the human parade as it passes by just like at the beginning of the movie Ice Age. And believe me humans come in all shapes, sizes and just weird shit.

Hong Kong

My favorite soup used to be my dad's chicken noodle soup. But, these days without question my favorite soup is Won Ton Noodle soup. And believe me I've had this soup in a million different soup kitchens... but my all-time favorite is off the beaten track in Hong Kong. I couldn't even tell you the name of the joint as it's written in Chinese. I can tell you that it sits on a side road off the main drag running through Hong Kong - Nathan Road.

This place is one of the wonders of the world - it's very small maybe six or seven tables of the old fashion kind you know the ones I'm talking about with chrome and Formica tops with a very dinky kitchen. But man oh man the Won Ton noodle soup there is as Tina Turner would put it: "Simply the best!"

Whenever I'm there which is every time I go to Hong Kong I only order two things: A bowl of Won Ton noodle soup and a bottle of coke.

The coke bottle is old fashioned as well - it's one of those 1950's numbers - small bottle with the extra thick green glass... I love it!

Si Senior

Closer to home, and when I refer to home I still mean the San Francisco Bay Area, an absolute must for us is to sneak into a Chillis (one of those brightly lit fast food Tex-Mex chains that runs the length of California). They serve the world's best Margaritas from a list of more than 20 varieties.

At around four in the afternoon, before the dinner rush, it's time to cozy up to a Cadillac margarita (Sauza Gold Tequila, Patron Citronge Orange Liqueur and GranGala) with a basket of warm, freshly-salted corn chips along with a bowl of hot salsa that'll make your tongue curl. Heaven.

Turkey McNuggets

I just love Thanksgiving - that's an American Thanksgiving - food, family and football with no gifts or cards to worry about. What could be a better combination?

One year, some Kiwi friends wanted to cook a special Thanksgiving dinner for me. Remember the seasons are reversed Down Under. At this time of the year New Zealand is steamy and hot and filled with brilliant blue skies. It's very tropical. That's because it's the start of the summer season. When I arrived, I was escorted to the backyard where they had the barbie (barbecue) fired up. They had carved the entire turkey into little bite-sized chunks (think Turkey McNuggets) and they were charcoaling them beyond recognition on skewers.

No drumsticks, no mashed potatoes and gravy, no pumpkin pie. I fought back the urge to wipe a tear from the corner of my eye. No family and definitely no football either. Somehow, I realised, it would never be the same Downunder.

Comment One: And here's another holiday that is completely bonkers: Bing Crosby's "White Christmas" isn't a big seller at the bottom end of the world. Instead of "Dashing through the snow in a one-horse-open sleigh," or "Chestnuts roasting on an open fire," Kiwis are busy slapping on copious amounts of suntan oil down at the beach in sweltering one-hundred-plus degree heat on Christmas day.

Comment Two: And for some reason a lot of kiwis say 'Happy Christmas' instead of 'Merry Christmas'.

When I took Jennifer home to America to meet my family at Christmas we bumped into a friend of mine and Jennifer greeted him with 'Happy Christmas', the look on his face was priceless... he looked at me and said with a stunned quizzical expression: "That's not right? It's 'Happy New Year' and 'Merry Christmas". I was laughing my tits off!

Comment Three: And Halloween is another holiday all out of whack down here. By the time Halloween rolls around we're already in Daylight Savings so it doesn't get dark until around 9:00pm. Trust me when you're running around wearing a ghost costume there's nothing spooky when there aren't any dark shadows and the sun is shining brightly.

Bucket List
New Zealand, however, has introduced me to one of the world's most pleasurable food experiences.

If you want to enjoy a delicacy that is just out of this world like having sex with all your clothes on you'll just have to make the trip Down Under to enjoy a Bluff oyster. Juicy and shivery, these plump jewels from the sea will be worth the trip.

Bluff is the last wee fishing village at the bottom end of the South Island. Kiwis love their Bluff Oysters so much there are never enough to export. Aficionados have them flown from one end of the country to the other at the start of the oyster season so they can gulp down a few of these treats.

Add them to your 'things I must do before I die' list.

U.S. Airspace
One day, I visited the United States embassy in downtown Auckland with my Australian producer buddy, a guy who resembled a walking ashtray. He has exceptionally bright yellow nicotine stained fingers, always has a rolled cigarette stuck behind his ear and is constantly rolling another cig.

As we entered, he was rolling a smoke, as was his habit, but with no intention of lighting it inside. He was tapped on the shoulder by an ageing security guard who sternly warned him: 'No smoking in US airspace.'

His manner indicated that my buddy's potential cigarette smoke was a threat to America's national security. I thought this was hysterical and started laughing.

I couldn't help but use the line made immortal by tennis legend John McEnroe: 'You can't be serious!

My loud outburst immediately had every official head lifting from their document scanners to see what the fuss was all about.

Oops. Now about those nukes... No, I didn't want to go there.

China

Let me say this right from the get go... straight from the top... I love going to China... the place is just a fantastic beehive of activity... nobody is sitting on their asses in China... walk down any of their trillion back yard alley ways and you'll find people making clothes... printing posters and leaflets... welding heavy machinery... stacking glass windows... loading pipes... doing pottery... slaughtering pigs and chickens... it's all go in a Chinese alley... these are extremely busy people.

In fact one morning I saw a Chinese guy walking down the main boulevard of Guangzhou with a huge helping of a pigs entails or a cows stomach or some such animal... there he was walking down the road with his hands full heaped high with animal guts with the intestines hanging off like vines and I just assumed that he was going home for a morning fry-up. And the thing is nobody paid him any attention at all - like this was a regular occurrence and nothing to get excited about... unless of course he was gonna invite you over to enjoy this feast.

I find it a most intriguing place to travel mainly because so few people speak any English at all in the far flung places Jennifer and I visit... you have to rely on your wits and perseverance to get by...

For instance one time we were in apparently the small city of Nantong which is a port city on the Yangtze River but it also has a population of over 7 million - small city indeed...

Anyway there we are running around this place and nobody and I mean absolutely nobody speaks any English and we see no other Europeans in any shape or form... we're it... and everywhere we go we are stared at intently by the populace... we went in to a restaurant and ordered some food by pointing at the pictures on the menu board and all the chefs and cooks and wait staff came out to inspect us... hilarious...

We were staying at this most beautiful 5-star hotel that was just built and they had imported palm trees to put in the lobby... great hotel... the next morning we went down to have breakfast in their buffet which was just exquisite and I walked up to the chef behind the egg counter and said, "How ya going... I'll have two eggs sunny side up thanks"... the guy just looked at me blankly...

Jennifer came over laughing and reminded me that this guy didn't understand a single thing I had just said... he doesn't speak English darling... doh... I just forgot... but that's cool that's ok it's their country and I'm the visitor so it's me who has to adjust and in my opinion that's good for you... good for your soul... go out there and experience different ways of living… get out of your rut man!

Comment: And just to show what a small, small world it can be... when my son Sam was a junior in high school we had a senior Chinese student come over to the house every week to tutor him in math... one day I asked this kid where he was from in China... he said oh just a city you wouldn't have heard of... ok I said try me – where... and he said Nantong...

I told him that not only had I heard of it I'd been there and had a great time exploring the place... only I never got my sunny side up eggs... of course I told him that story and he just laughed.

Shanghai

Generally speaking, I don't find Chinese people that funny. But, on my very first trip to China I discovered one Chinese gentleman in Shanghai to be absolutely hilarious. I was on a business trip with my wife Jennifer and we had just checked into the Majesty Plaza which I renamed The Mystery Palace because every day it seemed something wacky happened inside this lovely old hotel.

Everything in China is massive and crowded. The Mystery Palace is located at the top end of Nanjing Road which is a pedestrian walking road or I should say a massive walking boulevard.

When we came out of the train tunnel at the top end of Nanjing Road the shock of it stopped me dead in my tracks. I just stood there and stared. In front of me more than a million people were walking down this road.

After we checked into our room, we went to put our passports and valuables into the room safe.

The word 'safe' here was an oxymoron. You could pick up the hotel room safe and just walk around with it...it wasn't attached or bolted into the wall. Like I said all kinds of wacky shit happened in this place.

So, we called the hotel manager and when he walked in our room Jennifer picked up the safe and carried it into the hallway and set it down in front of our room.

The manager looked at the safe then turned to look at us and then looked back to the safe and in the best traditions of that great Chinese philosopher Confucius with a pointed finger he whispered:

"Ahhhhhhhhhh... safe... not safe!"

Jennifer and I both had stomach cramps from laughing so much and every time we saw the guy at reception he would utter that line... very cool guy.

A.J. Foyt

Whose space is it anyway? Ok here it is... like most Westerners I have more than once sworn at the driving antics of an Asian person... but now that I've been to China several times I take what they do behind the wheel with a grain of salt... it all comes down to your philosophy in regards to space... in the Western world if you dare to enter another drivers space and this could be anywhere from 3 to 4 to 6 car lengths or more you'll get the blaring of horns and the gesticulating with the hands and the driver mouthing you Fuck-wit... etc... it's unfortunately the modern day road rage of 'I will protect my space at all costs'... so ya gotta ask the question - who exactly gave them this Divine right that all of that particular space belonged to them and no one else...

If you drive in China everywhere you go the joint is absolutely crowded jammed stacked to the gunnels... there's very little space... there, any space is fair game for a car... and I mean any... if there's an inch... just a measly little inch... a Chinese driver will edge his car in and I'm not exaggerating in the least bit here - it's funny as a fight to me but it seems that all Chinese drivers think they're A.J. Foyt when they get behind the wheel, causing my sphincter on numerous occasions to tightly clench itself into a knot as we've screamed down roads barely missing semi-trailer trucks... squillions of motorcycles piled high with goods – chickens and the entire family... people on bicycles... you name it and if it was on the road we barely missed it...

Once when driving from the train station to our hotel in Guangzhou which was over an hour away our driver was driving a stick shift in a really beat up old wreck of a tin pot car constantly down shifting and revving the shit out of his motor as we kept changing lanes every 200 feet in peak hour traffic... I'm not kidding this guy was amazing to watch as he was in and out of the smallest spaces and always managed to wiggle his way into another space so we could change lanes and then repeat the process all over again... it was, in a word, ludicrous where this guy wedged his car... really it was just like a wild ride in a cartoon... bending and zooming in and around every obstacle in our path...

So Chinese driving just seems normal to me now I understand where its coming from... so when I get back home I'm always amazed by how angry motorists get if you pull out in front of them when there's enough space for an 18 wheeler to pull in... in China that's enough space for an entire fleet of cars to pull in... like I said it all comes down to your philosophy, because no matter how much the Chinese interact with the Western world they do at times still just get it all ass-backwards... case in point:

Every year Jennifer and I went (before Coronavirus) to the international market in Yiwu which according to the World Bank is the largest small commodities market in the world with well over 75,000 stores... in fact this building is so large it would take you 2 hours to walk from one end to the other end... it's huge folks... so yeah these people deal with the Western world all the time... and yet one day we were in one of the thousands of hat stores and Jennifer and her Chinese agent Andy were doing business with the owners when I look at a beautiful beanie hat on display with a lovely boldly embroidered logo in reference to Disneyland... but instead of saying 'Mickey Mouse'... it said 'Mouse Mickey'... so just keep that in mind when an Asian driver makes an inexplicable move in their car.

Language As A Weapon
One year Jennifer took the trip to China by herself... so she's talking to me on the phone standing all alone on a deserted train platform in the middle of nowhere... at one point in our conversation she went uh oh... and I immediately exclaim: "What's up... what's wrong"... she told me that a group of rough looking guys were approaching... so what does Jennifer do... she immediately starts stamping her foot and in a low growling guttural voice she speaks in Maori... Ngaruwahia (which is a town in the North Island)... Manaakitanga (which means respect for the hosts)... Turangawaewae (which means a place to stand)... and like magic these strangers decided this woman was a nut job and they turned around and left... most likely these guys were just curious like everyone else to see a white woman... but why take chances when a good guttural Maori chant will do the trick.

Qingdao

On another trip to China we're in Qingdao which is a beautiful city... but instead of smelling all their lovely roses I land in their hospital with a very bad kidney infection... like most things the Chinese don't do hospitals like the Western world... again nobody in the joint speaks English and I'm the only white dude in the place so I'm getting the once over by everyone... people just walked right up to me only inches from my face and intently studied me like I was an alien species from another planet... I would have found this highly amusing except I was in intense pain by this stage... luckily the hospital had an interpreter... ok so this is the drill in a Chinese hospital: Nurses and doctors do not attend to you... that is done by your family... every patient in the place has their family with them or if you don't have a family like the guy next to me he hired an off duty nurse to look after him...

Everything in China is on a jumbo scale... they put me in a bed in a room with 400 other patients... it was like a vast football field of beds as far as the eye could see...

Next you walk over to the nurses station where they take your blood... in my case I hobbled over...

After that I was wheeled in a wheelchair by Jennifer and the bell boy from the hotel where we were staying (the Chinese get very nervous if anything goes wrong with white people in their care) and Barbara (one of the business people Jennifer was seeing) and our interpreter down endless corridors to the CT scanning room.

They wheeled me in and got me up and onto the scanning table which took some effort as I was in so much pain now I was doubled over and could barely move... and then they had to scramble out of the room as the Chinese guy behind the glass partition was yelling at them before he turned the machine on... after that they wheeled me back to my bed where after the results came back from the blood tests and the CT scan a nurse gave Jennifer a medicine chit...

Jennifer then went to the medicine room and presented her chit... they gave her the medicine I needed after she paid them of course... and just a side note here the CT scan only cost $125 bucks which is extremely cheap...

Anyway back she comes with my stuff which she gives to the nurse who then hooks me up with a drip for the antibiotics and I get a pole to hang the bag from...

I only mention the pole because this was a luxury for me and the room because none of the Chinese patients get a pole instead one of their family members stand behind them holding their drip bag with the medicine in it up in the air... trust me that just looks weird...

And meanwhile with all this going on I still have a steady stream of Chinese visitors coming up to me to give me a closer inspection... but now I'm feeling better with the antibiotics being pumped into me so I'm laughing and carrying on a one sided conversation with all these people to myself because none of them speak English... hi how ya going... you good... I hope you're not too unwell...

Finally the head doctor comes over and gives me the analysis from the CT scan which is spot on and I know this because I've had many a CT scan and what he says marries up with what the doctor's in Auckland have told me... then he suggests that I should stay in the hospital overnight and without thinking or blinking an eyeball I immediately respond with: "No fucking way Doc... when that drip is done I'm done... thanks…"

And that was it when that drip finished around 10:30pm that night they unhooked me and I left without speaking to anyone else... and I gotta say while it was vastly different to what I was used to the care they provided was excellent and we carried on with our trip without any more kidney problems.

Comment: Ok I honestly don't even know how to explain this next story...I know you're gonna think that I made it up...but no, this is exactly what happened:

Jennifer and I are in Qingdao... we check into our hotel and I'm gonna take a shower... I walk into the bathroom which is about the size of a shoebox... a small shoebox... I go to the toilet...

While I'm sitting on the toilet I'm looking directly at the bathtub and what looks like to me a shower nozzle hanging out of the wall... but there isn't a shower curtain and there's no place to hang the nozzle on the wall like you do when you're taking a shower... very strange I'm thinking but then again this is China...

I take a shower which is difficult to say the least trying to soap yourself with one hand while holding the shower nozzle with the other... but I manage to do it and also to not splash too much water out on the floor...

I get out dry myself and walk into our room where I say to Jennifer... "Wow that's a very strange shower arrangement they've got in there and there's no shower curtain"... Jennifer just gives me the most quizzical look and says - "What are you talking about - there's a glass shower box in there"... I say - "No there isn't"... and Jennifer exclaims - "Yes there most definitely is"... so I go back in and look and blow me down there it is a beautiful glass shower box that is right next to the toilet...

We're talking about an inch from the toilet...

While I was sitting on the toilet I could have bumped the shower with my elbow.... ok so here's the deal I'm in this tiny bathroom... I'm on the toilet... I'm at the sink... I'm standing in the bathtub... I'm all over that fucking joint... and yet I miss the biggest object in the room... how is that possible?

I mean we're talking about the elephant in the room... the world's biggest elephant in a very tiny... tiny room... hell Stevie Wonder would have seen that shower... I would have sworn on a stack of bibles that there was no shower in that bathroom... somebody please explain that to me!!!

Silence is Golden

Sometimes... just sometimes being loud is definitely not necessary to get your point across. Sometimes silence speaks volumes. While we were in Shanghai naturally we had to do some shopping. So, there we were Jennifer and myself in the ladies' department at Marks & Spencer's in downtown Shanghai. After walking down umpteen rows where Jennifer seemed to finger every piece of clothing on offer, she handed me her purse to hold as she entered the dressing rooms with mountains of items to try on. I sat down on a long bench just outside the dressing rooms. I turned to see a grizzled old Chinese man sitting at the other end of the bench. He too was clutching his wife's purse. I looked at him. He looked at me. I looked at his purse. He looked at my purse. Then we both looked at each other and simultaneously just shrugged our shoulders.

Breakfast

Absolutely the best ever breakfast I've eaten was at the top of the Shanghai Sofitel on Nanjing Road. I started out with beautiful one-inch-thick triangle cut chunks of the sweetest watermelon I've ever eaten... and of course they took out all the pips.

And I have to confess here that I probably add something to my watermelon that most people don't - salt. Yeah I just love to salt my watermelon.

Up next I had beautiful smoked duck... and I mean just tender and succulent to the point it was ridiculous it was so tasty... and then I topped that off with one of the best bowls of prawn Won Ton noodle soup I've ever eaten...

It was just one of those situations that came out of the blue... Jennifer and I merely went upstairs for breakfast and we landed in food heaven... all the elements just came together seamlessly.

I don't ever expect to duplicate that experience. It was a oncer.

One Hour

Ok, so Jennifer and I fly into Shanghai one night on another business trip and I'm standing in front of our hotel while she's taking a quick shower before we go out to grab a bite to eat. It's a nice evening and the city's night lights are all aglow when this rather stunning beautiful young Chinese woman is in my space and starts up a casual conversation... okay yeah I should have been immediately alerted that not all was on the up and up here... but hey I just got off a 12-hour plane flight and I was still very jet-lagged... anyway it's the sort of conversation that goes along the lines of:

Chinese girl: Where are you from?
Me: I'm originally from San Francisco...
Her: Oh that's a beautiful city...
Me: Yeah, it is... where are you from...?
Her: Right here in Shanghai...
Me: yeah, well this is a great city too...

Yeah I know riveting conversation.... it continues...

Her: What are you doing tonight...?
Me: I'm just waiting for my wife who's upstairs taking a shower...

That's when her eyes lit up and she pounced on her opportunity propositioning me right then and there... she looks up at me and demurely bats her eyes as women are wont to do and says if I like I could go with her for an hour and my wife would never know...

I looked down into her smiling face and said: It would be more like two minutes tops and my wife would definitely know... so no thank you.

I know it must be a male thing but I was kind of pumped that I had been propositioned like I'm some kind of stud when in reality it's just business as usual for these gals... oh darn! And yes I told Jennifer.

911

If I ever needed reminding of where my loyalties lay, the events of September 11, 2001, took away any doubts.

I was in a deep sleep six thousand miles away when terrorists flew their hijacked aircraft into the Twin Towers, the Pentagon and the heart of America.

Jennifer was out of town on business and I had been up half the night with 18-month-old Sam, a baby not noted for his ability to sleep for long spells. A thud woke me up and my fuddled brain immediately worked out that Sam had rolled out of bed.

In the background, I could hear the shrill sound of the phone ringing. I don't know about you but to me, the phone always seems extra loud when it's bad news.

I scooped up my wailing son and grabbed the phone.

My father-in-law was on the other end and in a heavy voice he said I should turn on the television.

With dread, I watched the news coming in from my homeland. My immediate thought was to call Jennifer to make sure she was safe.

And then I had this insane urge to go home.

America was under attack! I needed to be there.

Why - and exactly what I was going to do when I got there - I didn't know. I just knew that I had this immense yearning in my gut to go home.

Yes, home.

In that moment, as much as I enjoyed my life Down Under, I knew where home would always be.

Of course, as I came to terms with what had happened in America, I realized there was nothing I could do and my urge to go there was driven by emotion and a feeling of helplessness.

Instead, I held Sam to me, clinging to the son my new life had given me, and I wept.

Comment One: Although I gotta say at the time of writing this with the way Benedict Arnold and all his fake followers are trying to pretend the Coronavirus pandemic doesn't exist in America being the total dumb shits that they are it has become clear, Americans are willing to risk their lives and the lives of everyone around them to do whatever they want. With that in mind I'm more than happy to stay put in my adoptive home... thank you!

CHAPTER TWO

How to Survive as a Big Actor with Small Parts
Learning to act teaches Dybvig some vital life skills - and shows him what Hollywood actors are really like.

Always Start with a Sex Scene
She had a nice body, all curvy in the right places. Her blouse was unbuttoned and her skirt was hiked up above her knees. The second floor hotel room was small. The young woman appeared tiny.

Nobody said anything. Tension came along for the ride.

Her hair was unruly as she lay back on the bed with legs that never quit dangling over the side. She had that come-on pout look.

I got down on my knees and my head disappeared under her skirt. She started to moan. Loudly.

'Cut.'

'That's a buy,' yelled the director.

I had just earned my first credit as an actor. I ravished a wanton young actress in the Shakespeare Tavern in downtown Auckland, New Zealand's largest city. It wasn't a porn movie. It was a short film. I didn't get paid. I did it for the experience. No! Not the going down bit. I needed the acting experience, being on a film set.

Before the cameras rolled, my new actress friend and I discussed the protocol needed to complete this delicate scene. We agreed I would munch high on the inside of her thigh. I munched with gusto. She was wearing grey bicycle shorts under her skirt.

I got lip burn.

Comment: That was my very first time being on a film set and I immediately discovered something. Namely that the director is not going to direct you in every little detail. This was a very delicate scene with me going down on this complete stranger and I kept expecting the director to come over and talk us through it... but she didn't. So, on my own initiative I got together with this actress and we discussed how we were going to do the scene.

In the Beginning
How did I end up shooting movies in New Zealand?

By accident of course. My controversial profile landed me a job as a sports anchor on a cable television network.

While working there, my television producer, a pear-shaped Australian beatnik, suggested I take acting lessons thinking it would give me more scope in my presenting roles. I agreed on one condition — that he sign up too so we could support each other.

We enrolled as drama students at the Auckland Performing Arts School which would eventually lead me to learn the Meisner Technique of acting. Sanford Meisner is a legend amongst acting circles, but mostly unknown in America. He was one of the founding members of Group Theatre and taught at the famed Neighborhood Playhouse in New York for more than 50 years. Students of his technique include film stars Gregory Peck, Steve McQueen and Sandra Bullock, and the star of television's Sopranos, James Gandolfini to name a few.

Being cast as the strong silent type was not exactly what I was used to, in or out of the studio. I had always considered myself a tough guy.

Acting challenged me to think again. Despite having my producer there for support, I initially struggled at the drama school, especially when it was my turn to try out in front of the class.

The thought of opening up emotionally in front of strangers scared me shitless. Hell, the advantage of being loud and outrageous was that strangers didn't want to get too close to me.

My first scene at the school with a female actor was a terrifying experience and a complete washout but it helped change my life.

There's a scene in the movie Broadcast News where actor Albert Brooks (Mel's brother) gets his first big break to read the evening news. He was so nervous he couldn't control the rivers of sweat pouring down his face. Well, I had those same rivers of sweat pouring down the sides of my face for my very first close-up acting scene.

We were sitting in chairs, our faces so close we could each feel the heat of the other's breath. I could see the tiny hairs on her upper lip as I mouthed some scripted endearments to her, a fellow student but still a stranger.

I felt trapped. There was nowhere to run.

The instructor and the rest of the class were staring at us with enough intensity to melt steel. I was drowning. I ended up soaking wet. But something happened. I was hooked enough to go out and purchase a wetsuit and persevere and for the first time in my life I started to tap into my inner emotional being.

Comment: I became a drama student: I enrolled in class after class... more on technique... another on Shakespeare (that was wild)... stage classes... voice classes... and finally the Meisner Technique.

Hollywood & Vine
Like I've said I've had plenty of acting classes in New Zealand... but I've only taken one acting class in America and you couldn't get any more cliched than this...

One night when we were visiting my older sister Nancy in Carlsbad, California which is a city near San Diego, I drove the 125 hundred miles to Los Angeles to take an acting class from Jeremiah Comey... And you'll never guess where his studios were located... ok I'll tell you... none other than at HOLLYWOOD & VINE... I mean come on you can't possibly get more cliched than that... this used to be the absolute birthplace of Hollywood... the intersection of Hollywood Boulevard and Vine Street in Hollywood is a district of Los Angeles which became known in the 1920's for its concentration of radio and movie related businesses... and just to top it off as the beating heart of the acting world... the Hollywood Walk of Fame is centered on this intersection.

Unfortunately for me no agent spotted my talent that night and that was that.

Rick Springfield

One of Meisner's tenets was to have "truthful moments", to live truthfully under imaginary circumstances.

I had an embarrassing unintentional truthful moment on a series called 'High Tide'. This was a cops and robbers show that constantly had beautiful buxom young girls flouncing about in bikinis. I was playing a hard-nosed police sergeant (what else) and Rick Springfield, (#1 single 1981 - Jessie's Girl), was an undercover agent disguised as a surfer. My first day on the set called for me to roll up in my cruiser and arrest Rick at the beach.

I was right in the middle of the scene reading Springfield his rights when something happened in the immediate background that didn't happen when we had rehearsed the scene just moments prior.

A swell of well-developed breasts with just the tiniest bit of bikini top covering them started to glide by in the background. I was okay until one young lady bounced by with so much ampleness her breasts did that little jiggle thing on top. I lost my concentration. The director called out, "What's the problem, John?"

"Nothing," I sighed. "I was just having a truthful moment."

Greg McGee & Chris Bailey

Everyone at one time or another needs a domino tipped in their favor to get the ball rolling. The role in 'Fallout' proved to be my acting domino. 'Fallout' was a political drama. I was known around town as a sports presenter and a former basketball bad boy. When I was involved with a game it usually turned into something out of the WWE. During one game I got so frustrated, I jumped up off the bench, ran one way, ran the other way, then ended up by the scorers' table, where I grabbed a gym bag and hurled it as high as I could into the air.

Turned out this bag belonged to the referee upon whom I was venting my frustrations. Everyone in the stadium looked up as his shirt, pants, socks and underwear all floated down onto the court. The joint erupted.

So I certainly wasn't the first pick for serious acting roles. In fact, I was finding it damn hard to get any serious auditions, period.

The writer of 'Fallout' Greg McGee wanted a real American for the part of Richard Armitage. He didn't want a Kiwi actor using a fake American accent. He got me an audition. He went even further. He got the director Chris Bailey to audition me.

Yes, I was in with a shot. All the hard work I had done in my acting classes had paid off. I nailed the audition.

But, the production house, South Pacific Pictures (Whale Rider - Keisha Castle-Hughes) wanted to play it safe and give this role to a more experienced performer.

However, unbeknown to me at the time both Greg and Chris went to bat for me to get that role. Their belief in a rookie actor was the domino that tipped my acting career into action.

Thanks guys!!!

Hercules

I was as far as one can get from Hollywood when I started my acting career. But, as luck would have it Hollywood came to me. The popular camp shows 'Hercules' and 'Xena' were both filmed in Auckland, New Zealand.

Appearing in those shows was a lot of fun. You got to dress up in outrageous costumes and in my case play monsters and bad guys in dungeons and castles.

And they paid you good money to do it.

The Mummy

Busty blondes are type cast and big burly men get the same treatment. The character descriptions for the roles I was put up for all had the same ring: Strong, pushy, aggressive, tough and hard, mean-looking, evil; I played thugs, slave-traders, pirates, henchmen, warlords and insane maniacs. My parts were mean, nasty and basically self-explanatory. I was never, ever going to end up with the girl. In my first major guest role in 'Hercules' I played a Satyr. I was the leader of a group of bandits terrorizing a village. Sound familiar?

This role called for three hours of make-up. I had to wear a prosthetic. They needed a bust of my head so I went to a special effects company where they plugged my ears with wax, dunked my head in a bucket of rubber jelly and then encased my entire head in strips of plaster of Paris. I got a solid idea of what a mummy must feel like as the plaster hardened. The process took about forty-five minutes. I could breathe only through my nose. This definitely wasn't a part for a claustrophobic. After that I went to an eye doctor to be fitted with yellow contact lenses.

Comment: I struggled with those yellow contact lenses. They were never comfortable on my eyes and getting them on took a lot of will power on my part. However, they looked fantastic. On the set on the day of the shoot the make-up gals had a real struggle getting them on my eyes.

They practically had to hog tie me to get them in. I was only supposed to wear them right before shooting my scene. But, as often happens in the movie business there were delays and believe me the make-up gals did not want to have to put those damn contact lenses in again so I had those suckers in way too long. My eyes hurt like hell. On the way home my eyes suddenly just shut down... I didn't know what was going on... but I literally couldn't open my eyes.

I had to swerve off the motorway and stayed put for about an hour. I could have easily crashed and killed myself that day. Eventually my eyes adjusted and I could carry on. Ya just never know what's going to happen in the land of make believe.

Nasty Max
The funniest and best bit of drama for that episode took place off the set. Along with all this exotic make-up I also had a pack of killer dogs. Universal brought in a special dog handler with four vicious Rottweiler hunting dogs. Just as we were about to go into the woods to shoot a scene an elderly gentleman with the most beautiful snow white hair and his geriatric pet Labrador out for a walk approached. I was standing there in a furry animal suit with a festering oozing prosthetic on my head wearing bright yellow contact lenses. The old guy paid no heed to me; it was like he came by Satyrs all the time.

The Rottweilers were an altogether different story. When they saw fresh meat in the shape of a friendly tail-wagging ancient mutt they went ballistic. The Rottweiler's dog handler, a big tough dude with tattoos and muscled forearms, was straining for all he was worth keeping his pack of compact snarling dinosaurs under control. This beautifully dressed older gent looked straight down his nose at the dog handler and his frothing beasts and in delightfully clipped English vowels commanded, "That's right you'd better keep your dogs under control. Old Max here can get frightfully nasty, very nasty indeed." You could have knocked me over with a feather. I actually fell down on my knees because I got stomach cramps from laughing so much.

116

Comment: This is what happens when there are no unions involved: The set for Hercules in the Underworld was a maze of enclosed tunnels and to create the atmosphere for the Underworld they had actually set up lit barrels of oil at the entrance and exits of every tunnel. The smoking oil barrels filled the entire set with - yes you guessed it - thick billowing clouds of black oily smoke.

When the director came up to me, he looked exactly like a character out of a Mad Max movie - he was wearing goggles and had a huge checked scarf wrapped around his head and nose. I remember Hercules star Kevin Sorbo telling me in our first scene that only in New Zealand could you have actual smoking barrels of oil infiltrating the set. Definitely not the healthiest of conditions.

Hollywood Star

My first encounter with a precious actor came on the set of 'Xena' where I was playing another thug making a move on Lucy Lawless. I arrived in the wee hours of the morning, did my wardrobe and make-up and retired to the guest actor's campervan. I was reading the morning paper and sipping a cup of coffee when in walked actor Robert Trebor, who had a regular role as Salmoneus in both 'Hercules' and 'Xena'. We hadn't met, and seeing as I was going to kick his butt that afternoon I jumped up and stuck out my hand and blurted, "How ya doin'? I'm John Dybvig."

Nothing. My hand was hanging out there in empty space while Trebor just stared at me like a stunned mullet. I kept smiling. He kept staring. Finally he came around and stammered, "Can I help you?"

"Nope, I'm fine," I exclaimed. "Just reading the paper."

Trebor then went into a slight tremble and stuttered, "But, you're in my trailer."

"What?"

"My trailer! This is my trailer."

"Oh."

It finally dawned on me where he was coming from; this was my first close-up encounter with a Hollywood star. I had previously worked with the lead star of 'Hercules' Kevin Sorbo in a Jim Beam ad, and he was about as friendly and down to earth as anybody you'd meet. The same can be said for 'Xena' star Lucy Lawless. I knew her before she put on the leather breastplates and she hadn't changed much. Lucy was always a hard working professional woman who treated people with respect. Lucy can kick my butt any day and she did in several episodes. But now I found my butt getting kicked out of a campervan. While I was collecting my belongings, Robert Trebor stepped out of the van and accosted producer Eric Gruendemann. Trebor was extremely excited as his words came tumbling out in a torrent:

"Eric, there's another actor in my van,' he whined.

"That's my van."

"It says in my contact that I get a personal van."

He kept repeating himself, "Eric, there's another actor in my van." "That's my van." Gruendemann calmed Trebor down and told him he'd fix the problem.

Later when I walked by there was a neon sign flashing Trebor's name on top of his campervan, in big bright lights.

Only kidding, but there was indeed a new sign on the trailer with Robert's name in big bold letters. I just laughed.

The sad thing to me was that Trebor was so uptight about such a trivial misunderstanding. I did enjoy working with him and he taught me a few things; so all in all everything worked out just fine.

So long as I stayed out of his goddamn van!

Number One

This is strictly unofficial of course, but I'm staking a claim for a bit of fame here, in the very first episode of 'Hercules - The Wrong Path' - I deliver the very first line of the series. I'm playing a thug (what else) in the opening two-minute teaser where my band-of-heartless bandits are robbing the local tavern. I'm holding a knife to the throat of a lusty wench and just before Kevin Sorbo (Hercules) and Michael Hurst (Iolaus) strut in to kick my ass I growl out these immortal words in my best gravelly sneer:

"Hurry up and get the money." Too bad I didn't shout, "Show me the money," (Cuba Gooding Junior's famous line from Jerry Maguire starring Tom Cruise). I could have been years ahead of my time.

Ron Silver

When my wife Jennifer and I attended the pre-production drinks of an HBO movie called 'Exposure' starring Alexandra Paul, possibly Hollywood's nicest human being and the only actress in Bay Watch with real natural breasts, and Ron Silver (Chicago Hope, The West Wing) a complex man if ever I met one, Jennifer was pregnant and way overdue, ballooning to the point of looking like the Goodyear blimp. When it was time to go Jennifer told Ron it was a pleasure meeting him and indeed they got on like a house on fire, which I just love about my wife, she can hold her own with anyone and gives back as good as she gets.

Silver suddenly got very serious and gave Jennifer the full Hollywood treatment. He took Jennifer's hand in his and gently caressed it and then in complete sincerity he gazed longingly into her eyes and purred, "I know we've just met Jennifer... but could you... would you...and here he took a moment to cast an eye over the enormous mound nestled between them... could you call me first?" And without missing a beat my wife shot right back, "I can do one better Ron, do you want to be there?"

Silver had that momentary stunned look like he hadn't really heard what he had just heard. After all he didn't know Jennifer, they had just met that night and she said it in all seriousness and held his gaze. He looked at her, hesitating slightly, then he just threw back his head and roared with laughter slapping my back exclaiming, "You've got a good one here, John!"

Thanks Ron, I know that.

Explosion
Ron was very intense on the set but he also had a wonderful streak for humour. For instance: In one scene a local actor playing the receptionist only had one line when the director asked her to speak an additional line. She squealed, "But I only learned one line." Yes, she was blonde. Silver immediately pulled out his cell phone and bellowed, "Hey call her agent! You can double your money." Everyone on the set just busted up.

I only had one scene with Ron but it was very memorable. We shot this scene in the dead of night, near the end of the movie, and the director wanted to keep it moving so he cut my four-line interchange with Silver down to two... no big deal really. I wasn't fazed. But Ron was. When we did our block through Ron exclaimed, "Hey John you've got two more lines here." I explained what the director wanted and he just said, "Bullshit!" and screamed out to the director, "David I think the scene works better with John saying his entire piece, you don't mind do you?"

And of course, he didn't, who's gonna argue with the star of the movie? And just to make this scene more interesting Ron changed tracks right in the middle of shooting just to keep me on my toes. In the block through, he played his part very low key in shock at news of his friends' death, but when we shot the scene he literally exploded in a rage and came at me like a bull in a china shop! Fortunately, I had the presence of mind to hang in there with him. Afterward he gave me a hug and said in all sincerity, I hope you didn't mind that John? I just went with the moment." Of course, I didn't mind, it was a pleasure and a thrill to have worked with Ron.

Comment: I was shocked to learn that Ron Silver died of esophageal cancer on the morning of March, 15, 2009.

John Hurt

One soon finds out that not all the best action is captured on film. On this particular film set early in the morning suddenly time stopped. Everyone stood suspended and held their breaths as the twice academy award - nominated, triple Bafta award and Golden Globe winning English actor John Hurt, well known for his portrayals of Thomas W. Kane in the movie Alien (the alien pops out of his chest at dinner) and John Merrick in The Elephant Man stopped dead in his tracks, turned and stared.

One of the first films I worked on as an American accent coach was 'The Climb' starring Hurt and Oscar nominated American actor David Strathairn (Good Luck and Good Night).

It was the very first day of the shoot in a cold dusty Blockhouse Bay warehouse in the outer suburbs of Auckland, New Zealand. Hurt in character held center stage rehearsing a long monologue about his character's time as an engineer in the jungles of Venezuela, when he described the barmaid in this scene with skin as 'brown as a nut' the director suddenly interrupted with: "that's nut brown, John".

Hurt was visibly not impressed. The warehouse was eerily silent filled with the distant creaks and groans of a vast old building as Hurt just stood there rooted to the spot intently studying the director.

Finally he began his monologue again from the beginning and when he came to his description of the barmaid this time he carefully described her skin as 'nut brown' whereupon he proceeded ever so slowly from the far side of the set along with every set of the crews eyes over to the director who was sitting in one of those classic canvas, collapsible directors chairs, when he finally got there Hurt bent down so his face was merely inches from the director's and quietly purred: "Was that good for you Bob?"

The tension was palpable. Talk about an electric atmosphere this was the best scene in the film, only it wasn't in the movie it was real!

Comment: I had half a dozen local actors on that film and they all passed themselves off as Americans with flying colors. The only actor who got pinged for a wayward accent from the review in Variety magazine was English actor John Hurt. And the irony here was I wasn't allowed to work with him because he was such a big star.

And the thing is I could have easily corrected his accent... but ego monster played his hand once again which is fairly normal in the movie business.

Elephant Man

Later on the set of 'The Climb' I heard English actor John Hurt put an extremely bombastic journalist very nicely in his place.

This wordsmith was visibly more impressed with his own importance while he droned on and on and on... about the deep psychological abuses and acute suffering the 'Elephant Man' Joseph Merrick endured during his short life.

He pointedly asked John Hurt (nominated for an Oscar for his portrayal of Merrick) how he got those complex underlying expressions of profound anguish to shine through all the heavy make-up and the enormous prosthetic covering three-quarters of his body?

The journalist stood waiting for the reply (smugly pleased with himself), while I was totally exhausted just trying to keep up with the guy's marathon of inane babbling.

Hurt on the other hand knew exactly how to handle the situation: He studied this nincompoop journalist in disdain for a moment then titled his head slightly back and in his 70-smokes-a-day gravelly voice gargled: "It's called acting," then sauntered off.

Nice touch.

Likeable Rogue

Luckily for me I got to spend a good deal of time with John and found him to be a likeable rogue, (he could spin some great yarns after a few ales) and a beautiful actor to watch on set.

Although Hurt and I differed on one major point when it came to movies, sentimentality. John couldn't stand the overly sentimental nature of American films. 'Mr. Holland's opus', starring Richard Dreyfus, was playing at the time. I loved it. Hurt hated it.

He told me that sentimentality is by definition something that's not true, that it's saccharine, it's not real. I just laughed and exclaimed, hey man, you sure have a funny attitude about what is and what isn't real for a guy who works in the world of 'suspension of disbelief'.

John Hurt worked hard to come across as a bit of a crusty curmudgeon, but underneath he was just a big softie. When he was finished with his part in the movie, they held a huge wrap party just for him as suited his stature in the business. Late in the night when he departed somewhat worse for wear, he slurred some unintelligible sentiments in my ear and then with misty eyes he grabbed me with both hands and planted a big wet kiss on the top of my bald head. Very sentimental and very... very real.

David Strathairn

Another wrinkle that came out of that first job was my beautiful lovely wife Jennifer, who hasn't a mean bone in her body, ended up disliking the very likable David Strathairn immensely and I need to explain why: My mother used to always tell me: "First impressions are lasting impressions until secondary ones can be made, so it's best to always put your best foot forward when meeting people for the first time."

Unfortunately, this didn't happen when Hollywood's most humble actor David Stathairn met Jennifer. Strathairn is one of the world's nicest human beings. I spent a month with the dude on the film set of 'The Climb'. I even played basketball with him (nice jumper) and his kid at the local YMCA. Nice man. Good man. Humble man. Jennifer thinks he's a jerk.

She's only met him once and as far as she's concerned once is enough. I introduced her to Strathairn at John Hurt's wrap party. Jennifer tried unsuccessfully to engage David in conversation several times and he completely ignored her. It was embarrassing and the situation was made even more awkward because we were all crammed into booths facing each other.

While Jennifer politely tried to engage Strathairn in conversation he was intent on propping up one of Hurt's ex-wives who was so totally drunk off her face she couldn't sit up straight let alone say anything. David was incredibly rude to Jennifer and I have no idea why. To me it was totally out of his character, but as far as Jennifer is concerned that is his character.

So now every time Strathairn pops up in the news or in a movie we're watching I can't resist chuckling, "Hey, hon, there's your buddy David Strathairn." And predictably Jennifer always glares.

Comment One: This is another tale that you're probably gonna think that I'm exaggerating but honestly this is the way it happened. They always get a lot of young eager beavers to work on any movie set and 'The Climb' was no different. And the thing is these kids are lovely but often don't really have a clue.

Ok so we're right in the middle of the shoot and it's always about this time that they schedule the group photo of the cast and crew. On this particular day the photo shoot was to be done right after the lunch break. I wasn't working that day and neither was my acting buddy Mike Saccente who had a very nice part playing John Hurt's son in the movie, so we arrived right at lunch time figuring to have a quick bite to eat with the rest of the cast and crew before the photo shoot. We're standing in line with David Strathairn yacking away as you do when one of the young... very young assistant directors marches up to Saccente in line and loudly tells him that since he wasn't working that day he wasn't allowed to have lunch because he wasn't catered for in the count. Of course Mike was totally embarrassed and I didn't help much because I was laughing my ass off... and then everybody in line started laughing when Strathairn said to Mike, "Don't worry about it Mike, I'll get you an extra potato."

See, the thing is and anybody who's been on a movie set will know this... there's always way too much food... there's never a shortage of food... so her declaration that Mike wasn't in the count... one measly person was a total nonsense. But still ya gotta laugh... at least we were... Mike wasn't.

Comment Two: One day when Mike and I were both on the set we talked the video operator into showing us a scene on his monitor that Mike had just shot. We're standing there watching it when suddenly we felt the presence of someone else. That someone else turned out to be the director of the movie Bob Swam. He didn't look pleased. Some directors don't mind if you look at the footage on the set, but a lot of directors do mind and Bob was one of them. This was very early in the movie like about the third or fourth day and Swam looked directly at us about an inch away from our faces and said in no uncertain terms: "If either of you do this again, I will fire you on the spot!" Oh, okay.

Comment Three: But when the movie was finished Bob Swam paid Mike the ultimate compliment. Mike did a great job with his part... personally I think Saccente is an outstanding actor and apparently so did Bob. On the last day of the shoot, Swam told Mike that he had elevated his part beyond what it was... that's cool!

Carl Lewis

About the time my little guy was struggling with his first words, "She no share," in reference to a little playmate who wouldn't share her toys, Olympic sprinter and winner of nine Olympic gold medals Carl Lewis was in town and he too was struggling to get his words out.

I was working on a B-grade disaster flick called 'Atomic Twister' starring Sharon Lawrence from NYPD Blue fame (she plays the DA always at odds with Sipowitz) who's in one of my all-time favorite scenes from that series.

The scene has Lawrence and Dennis Franz in the shower just after she's moved in with Sipowitz. Franz in character as Sipowitz is so uncomfortable it hurts to watch him as Sharon takes the soap and reaches down between his legs.

Sipowitz - in that great hesitating style of his character starts scratching his forehead for the zillionth time - explains that he's "Ahh - already washed down there." Sharon bats her beautiful eyes and gives him a knowing, sensual smile... To which Sipowitz concludes and stammers: "Ah, yeah, I guess we could wash there again."

I loved the scene and I told her. I think people in any field enjoy knowing that people appreciate what they do. You don't have to be all gushy and silly about it, just be honest. Lawrence was delightful, providing Champagne and nibbles for the entire cast & crew on her last day. Classy.

Corbin Bernstein from LA Law also starred in 'Atomic Twister', he was a little chubby telling the photographer that he could only shoot him from the chest up which caused me to laugh to myself. But he was one helluva nice guy to talk with.

Stay Calm
This was to be Carl Lewis's very first acting role. When he walked into the hotel conference room for the cast read-thru he was shitting bricks, visibly nervous, uneasy, jerking his head everywhere like a bird surrounded by cats and scratching imaginary itches. I was fascinated watching him squirm in his seat. Here was one of the all-time greatest athletes ever, a guy who had performed in front of billions of people under enormous pressure and yet in this room with just a handful of actors he was uncomfortable - nervous as hell! Definitely out of his element.

When his turn came up during the read-thru he completely mashed his few lines. Carl was playing the security guard who is the first person to die trying to out-run the twister from his little guard shack to the main building. A stock scene in any disaster movie.

On the set when it came time to shoot his scene, Lewis was constantly talking to himself trying to calm down, "Ok, Carl, you can do this, stay calm, just relax you can do this." He eventually got through the scene, he was a little wooden, but it was fine. Just something to keep in mind, it happens to all of us no matter what lofty heights we reach.

Seabiscuit

As every serious angler will tell you about the big one that got away so it is with actors - we've all got dozens of hard luck stories about roles lost through unusual circumstances.

Originally a friend of mine Michael Saccente had the security guard role, but, once you're in the game something you quickly discover is that keeping or landing roles is not easy. Does it come down to looks, talent, reputation, your agent...What? In reality it's not like Coca-Cola or Kentucky Fried Chicken, there is not a proven recipe. My friend got a call back with the director. Seeing as the security guard has to sprint for his life the director asked Mike only one question, "You got any problems running?"

My buddy enthused that he could run like Seabiscuit! He wins the part. He calls me and together we gush, cheer and verbally celebrate...Next day he calls again in disbelief as he expounds upon losing the part. The following is the actual conversation I had with my friend, something that Jerry and George would have done on Seinfield:

"Who got it?" I asked.
"You won't believe it!"
"I will. Who go it?"
"You just won't believe it!"
"I'm telling you I will!" I screamed. "Who got it?"
"Carl Lewis."
"THE... Carl Lewis?"
"Yeah."
"Carl Lewis the Olympic sprinter?"
"Un huh."
"Carl Lewis the winner of nine Olympic gold medals got your measly little part?"

"Yes! THAT... Carl Lewis." My friend was miffed.
"Wow. That's weird." I finally exclaimed!

Comment: Saccente had to laugh when he told me that when he learned who got his part he exclaimed: Wow, I can run, but I can't run that fast!" I also found out that not only was Carl Lewis represented by the same agency in Los Angeles that the wife of the owner of the film company shooting the movie worked for - but also the owner's brother went to the University of Houston with Carl. I guess you could say Carl had a couple of strong pluses going for him to get that role, besides the fact he was frigging Carl Lewis!

Tom Selleck and Me (Almost)
We celebrate birthdays. Birthdays are a big deal in our house, they never ever go unnoticed (sorry Jehovah's Witness). Jennifer insists on this believing that it's a person's very special day and should be duly noted and I love her for it. Both kids have had memorable birthdays early in their young lives. For instance it's not every day that you get to celebrate your birthday twice on the same actual day. Lily was born on the13th of May. On her third birthday we had a beautiful New Zealand birthday party for her, then later in the day we boarded a plane for a twelve-hour flight to San Francisco. Because we crossed the international dateline we arrived on Lily's third birthday again (talk about 'Back to the Future') so we celebrated it all over again with Lily's American family. I can tell you that she was one very tired little girl at day's end.

Magnum P.I.
On Sam's fourth birthday I got a very unusual call late in the afternoon. We all have our favorite television shows, one of mine is Magnum P.I. I loved every character in the series and at one time I lived in Hawaii, so it always brought with it a flood of pleasant memories: Back then I filled in my days perfecting my tennis game, whacking endless buckets of golf balls, going to any number of fantastic beaches and working on my whopper burger intake... ahhhhhhhhh life in paradise those were the days, but now on the far side of the world, many years down the track and completely out of the blue, I suddenly had an opportunity to hang with Magnum.

Tom Selleck was in New Zealand to shoot 'Countdown to D-Day'. This was a CBS movie of the week about the final crucial days leading up to the invasion of Europe being shot in Auckland. And apparently they desperately needed a sexy hunky body double for big Tom. And even though I'm a balding middle-age suburban father of two very young children walking around with my kid's snot and food stains on my clothes, I got the call.

Sometimes you have to go with the flow, with the moment, "I'm your man!" I shouted. The money was laughable. But the money wasn't the point. The point was the opportunity to hang with Magnum.

I was asked to meet the director and DOP (director of photography) late in the afternoon on my son Sam's fourth birthday. Great timing. Sam's party was at 5:30 that evening so the pressure was on big time for me to get to the meeting and get Sam and his two-year-old sister Lily back in time for all his gifts. I gave all this about two seconds thought, looking at the kitchen clock which read 3:15 (great besides the normal late afternoon traffic I had to fight the school's out crush) and exclaimed, "I'm on my way."

Naturally the set was completely on the opposite side of town as I twisted and turned and revved the motor endlessly, like you do when you're in a hurry. Finally I screamed onto the lot with my two kids in tow. One of the assistant directors kindly offered to mind them while I had my meeting.

I was standing in a war room with actors milling about in WWII military uniforms when the director suddenly burst into the room - wham - with enough energy to light up Auckland for a year if we had a blackout. He and his DOP immediately sized me up like a prime bull; they kept circling me, looking me over like a jumbo steak and they hadn't eaten in a month. I thought this must be how a woman feels being undressed whenever she walks by a group of men.

Mumbling

While all this angling and gazing on their part was going on I was distracted by an actor sitting in the corner of the room mumbling to himself (he was going over his lines for the next scene) and I know I know him but I just can't put a name to his face. I chuckled to myself listening to his mumbling because I'm always walking around the house talking to myself when I have an upcoming part, and it drives my wife nuts, not to mention my neighbors if I'm outside in the garden shouting at imaginary people.

Meanwhile the two carnivores were intently discussing my physical attributes. And I'm standing there fidgeting like a little kid because the clock is ticking and the pressure is mounting. Finally the director asked if I could wait a minute.

"One minute." I immediately barked back! He looked startled. I told him yeah, but only for a minute because I know a minute in movie time is really three hours. He gave me a curious double-take when I fairly screamed that it was my son's fourth birthday.

Everyone in the room looked up, mortified that I'd say that to the director. But, hey, a four-year-old kid doesn't give a hoot or a holler about Tom Selleck, all he knows is when he gets home he's getting presents. If Dad gets him home on time.

I think the huge difference with being an older parent is I want my family around me as much as possible, everywhere I go the kids go. They tag along with me to my acting auditions and television work. I have the confidence that comes with age to make that work and I'm definitely not intimidated about how important others think these situations may be because my children are far more important to me than any interview or acting role I might get. When push comes to shove I'm not out to impress anybody except my family.

And then the mumbling actor in the corner finally says something out loud and bingo I instantly know who he is, which surprises the heck out of me: None other than Tom Selleck.

Yeah, go ahead and laugh, but this is not the Tom Selleck we all know and love. There's no thick moustache, no wavy hair. In fact he's sporting a number one with half his head shaved. Now I know why I'm suitable to body double for this Hollywood hunk. We're both about the same size, shape and we have the same haircut.

My Bottom

The director comes back and gives his slab of beef (me) the once over again and then calmly says thank you. I hesitated for a split second. I'm expecting him to exalt, "Yes! You are too sexy for your shirt, you're our man." But, he doesn't so I nod, say thanks and grab my two little darlings and scramble out of there. By now the traffic has risen like some snarling gigantic dragon hell bent on keeping my boy from his booty. But there is a God and by some miracle I managed to snake my way through every back alley shortcut I could think of and we duly arrived just as all the presents were arriving. Yes!

Naturally I was flushed with excitement with my close encounter with Tom Selleck, even though I didn't think I had gotten the job. Still it made for a great story and everybody had a good laugh that I had failed to recognize him. But the movie business moves in mysterious ways and a few days later I got another call from the production office to go out there and get measured. I'm still in with a chance here, I received the full measuring treatment; every limb and every ounce of flesh that hung on my frame went under the tape. The wardrobe gal even took my wallet out of my pants.

Yes, let me repeat that, she took my wallet out of my pants to get a precise measurement of my butt. She informed me in a most serious hushed tone that the producers were very particular. That didn't bother me, what bothered the raspberries out of me was she forgot to put my wallet back in my pants. I discovered this when I stopped off at the zoo on the way home to give the kids a treat for being so patient.

Sally Field once cried at the Oscars, "You really like me. You really, really, really, really like me!" Well, those producers said the same thing about my bottom, they like it just fine and I got the job. I got a contract, a script and a call time for my first day hanging out with my new twin brother, big Tom. This was gossip too good to hold in, my fingers got button burn from the speed at which I was punching in numbers to gush forth to all my friends about what a cool job I had landed.

I even told strangers, I told the guy pumping gas into my jeep. And the reaction was always the same. Wow! They all loved Magnum. There's guilt by association and there's status by association; some of that old Tom Selleck magic had dusted itself off on me. Then late on the night before my very first day being Tom Selleck's twin I received one last call from the production office.

A disembodied voice simply informed me that the gig was off and before I could even utter a feeble "golly jeepers" the line went dead. I stood there holding onto the receiver like a kid with a quivering lower lip because he's suddenly lost his favorite toy. It seemed the producers simply asked one of the nicest men in the movie business if he wouldn't mind sticking around for the extra time it required to shoot his body double shots himself? Big Tom flashed that famous grin of his, flipped those bushy eyebrows a couple of times and purred, "Sure, no problem." And just like that all my magic disappeared.

Comment: So, now whenever I see a rerun of 'Magnum' I dreamily think, "Yeah, me and Tom Selleck (almost)."

Peter Jackson
No Big Hairy Ape

The thing is, don't lock yourself into assuming you know just how your life will go and just what will be of value to you. As John Lennon sang, 'Life is what happens to you whilst you are busy making other plans.' Seize the day or the moment. For instance: I received a call from my agent that I was being offered a small one-line part in Peter Jackson's remake of that 1933 classic 'King Kong'. I was thrilled and immediately accepted. What's that old saying about there being no small parts, just small actors? I then got another call saying that they had to reschedule my shoot dates and was I still available? Are you kidding? You bet, I still had my hand up. Well, wouldn't you know it, I went from a single line to having one of the longest monologues in the movie.

15 Seconds

Andy Warhol once proclaimed that everyone would be famous for fifteen minutes. I'm not a greedy kind of guy so I was very happy with my fifteen seconds. It was one of those breathlessly hot dry summer afternoons and I was wearing a full button down 1930's thick woolen New York policeman's uniform. I felt like the luckiest guy in the world,

I was on cloud nine as one of Hollywood's most powerful directors casually picked his way through the throng moving closer to me. Finally, Peter Jackson looked up, "That's not going to work, is it John?"

I looked down and shook my head, "Nope." This was the very last scene in 'King Kong' and I was playing the New York policeman attempting to disperse the crowd after Kong having gazed lovingly one last time into the beautiful eyes of Naomi Watts, then falls a hundred or so stories off the Empire State building so Jack Black could make his entrance and utter that most famous of lines, 'It wasn't the airplanes... it was beauty killed the beast.'

Originally, I had one line: "Come on boys, move on! Show's over!" Well, that just wasn't going to cut the mustard with the amount of space that I had to cover. There were over a thousand extras on the set for that scene, talk about an adrenalin rush.

Peter was deep in thought when he remarked;" You probably know how to do that American cop crowd stuff, don't you?"

"Yeah, I do." I grinned.

"Good, do that then."

Yes, I was just given carte blanche to do whatever lines I wanted, in one of Hollywood's most expensive movies. I did the usual cop banter, "All right folks, the show's over, move along, come on let's clear this area, keep moving," and then when I got to the photographers I snarled: "Okay, shove off boys." Then after several takes' I couldn't resist throwing in one of the all-time 'classic cop' clichés:

"Nothing to see here."

Seeing as there was a twenty-five-foot mutant gorilla lying prone in the middle of the street Universal decided not to use that line. Apparently, they didn't see the irony of the situation. "Nothing to see here" that's funny folks, really... that's funny... oh well I guess it wasn't supposed to be funny in the end. My wife Jennifer certainly didn't think it was funny when we saw the movie... she was crying so much when Kong literally bit the bullet, she almost missed my performance. Upstaged by a monkey... Bananas! Double Bananas!!

Disneyland

Finally, when the day's shoot was over and everybody had hugged and kissed and congratulated each other on a job well done, I walked off the New York set and it reminded me exactly of walking down Main Street out of Disneyland when I was a kid and knowing that feeling of the magic disappearing. Little was I to know at the time, but just a few days later Peter Jackson and I would hook-up one more time and get down to the real nitty gritty.

You Could Have Fooled Me

The King Kong production was first class in every aspect. I was discussing with my wife what we were going to do when I flew from Auckland down to Wellington, car wise? Would I drive myself and leave the car at the airport or would she and the kids drop me off? Then I got my travel itinerary and voila, a corporate cab would pick me up at home and transport me to the airport. That's probably not a big deal to most actors, but when you're an unknown, that's very cool. It's nice not to have to worry about the hassle of parking. It's a quick one-hour flight down to Peter Jackson's hometown where I'm picked up and whisked to my hotel, which is right on the edge of a beautiful harbor very similar to San Francisco Bay. Later I was to discover that Wellington had a lot more in common with my home town.

The next morning we drove out to the lot where Peter had built his New York set, and I have to say, when you see it up close it just takes your breath away. You can throw in all the adjectives, the buildings were perfect in every detail, the layout was spectacular and most importantly the feel was there. I was sweltering in the heat but this scene was set in mid-winter in New York so there was plenty of snow on the ground and yes I just had to reach down and touch it, it looked so real but wasn't. Even though I'm in the movies I'm still a big kid at heart. When I was filming 'Atomic Twister' we shot the beginning of the movie in the house where Sharon Lawrence's character lived, and then several weeks later we came back to that same house to shoot the final climatic scenes in the aftermath of the twister. When I rounded the corner on the set which was in a real life neighbourhood I was momentarily stunned because the movie carpenters had turned the house into a shambles all busted up as if a twister had run through it - honestly it was so real I just forgot that I was on a movie set. But that's just me I can easily just get lost in the moment anywhere anytime.

Buddy Holly

Watching Peter Jackson work was awe inspiring, he was so respectful of everyone that he came into contact with, it was beautiful to watch and even more of a blast to be involved kind of the way you think movies should be, fun and creative.

Upon arriving on the set I went to wardrobe, then make-up, and then went over to my camper to lounge around with the other actors. I love this lull before the storm of being called to the set, there's this beautiful underlying tension in the air that everybody does their damnedest to ignore while trying to act cool-as-a-cucumber. Me, I just soak it all in, I'm there for the entire experience, I don't have time to be cool.

The date just happened to be February 3rd, and seeing as Buddy Holly has always been one of my heroes it was a natural segue for me to slip into the conversation that today was: "The day the music died." Another American actor in our group (one of the photographers) piped up that it was his birthday and then waxed lyrically about how he was born on the day the music died in 1964. He looked chuffed (kiwi slang for being excited) imparting this bit of his personal history to the group. I had to be the one to burst his bubble. I looked at him in amusement: "Wrong there Kemosabe... you missed the tragic event by five years."

"Whaddaya mean?" "I mean Buddy Holly, J.P. 'The Big Bopper' Richardson and Richie Valens died on February 3rd, 1959... that's what I mean."
"No way!"
"Fraid so."

This conversation see-sawed back and forth finally ending with the ever classic: "Wanna bet?" In heated animation... of course! This was a very surreal bet, the other actor was so positive, so cock sure and yet I know he's dead-ass wrong. Life can certainly be a funny business at times.

Comment: When we all got back to Auckland my fellow American phoned me and said he 'Googled' and that I had shattered a life-long image he had held. He actually sounded sad like it was my fault. What can I say? The guy still owes me twenty bucks.

Don McLean

That conversation reminded me of the time I met Don McLean: Years before back in the eighties when Don McLean, who sang 'Bye Bye American Pie' (the day the music died) was touring New Zealand. I tagged along one day with a journalist buddy who was interviewing him. The interview took place poolside at McLean's hotel. It was a blistering hot afternoon (hot enough to fry an egg on the sidewalk) so I was wearing shorts, my journalist friend was wearing shorts and surprise-surprise so was everybody else poolside... except dandy Don. He came sauntering out to the pool deck wearing black slacks, a black shirt and a heavy black leather jacket. Talk about the odd guy out. I watched the interview for several minutes flicking the sweat dripping off my nose while watching rivers slide down the side of Don's face until I couldn't contain myself any longer and I just blurted out: "Hey man, you gotta be roasting in that leather jacket?" My journalist friend rolled his eyes, McLean looked puzzled.

Finally, he mumbled: "Yeah" and took it off. Wow the price of being cool.

Shake Rattle and Roll

When we eventually made it onto the set the first 'take' took me completely by surprise. When action was called the rush of the crowd almost knocked me over (a very truthful moment), and I'm not a small guy. I did literally have to fight and push to keep them back, and of course Jack Black never came close to making it through this dense pack of actors. Peter strode out and told the extras that they were doing a great job and to keep it up, and then he worked out a plan with Jack to get him through.

Peter Jackson has a beautiful low-key manner when handling his actors, at one point the actor who mistakenly thought he and Buddy Holly had a spiritual connection did a little ad lib with the "airplanes got him" line. Peter, with a nice bemused smirk on his face, casually mentioned that that was one of the most famous lines in the original movie so he'd appreciate it if he stuck to the script. He was light hearted about it, but he made his point and no one was embarrassed.

This was a serious scene so the normally manic, funny, outrageous Jack Black was low key and sombre, a true professional in every way, working hard to get this vital scene just right. When the day was done Peter Jackson was very gracious in thanking me for coming down. In fact, everybody that I came into contact with on that production from the assistant AD, who made me a great flat white, to the drivers, the sound guys, the make-up people, everyone was first class and a pleasure to work with. This was truly one of those jobs where you're thinking: "I can't believe they're paying me to do this." However, I got my biggest thrill the next day, bright and early before I flew home. A little after six a.m. an earthquake shook me right out of bed, and naturally being from San Francisco, I was up and out the door and down those nine flights of stairs in a flash.

The receptionist in true kiwi deadpan fashion greeted me with, "That was a good one mate, wasn't it?"

"Uh, yeah."

Comment: I was so rattled that I wouldn't go back up to the 9th floor to have my breakfast in their private dining room and trust me they had a feast all laid out up there for the penthouse guests. Uh huh, I ate a stale Croissant in the restaurant on the ground floor.

Just Let Go
One of the very weird things about being a house-husband actor is the sudden shift in your surroundings, one minute I'm staying in a plush top floor hotel suite that was as big as our house; I had a camper van with a double bed on the set and a whole host of swell people to look after my every need. Ahhhhhhhhh, bliss! That's a definite bonus when you get to travel out of town for a role, you can just let go and let somebody else worry about all the small stuff. You don't need to plan anything because somebody else has your schedule all laid out for you, that is pure heaven, that and you can actually sit down and read a book without two little munchkins climbing all over you.

But, then just as quickly as I flew back, I hopped into my corporate cab, shot home and immediately took over the duties of looking after the kids, playing hide and seek, making lunches, going to the playground and tending to boo boos. They say variety is the spice of life and it doesn't get any more varied than that.

King Kong Part Two

Two days later I was still bathed in that exotic rush that can only come from being on a movie set when I got one of those 'out-of-the-blue' phone calls. Just before ten p.m., which is that peaceful quiet time after we've bathed the kids, read stories and tucked them into bed, my wife Jennifer and I were having a nice cuppa (tea) and a biscuit when the phone rang. We both looked at the phone simultaneously thinking, now who in the world is calling at this hour? The casting agent for 'King Kong' was on the other end of the line. She quickly explained that Peter Jackson had written an entirely new scene and requested that I play the lead role. Talk about an instant shot of adrenalin, I was so excited I almost snapped to attention. They wanted me to fly down early the next morning. No problem, however Peter Jackson didn't hold as much weight with Jennifer, she just gave me her 'mother' stare and told me that before I went anywhere I had to organise our nanny, which was a mad scramble on such short notice. Life goes on whether you're a sudden movie star or not and the kids' well-being comes first, even before Mr. Jackson.

Comment: I wonder if Brad Pitt has to go through this when he gets a part?

WTF

It always makes me laugh how people in the movie business treat actors with such 'kid gloves', like they'd break having to deal with functioning in the real world.

There was a possibility that my plane might be diverted to another town about a hundred miles from Wellington, because of fog. This casting agent hummed and hawed tap dancing around the question of whether it would be possible for me to pick up a rental car and drive in to the Capital? She asked this with such a feeling of trepidation that you could be excused for thinking that I was mentally handicapped. She obviously didn't know that I was Super Dad in my private life where no problem was unsolvable. "No problem," I shot back. However, we did eventually land in Wellington, but not before the pilot scared the living daylights out of me. I'm not a great flyer to start with and as we were approaching the Wellington airport which was shrouded in fog the pilot came on the loudspeaker and in true laconic kiwi understatement told us that while the airstrip was indeed fogged in, he could see a small sliver of clean air so he was going to have a crack at it. What the fuck!

Comment: The Wellington airport is famous for being difficult to land on. The runway sits right on a bay and the wind factor is enormous making for at times a hair-raising landing as the plane literally tilts back and forth like a limp rag doll in the wind. One night when I was flying into Wellington we just touched down when suddenly the pilot hit the Thrusters full throttle and we immediately took off again which was kind of thrilling in its own way... this runway is not the longest in the world and apparently, he misjudged his approach. That's the only time in all the flying I've done that that has happened... the guy next to me had to grab the vomit bag as he just let it all go. Yuck!

Sadistic Sergeant
My new dialogue for this scene was absolutely in my wheelhouse. I'm in a military truck racing through the streets of New York and we're after the 'Big Monkey!' I'm a grizzled, mean looking army sergeant, in fact my character's title is, "Sadistic Sergeant," and I'm staring in disgust at the frightened faces of a group of young soldiers.

All these actors were in fact guys who worked at Weta (Jackson's special effects department), including Christian Rivers who later picked up an Oscar for outstanding special effects for 'King Kong'.

As we were all sitting cramped in the truck making small talk while they positioned the camera it was obvious that the Weta boys were very nervous with the prospect of being in front of the camera. So just before we started to shoot this scene Peter Jackson sidled up to the back of the truck, peered in, and calmly and reassuringly told everyone to relax that we were going to shoot this scene a lot so there was no need to panic that eventually we'd get what we wanted. Peter Jackson has such a calming effect when he speaks.

Comment: The thing about this second part is I get killed in it along with all my men. But, I'm in the very last scene of the movie which we've already filmed. I asked Peter about this and his reply was classic Hollywood: Peter just nonchalantly said, "We'll put a moustache on you and no one will notice the difference." I just busted up! Yeah okay. The other thing was my voice... I've got a very distinctive voice... it stands out. I was told by one of the lead writers that if my Sadistic Sergeant scene made the cut they were going to get Bruce Willis to voice over my part in the last scene... cool... or should that be super cool! The other thing I discovered was in the original script the last scene with this dialogue: 'oh no, it wasn't the airplanes. It was beauty killed the beast' was to be between the cop I was playing and an old lady... and that old lady was none other than the original star of the 1933 classic Fay Wray... that would have been way beyond cool for me... but unfortunately Fay Wray who was in her 90's passed before any of that could happen.

Rock Solid
Maybe this was an omen, normally I'm rock solid when it comes to dialogue and for the first hour of shooting I was just fine. Then for some unknown reason I got the yips jumbling up my dialogue, I was getting my apes and gorillas in the wrong order which was throwing me off my rhythm. Thank god the dialogue coach Liz Himmelstein was there, she reached through the back of the truck and tugged on my coat and calmed me down, so thank-you Liz. Now I knew firsthand how my actors felt on the set when their nerves were shot, when I was the dialogue coach. It also reminded me that like most things in life it's a team effort. Check out my dialogue for this scene:

"Listen up! This is New York City and this is sacred ground - you hear me!?! It was built for humans, by humans - not for stinking lice infested apes!"

"The thought of some mutant gorilla crapping all over the streets of this fair city fills me with disgust."

"So this is how it's gonna be: We find it, we kill it - we cut its ugly head off and ram it up its ass!"

Only I don't get to complete that last sentence because just as I'm saying 'ass' we all look up in complete horror as this gargantuan monkey paw sweeps through the air smashing us and our truck to smithereens, which is a classic example of Peter Jackson's sense of black humor.

Peter did this scene as a 'piss-take' on the John Wayne, American 'gung-ho, we're going to save the world' that we Americans love to portray in the movies. Which is exactly why I thought the part was perfect for me, I'm about as American as you can get and proud of it! Where's my flag!?!

Comment: Unfortunately, this was one of many scenes that didn't make the final cut into the movie, but it's in the Director's set on DVD. Peter told me that I did such a great job with the New York policeman's role that he thought I'd be perfect for this role. And yes, I was pumped hearing this from one of the world's top directors. I got so much from my involvement with that movie, it may have been a small role but the experience for me was bigger than Kong.

Kimball Bent

I was a sports presenter when I got into acting. The closest I had come to anything theatrical was in hosting a big-time wrestling show. Now that was genuine suspension of disbelief territory!

I grew up like most American kids playing cowboys and Indians so when I landed the plum role of Kimball Bent in a television series called Greenstone I was in my own personal Blue Heaven.

This was an eight-part mini-series on the Maori Land Wars fought against the British in New Zealand during the 1800's. The Maori people are the indigenous people of the country and one of the last sections of the globe to suffer British colonization. As in days of old it did not go smoothly, Greenstone was a chance for New Zealand to explore its wild-west roots.

And I was the only American in the production. My character was based on a real-life soldier and adventurer named Kimball Bent. Bent was born in Maine (1837-1916) and worked a merchant ship over to England where he jumped ship and joined the British army. He served in India and then when they stationed him in New Zealand he deserted and joined forces with the Maori chief Titokowaru and got caught up in the Land Wars against his former employers.

I had an absolute blast playing this character. I got to ride this beautiful retired racehorse and the costume I wore came right out of Sam Peckinpah's Wild Bunch... A big black cowboy hat, leather pants cowboy boots with spurs, a red bandana and the heaviest dust coat (it literally weighed a ton) I've ever worn in my life. Walking around in that coat was a total workout in itself. It was one of those full-length butt ugly numbers... Charles Bronson wears one as he steps off the train to face a bus load of bad guys in the movie 'Once Upon a Time in the West'.

You know the coat I'm talking about: It looks like it's survived every dust storm known to man and actor... Plus - to top it all off - I got to carry this double barreled shotgun. And like the sister sang in "Shaft" - 'I was a baaaddd mutha-f*****... Watch your mouth!?!'

Hurry Up and Wait
One thing you quickly learn about in the acting game is the waiting game. The acting motto seems to be: hurry up and wait. The schedule goes along these lines: Wardrobe, make-up, sit. 'Hercules in the Underworld' was one of the five television movies that preceded the series: 'Hercules; the Legendary Journeys' and this is where I learned the art of waiting. I had to be in wardrobe at six a.m., I wasn't there long, I wore only my jockey briefs and a stringy grass skirt.

Make-up was a different story. I had my entire body covered in green slime. This mud was made up from a green powder and KY jelly. Let me tell you cold KY jelly is not much fun at six in the morning. It was everywhere in my beard, mustache, hair, armpit hairs... I was caked in it. One day on the set after getting my slime treatment I sat until lunch. After lunch I sat until afternoon break, then I sat some more. I never made it on set that day. I sat around for twelve hours. That's the way it seems to be in this business; sometimes you arrive, do your scenes and skeedattle, but mostly you wait.

Bobby Flay
I've sat with a lot of actors who constantly bitch about having to sit around all day long. I mean come on "get a life" sitting around having a personal minder, drinking coffee and eating snacks all day? I had one of the best steak sandwiches I've ever eaten on the set of a Disney movie called 'Eddie's Million Dollar Cook Off'. Absolutely delicious and I got paid to eat it as well - so what's to moan about, darlings?

Take my word for it, it beats the hell out of the heat and sheep shit of a woolshed and the stink and sheep shit of a slaughterhouse. The funny thing about that movie was I spent a day on the set with New York celebrity chef Bobby Flay who was a perfect gentleman in every way, nice man. Now the weird thing was I had never heard of the man, but the night before I was to meet him I was watching an episode of 'The Soprano's' when one of the characters in the series suddenly asks Artie in his restaurant, "Who do you think you are, Bobby Flay?" And then the very next day I meet the guy. I ask you, is that a sign or what? Truly a Zen moment.

And he too never made it on set his first day even though he was ushered onto the set with lots of fanfare at 7:30 am.

Flay was very fidgety and unsettled waiting around, he kept asking me why he had to be on the set so early?

I in turn asked him why he was doing the movie in the first place and he gave me one of the best answers I've ever heard to be in a movie: Flay lit up when he explained, "My little girl just loves the Disney channel and this is going to make me a great big hero in her eyes when she sees daddy in one of their movies." Beautiful.

Comment One: My philosophy about sitting around is very simple they've got me for the day, it's their dime and they can spend it any way they see fit. So, you might as well settle back, relax and enjoy the ride.

Comment Two: This story really illustrates what a small... small... small... joint New Zealand is. Because I was working full time on the Disney Channel's movie 'Eddie's Million Dollar Cookoff' I had to get our nanny to look after young three-year-old Sam every day Monday thru Friday. No problem, she was a lovely young gal and Sam adored her. The problem arose when the entire kiwi crew got into some kind of beef with the American director and walked off the set. I was like... wow never seen that before they must have been pretty pissed off! They made their statement but within a day the movie had another entirely new crew... plus Disney sent out one of their top executives as a trouble shooter to keep everybody in line.

The first thing that happened with the new crew was I got a polite telling off by the first AD (Assistant Director) when I walked onto the set and began working with one of my kiwi actors in the movie. I just forgot that everybody was new... but it's protocol for anyone that walks onto a set to first introduce yourself to the first AD... technically it's his set and he's responsible for everyone on it. I apologized and it wasn't a big deal... he was cool with it seeing as it was a pretty hectic time. The second thing is still amazing to me as I write this: The Disney executive who came out swiped my nanny. Yeah, that's right, this woman took my nanny right from under my feet. There's a couple of million people in Auckland with I'm sure more than one nanny and this gal takes mine. What are the odds? I couldn't really get mad at my nanny because she was getting paid five times what I was paying her... so I perfectly understood where she was coming from... but it did put a lot of pressure on me on short notice to hustle up another nanny.

Marlo Thomas

And of course, there are all kinds of reasons for delays on a movie set: One Sunday evening I got a call from the film set of the movie 'Deceit' starring Marlo Thomas. I grew-up watching her father Danny Thomas (Make Room for Daddy) and I always liked her television show 'That Girl.' The producers were in a panic because one of the young kiwi child actors was having some trouble with his American accent for a crucial scene so I got the call to come in and tweak his drawl. When I arrived on the set I ran into the film's lighting director, a guy I'd worked with on several other projects and just casually I asked him how the shoot was going as you do? He immediately exhaled and with a very pained expression snorted that it was going as slow as molasses running uphill. I shot him a puzzling look and he explained that he was required to light Marlo, who was 60 plus, into looking like a 40- year-old. I laughed.

Blowtorch

Sometimes even people who are supposed to spot interesting behavior wouldn't recognize it if it came up and bit them on the ass. Case in point: I was doing some accent work for a local community theater that was putting on an American play. One night I'm watching the male and female leads rehearsing a scene that required the male actor to light a candle. The guy pulls out his matches and naturally the first two matches don't light... and he goes through a scene that everybody in the audience would have sympathized with by repeatedly striking the dud matches and getting nothing more than a faint spark. Meanwhile the female actor is intently watching this process, and through her behavior is urgently willing the match to light. It's as plain as day. Finally this frustrated actor rips out a third match and strikes it and gets a very low flame - so he gingerly tilts the match down willing the flame to get brighter, which it does, and he lights the candle and they carry on with the scene much to the relief of everyone watching. You could almost hear a Collective Sigh. It was beautiful truthful behavior. The director called out when the scene was finished: "Don't worry about lighting that candle I'll have that fixed."

"You'll do what!?! Whaddaya gonna do give the guy a blowtorch?"
The director may have been watching, but he certainly wasn't seeing.

Goofy Shit

All kinds of goofy shit happens on a set on any given day as the following stories will indicate - you just never know what's going to come up - which is one of the things I enjoy - being challenged. And sometimes I even challenge myself. I was playing the part of a United States mountain instructor in a documentary about the Mt. Erebus disaster where an Air New Zealand plane had flown into the Antarctic volcano killing all on board. The first scene had a group of New Zealand policemen coming off a cargo plane to collect the bodies. I was to greet them as they came off...I marched up to them and shouted out my greeting: "Hey guys welcome, I'm John Dybvig." I just did it so naturally... it took a second or two for everyone including me to realise what I had done and then we all busted up. But that's me... I can get completely lost in any moment and just do what comes naturally to me. During the forty years I've lived down here because kiwis are so slow in coming forward I'm always greeting people with: "How ya going - I'm John Dybvig." And so naturally that became the catch cry for the shoot - "Hey guys welcome, I'm John Dybvig." I've never had any serious mishaps on a set but I have had a few close shaves.

One time I had to ride up to the two lead characters in the mini-series Greenstone, bark out some dialogue and then - as they rode off - turn back in the saddle to deliver some more lines to my band of men. Just as I turned my race horse suddenly bolted and took off in hot pursuit of his racehorse buddies just about whipping me right off his back end. And believe me when I say this horse was screaming down this country lane - I mean he was motoring as I barely recovered and clung on for dear life. The director God bless his heart came up to me and in a classic understatement said: "John, you're supposed to stay back in this scene."

"Thank-you," I panted. "Would you please give that direction to the horse."

Comment: One of those lead characters in Greenstone was a very young Matthew Rhys a Welsh actor who went on to huge roles in America. He starred in Brothers & Sisters and The Americans for which he received two Golden Globe nominations and a Primetime Emmy Award. He also had the lead role on the HBO period series Perry Mason.

Danish Pastry

I also witnessed first-hand how goofy some actors can be in going the extra mile to make their performances as realistic as possible. I was working with a very innocent eager-beaver British actor on the set of 'Greenstone': On one particular day we were lounging around in the actor's campervan preparing for our next scene, which was to be a huge battle in the Maori Land Wars, where my preparation involved jamming on my boots, grabbing my cowboy hat and bandana - along with brushing off the squillion and one crumbs scattered all over the front of my costume from the rather large Danish pastry I was stuffing into my mouth when we got the call.

My young English actor friend was supposed to be harbouring a shoulder wound during this battle - so he actually punched three large pointy tacks into his shoulder to simulate his wound. I winced with each puncture, and put a piece of tape over the spurting blood to hold them in place - what else could I do? - I just stood there wide-eyed and exclaimed, "Wow! That's some dedication brother!"

Comment: It seemed way over the top to me and reminded me of the famous conversation between Dustin Hoffman and Sir Laurence Olivier, on the set of the movie 'Marathon Man'. To prepare for one of the scenes Hoffman went for a few days without sleep and looked pretty rough. Olivier asked why he was putting himself through such an ordeal and Hoffman replied that he was trying to be convincing in the role. Olivier replied, "Try acting dear boy."

Joe Pytka

This guy is the real deal but also kind of a goofy nut job. Interesting combination. I found this out one day when I was acting in a Gatorade commercial being directed by Mr. Pytka. First let me lay down some credentials for this master craftsman: He's worked with Michael Jackson, Madonna, Michael Jordan, Tiger Woods, Henry Kissenger and oh yeah John Dybvig... ha... only kidding about putting my name in there but it's not everyday you can stick your name in that hall of fame line-up. One of my all time favorite TV commercials was the McDonald's ad featuring Michael Jordan and Larry Bird playing a game of 'Horse' which was directed by Joe Pytka. He also directed Jordan in the movie 'Space Jam'. Plus he's got more honors than I can list and over fifty pieces of his work in the permanent collection of New York's Museum of Modern Art. So here he was... this giant in the ad industry in little old New Zealand directing a commercial for Gatorade of which I had a part.

Okay this is where it gets weird: We're on the set right in the middle of shooting this epic TVC and suddenly Pytka stops and just starts throwing around an American football with another American who was a former football player in the States and was a consultant for another part of this commercial while the rest of us actors and crew just stood around and watched them. He didn't make any kind of announcement 'like take five guys'...nope he just suddenly stopped and picked up a football and started throwing it. This game of catch went on and on and on and the entire cast and crew didn't move a muscle we all just stood where we were kinda frozen and watched this ridiculous spectacle on the set as it seemed to me that Pytka was showing everyone that 'yes' he had the biggest 'dick' on that set.

Finally, Joe got his itch for throwing an American football around scratched and we resumed work. What Joe said next really takes the cake...strangest thing I've ever had said about me: At this point in the script they're going to shoot an extreme close-up of me so Joe asks his First Assistant to maneuver me into position for this delicate shot. His First Assistant is a black guy by the name of Randy who was from my home town San Francisco. Randy grabs me by the shoulders and starts maneuvering me into position.

Okay time now for just a bit of explaining here. I've done this like a lot of times in the business and what happens is the guy pushes you back one way and director yells out "no, too much". So, then he grabs you and pulls you back in the other direction and again the director yells out, "No, too far," and so it goes this human tug of war trying to get into the right position for the shot. And for an extreme close-up it's gonna be an even tighter tug of war.

So, knowing all this and having been through all this before I put in a little bit of resistance taking tiny crab like steps when Randy starts pushing me hoping to keep it in a tight space cutting out the back and forth tugging and pushing to the extremes.

Now while Randy is pushing me Joe is urgently yelling at the top of his lungs, "Randy, I said get the actor in position" and Randy yells back, "I'm trying Joe but the actor is resisting". And I'm thinking to myself: No, I'm not resisting, I'm actually trying to help. And Joe Pytka yells back:

"Maybe the actor's not used to having a black man touching him".

Comment: What the fuck! Having grown up in the San Francisco Bay Area and having been involved in basketball playing against all black colleges and then recruiting a host of black players in my coaching days I was just flabbergasted to hear such a weird thing said out loud about me. My immediate reaction was to tell Pytka to go 'fuck himself' but in the end I kept it professional on my part and just thought... what a weird fuck! On the other hand there's a part of me that likes that kind of 'weirdness' Dr. Jekyll and Mr. Hyde anyone!?!

Bubonic Plague
Dying some kind of horrible death is always a lot of fun in acting.

The best death role I've had was on a hospital drama called 'Mercy Peak'.

I had three large pus-filled inguinal buboes in my groin, or in other words I had the Bubonic Plague. The ugly American. That's what you get when you're the American actor in local overseas productions. Forget about being the hero. You're going to be the villain so you might as well relax and enjoy your evilness. This is what the lead doctor in this series had to say about my character: "I never thought I'd see it. The most advanced nation on earth - so they'd have us believe - and they come to us bearing the Black Death". I questioned if Bubonic Plague was still around only to have it promptly explained to me that apparently you can still get the Plague even today in California. About a dozen cases a year are reported. The Plague is endemic in certain animals, chipmunks (even Alvin?) squirrels and the fleas they carry. So you'd better keep that in mind the next time you're tempted to feed something to one of those cute little critters in the park.

As it turned out they weren't going to show the television audience my grotesquely swollen balls so they needed some way to let the audience know the gravity of the situation. The solution was to have one of the handsome young doctors stick his handsome, young head down my boxer shorts. And then when this doctor's head re-appeared for an extreme close-up, his young horrified medically qualified expression would make it plain to one and all that no one should be sticking their heads down this man's boxers ever again.

Filming this scene came straight out of a Marx Brothers script. The actor who was playing the handsome young doctor was a bit timid about getting up close and personal with my fruit basket, so he just gave it a tweezers-like tug to the front of my boxers, giving him about an inch to sort of peek inside before delivering his diagnosis.

The director immediately yelled, "Cut" and came rushing onto the set screaming, "No, no, no! That kind of look is never going to sell the gravity of the situation to the audience." He loomed over me and barked, "Do you mind, John?"

"No. Of course not, be my guest." I smiled back. Where upon he took hold of my boxers, like you do when you grab a cat by the scruff of his neck and yanked them clear up to the ceiling, and then stuck his entire head down my shorts and had a real good nosey.

He popped back out and exclaimed, "You try it. You don't mind, do you, John?"

"Hell no. I could lie here all day and have the entire cast and crew take turns eye-ballin' my gonads."

Rock Hudson

However, in one of life's ironic twists I had to do a reversal and actually come out of the heterosexual closet in my first major role. I was playing the American hard ass in a New Zealand mini-series called 'Fallout'. In 1984 New Zealand said no to Big Brother. The Labour Government (Democrats) passed an anti-nuclear bill officially making this blip on the radar screen a nuclear-free dot in the ocean. This meant that U.S. war ships could no longer dock in New Zealand ports because the United States has a "Neither confirm nor deny" policy when it comes to whether or not our ships are nuclear armed. Consequently, all military ties between the two countries were severed. What? You didn't notice!?! My brother in San Francisco certainly noticed. One time when I called him he exclaimed: "What the Hell's going on in that little tinpot country you're living in?"

I played the role of Richard Armitage, a Vietnam veteran, who was the Assistant Secretary of Defense at the Pentagon. After that he became the Assistant Secretary of State under Colin Powell and today he still works in Washington. My first day on the set was hectic beyond belief. Every other scene required me to change into another costume. I would literally be undressing on the run to wardrobe.

During one lightning quick change one of the sweet young wardrobe boys was down on one knee putting my shoes on when my pants slipped and dropped around my ankles. Well, this budding Rock Hudson could barely contain himself; he eyed up my package only inches from his face and squealed, "Oh, my, my, my."

I just pulled up my pants and laughed, "Not my kind of ball game, big guy."

Sound Effects

On the set of 'Hercules,' I once had my little finger nail completely ripped off in a fight. Another actor jammed the point of a metal spear all the way up under my nail. Yeah, I swore just a little bit. Son-of-a-bitch that hurt! In the early days of that production they actually used real metal swords and spears! Sure they were blunted but hey... I remember worrying about fighting Michael Hurst (Iolaus) in a big fight scene from my Saytar days. I'm six three and weighing in at the 250 mark. Mike is maybe a smidgen taller than a Smurf and has all the body weight of a wet noodle. Plus I know I was using Arnold Schwarzenegger's sword from 'Conan the Barbarian'. The thing weighed at least three tons. I'm not kidding it was the biggest gawd damn sword I've ever seen. Somebody eventually wised up and queried the use of real metal when rubber with sound effect is just as effective. Doh!

Handshakes

On the set of 'Young Hercules' (starring a very young Ryan Gosling) I had to mug a little old lady. One of New Zealand's pioneer actors, at eighty she was extremely tiny and frail. I had to rush up to her in the market place and snatch her bag. She on the other hand was supposed to scream and hold on to her bag.

This worried me. Suppose we got carried away in the adrenalin rush that goes with any scene. I once shook hands with a ninety-year-old gentleman whose skin was the texture of rice paper. I shook too hard in assuring him that I was pleased to meet him. The skin on the back of his hand split wide open like the parting of the Red Sea in The Ten Commandments. I'll never forget the sticky feeling of his blood on my fingers and looking in horror at what I'd done.

I seemed to have a history of out-of-control handshakes, my dad always told me to shake hands like a man, not a dead fish. I once gave singer Christopher Cross a hearty handshake and he immediately jerked his hand back wringing it gingerly in the air wincing, "Damn man, that's my guitar hand!"

And when I was introduced to the legendary basketball coach John Wooden I was so excited I started pumping his hand up and down like a crazed man trying to pump water from a dry well. Wooden, who was in his late 70's paled and they had to prise our hands apart.

So I was weary of older people when it came to the physical stuff. I came up with a plan. I told her that I'd just hold on to the purse and she could do all the pulling. I just went with her movements and it worked perfectly. The eighty-year-old came out of the scene with all her limbs intact. But, I can't take credit for this brilliant idea. Robert Trebor had instructed me to do the same with him when I had to grab him by his shirt collar and shake him around in that episode of 'Xena'. It works beautifully - in Xena it looks like I'm giving him a good old fashion throttling - but in reality he's doing all the work I'm just holding on going with the flow of his movements.

Comment: See, I told you I learned some tricks from him.

Mob
One of the funniest safety experiences I witnessed on a set was for a pirate series called Mysterious Island. In one scene we (band of pirates) were coming into shore in a rowboat and one of my pirate buddies had to slip overboard and swim the rest of the way to shore. The water was two and half feet deep but they had fifteen life guards surrounding him in bright orange vests. That's a really weird sight. He told me later that he prayed that nothing happened as he was much more afraid of getting trampled in the stampede of rescuers than of drowning.

Cement Wall
On the set of 'Atomic Twister' I came close to getting crushed by a runaway cop car.

It was a very simple scene; a Kiwi actor playing a deputy sheriff had to race up to a nuclear power plant in his patrol car at high speed, slam on the breaks and jump out, except for one small detail. The thirty-eight-year-old actor who was required to do this didn't have a driver's license and didn't know how to drive.

I looked at the director who just shook his head in utter and total disbelief. The safety officer stacked some heavy cement bags into a wall several feet from where the actor was supposed to stop.

The director yelled "action" and it was all on. Our rookie driver came screaming down the road in his police cruiser, a couple of tons of metal moving at high velocity in the hands of a novice who didn't understand the relationship between braking and space. The car exploded right through those cement bags scattering everyone.

Comment One: And I know you're not gonna believe this but we had another Kiwi actor on that set who was supposed to be a heavy truck driver arriving in an 18-wheeler in one scene. And guess what? Yeah, this guy didn't have a driver's license either and didn't know how to drive. The director who was a lovely Canadian joker just looked flummoxed and exclaimed: "What the fuck...!"

Comment Two: Although I have to say that when I first arrived in Napier, I too was stunned by the number of New Zealanders who didn't have a driver's license. Coming from California where having a driver's license is considered essential equipment, I just assumed that every adult in the world would have one.

Scrambling

The funniest moment on that production came one morning when we were out at a quarry shooting some of the big action sequences. I overheard the director on his cell phone talking to the owner of the film company in Santa Monica:

"You wouldn't fucking believe it."
"I'm watching them and I don't fucking believe it!?!"
"Yeah, they're running around right now pulling weeds."
"I don't know? Is it worth sending someone out now? We're right in the middle of the shoot?"

The problem was they had eight huge super powerful wind fans on the set that day and the art department had already used up all of its supply of brush, leaves, twigs and other assorted paraphernalia required for the entire day's shoot, just in the one rehearsal. Naturally you need that kind of background material when you're fighting a twister. Hence the mad scrambling but there's really not much vegetation at a quarry. The director was watching them shaking his head once again.

Comment One: I was the American accent coach on that movie and towards the end of the shoot with about three days left I finished with my last New Zealand actor in the movie so I walked up to the director and said, "It's been a pleasure working with you" - and it was - when he said, "Stick around John until the end of the shoot I enjoy your company"... see I told you he was a great guy and I picked up a pay check for another few days in the bargain.

Comment Two: And that wasn't the only time I've picked up a pay check for just lounging around. I was the American accent coach for an overseas TV commercial being shot in Auckland and when I arrived on the set on the first day I discovered that my kiwi talent wasn't required that day. So, I went up to the director and explained the situation. He just said that's okay John, stick around and get a feel for what we're doing... ha! I ate donuts and drank coffee and just shot the shit with the cast and crew all day and got paid to boot!

Comment Three: They say there ain't no such thing as a free lunch. While that may be true... one day I got paid $500 bucks to eat a free lunch. I was working as the American accent coach on a CBS movie of the week starring Thomas Gibson and Poppy Montgomery when they were shooting a scene at a local yacht club. I was only working one scene that day and was given a time to be on set. I arrived just before lunch to be told that they had rescheduled the scene and shot it in the morning. So, I had my free lunch with the cast and crew and got paid for the day to boot. And the best was yet to come... when I walked up to the director to tell him that I was done for the day he actually said this to me: "That's great, John, I want to tell you that I really enjoy working with you... you do a great job and you're not always getting in my way."

Yeah baby, love to hear a compliment like that on a day when I did absolutely zero work and had a great lunch to boot. but I knew what he was talking about... being an American accent coach on a set is at times a tricky business... you have to know when to and when not to walk onto the set to help out an actor who might be struggling a bit with their accent... you've got to keep an eagle eye on the director because there are times when you know that he doesn't give a shit about the accent as he's trying to get a performance out of the actor on film... at those times you've just got to stay back and keep your powder dry.

Comment Four: On the set of Atomic Twister they picked a young kiwi kid who lacked so much energy he could barely act let alone do an American accent. That's one of the key elements in perfecting your accent... you've got to have some energy. I remember asking the producer why they selected this kid in the first place and he just kind of shrugged his shoulders. Yeah, I thought to myself bad choice. This kid was struggling so much that one day when I arrived on the set the director came up to me and said, "John, this is no reflection on the work you're doing... but I'd rather you weren't on the set today... this kid doesn't need any more distractions and I need to get a performance out of him today."

Comment Five: Just going back to that CBS movie of the week. Thomas Gibson who was the lead in 'Criminal Minds' for many years was a true professional in every way. Whenever anyone walked onto the set who was new like me Gibson would always go up to them and introduce himself... nice touch I thought. Poppy Montgomery on the other hand was difficult to say the least. I remember standing on High Street... our first location... in down town Auckland on the very first day of the shoot when she sauntered onto the set and declared loudly to no-one in particular that she wasn't gonna be a problem on the set. Yeah, right I thought to myself. Poppy had more than a few problems but this one kind of tells it all.

The movie was called 'Raising Waylon' which was a custody battle over a young boy. At the end of the movie we're in court and Poppy's attorney, who is none other than my good buddy Michael Saccente, wins the day for her character. Whereupon according to the script she's supposed to hug her attorney. A standard reaction one would have thought. I remember watching the scene as Mike goes to hug her with outstretched arms and she brushes right past him. They should have kept that scene in the movie because the look on Saccente's face was hilarious. Cut! "We'll shoot again," yells the director, then he brings up the fact that she's supposed to hug her attorney and Poppy simply says, "I'm not hugging him." Why? Who would know? I'm the kind of guy who'll talk to anyone... anywhere... anytime... and yet for the five weeks I was on set with Poppy Montgomery I never said one word to her even though some days I'd be standing right next to her for hours.

Serious
And this is some real goofy shit here: Sometimes the hyperbole from ad agencies can be absolutely hilarious. For example, the following is an audition script I was given for a 60 second TV commercial for a bank.

Casting brief: Lead characters:
People who I think (ad man) could carry this off successfully: Danny Devito, Alexi Sayles, Rowan Atkinson, Steve Martin, Julian Cleary, Rudolf Valentino, Ronald Biggs (Ha Ha) Biggs pulled off England's greatest train robbery.
Opening Sequences: Maxwell Smart opening sequence rip off. Down the tunnel of opening doors. Star Wars, Princess Leah and Luke Skywalker on the ledge with a 200 foot drop down into the space dock below them scene rip off. The actor walks through a door to be trapped on a ledge with a huge drop below. But below is a huge pool of money. A diving board automatically appears in front of him and he decides to take the plunge, a la Scrooge McDuck rip off. He dives into a sea of money then leaps up out of it heroically, flamboyantly throwing coins into the air. He proceeds to frolic in the sea of coins, remembering to keep his tongue firmly resting in his cheek. He skips across the sea of bullion relishing his freedom from autocratic banking procedures.

This is the celebration. Excite me, amuse me, surprise me, interpret this script. I won't knock back anything that is over the top. Equally, an anti-performance is always refreshing and exciting. Let them read this brief prior to casting. If they don't like it, or at least understand Tarantino, Black Adder, Max Headroom, stay home. If they don't understand Jeff Koons, Busby Berkley, or Warhol, they will not understand how well a piss take can communicate a serious message.

Appearance is secondary, but I would imagine that we would unfortunately need to lean slightly towards a European look. Pretty wise, I don't really mind if they had to break the mould after birth. Texture and versatility is very important. Some athletic ability will be required, but they certainly don't need to be Michael Jordan.

I relish the unexpected and spontaneous. Encapsulate and chase identifiable preconceptions and characterization that the audience will identify and understand. In reality, if Christopher Lloyd's character from "Taxi" (Jim) or Marlon Brando from "The Godfather" played the role, it would work, purely due to a fully developed sense of who their character is.

Comment: Could this bozo drop any more names? I think in reality Christopher Lloyd (Taxi) or Marlon Brando (The Godfather) could play any damn part they wanted and it would work mainly because they're Christopher Lloyd and Marlon Brando... I mean come on give me a break here - the horseshit this guy shoveled out was phenomenal to say the least! And just for the record the role went to a nondescript white geek and the ad was underwhelming and instantly forgettable.

Dang

That experience reminded me of the time I walked into a recording studio a bit early and got ambushed by the writer. I was playing a Texas truck driver and this wordsmith who was a budding Tolstoy much like Bozo the clown from the bank ad, this kid (he looked all of three) wanted me to go the 'whole nine yards' with tears in my eyes, snot in my nose and wax in my ears as I portrayed the profound anguish of the entire American nation with just one word; 'Dang!'

I was limbering-up stretching all the boundaries to allow every emotion known to mankind to fill me to the brim which resulted in 'Dang' coming out long and slow like a record being played on the wrong speed. The director was there by this stage and he immediately barked out: "What the hell are you doing, John?" "We hired you because you've got a loud booming forceful American voice." "So, let's just say 'Dang' with plenty of gusto like you mean it!"

"Oh, ok?"

Comment One: Yeah, they actually had a writer for one word.

Comment Two: And then on the other side of the fence you get writers who can't just shut the fuck up. They have to show the whole world how fucking clever they are by filling the script with an enormous amount of un-necessary words.

I had a voice over job to do a Barry White voice... no problem. If you know anything about Barry White it's that he talks in a slow low rumble... that's him... that's his voice. I walked into the studio and was given a script for a 30-second ad. The script was two pages worth crammed from top to bottom with endless words... so many words... speed reading I could barely get it all in in the allotted time.

I just looked at these two young, and I mean extremely young, whippersnappers and said - "hey guys that's not gonna work and in fact it's not even close for a Barry White voice." These numb nuts had no clue... when you're doing a voice over it's not just about reading the words - it's all about a performance with the words and like I said Barry White is 'slow' personified... so you have to take that into account when writing your script. Anyway in the end they scrapped Barry White, fired me and hired someone else to do a hip hop version... with lots of words.

Out of Tune

It's one thing to learn how to act - it's another to land a part. New Zealand is a small country with a limited number of acting opportunities for a bald American with a loud voice, so I quickly learned it was essential to try for any role that came along. But even I drew the line when my agent rang to say I was wanted to audition for a musical play.

I turned it down for the simple reason that I couldn't sing. And when I say I can't sing for me I sound worse than someone pulling on the tail of a screeching cat - yeah, it's like mission impossible. But the casting director for the play persisted and said they really wanted to see me.

Apparently, I had all the personal characteristics for the part and surely, I could hold a note long enough to get by. In the end, I agreed to give it my best shot.

I learned a song from the musical West Side Story and went to the theatre where I nervously waited for my turn among the line of stage hopefuls.

Eventually, my name was called and I clambered onto the stage, getting myself ready next to the waiting piano. I briefed the pianist and we launched into the song that had helped make many a star off Broadway. That's Broadway, New York. Clearly it didn't work as well, off Broadway, Auckland.

You know when you're bad, and when the song reached its inevitable climax, I knew I had been worse than bad. But the director bounced up onto the stage and exclaimed: "Okay, John that was great, good to clear out the old cobwebs, loosen up the voice box." It was his attempt to boost me up. Then he carried on, "let's do the song again and this time keep in tune with the piano." I'm immediately thinking: "in tune". What the hell's that? I know nothing about keeping in tune with anything let alone a piano.

So, as the director jumped down off the stage to return to his seat I inched over to the guy playing the piano and whispered, "hey man, can we reverse those roles and you keep in tune with me?" He nodded in the affirmative and off we sailed into another disaster. In the middle of my butchering another attempt at sounding musical I could hear some noise coming from the dark depths of the theatre. What's that?

Then it dawned on me that I was hearing the suppressed giggles coming from the producer and director. They couldn't help themselves they just couldn't hold it back any longer that's how bad I was.

Comment: When American Idol first appeared on television they used to single out a really bad singer so Simon Cowell could make some funny pithy statements about how tragic he was while rolling his eyes and then everyone had a good laugh. They even featured these guys on their show and some of these terrible singers actually got their 15 minutes of fame by being so bad. I was equally as bad (Simon Cowell would have had a field day with me – oh boy)… if not worse than those guys... but all I got was being laughed out of the theatre.

Deja Vu
Okay so one would have thought that that would have been the end of me trying to be musical.

Wrong.

Several years later I was acting in a Disney Movie called 'Ready to Run'. The last scene was a big bar-b-cue hoedown with all the cast involved. I was only required to say a couple of lines to those around me while I was helping myself to a hamburger. No big deal.

But, when I arrived on set for the scene the director came up to me and said: "John, we've changed your bit, instead of getting a hamburger we want you to dance around the floor in front of the band with one of the leading actresses in the movie.

And I'm thinking, "Why me?" Why the hell would they think I'm a twinkle toes type of guy?

Inside I'm panicking big time my dancing skills rank right up there alongside my singing ability. Gene Kelly... Fred Astaire I ain't! This actress just happened to be one of those Latino women who could dazzle you with her moves on the dance floor. But, if that's what the director wants then a man's gotta do what a man's gotta do. As we pair up I'm like Herman Munster dancing with a slim ballerina. So here we go again in the let's be embarrassed stakes - during the rehearsal when the band fires up she's off with a hiss and a roar fliting around light as a feather while I'm barely hanging on lumbering around her trying my damnedest not to crush her dainty feet and the crew is pissing themselves - laughing their asses off. Doh!

Comment One: The director for this movie was a very nice guy but also a very explosive kind of guy.

When I auditioned for him I had two parts I was going for... one was for the bad guy in the movie and the other was for the track announcer.

When I walked into the room the director and producer were sitting next to each other heads down intently looking over a pile of notes. These two were no light weight guys either - the director was Duwayne Dunham who had worked with George Lucas on his Star Wars movies and the producer was Bill Borden who produced Disney's High School Musical movies amongst other huge projects.

I asked them which part I should do first, and Duwayne just waved his hand and said just do it without even looking up. Ok, I thought I need to get this guy's attention to get a part in his movie. I chose to do the track announcer first.

So, while the director and producer were sitting over to the side huddled over their notes I quietly strolled directly behind them and WHAM... and I mean...WHAM... WHAM... WHAM!!! I verbally just blew them right out of the room with my booming mile-a-minute race track calling. Both of them jumped three feet in the air scattering their notes everywhere. Duwayne turned around and said, "That was good." I got the track announcer role.

Comment Two: Ok I just gotta tell this story... on the day I was fascinated watching it... this was a great scene. Like I've said before there are so many great scenes happening behind the cameras. We're on the last day of the shoot for "Ready to Run" and time is short so the producer Bill Borden is directing the second unit at the same time Duwayne Dunham is directing the first unit to finish up the movie. I'm standing off to one side watching a scene that Duwayne is directing when we can hear some noise in the background. Duwayne shouts out: "Tell whoever is making that noise to shut it down... now!"

He yells this to a young kid who is one of the assistant directors on the set.

The noise continues... Duwane shouts out louder to shut it down! Right Now!!

The young kid is stuck in between a rock and a hard place. The noise is coming from a scene that Bill is shooting and the kid doesn't know if he can tell the producer to be quiet. I figure the kid is thinking that the producer of the movie is higher up in the pecking order. Duwayne is getting madder and madder... but finally Bill's scene is shot and the noise is gone. Duwayne then completes his scene and then marches up to the young kid and shouts right in his face: "This is my fucking movie... do you fucking understand that!" He continued: "And when I fucking tell you to fucking shut down the fucking noise... I mean shut the fucking noise down... do you fucking understand that!?!"

The kid is shaking by now and feebly nods in the affirmative. Duwayne then turns to leave but abruptly turns back and yells at the kid... "But I'm not fucking angry with you - ok?"

I just thought the whole scene was hilarious because the poor kid was scared shitless and kept swiveling his head one way in Bill's direction and then the other way back to Duwayne... and he just didn't know what to do. I don't think the kid thought it was that funny.

Side Note: And you might think that I was exaggerating the number of times Duwayne said the word 'FUCK' but I'm not. He said it in every sentence loudly and with emphasis and that's mainly why I thought it was so funny... Duwayne was like a 'FUCK' popcorn machine unleashed... yeah I know I have a weird sense of humour - but there ya go.

Comment Three: And this is some more goofy shit that happens on a set on any given day. Again, we're on the set of "Ready to Run" with Duwayne Dunham directing. We are in a small barn for the most delicate scene in the movie. In this scene the young girl who is the lead in this movie is talking in a soothing voice to a giant black stallion trying to get the stallion to lay down. The horse trainer shows her how to do this using a tooth pick to gently prod the back of one of the stallions' front legs... that's not as easy as it sounds... it takes a great deal of concentration and patience.

Meanwhile I have a part to play in this scene in the background that's killing me... yeah I've gotta sing once again... this time it's Wilson Pickett's Mustang Sally. So, I'm standing in the back softly singing Mustang Sally while the young girl is talking to the horse and gently trying to get it to lay down... this is a very dramatic and tense scene and is taking some time to complete so Duwayne is silently winding his arm in the air giving me the signal to keep on singing.

Now I'm just completely making up new verses ending each one with: "All you want to do is ride around Sally (ride Sally ride)." The young actress has just about gotten the horse to lay down which is really a beautiful thing to see with the horse being so big and the actress being so tiny in this enclosed horse stall when suddenly the sound engineer shouts out that he's run out of batteries... the horse bolts straight back up and Duwayne also bolts straight out of his chair as angry as anybody I've ever seen.

I can tell he wants to just smack the sound engineer... but because he also realizes this he just marches straight out of the barn to cool off. The friction in the air was terrific! The thing is they could have added the sound after the fact... the sound engineer ruined the scene needlessly. They had to take a break and shoot the scene later so the horse could quiet down. Delays cost time and money in the movie business.

Comment Four: And finally one last comment on 'Ready to Run." Again, this involves me and involves a big surprise on the day of my shoot.

I arrive on the set ready to do my track announcing scene. I had about 8 bits of race dialogue memorized for my scene. No big deal... something I could do in my sleep.

But right as I'm getting settled into the announcer's chair Duwayne bounces up to me and says: "John, we want you to announce the entire race so we can cut where and when we want to." Immediately I'm sweating a monsoon... the entire race is several pages long and of course I haven't memorized them. Duwayne tells me no problem... what they did was they printed the entire race in big block words on several huge pieces of cardboard and had people walking back and forth a distance away in front of me carrying them... so it looked like I was following the horses around the track. Fortunately, my eyesight was in great shape and I could read very, very well. Whew!

Comment Five: This is definitely my last thought on this movie. I was the American accent coach on that movie and I had a very nice part in the movie and then they gave me another job - they wanted me to stay on set and do the main horse's lines for the actors who had scenes with Thunder Jam and then on top of that I voiced all the horses in the movie for the producer Bill Bolden so he could time them out in the movie. When Duwayne brought the movie back to New Zealand for a cast and crew special showing he told me that his 15-year-old daughter told him that they should have kept my voice for the main horse Thunder Jam. Thank you young lady.

Mission Impossible

I'm the type of guy who hustles. I hustled when I was a hoopster and naturally, I hustled when I entered the acting world. Although not all my hustles panned out...

Case in point: When they filmed 'Mission Impossible II' in Australia I hustled my ass off to get a part! A director friend of mine gave me the address of where the American big wig (Paula Wagoner, Tom Cruise's business partner) producing the film was staying. I sent her my show reel.

However, this was NOT your run-of-the-mill showreel. I flew over to Sydney and put together a Mission Impossible themed showreel.
I did the whole opening Mission Impossible bit about "the tape you are now watching..." Then it progresses to me clearly identifying the target. The target was ME getting a part in their flick! Snippets of me followed... Shots of me appearing in different shows flashed up and at the very end of the tape I returned to assure them in person that "NO, this tape won't self destruct." Especially if I get a part in your movie! This was a creative hustle by a lone unknown actor trying to hustle for a part, and all I got was my show reel and accompanying letter back in the mail with the ultimate put down: No comment...they totally ignored my effort while they actually put in some effort of their own to make me seem small and insignificant - normally if it's a 'don't call us - we'll call you' situation they just toss whatever they've been sent in the waste basket.

Comment: I don't believe people today recognize genuine 'effort' and that's sad. It's not like in the movies when the hero does something goofy to win the day.

In 'real life' these days it seems to me that an awful lot of people out there have lost their sense of humor. But you know what? That's the way it goes sometimes, the thing is you can't berate the other guy for not wanting to play your game.

If you knock on someone else's door and they don't want to open it, "TS"... which - as my older brother used to say - stands for 'Tough Shit." Get over it. Move on.

No License

When I flew back to Washington, D. C. to film the location shots for 'Fallout' our first scene was on the top of Capital Hill, what a majestic building. I had never been to our nation's capital so I was pumped, and not only that I was being driven around in a chauffeured black limo and another actor was dressed in military uniform hopping out and opening my door. Even though it was only make-believe the public didn't know that and a lot of heads turned to look in my direction, damn it was a blast!

We were blocking thru the scene and I was talking with the director when a Capital Hill police car approached. The director immediately whispered to me sideways to let him do the talking.

"Why?"

"Because we don't have a license to be shooting here."

"Oh, that's great; I'm going to get arrested in my own country."

The cops weren't the smiley type and made us move on and we had to scoot around to the front of the Capital building to the public area and shoot the scene there.

Our next location was the Pentagon. I looked hard at my director. He just smiled.

Atomic Meltdown

You also find that not all the drama is going on the screen during the filming of a movie. One afternoon I was sitting directly behind the director of 'Atomic Twister' when they were shooting the most dramatic moments in the movie. This is the scene where our heroes save the nuclear plant and themselves from a meltdown and avert a world disaster.

Now, while all this drama is taking place right in front of us, the director got a call on his cell phone (silent ring). It's his wife. They had just moved from Los Angeles to Vancouver where she doesn't know a soul. Then he's taken off half way around the world and is sitting in a dusty decrepit warehouse on a film set and their eighteen-month old baby boy has an extremely high fever. His wife is hysterical with worry.

I'm listening to this jumping out of my skin; the director's boy is the same age as mine. The director's wife is panicking, but he's sitting there as cool as a cucumber. He's still watching the monitor of this hugely dramatic scene while a nuclear reactor is reaching critical melt down with a multitude of actors rushing around in various stages of action, and right in the middle of all this incredible tension he calmed his wife down, called a doctor he knew in Vancouver and called her back to say the doctor would be right over in five minutes.

"Cut! That's a buy, moving on."

Comment: I was so impressed with how calm, cool and collected he was. When it comes to my children, I wear my heart and emotions and almost every other organ on my sleeve loudly! In that situation if it was my kid, I'd be going completely bonkers... fuck the atomic meltdown! I'd be in meltdown!!!

Who Gives A Fuck

I had a very small... small role as a high school principal in a film project called - 'The Subtle Art of Not Giving a Fuck' which is an adaptation of Mark Manson's book of the same name... the main reason I'm mentioning this is because I just loved the title of Mark's book - The Subtle Art of Not Giving a Fuck... brilliant for the times we live in!

The other reason I'm mentioning this is because personally I like a lot of Mark's ideas so I recommend either reading the book or go to YouTube where Mark gives a great summary of his ideas in the book.

Listening

Acting has taught me a lot. For one thing it's taught me to listen, to really, really, really listen, not only to my wife, but to my kids. To focus on the other person and actually hear what they're saying. When acting is slick and glib with little connection between the actors it's because there's a lack of involvement, they're not letting the other actor's words sink in because they're concentrating so much on what they're going to say. Their chief concern is their point of view, kind of like in real life. Which is mostly, no make that entirely how I behaved before I learned the Meisner Technique. Before I actually learned to 'listen'.

Michael Saccente

Another thing becoming an actor taught me was the absolute power of 'Emotional Preparation': Emotional preparation in acting is really 'believing' that the imaginary circumstances you're in are true. You give yourself up to the imaginary circumstances. My old self was so shallow that I would never have been able to do that, but acting classes prepared me to let go and not be threatened by my emotions. My Meisner acting tutor Michael Saccente who studied under the legendary teacher in New York, once gave me an acting assignment one night in his class, that blew me away: I was to sit at a desk in front of the class and write a letter to his mother about attending his funeral. I completely gave myself over to this task and was so absorbed that when another actor walked in and asked me if I was alright (the pinch), when I tried to explain what was wrong (even though Mike was sitting in the back of the class) I felt this emotional tidal wave sweeping over me and I broke down crying like a baby, (my ouch). What a rush.

Comment: That was definitely my break-through in the acting world... to finally just let all my macho bullshit go and get involved with my emotions. To embrace the 'Suspension of disbelief'.

Brandon Lee

On the set of 'High Tide' starring George Segal and Rick Springfield (Jesse's Girl) I had to get shot at point-blank range.

Even when it's make-believe, having someone point a gun at you up close is spooky. Especially when the armourer on the set had just told me how Brandon Lee was shot and killed on the set of 'The Crow'. Apparently there was a wad of cardboard in the chamber and it wasn't checked before they put in a blank flash charge. The gun was a .44 Magnum so the cardboard wad was lethal enough to kill at close range. Another Lee was gone too soon. When we shot the scene and I got shot I know I winced that little bit extra as I saw the flash. So in terms of emotional preparation, the armourer scaring the living daylights out of me with his story was a good move.

Comment: After hearing about that wad of cardboard stuck in the gun - I told the first AD that I wanted to check the gun before we shot the scene. The director heard about this and told me that if I wasn't comfortable with the scene, we could do it another way. I told her that I appreciated her concern but after checking the gun I was cool with the scene.

Cameron Duncan

Although one night, I found myself on the set of a short film where I had to actually shut down my emotional senses otherwise I never would have made it through the night.

By far and away the most moving film experience I've had, in a real life sad way, was on the set of a short film called 'Strike Zone.'

I got a call, as you do in New Zealand, late one afternoon from a producer friend who wanted to know if I was available to film a scene that night.

'Strike Zone' was written, directed, acted and edited by Cameron Duncan (1986-2003): It's a semi-autobiographical film about a young cancer battler's quest to create a team of champion softball players in the remaining two months of his life. It doesn't get any more dramatic or emotional than that, but for me it did. Cameron's dad, with whom I've worked with on several projects, was the cameraman shooting the film while his son directed his own funeral.

I almost lost it at one point thinking of my own son and how I'd react in this type of situation. I had to mentally force myself to shut down emotionally from a personal standpoint and not think about the circumstances surrounding this film, and get on with the job.

Cameron Duncan was an outstanding young New Zealand film maker, having won several awards for his short films and television commercials. Academy Award winning film director Peter Jackson was so captivated by young Cameron's talent that he invited him onto the 'Lord of the Rings' set and included two of Cameron's short films 'DFK6498' and 'Strike Zone' on the extended DVD of 'Lord of the Rings - The Return of the King'. Peter Jackson and his partner Fran Walsh supported him throughout his illness. Fran, who wrote the lyrics for 'Into the West' sung by Annie Lennox, which won an Oscar for best song, dedicated that song to Cameron's memory during her acceptance speech at the Academy Awards. Several months after 'Strike Force' was shot Cameron Duncan succumbed to his illness. This happened during the final stages for the completion of 'The Return of the King', Peter Jackson's third installment of The Lord of the Rings trilogy.

Deadlines loomed large and the pressure was on for Peter to deliver this huge film, which was to eventually be honored with 11 Oscars, but he dropped everything and flew up to Auckland to attend Cameron's funeral.

That was my first encounter with the great filmmaker. I was astounded at how down to earth he was as he spoke simply from his heart when he told the gathering that he had hoped that the magic of film making might somehow pull Cameron through, but it wasn't to be.

Christopher Lloyd
However, the best emotional preparation I was ever going to have for a role came on the set of 'Kid's World' starring Christopher Lloyd. When I met Lloyd we shook hands and he studied me intently, never saying a single word, and then walked away. That was weird I thought.

It was only later that I realized he'd done a Jim Ignatowski (his character in the hit television sitcom Taxi) on me and never explained himself. Nice.

He was also a very accommodating Hollywood star: One day after shooting his last scene for the day in a local neighbourhood, he hung around for a half hour signing autographs and shooting the breeze with the enormous crowd that gathered to catch a glimpse of him. Nice man.

Still, my first day on the set was very emotional. I was playing the Dad to the fourteen-year-old lead.

When I arrived the First Assistant Director announced to the other cast and crew, "This is John Dybvig, he's the Dad."

I just stood there beaming at hearing those words.

And finally I fairly screamed, "Yes! Yes, I am the Dad!"

Everyone stood there, mouths agape like I was a total nutter, until I gushed forth that my lovely wife Jennifer had told me that very morning that I should start preparing to become a dad in the real world. I was fifty at the time and Sam was my first child, so yeah I was completely bonkers and over the moon for that shoot.

Love Your Work Doll

I was forty-two when I characteristically barged into this narcissistic world. Previously I was a jockstrap, a caveman dragging my knuckles on the ground.

Macho was in, emotional displays never, especially hugging other men. Strange men with high voices, yech!

It took me a while to warm up to the idea, but now I'm a regular huggaholic. "Baby, sweetie, love your work... hug... hug... hug" And I'm not threatened by the experience.

Unexpected Fame

Another kick to being an actor is when one of your shows pops up overseas. My aunt in Los Angeles couldn't sleep one night and was channel surfing at 2:00am in the morning and caught my appearance in 'High Tide' much to her delight. And my travel agent here in New Zealand caught one of my 'Hercules' episodes while vacationing in Canada. But the absolute best was when my wife Jennifer was on business with her mother in Florence, Italy. They checked into this lovely small boutique hotel smack in the middle of town surrounded by acres and acres of some of the world's most stylish architecture steeped in the rich history of the Renaissance. Once inside their room they casually flipped on the television and suddenly I popped up talking a million miles an hour in the Disney movie 'Ready to Run' calling a horse race in fluent Italian. Jennifer told me she and her mother were shrieking and hooting so loudly that several hotel employees rushed in thinking something terrible was happening. That's cool.

What is Acting

I gotta say being an actor is a total rush. It's a joy and a struggle at the same time... countless auditions - countless rejections. There's no in-betweens for the majority of actors in the world.

It often seems that one minute you're totally immersed in a project with highly skilled directors, producers, crew and fellow actors and it's an opportunity to be treasured. You're on this incredible high for a few days, a week or a couple of months. It's like floating on a cloud above life itself.

Then bang. The needle is yanked. Cold turkey. No work.

But the craving and frustration never leave until you bag your next hit, your next working gig. It's the creative rush that keeps you going.

I'm a house-husband in New Zealand who got into the acting game late so I've only been in it a short while but this is what I've learned.

In reality acting is not like Coca-Cola or Kentucky Fried Chicken, there is not a proven recipe. The one thing you can do consistently is to do your job. Go to as many auditions as you can, know your lines and be on time.

If the gods are smiling and that X-factor we call talent shows up on the day you may come away laughing. Either way prepare yourself for the next audition. If you're not comfortable walking side by side with rejection, well... you should probably think about another career choice.

If you fit the current description of whom the director thinks he wants in the part at that moment, and believe me that 'vision' is always under review your mug shot might get pulled from a pile and you'll be called to the audition. Parts are won and lost for many a reason. Not all of them 'artistic'... Unless you go unprepared and really screw up the audition don't take it to heart. The better you are the more the law of averages is in your favor. The business has natural flood gates in place to sort out the wannabes from the contenders.

Enjoy the process as the system weeds out the dreamers from the actors. People who 'tried it once and found it wasn't for me' got flushed at the first post... believe me! Persist! But with intelligence! So the big question is: "What is acting?"

To be perfectly honest it beats the hell out of me, but here's what I think: Acting is doing... living truthfully under imaginary circumstances... instinct... the heart... repeat... repeat from a point of view... energy... pinch and ouch... working moment to moment... letting the moments pile up... letting the stone hit the bottom... listening... really listening... having long will.

And of course having the right agent.

Get The Job Done

This is a huge shout out to every crew member I've ever worked with on every set I've been on... one of the things I enjoy most about working in the film industry is being surrounded by the crew... it's one of the greatest work environments I've ever been in...there's absolutely no bullshit... no excuses... no slow approach... no I'll get to it in a minute... it's full steam ahead always and no problem is too difficult for the lighting guys... the props people... the make-up gals... the wardrobe people... the carpenters... the special effects people... the stunt women and men... the camera operators... everybody on a film set just busts their asses to get the job done... like I've said it's such a pleasure to be around that kind of work environment... so I salute everybody who works behind the camera... you beautiful people are truly amazing!!!

The Joke

Of course I can't leave you without regaling you with my favorite acting joke which if one thinks about it isn't really a joke - it's true:

One day an actor who is totally down on his luck hasn't had a job in months is driving home from yet another fruitless audition.
He's driving towards his house set in the hills and off in the distance he can see some rising smoke. The closer he gets to his house the more smoke he sees until finally he comes up over the last hill and looks down to where his house is and all he can see is clouds of billowing smoke.

He races down the hill and in front of him are half a dozen fire trucks and police cars. His house much to his horror is completely burnt to the ground. The fire chief comes up to him and gently explains to him that his wife and children have perished in the fire. The actor starts to sob uncontrollably. And then the chief says: "And your agent also perished." The actor is still wailing when all of a sudden he stops, looks up and says:

"Wait... what? You said... my agent was at my house."

CHAPTER THREE

How to Survive as a D-List Celebrity
Dybvig looks forward to life on the red carpet - but finds himself flipping 'burgers.

The Kid

It was meant to be the peak of my career as a celebrity. I had my own television show; my own radio show; appeared in movies, and was known throughout New Zealand as the 'Loud American'.

Flushed with my success, I cruised through town in my 1975 green Mercedes (I loved that car) and stopped for a red light. This filthy ragged-looking kid hustled up to wash my windows. He quickly threw the dirty soapy water on my windscreen and in the same motion he began frantically wiping it off. He was hurrying because time was short and the lights would change soon. Suddenly, he stopped and peered at me through the windscreen.

You could see his thought process as his memory banks ticked over. Then, he blurted out: 'Hey, man, are you that Dibby fella?'

'Yeah, man,' I said, repaying his recognition with my best effort at a showbiz smile.

I wondered what he'd say next - maybe something about my achievements in sport, television or acting.

He leaned back, slowly shaking his head before he quietly and almost conspiratorially poked his head next to mine.

'Hey, bro,' he whispered, 'you've put on some weight.'

Not expecting that comment I had that little bit of a stunned mullet look... oh.

As I went to give the kid a dollar.

The larrikin held up both hands in mock insult.
'Freebie, bro, freebie.'

I laughed and kept laughing and still laugh today when I think about that experience. So much for being world famous in New Zealand.

The Wise Crack
Notwithstanding my weight problem, I became a D-list celebrity in one of the world's smallest nations, on the furthest reaches of our planet.

When I was back in the States one year on a visit, I told senior sports journalist Mark Purdy of the San Jose Mercury News (San Francisco Bay Area) that I had moved to New Zealand.

Without hesitation, he asked:

'On purpose?'

Gawd, I laughed! And that's something that I love about America that is uniquely ours: The Wisecrack. Nobody in the world can 'wisecrack' like us (until Trump came along). My all-time favorite was by President Ronald Reagan when he was checking sound levels on his microphone before a national broadcast:

"My fellow Americans. I'm pleased to announce that I've signed legislation outlawing the Soviet Union. We begin bombing in five minutes."

Comment: Where'd It Go: What happened America? Where'd it go? We used to have a great sense of humor. We'd laugh at anything and everything even ourselves. There was nothing we wouldn't wise crack about. Under Trump that's all gone. Today it's all about division. Hate. Sides. Tribal politics. You literally cannot joke about anything in America today without someone taking offense. Sad.

Speaking American
No matter where I went, I couldn't hide the fact I was an American. All I had to do was open my mouth.

Like I said, half the time I didn't have a clue as to what these people were on about. I spoke American and they spoke the Queen's English... big difference... massive difference. And for all of the new-fangled gadgets we have to communicate throughout our universe there is still one fundamental problem:

The Communication Gap.

Because no matter how you slice it, dice it or chop it you still have to get your ideas across to the guy sitting across the desk from you.

Communication Gap
'It's not just what you say... it's what the other guy hears... ... there's not only the difference between what you say and what you mean... ...there's an enormous difference between what he thought you said and what he thought you meant to say!?!"

Therein lies the 'Communication Gap'.

Hi Ho Silver
Let me illustrate: One day the Lone Ranger and his trusty horse Silver were out riding through some dangerous Indian territory... they were clomping along nice and easy when all of a sudden, a band of marauding Indians came charging after them. The Lone Ranger with a throaty "Hi Ho Silver" took off!

It quickly became apparent that he couldn't outrun these pesky Indians so he rode behind some rocks, jumped off Silver, whispered in his trusty horse's ear, slapped him on the rump and Silver took off over the hill. Then the Lone Ranger drew out his six-guns and started shooting at the surrounding Indians. A little while later Silver came charging back over the top of the hill carrying a beautiful blonde woman on his back:

Naked!

Buck naked!

Not a stitch of clothing to be seen.

Silver roared up to the Lone Ranger skidding to a halt in a cloud of dust - the Lone Ranger looked at Silver, shrugged his shoulders and slowly shaking his head in total frustration exploded:

"Mannnnnnnnn...I told you to bring back a...

...Posse!"

Comment: When I told the above joke to one of my American accent classes one night... right when I said "Indian territory" the hand of one of my very young female students suddenly shot up urgently wanting to say something. I stopped in the middle of my joke looked at her and said: "Normally it's polite to wait until one is finished with one's joke before interrupting." But she blurted out: "You can't say 'Indian' they're native Americans - you have to say native Americans." I started to say: "It's a joke... but then I realised how futile that would be with today's younger generation.

Comment Two: Whenever I've delivered this joke to a room full of people - because it's a word association joke... on the punchline there's a very brief moment of silence as their collective minds tick over and then like magic when they all click in unison... WHAM!!! And I mean - WHAM BAM!!!... The entire room just erupts in laughter... EXPLODES... it's a great rush... it's such a buzz when you connect with an audience that way... I love it every time it happens.

Barrack Obama

When two different cultures bump up against each other the results can be bizarre, hilarious and downright weird to say the least - check out this very real lesson in the communications gap that took place during President Obama's swearing in ceremonies:

Radio Host: We've got Tom on the line all the way from Santa Barbara, California. Hello Tom, tell me your first impression of President Barack Obama in Washington D.C. this morning?
Tommy: "I hear Snoop Dog's in the house."
Radio Host: "Pardon?"
Tommy: "Yeah, Snoop Dog's in the House!"

I worked at this station in Auckland with my 'Letter from America' show so I was invited onto their breakfast show as the local American covering one of America's most historic occasions - namely the Inauguration of its first Black American President.

I had given the radio host Tommy's number so they could get some on the spot reactions from the States. Tommy's sudden news flash had everyone in the station scrambling... the host even Googled and during the commercial break breathlessly told me that he couldn't find anything about Snoop Dog being at the White House. I just sat there and looked at him in disbelief thinking:

"Wow, I'm definitely not in Kansas now."

Thus, I became the local interpreter translating what my buddy from the colonies was trying to get across:

"Look guys Tommy was just talking 'smack' pulling your chain, it's just an expression, he was being an American wise guy and it didn't mean anything really - of course Snoop Dog's not at the White House today of all days... both guys are black... White House... Snoop Dog's in the house... that's funny."

Then came the coup de gras: The morning host was waxing on and on and on about what a brilliantly smooth orator Obama was when Tommy interrupted with... "Yeah, but I'm still not drinking the Kool Aid".

I was howling what a killer segue! Tommy was pure gold with the stuff he was dishing out that morning. The morning host was mortified, he had the most dazed look of "What the..." plastered on his mug that I've ever seen. He was so stunned he had absolutely no come back - for all he knew Tommy might as well have been speaking jibberish. In total confusion he looked in my direction with an expression that screamed please explain!

I took over once again pointing out to him, our listeners and everyone else in the studio that Tommy was referring to another incredibly smooth American talker - 'People's Temple' cult leader Jim Jones who not only convinced his American cult into moving from San Francisco to Guyana but once there he sweet talked them into thinking that it'd be real groovy if they all quenched their thirst in this hot little South American country with a nice cold glass of poisoned Kool Aid resulting in the deaths of over 900 people, one of the largest mass suicides in history.

I was still getting some queer looks so I spelled it out for them in black and white:

"All Tommy is saying is he's not swallowing everything that Obama is coming out with without seeing some real action first... he's not getting all giddy just because the man can string a few sentences together and he's definitely not taking his word on all those promises on blind faith... the man's a pragmatist he wants to see some cold hard results."

I finally got some nods... Oh!?! I walked out of there feeling like I had done a translator shift at the United Nations.

Rat
Another example of miscommunication got me offside with a basketball player I was coaching in Napier.

In America, we use the term 'gym rat' to describe someone who spends a lot of time in a gym, working on their game even if it's casually shooting baskets alone. A gym rat may spend as much as eight or 10 hours a day in a gym shooting or playing one-on-one so for a basketball player to be called a gym rat is considered a compliment - in fact, it's seen to be cool.

One day, I told the President of the Napier Basketball Association that we had a young kid who was always hanging out in the stadium. I described the kid as 'a real gym rat'.

Next day, this youngster accosted me on the street.

'I heard what you called me,' he exclaimed indignantly.

'What?' I said, confused.

'A rat!' he spat. 'You called me a rat.'

I gave up and walked away, chuckling and shaking my head.

Man-oh-man, where had I landed?

Bulldog 'Bob' Brown

My public profile had started through basketball. At first, I was the loud and gruff coach who ranted and raved up and down the side of the court. Then I was the walking headline - the coach who was banned from one town for life. Someone in television obviously thought I would be good for ratings - a loudmouth who could shake things up.

I found myself presenting and fronting any sort of American sports event that was worthy of broadcast in New Zealand. Football. Basketball. And wrestling.

I caught the lead surfboard in the wrestle mania wave sweeping the world and my job was to make it appear that I knew what was going on in the ring - whether I did or not. My greatest weapon was my booming, gravelly voice.

'Wop! It's a smack to the kisser followed by an Inverted Atomic Drop. I tell ya in this game it's punish and win. If you're outgunned you can always even things up with a good poke to the eyes. Yes! It's a Big Belly Suplex with a Flying Knee.'

I even got creative and came up with my own shit. I invented the 'Reverse Sunset Flip - with a Shoulder Crank.'

I'm the author of the San Berdoo Butt Drop and the coiner of the Bigbelly Flapjack. Yeehaw. Not a lot of people can say that. Most likely not a lot of people would wanna say that.

The drill is the same the world over. Except in New Zealand they got the inexpensive wrestlers. Wal-Mart specials... They didn't get the 'Rock' (who, incidentally, lived with an uncle in New Zealand for a short time when he was a kid) small world.

No... instead they got 'Bulldog Bob Brown.' Bulldog may have been a real warrior back in the days of Tyrannosaurus Rex (the dinosaur - not the band), but by the time they found him his body had already lost the battle with gravity.

What once may have been muscles now hung in overlapping folds from scrawny shoulders, like drapes over old theater curtains. His gluteus Maxima had so given up the ghost that it looked like he'd taken a dump in his trunks. His bare legs were a blaze of purple and red with varicose veins and ruptured capillaries.

Bulldog was not a pretty sight.

However, a man's gotta do what a man's gotta do and seeing as I was the expert wrestling commentator for this pathetic scene, I put on my best Ventura sneer and soliloquized.

'Look at those rippling shoulder muscles! This gladiator is some athlete!'

For his first bout the old geezer tottered over and attacked the smallest, most feeble-looking guy in the ring - Bulldog commenced to gum his eyebrow.

'Whoa!' I cried. 'Bulldog Bob's gone berserk. He's attacking the manager.'

'No,' cried my co-commentator, 'that's the Samoan Warrior.'

'That little guy in green is a wrestler?' I exclaimed in total bewilderment.

'A novice wrestler - he's here to get some experience.'

'Oh?'

Bulldog won that bout by lavishing his opponent with a severe slobbering to his forehead.

On his way back to the locker room, Bulldog had a sudden rush of blood and got cocky, thinking he'd try the ever-popular crowd charge.

The old man picked two small kids, glowered menacingly and raced towards them.

The small kid stood his ground giving Bulldog the finger. The bigger kid (the 13-year-old) waited until he got in range and popped him with two quick left jabs and finished him off with a sweet right cross. No respect for the elderly. Bob staggered, but held his feet... barely. The security guards stepped in to save the old fart from a more serious beating.

Jesse 'The Body' Ventura

Hunter S. Thompson once said, 'When the going gets weird, the weird turn pro.' I never knew what that meant until I joined the professional wrestling circus.

The behind-the-scenes shooting of this farce was stranger than anything that happened in the ring.

The television producer for this three-ringed circus was a perky little English dude whose catch-all reaction to any disaster was always: 'Don't worry about it, mate.'

Even telling him I didn't know shit about wrestling didn't faze him.

'Don't worry about it, mate,' he enthused. 'Just give it heaps of this (talking gesture with his hand) and lots of the old energy.'

You do what you can... I got hold of a couple of WWF (World Wrestling Federation - before the real WWF - World Wildlife Fund - took them to court and forced them to change their name to WWE) tapes and spent my days studying Jesse 'The Body' Ventura.

I actually took notes. Homework. My house began to resemble Westlemania-101 for beginners. One day, there was a knock on the door. My mind was fixated on all the wrestling information laid out before me and I yelled for whoever it was to come inside.

In walked two Mormon Elders looking for new converts. They found me transfixed, watching wrestling videos surrounded by piles of wrestling magazines and posters of half-naked females under headlines like Naked Pussies Cat Fight!

I was popping my eyeballs and shouting at the screen, 'Yes, it's a flying Suplex, Atomic-drop-Screwdriver-Brandy-Alexander.' The Mormons silently excused themselves.

Comment One: Some people are beyond saving.

Comment Two: Since I really didn't know squat about big time wrestling lingo I just made shit up as I went along: In the corners of the ring where the ropes meet at ninety-degree angles, there's a geegaw called a turnbuckle. You hardly ever hear of it in boxing matches, but in wrestling it's used a lot. Guys climb on it, slam each other's heads into it, dive into it and so on. But for some unexplained reason every time I came to mention it I got this block. I called it the belt buckle:

"Whoa!" I'd cry, "the Russian Brute crashed into the belt buckle."

I also had trouble with the oldest and most commonplace throw - the Flying Mare. I'd call it a Flying Horse (actually my favorite Chinese restaurant) or a Mare horse or a Nightmare.

"Whoa, oh, it's a Flying Mare horse right into the belt buckle."

Snuffgrumphullphallous

The promoter was an ex-professional wrestler with the tag name Marvin the Mangler. Oh, yeah. He was a mammoth gnarled beast. He looked like an aging overweight walrus, not unlike pro golfer Craig Stadler, but with a lot more dents in his head. Marvin was the wrestling equivalent of boxing hustler Don King - but without the mouth. Of celebrities who insure their valuable body parts, Marvin's mouth received a valuation of 50 cents from Lloyds of London. He must have taken some vicious blows to his windpipe because his entire vocabulary consisted of one word: 'Snuffgrumphullphallous.'

He spun this single word, and all its variations, to amazing lengths, the shortest taking about twenty minutes. I did not understand a single thing this man rasped during the entire shoot; whatever he was saying had nothing to do with me or my fellow commentator.

All the fights were carefully choreographed, as is the natural world of professional Big-Time wrestling. They knew who would win, how they'd win and when they'd win. But we never knew beforehand what stunts the wrestlers were going to pull. Honest. I'm not making this up.

It had to be the only professional wrestling show in the world where the commentators were at the same level as the audience when it came to knowing what was going to happen. I couldn't believe it throughout the entire shoot I kept expecting the bubble to burst and find myself at the skulduggery meetings... but it never happened. So, we just kept making it up as we went along.

My New Zealand co-commentator was the strangest duck I've ever worked with. He just topped five feet and had at least a four-and-a-half-foot nose. He closely resembled a rat (no, not a gym rat but a real rat). I immediately started calling him Chuck E. Cheese.

The commentary was going to be a three-way thing: The rat was the straight Good Guy commentator and surprise, surprise, I was going to be the Ugly American - the mister shout guy - while Marvin the Mangler would be the New Zealand wrestling expert.

Like I said, the cameras should have been turned around.

Don't Do It
I was constantly receiving well-meaning advice from media colleagues to distance myself from this absurdity for the sake of my credibility.

They were equally assiduous in disassociating themselves from it and did so at every opportunity. They'd whine, 'I've never seen it myself, you understand...' before going into details that the most fanatical supporter would have missed.

'So, you've watched it?' I would challenge.

'Well, you know, the kids watch it, so you can't help catching some of it.'

My over-the-top reaction didn't help. 'Hey!' I'd bellow, 'I can't give up wrestling. Big sweaty men in tights are my life.'

The difference in attitude between adults and children was interesting. The kids seemed far more mature. They were less concerned about insults to their intelligence. I don't think for one minute they actually thought the fights were for real - any more than they believe they're piloting a real rocket at the video arcade. The kids were just happy to go along with the fantasy. But adults - all kinds of intelligent and educated adults - seemed to require reassurance.

'Boy, those wrestlers, huh, I mean, they're not for real, are they?' I didn't help there either. 'What do you mean, they're not for real? Are you saying they fake that stuff? You calling me and my buddies liars?' When you discuss movies with someone do you feel the urge to let everyone know that the actors were only pretending?

The Usual Suspects

The wrestlers for this gig turned out to be the 'usual suspects' in a fight to the death between the Good Guys and the Bad Guys. The first bout featured the Wild Thing Stevie Ray, who was doing a lady killer shtick. He had long blond hair and did a great imitation of a man deeply and shamelessly in love with himself. His ring attire was a pair of pink tights with a bulge in front that looked like he had an outboard motor down there. Stevie Ray spent most of his time running his fingers through his hair and the rest fondling the drive shaft on the Evinrude. A real snapperhead. He was up against Chief Mark Youngblood who had an entire wardrobe of Apache chic outfits featuring tassels and feathered headdress. Perfect.

The commentary booth at this stadium was waaaay up in the rafters. You had to climb umpteen steps to get there. Marvin the Walrus hadn't even started when I heard our director count us down. We were about to take off and the only person who knew anything about flying was still on the runway. So Chuck E. Cheese and I did the only sensible thing we could in such a predicament - we winged it, which meant getting hysterical and saying the first thing that came into our heads:

<u>Me:</u> 'What would you know about it, Chuck? The only thing you ever wrestled was your conscience. Looks like you lost.'
<u>Chuck E. Cheese:</u> 'Clean wrestling, John Dybvig, that's what we like in New Zealand. Oh, and back comes Stevie Ray with the Slammer, Jammer, Glammer, Hammer!'
<u>Me:</u> 'Boy, that guy's some athlete. The Glammer Hammer is one of the hardest moves in the game!'
<u>Chuck:</u> 'And the cleanest.'
<u>Me:</u> 'Shut up, you little weenie.'

Since neither of us had a clue about the holds, we agreed with whatever the other made up. If I called something a Sawback-Screwbelly-Suplex, Chuck E. Cheese spent some time validating it with a sage comment about what a great move it was. The Mangler finally arrived and couldn't believe his ears. He joined us just in time for the second bout between the Russian Brute and some local nobody. One guess as to who won.

The Russian Brute was the primo Bad Guy. This monster was a genuine 6'8" and more than three hundred and forty pounds. This was a pleasant surprise as most of the wrestlers had a bad case of dwarfism on the flight over, that being the reason I wasn't allowed to do interviews. It's not a good look when the announcer towers over the star wrestler.

Comrade

The Russian Brute pushed me into a corner and jammed a stony finger deep into my chest and in an accent thick enough to walk on, he grunted: 'What you say about Brute?'

He had me going. I went into my routine about the rampaging monster who smashed the iron curtain with his famous heart punch. He seemed to like it.

The accent disappeared and it was like talking to my brother. Turned out in real life he ran a hardware store in Independence, Missouri. We shot the breeze for a while about the difficulty of performance and the demands of showbiz. He was just a jobbing wrestler on the road.

The Mangler started to describe to us the legitimate names of the moves. 'That hold is called a Snumphallagrampus, also known as the Snumlamphalligantullus, but more correctly a Snumpurastabaaga Lock.' By the time he finished, the Russian Brute had rearranged the nobody into three different shapes and was busy strangling him with the Russian flag. The fight was over and Marvin baby was still describing the first hold. Something wasn't quite right.

'Well, Chuck, that fight was a lot like you, far too short.'
'I suppose that passes for wit where you come from, John Dybvig?'
'Eat my shorts, squirt.'
"Well, I'll tell you one thing I like about you, Chuck, you're so dull you make me look even more exciting than I am."

Strut

I had one thing in common with all the Bad Guys; they all had adopted the gravel throat delivery that I had been perfecting at home in front of my TV. When we were talking together it was like a tribe of Neanderthals had stumbled across a case of bad Listerine. Ruptured mucous membrane and strained uvulas everywhere. The other thing I loved about the Bad Guys was their strut. You hold your arms out from your sides like you've got jock itch in your armpits and you pull in your butt real tight like Stevie Ray just started the outboard, then you walk around real slow and careful. I tried it for a while, but people kept asking me if I was feeling alright, so I dropped it.

Mullet

I did one interview, which I ended up regretting. The Monoglian Mauler came in at a true 6'5"and about a trillion pounds, give or take a couple. He resembled the Goodyear Blimp forced into a giant scarlet leotard. We're talking blubber guts, porkola, fat city here. You can bet your last Dinar he wasn't born in your actual oriental Mongolia. More likely Mongolia, Illinois.

And yes, even the interviews had a twist: The Monoglian Mauler did a party trick with an aging mullet.

I popped my first question: 'Mongolian Mauler, I believe you...' Mongo hit himself on the head with the fish and took a huge bite out of the mid-section. A putrid spray of guts and fish goop spurted all over my face. I went back to the commentary booth smelling like the tarpaulin off a trawler.

Television Tournament Belt

When all the wrestlers had beaten each other to within an inch of their lives so many times it got tedious to say the least we finally arrived at the big moment: The championship bout for the Television Tournament Belt (I wonder how long it took them to think of that gem). The final showdown came down to Siva Afi and the Bounty Hunter.

It's a pro-wrestling axiom that anybody of definable ethnic origins is a prince or a king or a chief. Afi was a high chief.

He had international fame as well: He worked on the set of B. L. Stryker as Burt Reynolds' bodyguard and as a stuntman. He also did some stunt work for Miami Vice.Afi really looked the goods, he had a full body tattoo and with his iron pumped musculature of lats and pecs and delts and with all kinds of other muscle groups all improbably stacked up on each other his arms in their resting state were parallel to the ground.

The Bounty Hunter came out screaming the typical wrestling insults challenging Afi to prove his manhood ad nausea, but he had a naturally soft and melodic speaking voice so the acid-gargle delivery didn't work. He sounded like Mary Tyler More doing a Satchmo impression. He was about eight feet of acne across the back, I've never seen so much bad skin in one piece. And just in case you thought there was any doubt about who was going to win this epic battle Marvin the Mangler was in Afi's corner as his manager. Bount did his dirty low down, mean and cheatingest best, but he was never really in it. Once they'd sorted out the hair pulling and crutch grabbing, Siva showed why he was the top draw card.

The man could fly. At the merest excuse, he clambered onto the top rope and used it as an ersatz trampoline. He did swan dives from up there. He did double flick flaks and Tsukahara's.

If Bounty boy took two seconds to abuse the audience - which was his best move - Siva would Nijinsky onto the top rope, execute a stunningly beautiful leap into the rafters and land with both feet in the deepest pock mark on the Bount's back. He took the Bount's legs and one of his arms and plaited them into an interesting tapa pattern.

Siva introduced body parts to each other which, to my way of thinking, should remain strangers. He arranged Bount into sixteen solo Kama Sutra positions. Chuck E. Cheese and I failed miserably to match Afi's masterful display. We were reduced to one word each: 'Afi ... unbelievable! ... Afi ... unbelievable!'

The bounty Hunter tried to counter by twisting Siva into the shape of a two-seater couch and lounged about on him waiting for his Bad Guy buddies, but they failed to show up. Finally, Siva got tired of this and wiggled off the couch, bounced up onto the top rope yet again and came down on the Bount in a rather unfortunate looking hold. The Bount had both his shoulders on the canvas with his legs back over his head kicking like pistons. Siva sat with his nose buried deep into the Bounty Hunters fundament (right up there where the sun don't shine!) while clinging desperately to the backs of his driving thighs. I was busting up, it was almost impossible to keep calling the play-by-play. I think it's called some kind of Cradle Hold, but I called it a Sunset Flip. By this stage of the proceedings I was calling everything a Sunset Flip. The referee held his count as long as he dared and finally smacked the canvas and it was all over but the shouting.

Mayhem

Marvin the Mangler himself, the present holder of the coveted Television Belt (why don't I find that surprising?), waddled into the ring. He held a microphone in one hand.

'Ladies and gentlemen, boys and girls.'

'Some time back when I ugurrggglebaaagghhh!'

The Bounty Hunter who had been lying prone - sensationally tired after a severe butt sniffing - wasn't a wrestler with a glass butt. He'd been nostrilled all right, but he put all that behind him. Now he sprang to his feet and felled Marvin with a blow to the back of his neck. From out of nowhere the Mongolian Mauler appeared and ambushed Afi. Picked him up and flung him out of the ring. Then they commenced to do all manner of Bad Guy stuff to poor helpless Marvin.

The rat and I were naturally taken aback... this ending was news to us. Siva gradually regained consciousness and dragged his mangled body into the ring just as Mongo and the Bount were running out of ideas for skulduggery.

Suddenly the lights went out. The entire stadium was plunged into pitch blackness. Erie. The rat made a virtue of it. Chuck E. Cheese:

'Yes, that's right! Turn the lights off! We don't want to see this! Kill those lights!'

Those lights were already dead. The place was a black hole. Whoever was orchestrating this was a genius. People were hysterical and that was just in the commentary booth. Then suddenly one sheer, icy, white shaft of light pierced the darkness, like God pointing his finger at the fallen. This was a master's touch. But unbelievably this master stroke turned out to be an accident. The lightning assistant had got up to go take a dump (great timing) and had accidentally kicked the plug out of the lightning control computer plunging us into the void.

That spotlight up in the rafters was the only light not controlled by the computer, so we had an operator up there to point it. It was pure luck that we had someone quick witted up there. She did a great job of tracking the action. Marvin lay in the center of the ring in critical condition - one foot twitching. Siva crawled to Marvin's side and tore at his hair in silent, slow motion agony. He reached out one imploring hand in a gesture of tenderness and compassion. He raised his eyes to heaven.

Me: 'Afi's a little upset.'

Okay, it didn't quite match the moment. I did better with my exit line.

Me: 'Chuck, this has got to be the saddest moment I've ever seen in sports.'

Comment One: Showbiz-wise, the audience got their money's worth that night.

Comment Two: All told we ended up producing 12 one-hour wrestling shows in four weeks. It took several months for my vocal chords to calm down. And believe me that was as far as I wanted to take my professional wrestling broadcasting career. But, it was by far and away not even close to the disaster my fellow media colleagues would have had me believe. I accepted the job for what it was and worked damn hard to make it successful. I gave it my best shot. If you're honest in your approach and philosophy about why you do something and how you do it then it will never turn against you or hurt you, you can only grow from it. And I did. I had a ton of fun and was given the opportunity to grow laterally and experiment as a television presenter. I left that show and experience a much better person. And besides now I had some great stories to tell. After wrestling, anything else would seem easy - but maybe not as much fun.

Do You Know Who I Am

Being a celebrity in New Zealand isn't the easiest thing in the world, nor the most difficult. On one hand, the small population gives everyone with even the merest of talents the chance to push their way into the spotlight.

At the same time, New Zealand collectively squirms at the very suggestion that someone has become a celebrity. When the courts suppress publication of a celebrity's name, the nation goes into gossip overdrive and before long the name is known to all those who want to know.

By the time the courts reveal the name, half the people say they already knew it. The other half say they'd never heard of the so-called 'household name' in the first place.

And most say they couldn't really care.

As D-list celebrities go, I've had no difficulty in accepting my place in the pecking order of celebrity life.

Microphones Up My Nose

I was subject to more media attention after I was banned as a basketball coach than before. I was loud, never short of a word, foreign and had a murky past. Perfect grist for the talk-show mill. Suddenly I found myself doing a host of chat shows. The next one I appeared on was being broadcast live. I was doing my usual shtick as Mr. Shout. The host came into the green room to chat with us informally before we went on air. She strode directly up to me and calmly looked up into my face and whispered, "John, this show is going live to air. I'd appreciate it very much if you didn't say 'Fuck'."

"No problem, I know lots of other cuss words." Talk about having a reputation. Ouch! Double ouch!!

Comment: I was more than a little irritated that she thought it needed saying at all. But that's the rub when you end up with a reputation. Most people you meet know only one thing about you: "You're the loudmouth American basketball coach who swore on television?"

Mr. Shout

On this particular show I was pushing a book I wrote. In return, I would manifest Mr. Shout for them. I had developed this five-minute, one-man act on coaching a game of basketball that I performed on the rubber chicken circuit. (After dinner speaking trail). That's coaching basketball Dybvig style:

I got up out of my chair and walked to the middle of the studio where I addressed an imaginary team:

"All right fellas, tonight we've got a great chance to win this game. We're bigger than they are. I wanna take the ball right to the hole. I want us to dominate the boards. You got that? All right. Let's go get'em."

The team huddle around me as I put my hands into the center of an imaginary group and yell: "Break!"

I describe the action play-by-play as it happens. I'm extremely loud and I'm throwing my arms about pointing out the action:

"Jump ball. We get the tip. My guard gets it and drives down the right side. He makes a quick snap pass to my forward. My forward takes it down to the corner. My center moves across the lane and posts up strong (I'm playing the center now). My forward gives him a nice two-handed baseline bounce pass (I play this action out as my forward). My center grabs it (I'm back in the post now), he pivots and gives a good head and shoulder fake, and takes it right to the hole... he's fouled (that's me) heavily but the ref doesn't call it!"

Now I go into full Bobby Knight mode (outrageous American basketball coach) and literally explode in a complete rage: My eyes are bulging and I'm frantically running up and down the studio stage screaming at an imaginary referee:

"That's a foul... th-th-th-thaaat's a foul! Goddamnit, ref! What the hell are you looking at? That's a foul! You owe me one, Goddamnit! Jeezzzz!"

Suddenly I shift my attention from the ref to my players and the opposition... watching intently describing the action:

"Look at those little guys out there pushing my big guys around."

I march over to an imaginary score bench and bark!

"Timeout!"

I make a sign with my index finger and hand...

"Gimme a timeout!"

My imaginary team are straggling off the floor... I scream at them:

"Get over here."

Now I'm hunched over as if I'm talking to my team in the huddle again.

"What the hell is going on out there, gentlemen? I called this timeout to talk about hustle. I don't like talking about hustle... hustle doesn't require any brains... hustle doesn't require any skill. Those little bastards are out hustling you and pushing you big guys around because they've got more desire... they've got big hearts... they want to WIN this goddamn game!"

Now I look up as if I'm addressing two taller players.

"And you two!? Did you fly over here from America to watch this goddamn game or to play it?"

Slowly I wheel back to the entire team and in a quieter but more menacing tone I hiss:

"Now, gentlemen, if we don't go out there and bust our butts... well then, I'm likely to get a bit irritated, and we don't want that... do we, gentlemen?"

I stand up straight, drop my hunched-up shoulders and smile. I'm back in the real world. The only extra thing I do with this routine in an after-dinner speech is when I start screaming foul at the ref I fly off the stage into the crowd and start banging on the tables causing the wine glasses to topple and break. It's always a great effect... shakes the shit out of the guests. The only drawback is once in a while I get a laundry bill sent to me.

The next day a dour journalist reviewed my book and referred to my television performance. In his opinion, anyone able to summon up that kind of emotion on the spot was PROBABLY far too phony for his liking, my basketball antics were PROBABLY fake too, and all in all I was PROBABLY an American jerk off and it was PROBABLY time for me to go home.

Comment One: Oh, and he didn't like my book either.

Comment Two: In an ironic twist several years later I was doing a basketball show with Anthony Ray Parker who played Dozer in the original Matrix. For this particular show they'd film the game and then cut it down to an hour then Anthony Ray and I would go into a sound booth and call the game. Believe me that ain't as easy as it sounds.

One weekend Anthony was away Swanning around doing his movie star routine at some resort so I had to find a replacement. You got it. I called on my dour journalist friend. This is what he had to say about the experience:

"I always expected John Dybvig to wind up in a padded room. I just never imagined I would share it with him. Yet there I was locked in a sound proof booth with the wild man of hoops, recording a commentary for Sky's weekly basketball show. I can now assure those couch jockeys at home that this lark with the microphone is not as easy as it may seem. There's nothing scarier than the split-second's silence before delivering your opening words. Stating the obvious I can sum up my performance by saying that I was a bit subdued compared to John Dybvig and Anthony Ray."

Bumped

I got invited onto several more chat shows until I got bumped by Mr. Ed.

I was all set to appear on yet another chat show... yes Mr. Shout was still hot. The producer called me in for an interview, and the date was set.

But as they say, timing is everything. I was lounging about in the Green room warming up my vocal-chords when Mark Todd walked into the room. That's New Zealand Olympic gold medal winner and horse equestrian Mark Todd. He and his trusty steed Charisma had just arrived home that very night from the Olympics. I was familiar with Charisma. I'd run an interview with him in my newspaper column:

"So, tell me, Charisma. Does Mark help at all or do you just kinda carry him around the course?"

I was a D-list celebrity while Mark Todd was an extra super-duper A-list celeb - I was bumped from the show... as Johnny Carson used to say on the Late Show, "We've run out of time folks and will have to have John Dybvig back on next time." Even horses get their revenge.

Crystal
I don't do drugs well. I'm not a prude. It's just the few times I've taken any they've made me feel unwell. I felt no thrill and the attractions of mood enhancement by smoke or pill have been a complete mystery to me. It must be my chemical makeup or something.

The one time I smoked marijuana, I spent the entire night trying to nail down a passing thought - any passing thought.

And the night I took an extremely small and almost insignificant crystal known as 'speed' I spent the entire night bouncing off the walls. I was talking a zillion miles an hour and just couldn't shut up. And I had this insatiable thirst for coffee which I was drinking by the bucket. Then, at four in the morning, I purposefully strode down to the freeway and hitched a ride to see some friends five hundred miles away.

Now, that was a trip.

But I didn't like it. I can't understand why anyone would pay through the nose for a one-way ticket to Palookaville.

And anyway, I was loud enough when I was straight.

Comment One: I know the general public just associates celebrities and drugs like you do with bread and butter, the two just naturally go together. But not for me. I'm glad I tried it in my limited way because I found out that it just wasn't my game.

Comment Two: Fast forward to now when I'm an old man and my attitude to drugs hasn't changed one iota. One night I inadvertently ate a slice of chocolate cake. Not an ordinary chocolate cake but one baked with some special butter. At first I didn't notice anything out of the ordinary... but it all changed when I went to get up. I couldn't move... I literally couldn't move a muscle I was so stoned. Eventually I was able to get up and stagger to my bed. And I gotta say I didn't like the way I was feeling then like I didn't like the feeling I had years prior. I guess you could say I'm just not a drug guy.

Comment Three: The other thing you could say about me is I'm not a celebrity type of guy either. I never considered myself a celeb... rather I preferred to be known as a 'known person.' Which when you think about it sounds like I'm on the FBI's Top Ten Most Wanted List... hmmmmmmmmmmmm?

Hissy Fit
When celebrities aren't trying to dance, skate, sing or cook for attention, they're accepting any invitation to appear in public.

In New Zealand, that can mean turning up at the smallest of events in the hope it will lead to a photograph or plug in a paper or magazine.

I was asked to do a charity event at McDonald's, working behind the counter. It taught me a couple of things — first, that making an ice cream cone is not as easy as it looks and second, they do brainwash their employees.

I was behind the counter, taking orders and doing fine until one customer ordered an ice cream cone.

The problem is you have to be coordinated enough to pull the ice cream lever straight out with one hand and at the same time twirl the filling cone to pile the ice cream high.

No matter how hard I tried, I just couldn't do it. My cones all came out lopsided. They looked a mess. I was such a bozo, I couldn't even make a lousy ice cream cone. I had to laugh.

At the end of my charity shift, I was cheerily told I could make my own McDonald's burger.

From the sounds of it, this was considered quite a privilege. I just exclaimed, "Cool, get me to the grill!" I dutifully flipped my patty and placed it on my bun with a squirt of mustard and ketchup.

Then I got out of line. Because I love diced onions on my burgers, I reached into the diced onion tray and grabbed a big handful whereupon my supervisor, a girl of 17, immediately seized my wrist (she had a very strong grip for a skinny kid) and carefully but forcefully explained that according to the McDonald's manual I was to put only six diced segments of onion on my burger.

She was serious. Her eyes glazed over and I swear she was in a trance as her voice took on the tone of someone following orders. I looked her square in the eye and grabbed an even bigger handful of onions and plopped them on my burger.

Hell, I might be only D-list but I could throw a hissy fit like the best of them.

Darling

At this stage of my career, I was not only working in the public eye I was also getting invited to spend my social life in the same place. They call it a 'celebrity event'. Like I said I never liked the word celebrity, so I looked it up in a dictionary. It comes from the Latin root 'celebro' which means 'frequented.' That didn't help me to like the word any better. Makes you feel like the busiest whore in the brothel.

Sometimes you can do your bit for charity by doing fun things like skiing or white-water rafting or wrecking stock cars or my favorite playing golf, but usually it's standing around at cocktail parties talking earnestly to other frequented people about how much you like their work.

'Oh, wow,' you gush, 'I really like your work.'

'Gee, thanks,' they gush back, 'I really love your work too.'

Then you stare into space for a while because you've already said the most important thing you're ever going to say to each other.

Star Wars
Being hauled into celebrity events means you can be flipping burgers one day and put your life at risk the next. I once sat in as a navigator on a professional car rally tour. Talk about a buzz. I absolutely loved it even if it scared me shitless at times! If you want to know how it feels to scream around hairpin corners flat out spitting gravel everywhere while the driver is pulling furiously on the handbrake to keep the car on the road I suggest you climb into one of those big commercial washing machines and set it at full agitate. Get somebody to strap the machine to a rocket sled and push it down a really steep toboggan run. Then hang on for dear life. It's a rush! Sliding around those hairpin turns at full speed didn't worry me too much rather it was when my driver cranked it up to over 200 k's per hour on a two kilometre stretch of straight road (dirt road... not smooth full of gravel) lined all the way with giant thick forest trees. The trees were so... so close like right on the road verge while the car was violently shimming back and forth as my driver was struggling to keep the car in a somewhat straight line as we screamed by tree after tree in a blur.

All I could think of at the time was of one of those Star Wars movies when with just the littlest mistake the fighter jet goes off course tilting just enough to hit some doo-dad on the Death Star and ends up spinning and cartwheeling completely out of control before exploding into a million pieces.

Snot
Another time I went scuba diving, for the first time, in a shark tank for the national Telethon. The diving instructor attempted to build up my confidence.

'The only thing you've got to remember is to keep breathing.'

'Aaahh ... Excuse me?'

'Oh yeah, people panic and hold their breath and, well, that can kill you.'

That's good to know. I never heard Lloyd Bridges mention that on Sea Hunt. So, I'm hanging bug-eyed in the water with these sharks ghosting by for a closer look, but I couldn't care less about them because I'm hysterically focusing on my breathing. It's like I've reverted back to babyhood and have forgotten how to breathe. In my mind I'm going: suck in - breathe out, suck in - breathe out.

I've got on a full face mask and my nose starts to run. Heavily. I've got five hundred pounds of mucus running through my mustache and I'm wondering what I'm going to do when the level reaches my nostrils?

Meanwhile my brain has gone haywire: suck in - breathe out, suck in - breathe out... I was hyperventilating. I'm wondering if snot has the same effect on sharks as blood. I've never heard of a snot frenzy, but in the mood I'm in it seems reasonable. I'm under water but I'm sweating. Finally, when I got the nod to come out, I shot out of the water like an intercontinental ballistic missile launched from a submarine.

Comment: I did do one practice dive in a local swimming pool. The instructor had me do a summersault under water and I immediately panicked as I went into a total whiteout... I was disoriented and had no idea where the surface of the pool was. I was so amazed about how totally confused I was - I mean come on the pool wasn't all that deep, but I was completely flummoxed as to where up was. Scared the shit out of me. All in all I didn't find scuba diving that much fun.

The Power of the Red Suit
I've had three goes at playing Santa Claus.

<u>Santa Claus One:</u> For several years when my kids were in grade school I would dress up as Santa and visit their class when they had their end of year Christmas party. I would ho ho it and hand out candy and make personal remarks to the kids that the teacher had given me beforehand. The kids loved it... and naturally my kids would accuse me of being Santa Claus and of course I'd always deny it. Who me... not me. I haven't a clue as to what you're talking about. The funny thing was when I drove over to the school in my Santa outfit when I would stop for a red light the people in the car next to me would always light up and start laughing as they all pointed in my direction - and I could hear them saying, "Hey there's Santa Claus."

<u>Santa Claus Two:</u> I was in no way prepared for my second attempt which occurred in the public arena. I was playing Santa Claus for the city of Devonport who were celebrating the opening of their spanking brand new library during the Christmas season. The Christchurch Wizard was also with me for this gig. The Wiz and I took the ferry over from Auckland and were dressed in our costumes when the ferry docked in Devonport.

The minute we walked down the pier towards the city center the Wizard might as well have been invisible... me dressed in that particular red suit that is known and loved by every child on the planet was an instant magnet to every kid in sight. I could see kids off in the distance looking up and excitedly pointing their fingers in my direction as they began running towards me. Suddenly I was the centrepiece in a flotilla of small and large children.

I felt like the pied piper everywhere I went... everywhere I turned whatever I did the kids clung to me for dear life. I was continually ho ho hoing it and remarking to all their requests as to what they wanted for Christmas. It was an amazing experience I just wasn't prepared for the instant power of that red suit.

<u>Santa Claus Three:</u> My last Santa Claus act was a real doozy. I was playing Santa for New Zealand's richest man Graeme Hart (he's in the billionaire class)... for his family and the families of several of his friends at his mansion in Auckland. And believe me a mansion it was... the guest house in the backyard was three times as large as my house. The scene was a bit weird... the mothers and the kids were in their living room by the Christmas tree while the blokes were out back by the bar-b-cue knocking back beers and laughing their tits off. Anyway no big deal I walked into their living room with my bag of goodies and boomed out, "Ho...ho...ho!" When one of the little bastards immediately yells out that Santa had an American accent... I quickly ho hoed back that Santa came from the North Pole... ha...ha...ha... know what I'm saying little man!

Then right in the middle of my handing out gifts and candy and whatnot this enormous Golden Lab comes bounding into the room and immediately latches onto me and starts humping my leg. So I'm standing in front of all these kids and their moms with a dog that's humping me faster than a jackhammer and I'm ho...ho...hoing like crazy while trying my best to shake this damn crazed dog off when finally I give the dog a mighty high kick that would rival anything the Rockettes could do and the dog flies off but he lands under the Christmas tree and nearly knocks it over as he's scrambling to get up and have another crack at humping my leg which has the entire crowd scrambling to save the tree.

Finally I finish my gig and depart around behind the house where I run into the guys... I stop for a friendly chat but get no response from these clowns not even the offer of a beer... not much Christmas cheer from this crowd (maybe that's why he's New Zealand's richest man)... so I grab my bag and round the house to leave... but just as I start down their airport long runway of a drive they close their fucking electronic front gate which isn't one of those see through iron gates but rather a massive solid slab of wood which is just a smidgen smaller than the Great Wall of China.

I start to return to ask the guys if they'd reopen the gate but seeing as I got the cold shoulder from them just a few minutes before and I'm thinking they probably closed the damn gate on purpose I decided not to.

Instead I threw my bag over the gate and climbed up over it which took a fair bit of effort on my part but luckily for me I was a former athlete... and parachuted down to the ground below. I was kinda hoping that a cop car would be cruising the neighbourhood and arrest me searching Santa's bag for stolen goods... at least that would have made the evening interesting... ha! Or should that be ho!

Wall to Wall Teeth

One year I had a great opportunity to bungy jump from a helicopter. I was on a Variety Bash (a fundraising event) for the Variety Club of New Zealand, a charity that looks after disadvantaged kids. I was asked if I wanted to 'have-a-go' in Kiwi parlance, at leaping out of a helicopter. You betcha, I shot back in good old plain Yankee slang. It was all set up for the following morning, but late that afternoon I got a call from the television station I worked for telling me they had just secured the rights to show Magic Johnson's All-Star basketball game that night against the national side and that my tickets were waiting for me at the airport.

That night I got an up-close look at the intensity of celebrity pulling power. After the game I was in this small anteroom off the main locker room where Magic Johnson would walk a short fifteen steps before easing into his waiting limo just outside this side door. The 'man' in charge of this operation came out before Magic and barked in no uncertain terms that Magic would not be signing anything. He repeated himself. He asked all of us packed in this wee room if we understood what he said, we all nodded.

Then this tiny space was filled from floor to ceiling with the greatest smile you'd ever want to see. Magic's teeth entered the room and it was like he was a walking Black Hole (no pun intended), drawing everything and everybody irresistibly towards him. I sat back and counted. Magic scribbled his moniker 17 times on an array of items before he got his exceedingly long limbs into the back of that limo.

Ego Monster

SOMETIMES it was hard to keep grounded. That old Ego Monster can be one sneaky son of a gun. He got me good one year.

I was at the television network, in a pre-production meeting and going over the commentary duties for the upcoming televised season of sport. The meeting decided my fellow commentator - a large man - would handle the play-by-play commentary and I would supply the color and expert comments.

I went home and relaxed with a Southern Comfort, water and ice. Ego Monster dropped by for a drink. He taunted me with images of my co-presenter. The large man. 'Fat Boy!'

Ego Monster started the conversation.

'So, you're going to play second fiddle to the Fat Boy, huh?'

'Getouttahere,' I snapped. 'I don't play second fiddle to nobody.'

'Oh, right. So, he's gonna call the game and you're gonna get to make a comment every now and then?'

'Shut up, man!'

'Okay. But he's the local boy. He's gonna make you look like chopped liver.'

'You really think so?' I said. Maybe Ego Monster had a point...

This hallucination had me by the short and curlies. I was completely engrossed in the idea that the bozos at Sky TV were demeaning me. I spent the week leading up to the broadcast focused on my own importance.

Just before the game, I pulled an insane switch.

'We'll share the commentary,' I blurted confidently to the production team.

'What?'

'Yeah, sure. Fat Boy will call a bit and then I'll call for a bit. It'll be great.'

'No way, John!' the producer said, shaking his head.

'Look, trust me. It'll work. I know what I'm talking about.'

The producer weighed up his options. Who did he least want to fall out with - the Loud American or Fat Boy?

'Well, okay...'

The broadcast was a disaster! Anybody with sense knows a good commentary team follows set guidelines. You have to use an incredibly controlled mode of speech to get your points across. Television is not about being long-winded. You have to be aware of what you're saying, how long you take to say it, what the director is asking, what's happening on the screen, and what your co-commentator needs. And somewhere in there you also need to be entertaining!

You're like the centipede who can't walk because he's thinking about his legs. My sudden switch created so much confusion that we either talked over the top of each other or left huge gaps of silence while each waited for the other to speak. Then, of course, we'd both start at the same time... or both stop at the same time.

I had succeeded in making everybody look like a fool. Fat Boy eventually gave up in frustration and I took over the whole show. That was exactly what my Ego Monster wanted. This allowed me to make an even bigger fool of myself.

And that turned out to be a good thing. My Ego Monster had overplayed his hand and I realized there was an idiot amongst us.

Me!

Having swallowed what little remained of my pride, I gave myself a well-deserved kick in the ass, and we returned to sanity for the future broadcasts. For the rest of the series, Fat Boy did his job as commentator and I stuck to my job, providing the expert analysis. We sailed through the remaining season and the finals... and they were some of the best and most enjoyable broadcasts I've done.

Vacuum

I've always been aware of my ego. I like it. I'm comfortable with it. There's absolutely no way I'd put myself in front of a camera if I didn't have an ego to feed. The trick is to be aware of it.

It makes sense to recognize you've got an ego and that it's a healthy condition. Just don't let it get out of control and take over.

The year I was a finalist for best supporting actor in a drama - having played Richard Armitage in Fallout, a television drama about New Zealand's banning of nuclear weapons - my wife, Jennifer, and I walked up the red carpet and into the theater where the award ceremony was being held.

As we approached the entrance, we were surrounded by a swarm of celebrity photographers only inches from our faces, snapping in a frenzy of popping flashlights. I blinked and tried to smile as the flashes blinded me. Suddenly, the flaring lights stopped and the photographers vanished.

Poof!

Gone in the snap of a finger... just like that - here one minute, gone the next.

They left so quickly we could feel the cold draft in the vacuum. My wife was stunned and asked what had happened.

I shrugged and explained that a bigger fish had just walked in.

In the New Zealand fame game, a C-lister trumps a D-lister every time...

Sir Peter Snell

There are times I find New Zealander's just so damn funny just for being themselves in real life.

I appeared in a television commercial with the great and I mean great Sir Peter Snell.

Peter was the winner of multiple Olympic gold medals in Rome and Tokyo and one of the few men to have won the 800 and the 1500 metres at the same Olympics. So we're shooting this insurance commercial with Peter being the star and he's delivered his first line to the camera. The director rushed up to Peter gushing with praise for his performance as directors are wont to do and then suggested that he deliver the line again, with a bit more oomph. I'm standing there in the background watching Peter who is about as stoic a human being as you're ever going to get when he looked straight into the director's eyes and in complete seriousness deadpanned, "Why would I do that, I just said that line?"

Comment: Peter Snell died on December 12, 2019 (aged 80) in Dallas, Texas, United States.

Wynton Rufer

Talk about being droll this guy takes the cake for stoicism! If anyone could be any dryer than Peter Snell it would have to be Wynton Rufer. I was playing in a celebrity all star charity soccer game against New Zealand's national side - the All Whites - at Mt. Smart stadium for the Ronald McDonald House which looks after children with cancer. We celebs had our own kiwi celebrity coach in Wynton Rufer who played professionally for the famous German club Werder Bremen. Rufer came into our locker room and gave us a rousing pep talk like we were going up against his old German Club. I was cracking up inside thinking - wow - this is one serious dude. And then he asked who was playing goalie and I put my hand up... he marched over to me and in all seriousness asked me," Did you being your goalie gloves with you?" What the fuck! I've only played a handful of soccer games in my life and they were all of the celebrity charity type games. We weren't professional soccer players... what in the hell made him think that a semi-fat out of shape aging celeb had his own goalie gloves is way beyond me. But the thing was he was deadly serious... he looked confused when I said, "...Ahhh no I must have misplaced them in my other life." I'll tell you how bad I was during the game they gave the guy dressed up as Ronald McDonald with his twenty-foot-long red shoes a free kick against me and he scored. That's not good folks... the ball barely dribbled into the far corner of the net. But hey, maybe if I had my goalie gloves I would have blocked it!?!

Bob Charles

Okay now I've got to go for the trifecta of boring kiwi sportsman. I've been to several of pro golfer Bob Charles media interviews and I have to say if anybody could put an insomniac to sleep it would have to be Mr. Charles. Bob is earnest but like Wynton and Peter he is so dead panned and so... so deadly serious.

When I first came to New Zealand I was down in Christchurch and I wanted to play a round of golf but had left my clubs back in Auckland. No problem I'm thinking as I bowled up to the Russley Golf Club and asked to rent a set of left handed golf clubs.

The pro told me sorry but they didn't have any left handed clubs. I looked at the guy and exclaimed: "Are you serious!?! This is a travesty... are you telling me that the home of the greatest ever left handed golfer in the world Bob Charles doesn't have any left handed clubs... you should be ashamed of yourself... the guy was stunned turning a bright pink and began to stammer... but... but... as I walked out of the shop.

The Mad Butcher

So now I want to talk about a kiwi who is the direct opposite of the other three kiwis... this guy is like a walking talking volcano about to erupt at any moment: Everyone at one time or another needs a domino tipped in their favour... doesn't even have to be a big domino sometimes just a wee little one is enough. I've known Sir Peter Leitch or, as he's more commonly known (AKA), the Mad Butcher for a fair number of years now and I can honestly say he's an honest bloke and almost as loud as me which is saying something... he's down to earth but he's also a whole lot smarter than people think. Peter started from scratch and built himself and his family an empire... clever, clever man! But he's also a very, very fun guy to be around... back in the day I used to do the Lion Red sports trivia quizzes in pubs around the country with Peter and Phil Gifford... wow what a trio we made a loud brash American... an outrageous Kiwi who would challenge anyone to a wrestling match and a studious looking calm front man in Gifford who gave us a modicum of respectability, and I can tell you that the three of us always had plenty of laughs... a ton of fun and more than a few beers along the way.

Sir Peter is also as kind and generous as a guy can be - case in point: There was a brief time in my unusual and varied career in New Zealand when suddenly out of the blue all my work just dried up... I found myself jobless... nothing to do... no income. Which in most circumstances isn't that big a deal... I've lived off the smell of an oily rag before but this time it was different... I had recently just gotten married (Jennifer) and we had a six month old baby boy so I had a small panic attack. It got to the point that I just needed a few bucks to tide me over so I called Pete and asked him if he could spot me a thousand bucks and without any hesitation on his part he immediately said yes. It allowed me to pay the rent and buy some groceries and then as if by magic right after that the jobs just suddenly started pouring in and I've never looked back. So like I said at the beginning sometimes just the smallest gesture is all it takes to keep someone on the straight and narrow so thank-you Sir Peter Leitch you're a champion... or in down to earth kiwi parlance - you're a good bastard!

The Art of Humility

Working in television and film, the spotlight is always shining in your direction and you're constantly surrounded by ego maniacs, where a big ego is considered basic equipment. Humility is to TV performers, and actors, what honesty is to politicians.

It's supposed to be the major attribute, but if you really had it you'd be murdered at square one by the egomaniacs in one game and the liars in the other.

The theory is a celebrity can't carry out their role unless their ego is correctly inflated and buffed. A celebrity with a saggy ego is thought to be a liability. Unfortunately, this creates monsters of stupidity and vanity who wander around devouring every bit of available energy in the drive to be number one.

Howard Stern versus Rush Limbaugh

Two of the presenters I first worked with in television turned out to be the New Zealand equivalents of Howard Stern and Rush Limbaugh. The corridors at the network simply weren't wide enough for the presenters and their egos.

I loved it. One was rotund and the other looked like a young and dashing Cary Grant (without the accent).

The rotund one (let's call him 'fat boy') went into rigor mortis when the red light on the camera flashed. He talked like Howdy Doody. And from day one he thought his doo-doo didn't stink.

'Hold all my calls!' he would bellow at the receptionist. Then he'd retire to his office to twiddle with his pencils until impatience got the better of him. Five minutes later he'd be back in reception.

'Any calls?'

'No.'

'Well, take messages. I'm far too busy.'

He'd spend the whole day repeating this cycle and never took it for strange behaviour.

Comment: And here's the very weird bit with this guy - because I'm an American whenever we crossed paths in the stations corridors he felt the need to 'high-five' me. And not just an ordinary 'high-five' but an over exuberant one like we'd just won a championship.

But, here's the weird bit - I actually had to teach this numb-nuts how to do a 'high-five'.

Yeah, I'm not kidding... the problem was when fat boy went to do his high-five' he'd throw his hand up in the air and away from his body. You actually had to hunt his hand down. We did this several times and finally I had had enough it was just too weird even for me.

I pulled him aside one day and we went into an empty office where I explained to him that to do a 'high-five' all you had to do was follow the line of your shoulder along with the other guy and your outstretched hands would naturally meet in the middle. We actually practiced this until fat boy had it down. I'm still shaking my head as I write this.

Mirror Mirror on the Wall

His co-presenter (let's call him 'Cary Grant (aka) the Adonis') relied for his success on his chiselled good looks. To be fair, he looked like a Greek statue. But when it came to life, he didn't know diddly about squat. To compensate for his lack of knowledge - and he had much to compensate for - he simply bunkered down in the make-up room with his weapons of highlighter, lip gloss and eyeliner, until there was a permanent imprint of his face on the mirrors. Every hair on his lacquered head had a pet name and was perfectly disciplined to do his bidding. His philosophy was this: appearance is everything. His burning ambition was to become a game show host. I was working with Dick Clark.

Yahoo

Among the vast array of egos that I learned to navigate through, there's also those who have their feet firmly planted on solid ground. And they're often the most talented.

In my early days as a presenter, I worked on a morning kids' television program called Yahoo. Of course my spot on the show was as a wrestling commentator when the kids on the show would arm-wrestle for prizes. The Yahoo set was a concrete bunker with bleachers for the audience. There was scaffolding everywhere with kid-type props hanging off it - balloons, skateboards, surfboards and it was all covered in graffiti.

Typical kids' show... what wasn't typical was its host - one Phil Keoghan. Forty years later I'm still world famous in New Zealand while Phil Keoghan is simply 'world' famous. Phil went on to host America's 'The Amazing Race' and now has a closet full of Emmy's and lives in Beverly Hills.

I Know Nothing

Having cornered the market as New Zealand's 'go to' commentator on anything American, I needed to break into more mainstream Kiwi activities.

I got my chance when I was asked to be the color guy for television's coverage of the Auckland Summer Racing Carnival.

There was only one slight problem. I knew one end of a horse from the other, and that was about the limit of my knowledge.

The on-air team already had plenty of experts so I decided to head in the opposite direction and to make a virtue of my ignorance. I would talk about what I didn't know since there was so much of it.

Enthusiastically, I wrote some Marx Brothers-type scripts highlighting my total lack of knowledge of all things equine. I went to extremes to make it abundantly clear I knew nothing about horse racing.

I couldn't make it any clearer.

'Hey, I don't know up from down about horse racing,' I told the viewers.

'They told me to watch out for a chestnut, I thought they were talking about food.'

'Where I come from, punting is something you do with a football.'

Betting

You get the drift. For my first segment, I set up the lady at one of the gambling windows. Earlier in the day, I had a quiet word to her that it would be really peachy if she would be part of our live broadcast. 'I'll just come in and ask you how the betting slips work. Okay?'

I forgot to mention to her that the whole thing was a spoof. I wanted some honest reactions from her to my dumb questions. The cameraman was ready to capture the fun, tracking my entry to the betting area.

As the camera rolled, I walked in, went into my energy surge and started talking louder and faster.

'Hey! I know a bit about gambling. I can play a round robin and trifecta a quinella with the best of them,' I boasted.

'Hey, lady, I want numbers two and three in race one bracketed with one and three in race two... '
'...then I wanna round robin number three in race four with four, five and six in race seven ...'
'...No! Scratch that! Gimme five, six and seven in race six. Got that?'

Well, of course she didn't. It was all double-talk. It was very loud and fast, my patter fired in machine gun bursts by a lumbering monster blinding her with a super bright spotlight and trying to wedge my microphone up her nose.

The poor woman froze in shock, which was the perfect reaction.

'Huh?' she mumbled.

I was having a ball with this.

Mr. Ed

Our next location was the stables. They were empty except for the horses. I started to march up and down the exceedingly long stables, doing a monologue about the inadequacies of horses to no one in particular.

For all the different words they have to describe a horse's movements - like gallop, trot, pace, canter - you'd think they'd have a word for the horse version of the Liverpool Kiss. Horses do it all the time. Since they're too tall to jam their forehead in your face, they raise their head as high as they can and bring their jawbone crashing down on the top of your head. Hurts like hell.

And they stand on your feet, and if you stand near their head they bite you, and if you stand near their ass they kick.

Meanwhile, all the horses kept staring at me in that expressionless way that smart animals do. It was hilarious.

I ended the piece by screaming at the horses: 'You guys are all bastards!'

Comment: I remember always being amazed by the number of people who thought that I had adlibbed my pieces to camera. I took it as a compliment that I was so relaxed and natural that it looked like I was just talking off the cuff. But my stuff worked because I had worked out tight scripts. I went in prepared. Even if you're going to make a dick of yourself you've got to work at it. I was flattered that people thought I could adlib that well, clever adlibbing is an art. I'm not nearly that talented.

Slagged Off
My attempt at offbeat humor crashed and burned. One of the country's most popular radio sports talkback shows was inundated with calls.

My name, or versions of it, came up an awful lot. Some wit called me 'Dipstick' - like I haven't been called that before. But it amazed me the number of people who thought I was setting myself up as an expert on racing.

They thought they had made an important discovery they should share with the rest of New Zealand.

'Mate, that idiot American knows nothing about racing. I know more than he does. Maybe TV will give me the job?'

One newspaper reviewer honestly thought my mile-a-minute betting spot was a genuine attempt to explain betting systems.

'They tried to scuttle the whole show by injecting the number one gobstopper John Dybvig. He bellowed at such a pitch about things like how to place a bet, it's a wonder the equines didn't bolt,' the reviewer wrote.

'The idea was right - many don't know a round robin from a box trifecta - but the man wasn't. He gave new meaning to the term idiot box.'

Ouch.

But beneath it all, I really wasn't all that bothered — I'd been slagged off by experts before and by people who actually got the point.

Comment One: I'm not a big race guy, but I got to do something that most punters will never experience. The absolute best time for me during the racing carnival was when I got to tag along with the racing camera crew in a camera van in the interior as we followed the horses around the track. We were right next to them about two feet away. It was great to be speeding alongside the horses where they all seemed to be going in slow motion - hearing the slapping of the whips, the thunder of the hooves, the jockeys swearing at each other. And the magnificent muscle culture of the horses as they were straining for all they were worth. Clods of dirt were flying in through the open door of the van. This was better than the rodeo.

Comment Two: I also came to respect the jockeys a lot more as I witnessed firsthand how they sit on a saddle as substantial as a leaf of toilet tissue and control these huge animals at top speed with what looks like a rubber band operating in a maelstrom of flying hooves and muscle. The men and women in the racing game are certainly a tough breed.

Fight Anyone
It almost goes without saying that there's a right and a wrong time to do things.

One year, I was in a pub in the far North having a few quiet ones with some friends when one picked up the jug of beer to pour another glass for me.

I quickly grabbed my glass and turned it upside down on the table, saying I was done.

Immediately, and I mean instantly, the entire pub went silent with everyone turning to stare at me.

I was copping some very ugly stares from a group of big-muscled guys in the corner.

What?

What had happened?

My host quietly informed me I had just challenged anyone in the pub to a fight.

No, I hadn't, I assured him. He explained that by turning my glass upside down, I was declaring that the service in this joint was crap and was inviting any local for a punch-up. So much for little-known New Zealand traditions!

I immediately turned my glass upright and got to my feet, giving the double peace sign made famous by President Richard Nixon and hastily apologising for my ignorance and bad manners.

To my relief, the locals went back to their beers.

Laughing
On another night, I was out late with my buddies from Sky TV, my beatnik Australian producer and my Cary Grant look alike, a very young and very naive television presenter.

It was 3am and we were standing at the counter of a mobile greasy spoon in Auckland, having ordered some food. A group of motorcycle thugs with plenty of attitude and a crate of beer pulled up and put in their order at the same time.

As I said, timing is everything. They slammed the beer on the ground, looked our way and our young presenter was instantly shitting his pants. I tried to calm him, whispering, 'Just take it easy: relax, be natural, it's no biggie, just go with the flow.'

The gang wanted to get better acquainted.

'How's it, mate?'
'Good, mate. You, mate?'
'Beauty, mate.'

That's the sort of monosyllabic grunting that often passes for conversation amongst drunk macho males in New Zealand. Especially those still out on the town at 3am.

'Have a beer.'

This was not so much a question as a statement of fact. In that circumstance, if you choose not to have a beer, you fight. We had a beer. So, there we stood, a bunch of rugged bikies making small talk in the wee hours with an Aussie, a Yank and a naive young kid.

One of the young warriors babbled some unintelligible comments about his old lady and what she was going to get when he got home. Everybody roared. We all laughed along with him and when I say 'we' I really mean my Australian buddy and me.

The naive kid was petrified by now and stood motionless until the laughter died and then for some reason he decided it was time for him to laugh. It was totally out of sync. I wanted to slap him.

And it took milliseconds for the drunken yobboes to shift into attack mode.

'What the fuck you laughing at?' one asked the kid.
'Nothing,' he said, his laughter having drained.
'You think my old lady's funny?'
'Of course not,' he tried to say, reassuringly.

Before things turned nasty, my seasoned Australian friend interjected with a cracker of a joke that diverted their attention.

Thankfully, the burgers were now ready and the bikies took off.

Comment: That incident reminded me that even the smallest and simplest of events have their sense of rhythm. And as any foreigner in any country will tell you, living abroad means you're constantly marching to the beat of a different drummer.

Stranger in a strange land

As much as I've struggled sometimes to accept the changes of living in New Zealand, I've never stopped trying to appreciate the local ways. I've eaten raw kina, downed an awful lot of meat pies (I actually love them now). I've also had my ears pierced (for an acting role), but have drawn the line at getting a tattoo. I'm not that hip.

I've also experienced what it means when Kiwis say 'she'll be right'.

For the first 12 years I lived in the country, I never bothered to get a driver's license. I drove everywhere, without a second thought. Eventually I was pulled over by a cop who asked for my license. When I explained I didn't have one, and that I was an American and I travelled back and forth between New Zealand and America, he said: "John, I see you on television all the time". Then he just simply told me he thought it might be a good idea for me to get one. He didn't write me a ticket; just let me go with his bit of laid-back advice.

A few months later, he saw me driving again and pulled me over to the side of the road. He just wanted to check I'd taken his advice - which I had - and he sent me on my way.

Thanks.

Pole

No matter how careful I was, I could still get into weird situations without even trying.

Soon after Jennifer and I were married, we lived next door to people whose cat was always attacking our cat. One day at the crack of dawn, we were woken by the noise of a cat fight - I knew it was that damned cat abusing our cat again.

I shot out of bed and ran through the house, and out through our French doors and into the garden. I grabbed a metal umbrella pole and rounded the corner to find the cats squaring off against each other, hissing madly.

Still slightly sleepy, I clumsily swung the pole at the neighbor's cat and missed by a country mile.

The effort of my swing threw me off balance and as I twisted around, the pole sailed from my hands and through the air. It flew across our neighbor's yard and through their kitchen window, shattering it.

I couldn't believe it - of all the directions the pole could have gone, it chose the only window within range.

By this stage, Jennifer had got out of bed and was standing at the back door, screaming at me to come inside. She was making a good point as I was standing there buck naked with my own pole at full attention.

Oops.

Mugged by the Media

It doesn't matter whether you try to come across as a grump or a nice guy, the media will decide how you're perceived by the public.

An example of how easily you can get mugged by the media came in the aftermath of the Rainbow Warrior bombing in Auckland in July 1985.

The night after French spies attacked the ship, I appeared in a television interview with a Kiwi journalist, wanting to get my spin on life in New Zealand.

Prior to the interview, the night before we had met and shared a few laughs over a beer. The next day before the cameras rolled, the journalist was making amicable conversation in the television studio, putting me at ease.

The floor manager warned us we were about to start recording.
He counted us in... '5 — 4 — 3 — 2 — cue.'

My interviewer asked his first question:

"John Dybvig, in the time you've been in New Zealand you've been variously described as a jerk, a slob, an egotistical, arrogant American, the ugly American, the Rasputin of New Zealand basketball, a foul-mouthed publicity seeker and on and on and on. In fact, in the course of talking to various people before I did this interview, I must confess I haven't come across one person who had one good word to say about John Dybvig in New Zealand basketball. In light of this widespread ill feeling that there is towards you, why do you remain here?"

This wasn't going to be easy.

'Who'd you talk to, The Anti-American League?' I replied, trying to loosen things up a bit.

It didn't stop him for long and he continued to wade into me as I tried to defend myself.

I'd fallen for his sucker punch, being seduced into thinking the interview would be soft. No such luck.

It dawned on me as I sat there that I already had all the answers to any question this journalist wanted to throw my way because I had a philosophy about what and why I was doing what I was doing.

And when you suddenly discover that you have something in which you truly believe, you want to jump up and scream: 'Come on, throw me your best punch because I'm gonna pulverise you.'

On that occasion I was lucky because I already had my philosophy but it did remind me to follow that old Boy Scout rule: Be prepared. Television is an outrageously artificial medium.

When you see two guys talking on the tube, you are not witnessing any kind of normal conversation.

Time is limited and you're talking to one person while trying to get your message across to millions of anonymous people somewhere out beyond the camera. That is not normal. Whichever side of the camera I found myself on, I learned my own rules of thumb.

Say it simple. Say it straight. Take no prisoners.

Comment: Today it's all about 'fake news'... especially due to Mr. Fake News Himself... yeah Trump. I've been on the end of my fair share of bullshit things written about me... and for the most part to me it's like water off a duck's back... I really don't give a shit.

However this one example has always stood out to me: I'm down in Wellington coaching my Ponsonby club against the Saints. It's close to the end of the first half and I've got two technical fouls called against me... one more and I'm out. Naturally another call doesn't go our way and in frustration I kick the end of the advertising hoarding right near our bench... no big deal... right? Wrong. This hoarding runs for the entire length of the sideline... it's like a hundred feet long... well the kick I gave it makes it start to wobble and eventually the entire thing crashes to the floor with a loud bang.

The referee is running down the floor when he suddenly stops and looks at the fallen board and then he looks at me and hesitates for the briefest of seconds and then wham he slaps another technical foul on me... I'm out... kicked out of yet another game.

But, just a bit of a plea here on my part... wouldn't you think an advertising board that runs the length of the sideline would be attached to the scorer's table or somewhere... I mean come on... I couldn't believe the damn thing wasn't tied down.

Anyway I purposely got up very slowly and relayed a few instructions to my assistant coach and then in a very composed manner which I did on purpose I slowly walked across the court calm cool and collected into our locker room. I made sure I didn't cause a scene on the way out.

This is just a funny twist to the story... so I'm sitting in the empty locker room when in walks Saints owner Nick Mills... the Saints mascot is a guy dressed in a gorilla suit running around the court and Nick says to me that if I want he'd let me wear the gorilla suit so I could go back out on the court... I laughed and told Nick that I appreciated his offer but no thanks.

The next day the story in the paper said that I had gotten kicked out of the game and when I left I stomped off the court swearing and gesturing to one and all in a very angry manner. Well, yeah... that was all a complete lie... plain and simple I didn't do any of that. I saw the reporter who wrote that article later in the day and confronted him with his inaccurate description of how I left the court... and ya know what his reaction was? Yeah he just shrugged his shoulders and said tough. It didn't bother him one iota knowing that he wrote a whole bunch of lies. So there ya go baby... sometimes you just have to roll with the punches... no use getting all uptight over split milk... it's just not worth the effort.

David Letterman
Given my reputation as New Zealand's loudest man, it's no wonder some people are careful to look the other way when they see me coming. But, then again for most New Zealanders just being noticed in public is embarrassing.

Not so the Prime Minister, John Key.

One pleasant day in 2010, I was sipping a coffee at a Starbucks in Auckland, setting up a shot with a camera crew who were working with me on my latest crazy scheme.

I was sitting in a chair on the outside deck when the Prime Minister sauntered past, his bodyguards a respectable distance behind.

'How ya going, John?' I boomed.

'Good, John,' replied the leader of the nation with a smile.

He stepped inside Starbucks and ordered his own drink at the counter.

My producer was most impressed and excitedly asked me how I knew the Prime Minister.

Now, I didn't really know John Key in a formal sense, but I was always bumping into him at the radio station I worked for and we usually had short informal chats.

But I couldn't resist giving the producer shit. 'Don't you know him? He's your Prime Minister,' I laughed.

The producer still believed I had some connection with the Prime Minister and wondered if he would help us with our project. Not a problem - I immediately went into the coffee shop and explained to him what we were up to.

I was fronting a series of You Tube clips aimed at convincing American talk show host David Letterman to come to New Zealand. John Key had already been a much-publicized guest on Letterman's show so he quickly understood what I was trying to do.

Within minutes, John Key was with me in front of a camera.

'Hi, Dave. Remember me? John Key, Prime Minister of New Zealand,' he ad libbed like a pro. 'You should listen to this guy. He's for real.'

What a result! I could never imagine bumping into the President of the United States and talking him into making an unplanned appearance in a video shoot. That's what I love about this joint, the place I call my adopted home. It's a no fuss zone. Beautiful.

The Letterman project was all about being loud, and unafraid to push hard in public for what I wanted. The idea came to me when I was watching Letterman on his show, and he said New Zealand was his favourite country of all those he had never been to.

Wham, there it was, just the opportunity I needed to show the world what a wonderful place New Zealand was. I wanted to showcase the country, and get one of the world's best known celebrities to make some noise about it.

I wrote some scripts and got a large cut-out of Letterman's face which I stuck on a pole so I could symbolically carry him round on my mission to bring him Down Under. I put out the word that I was looking for help with my project - no point in being shy - and offers came in. The film community here is small and caring and I ended up with one of the country's hottest young film talents, Simon Ward.

We filmed a trilogy of You Tube clips, all urging Letterman to visit New Zealand. In typical fashion, for the first one I ranted into the camera, warning him that Kiwis press their noses rather than shake hands, eat purple burgers and have a different understanding of rooting. The first video also included shots of New Zealand's wonderful scenery.

For the second video I featured the upcoming Rugby World Cup and got legendary former All Black captain Wayne 'Buck' Shelford to come along, supporting my message to Letterman. All I did was ring him and he was all for helping out — again, New Zealand is so laid back. And the third one found me sitting at that Starbucks where I was pitching a free cup of coffee if Letterman made the trip down to the Land of the Long White Cloud.

Phil Koeghan
The three video clips were uploaded to You Tube (just search for John Dybvig and you'll find them) and my next hurdle was to try to get Letterman himself to view them. I sent them to Kiwi broadcaster Phil Keoghan, the host of The Amazing Race, an American show that has won numerous Emmys. As I said he and I had worked on his kids' television show in New Zealand and I hoped he could help.

'Nice job,' he emailed back to me. But he warned that Letterman was about the most difficult show to get on — namely because even he couldn't get on it with his basket of Emmy's - the Amazing Race's publicist had been trying unsuccessfully for eight years to get The Amazing Race on the show, even though they were part of the same network. Wow, now that's amazing!

St. Heliers Primary

It turned out the solution was in my own backyard. I sent the You Tube links to my kid's school, St Heliers Primary. One of the mothers, who was in charge of class emails, sent the links out and included them in a mail to her extended family. One was sent to a relative in New York who happened to be married to the vice president of NBC who knew one of Letterman's producers. The producer sent an email back, saying they thought the clips were fantastic and they had been sent to Letterman's head writer.

Imagine that, from St Heliers to the boardrooms of CBS in New York in less than an hour.

I would like to report that our efforts had since brought David Letterman to New Zealand but sadly not - so far, that is. Mainly because Letterman has a huge fear of flying and the trip Down Under is no jaunt around the block.

Comment: The Letterman project proved to me that sometimes life is not necessarily about the end result but the rollicking good time you can have along the way. I know this is an absolute cliché but for me it proved to be so true: The journey is often more important than the destination.

Armani

I've never owned a suit in my life. I never wear a watch.

I'm more your casual jeans and T-shirt guy, and I like nothing more than throwing on a colourful Hawaiian shirt — something as loud as the guy wearing it. When I was fronting a television show, the network provided me with suit jackets, business shirts and ties because it would make me look smart and authoritative. But because of the hot studio lights, I would have sweat sloshing around inside my jacket before we even went to air. Some guys can complete a triathlon in a three-piece suit and pull up looking immaculate.

Me? I go for a short stroll in my slacks and jacket and wind up looking like I've been wrestling alligators

Being a smart dresser is a talent. I don't have it. I could be wearing a tuxedo and still look like an unmade bed.

Comment One: This is not a brag... but when writing this it suddenly came to me that I've never even ironed a shirt. In fact, in my entire life I've never ironed anything. What does that say about me? I guess I'm not too bothered by wrinkles?

Comment Two: I did have a lot of fun when I was trying to figure out what to wear... I suggested going extremely casual to one of my producers - like naked! Yeah... nah... yeah... oh ok nah! I did go to a few of Auckland's upmarket menswear shops where I tried on all sorts of monkey suits... some of them made me look like a pimp... no thanks. I called it a day when some guy light of foot in one store suggested apricot slacks and a peasant blouse and expressed way too much interest in my inside leg measurement... know what I mean!?!

A Big Fish in a Small Pond
I have stampeded through New Zealand like your classic bull in a china shop, with perseverance, determination and most importantly a strong sense of self. And I've had an absolute rollicking good time to boot. Along the way, I've earned a reputation - people know what they're going to get when they run into John Dybvig.

One example was the time when I spent the afternoon at a director's house in a quiet suburb of Auckland. We were in his backyard going over a scene we were planning to shoot. I was blocking out the actions for camera positions and going over my dialogue.

My voice was on full throttle. Someone in the neighborhood called the police.

Unbeknown to us, two cops knocked on the front door. The director's wife explained the misunderstanding, saying it was just an actor and her husband working through a scene in their backyard.

All the same, cops being cops, they wanted to see for themselves. The two policemen poked their heads through the back door, surprising the director and me.

When they saw me, they smiled in unison, nodded knowingly and looked smugly at each other.

'Oh, it's Dybvig,' said one, as if that explained everything.

Dogged Determination

Like I've said I can be single minded when push comes to shove. I've always had a good healthy dose of dogged determination to get what I want or to go where I want to go... take the case of Saatchi & Saatchi world wide boss Kevin Roberts.

I wanted to hook up with Roberts to see if he could possibly help me land a literary agent in the States (Roberts had published several books in America)... Roberts has a home in New Zealand where he headed up Saatchi & Saatchi here before he landed the plum role of being in charge of the entire ship in New York.

Ok so here's the deal I had read in the papers that Kevin was due to fly back to New Zealand... so I rang up his PA (personal assistant) and asked if I could have a meeting with her boss... her answer was short and to the point - NO!

Ok I said I know he's flying into New Zealand so could I meet him at the arrivals gate and just talk with him while he walks to the baggage claim - I only need a few minutes... again her answer was minimal - NO!

Ok so maybe I could give you a short note that you could pass on to him explaining my case... NO!

This gal was one tough cookie... it looked like a no go... but thinking about it I knew if I could get to Kevin he'd see me because I had done a few speaking engagements with him in New Zealand so he knew who I was and we always got on like a house on fire (another slang term from my grandmother)... but the problem with getting to any high flyer is getting their attention and all these guys are surrounded by people and obstacles designed to discouraged you so that you can't get to them...

But like I said when I get something in my head - well I'm still like a dog with a big butcher's bone... BACK-OFF... ok so I'm thinking how can I get his attention and then bingo it just hit me... Kevin Roberts is a fanatical All Black rugby guy... he sits on their board... he's a total rah...rah guy when it comes to the All Blacks... so what do I do... I'll tell you... I went down to my local post office and bought an All Black envelope... which really stands out with the big bold black letters declaring them to be the world's best rugby team against the white envelope... so I got that and wrote a short note requesting a meeting when he got back to New Zealand and mailed it to him in New York... I knew that that All Black envelope would stand out like a blinking neon sign in the New York mailroom and Kevin would immediately open it... and sure enough he sent me an email to get hold of his PA (who he also emailed) to arrange a meeting... I immediately called her and she was nice as pie and set me up for a meeting with Kevin Roberts... it was such a reversal on her part... in the beginning she was cold and stern and firm in her denials... but as soon as Kevin gave her the green light for me she warmed up like a lovely apple pie just taken out of the oven... all nice and cosy... there was no rancor on her part because she was just doing her job...still for me I found the change in her attitude towards me in the snap of a finger amusing to say the least... right...I get my meeting with Kevin and he gives me a half hour one on one... we talk and have a lot of laughs and drink a Pepsi (Kevin loves Pepsi) but alas he was to be of no help in finding a literary agent in America... he told me that while he's worked with a few of them he described them as 'strange animals' indeed... and I have to say I gotta agree with him... I've been trying for over 20 years to land one... maybe one day?

Comment: The point of this story is when a problem arises if you give it enough thought you can usually come up with the solution... of course not every time but more times than you think... just don't give up immediately at your first rejection. Work on it. Here's a trick I do when I'm trying to come up with an answer for something... I give it a lot of thought... twisting and turning it over and over in my mind... then I totally dismiss it... just leave it... walk away from it... and then later like magic I'll be talking with someone or reading something or just sitting and thinking and whamo the answer will pop up... try it... you'll be amazed by how many times it works.

Shopping Mall
But sometimes you can be caught completely off guard... one day I'm standing in a shopping mall minding my own business when this really old guy beckons me over. A fan? This guy's ancient like really... really old and he gets his words out at about one a minute. I have to put my ear close to his mouth to catch what he's saying:

"I... can't... wait... (wobble wobble)... till... they... kick... (wobble wobble)... your arse... outtahere..."

This guy was prepared to spend the last few breaths of his life insulting me. I was impressed.

Parking Lot
Being a big fish in a small pond, and I say that tongue firmly in cheek, can certainly have its funny moments when it comes to your ego.

One of the funniest moments I've had with the public came about in a supermarket parking lot. I had just climbed out of my car when a guy parked next to me was just about to get into his, he eyed me up and exclaimed: "You're John Dybvig, aren't you!"

I said: "Yeah, Yes I am."

To which he said in a very kiwi matter of fact way: "You used to be somebody."

Ya gotta laugh.

Somebody
And speaking of being a specific somebody for my whole entire life wherever I've been in the world I've been the only Dybvig. So, whenever anyone yelled out Dybvig it was always for me... always! The first time I heard one of my son's mates yell out, 'hey Dybvig'... I immediately went to reply... but before I could, my son Sam answered. Wow... that was a shock. A real shock... a very cool shock... but still a shock!

CHAPTER FOUR

How to Survive 103 Jobs and The Mob
Only John Dybvig could take on more than 100 jobs before his 40th birthday and survive - including a brush with The Mob in Las Vegas.

Employment
By my count, I racked up at least 103 jobs before I turned 50... and after that, I simply lost count of the jobs I've had. It's not that I'm lazy, or I can't hold down a job. No, it's because I've never been afraid to go after a job that looks interesting - and I've never been afraid to walk out as soon as I lose interest. My thirties were a blur as I blundered and bludgeoned my way through America, New Zealand and Australia. I charged through countless jobs and more than a few relationships in a reckless assault on life. Live that kind of life-style for a decade and even though you're working some high-profile jobs you're walking on quicksand. There simply isn't any foundation underneath you.

I have variously worked the usual type of mundane jobs: peach-pit sweeper, bartender, busboy, dishwasher, house painter, telephone salesman, barista, gas station attendant, plumber's assistant, forklift driver, security guard, metal factory gofer, smorgasbord food line manager, chicken fryer. I've also found myself behind the counter in the Sears catalogue department, being a teacher, Insurance salesman, Sports bookie, radio talkback host, newspaper columnist, television presenter, voice/over artist, American accent coach and a 'Subliminal Cybernetics' counsellor, just to name a few. I've appeared as an actor in movies (usually cast as a wild man), shovelled sheep shit to earn a buck and dodged aircraft in a hot air balloon.

Hot Air
Yes, I foolishly agreed to broadcast live from a balloon at the 2000 Sydney Olympics. My producer had found out that some guy was going to propose to his girlfriend on the balloon so that was our angle for a feel good story. I was thinking it would be tethered a few feet above the ground.

Instead I found myself 3,000 feet in the air drifting between clouds while swinging in the wind in an oversized picnic basket interviewing this couple after the young man got down on bended knee and proposed.

They were extremely excited about the whole experience... me, I was shitting my pants the whole time. I'm not great with heights in the first place and when I heard the balloon pilot radio in our position to Sydney's International Airport control tower I got whiplash snapping my neck around in every direction looking for large aircraft.

Comment: I just wasn't comfortable in that hot air balloon... I felt so naked... we were just so exposed and everything about it just seemed so very flimsy to me... like it might just blow apart at any moment.

How did all this start
It all started one day when I got the telephone call children dread. It was mid-morning and I was running late for a game of tennis. I had burst out the front door and was just about to slam it shut... when the phone rang. I caught the door and stood there. Perhaps it rang just that little bit louder. I dunno... but I came back in and caught it... It was my older sister. Our father had had a heart attack earlier that morning. He had been pouring cement in the backyard. He died instantly... and as I stood there clutching the plastic receiver - for what seemed an eternity - my world suddenly seemed a far colder place.

Fathers and Sons

When I was growing up we were always at odds with each other, he was a tough no-nonsense Norwegian. He grew up during the depression on a farm in South Dakota. Work was very important to him so he always wanted me to work. And I - like most kids - always wanted to goof off. But in the end he usually got his way. By the time I was thirteen I was picking fruit during the summer, by fifteen I was the chief fryer in a chicken restaurant. But, still we just never got along, never saw eye-to-eye on anything. During one period I didn't speak to him for over two years. We lived your classic father and son angst, each too stubborn to relent to the other.

Stuff

Then during my first and only season at Gonzaga University as an assistant basketball coach my parents came up to Spokane, Washington and stayed with me for three weeks. My Dad and I talked about stuff for the first time in our lives. Nothing in particular; just stuff. For the first time in my coaching career my Mom and Dad came and watched me coach, I was so proud I was like a little kid again seeking approval from his parents. We spent time together and they were both very proud of what I was doing, my position at the University, although my Dad 'God Bless Him' found it difficult to understand that I wore shorts to work. I was really looking forward to summer with the promise of some more time together as father and son having finally gotten to know him a bit better. Instead as fate would have it I went home two months early to bury him. C'est la vie.

7-11

My once ordered existence now seemed very vague. All of a sudden being a basketball coach just didn't seem that important to me. My father's death had thrown me into a tailspin, my life grinding to a halt. I found myself in such a different head space that I didn't know how to handle it. So I didn't. I put that whole part of myself into a box and closed the lid.

I tossed in my coaching position which I had worked so damn hard to get and moved back to California. I tried to comfort my mother. I needed a job. Any job.

I was in the neighbourhood 7-11 when I noticed a sign: "Clerk wanted," and the next thing I knew I was working the graveyard shift. An apt name because the creepy crawly hours of the night brought out every oddball going, there were moments when the store looked like an audition for Michael Jackson's "Thriller" video. One time some dude strolled in, got a six pack of beer, and strolled right past me without paying, smiling the entire time. I rang the police, who picked him up and later told me he was high on PCP (Angel Dust). Then one stone-cold quiet night at around 3:00am the phone went "Jing!" I jumped three feet in the air. I picked up the receiver and listened to a sexy female voice on the other end asking me personal questions:

"Do you work there sir?"

"Huh?"

"Can you please describe for me what you're wearing?"

"Huh?"

Brilliant phone conversation on my part, the mysterious sexy voice belonged to a dispatch officer for the local police department. Apparently the shop's silent alarm had been triggered.

I looked up and got one helluva fright. Two Robocops were aiming the biggest meanest looking tubes of metal (shotguns) I had ever seen directly at me.

What made this experience even more frightening was a friend of mine was in exactly the same position I was in then, only he was being held up, and for whatever reason he grabbed the robber's sawn-off shotgun and it discharged killing him instantly. Every synapse in my body shut down:

"Dead clerk standing."

I was ordered not to move. No problem. Then the approaching lead cop, holding a bigger handgun than anything Clint Eastwood carried in Dirty Harry, stealthily checked out the store and finally called the all clear.

That experience stayed with me for a long-long, time. Too much fire power in too small a space with me right in the middle of it.

Comment: When you work the graveyard (nice terminology) shift you think of the weirdest shit in the dead of the night. The store is lit up brighter than a Christmas tree and the surrounding area is in total pitch blackness and you're thinking - yeah like moths to a flame any crook or nutjob out there is going to be attracted to the only building with its lights on. And I'm the lone idiot behind the counter. I had weapons stashed all over the store just in case.

Glory Days
Funnily enough though, that brush with death didn't scare me off. It took a very innocent chance meeting with the local mailman to do that. Early one morning I was working overtime when Mr. "Happy-as-Larry" skipped in delivering the mail. He instantly recognized me from the local high school championship basketball team I played on. We shot the breeze for a while about what singer Bruce Springsteen calls "The Glory Days." Finally he chirped something about the mail must go through. He was almost out the door when he casually snuck a quick furtive glance back and as I looked up our eyes locked for the briefest of seconds. I suddenly felt small. The mailman was embarrassed. His look sadly winced, "Your star once shone brightly kid... but now at 30 you're clerking in a 7-11..." So much emotion packed into nothing more than a blink of the eye. That was it. That was the exact moment metaphorically I went out for a pack of "cigarettes," and never came back.

How Now Brown Cow

I landed in New Zealand. When I arrived I was an oddity. You wanna laugh, then introduce an American to the anal New Zealand culture. I bungled my way thru New Zealand with perseverance and a strong sense of self.

I took on two classic Kiwi jobs I would never have contemplated in the States; pressing wool and working in a slaughterhouse.

I can still recall with clarity the first time I saw a cow slaughtered. First, they attached a chain to one leg as this huge ungainly beast moved forward on a conveyor belt, and then they shot it point blank in the middle of its forehead. It dropped off the moving belt and hung over a white washed pit where the butchers waited. One took an enormous butcher's knife and sliced the cow's throat all the way around so its head immediately snapped back and a tsunami of blood and innards spilled out. It was one of the most disgusting sights I've ever seen. These were tough environments where the men were hard. More than once during the week we'd all hit the pub just down the road at lunchtime for jugs of beer. I didn't normally drink beer in the middle of the day but I did with my gang.

Comment One: We also ate well. Often one of the gang would pinch a leg of fresh lamb and another gang member would bring potatoes, kumara and carrots and we'd all sit down to a beautiful lunch of roasted lamb and roasted vegetables. The foreman would stroll by our table stopping and enquiring: "Enjoying your lunch boys?" Of course he could never prove we stole the lamb...but he full well knew that we did.

Comment Two: Our meat workers union was so strong that I know you're not gonna believe this - but it's absolutely true: Of course the meat company employed security guards to watch over the plant including the bins where fresh lamb was stored... but if they stopped and stared at you while you were working for longer than 10 seconds the union would order a stop work meeting for company harassment.

Comment Three: One week I was goofing off pretty good by splitting from work a couple of hours early every day. The foreman called me into his office to tear strips off of me... which didn't bother me as I was goofing off. But when I came out of his office our union rep was just hustling up to the office in a rush and he literally tore strips off of me. He roared at me: "If you ever walk into the foreman's office again without first informing me... I'll have your fucking balls!" Then he carried on into the foreman's office to tell him a thing or two... I have never in my life worked for a stronger union.

The Pits
Until then, I had already thought I'd worked in the messiest job possible. When working my way through university, I had a job that literally was the absolute pits. Bottom rung of the ladder. Lower than a snake's belly in a wagon rut... I worked as a peach pit sweeper in an enormous warehouse in the San Joacquin Valley. Hundreds of thousands of peaches were de-pitted there and sent to markets worldwide.

What the world didn't know was that some poor schmuck had to continuously sweep zillions of pits dropping through the gaps of a platform raised five feet off the ground. And in 1971 that poor struggling university student was moi!

Under the steady drip of Chinese water so were the days of my life, gallons and gallons of sweet, sticky peach juice slowly dripped over my bent and hobbled body. The only reason I bring this up is that I was positive that as far as menial jobs went, things couldn't get any worse.

Sheep Shit
But a decade later, at the ass end of the world, I found myself covered in shit. Sheep shit.

I was a wool sorter in a seven-acre wool shed. I worked the 'Bin Room,' a collection of chicken-wire cages where loose wool along with the dags were classified and stored. Dags are the wooly bit covering the sheep's ass. Yes, that's the smelly bit. My job was the lowest form of life in the wool shed, even lower than the ticks and fleas that inhabited the wool.

Pressing
In mid-summer we hit peak season with tons of wool, piled up as far as the eye could see. This turned out to be my big break in the wool business. They needed another presser. I shot my hand up so quick I threw my shoulder out of joint.

Pressing wool was like going from the mailroom to having a job with your own office. In wool shed terms, pressing was higher in status because it involved the use of a machine. It was certainly a hell of a lot cleaner, and it paid more. I had never been a status seeker before, but then I had never before spent my days handling sheep shit. I decided a rise in status wouldn't be so bad after all.

The Hulk
I worked in a woolshed the size of three airplane hangers, jammed to the gunnels with the fleecy white stuff. The pressing machine was a solid monolith of metal with hydraulic hoses and coils. The routine was fairly basic; you slapped a burlap sack into the Hulk (my pet name for my presser) and then with arms stretched wide, you scooped loads of wool from a holding bin and stuffed it into the sack in the presser.

You slammed the lid shut and hit the big green button and the Hulk sprang into life. It hissed and clanked and shuddered as it squeezed and compressed the wool deep into the sack. You repeated this process until no more wool could possibly be squeezed in.

Scoop, stuff, press. Rivers of sweat rolled off my body in the oven of thick, humid sticky woolen heat.

Scoop, stuff, press. My hands were baby soft from all the lanolin in the wool.

Scoop, stuff, press. Each bale weighed in at more than 300 pounds.

The toughest part of the job was tightly sewing the cloth lid on the sack. You used six-inch razor sharp needles laced with a heavy twine. Invariably you sliced your fingers and the twine at first cut deeply into my soft hands as I continually struggled to keep the twine taut using something I think was called an albatross half-hitch cross stitch that would challenge any boy scout.

Pressure

My first week of pressing was pure hell! I literally worked my ass off and got absolutely nowhere. I struggled to press sixteen bales a day with my fingers covered in band-aids. The rest of the pressing gang would knock off between fifty and sixty bales a day. I didn't get it. I couldn't work any harder!?! It never dawned on that I could work smarter until one of the older pressers took pity on me. This gentleman had been there so long he looked like a bale of wool with glasses. He taught me the finer points of pressing wool. And as I learned the technique and stopped fighting the machine, suddenly like magic I too began pressing fifty plus bales a day. And I wasn't working nearly as hard. Amazing.

That experience was a great lesson for me. For one thing it taught me that you can learn something anywhere, anytime. And I'm not talking about the finer points of pressing wool. I'm talking about the principle of "being prepared"... of how a solid foundation of skills and techniques behind you - in whatever task you attempt - is the true meaning of motivation.

I just couldn't get over how pumped I was at going from a meager sixteen bales to over fifty. I mean we're not talking rocket science here, but with a bit of knowledge I could now hold my own with the other pressers. And believe me I was under constant pressure when I was lagging so far behind when I first started pressing wool. Self-esteem is important no matter what kind of job you're doing. Still it took the simple clarity of a lesson from an old man - in a dusty warehouse at the bottom end of the world - to ram it home.

Hook

You lived and learned the hard way, and only once I hooked a falling bale.

I was stacking my just completed bale on top of a tall stack of bales, working with my gaffer's hook when suddenly my world began to tumble down around me. Well actually one bale began to tumble down alongside me! Like Batman with his Bat-a-rang so did my arm and gaffer hook fly into action... I snared that woolen bastard mid-flight and proceeded to tumble on down behind it! I landed heavily on my back with a thud. The veterans all had a good laugh. Then a smelly little gnome of a man with rotten teeth and Popeye-like arms smothered in tattoos told me no one should ever hook a falling bale. At more than 300 pounds, the wool wins every time.

'Thanks,' I gasped.

'Besides,' he chortled with a knowing half-wink, 'it's only wool, what harm is it gonna do if it does fall?' A good point, made a couple of minutes too late.

Liquid Death

My other messy job in Auckland found me working the late season in the freezing works. I always had a yearning to try something like this and I really did think it might be fun.

My amusement ride started when they supplied me with my work clothes. I held out both arms in front of a Buddha-shaped Polynesian who began slapping freezing work clothes into them (it was like being in the army).

Two pairs of woolen pants, two pairs of thick woolen socks, two wool jerseys, two wool shirts, a woolen cap, two pairs of wool gloves, two pairs of boots (not woolen), one pair of white overalls, one white overtop and several other bits and pieces of gear all of a woolly nature. So that's where all that wool I pressed into bales had ended up.

I met the safety officer who took me on a tour of smells. Slaughterhouses are a maze of rotting buildings with openings into dark tunnels. And they stink! Every corner we turned we were met by a nasty new smell that clung to you as you moved through it.

We finally arrived at our destination, a five-story freezer. We went in and out of freezers for a tour that seemed to last for hours; big ones, little ones, long, short, wide, narrow, empty and full and they were all freezing cold.

The safety officer told me the greatest danger in a freezer was the ammonia, warning if it leaked it would attack the eyes, nose, mouth, ears and any cuts or sores. It was absolutely deadly. Ammonia is what kept the freezers freezing and each freezer had masses of the stuff piped around it.

Great, I thought, I'm working in Siberia, surrounded by liquid death.

Gangs

With Auckland being the largest Polynesian city in the world, it wasn't surprising that the gang I was assigned to consisted entirely of macho brown skins; Maori, Tongans, Samoans, Fijians and every other South Pacific nation was represented.

Oh yeah, and one white dude from San Francisco.

As with all gangs nicknames were a must: We had "Guts," "Empty Space," "Sidewinder," and "Flinty," amongst others.

They immediately gave me "Septic Tank," as most New Zealanders think Americans talk a load of bullshit.

I didn't try to deny this, I merely explained to them the historical events that led up to this tarnished image.

Noah

"You see guys it all started way back with Noah and his Ark. Noah got all the animals two-by-two on to his Ark just as the forty days and forty nights of heavy rain lashed earth. Well, that old Ark was out in all that water just bobbing away when after a while two huge bulls approached Noah and wanted to know where they could make their deposits. "Oh yeah," mumbled Noah as he scratched his head looking this way and that way throughout the crowded Ark, for a suitable spot, finally he pointed to an area way over on the far side. These two huge bulls slowly ambled over and began dropping some monstrously huge deposits causing the Ark to list badly to one side - in a panic Noah grabbed one of the two shovels he had on board and started slinging this mountain of bullshit over the side of the Ark. And then five hundred years later Christopher Columbus discovered America!"

The Joke is on Me

Yes, of course I was just pulling their leg, but it makes for a good story and usually breaks the ice between different cultures, you know making fun of yourself.

We were cogs in a machine and our job was to move meat; hot meat, frozen meat, any kind of meat. Move it all and keep it moving from room to room and from place to place. We had two basic jobs; one was to fill freezers with freshly killed lamb and the other was to empty the freezers of frozen lamb.

I remember the distinctive sound we made as our hands slapped the flanks of the newly slaughtered lamb suspended in the air hanging from hooks.

Pitty pat, pitty pat.

We'd spread out three feet apart down long dank corridors. The lamb hung on rails above our heads. The first guy in line would grab the carcass and give it a huge push. As it sailed by, another pair of hands would slap it along to keep the momentum going.

Pitty pat, pitty pat.

Soon, hundreds of sheep were flying towards the freezer until it was full.

Combat Pay

Moving frozen lamb was more fun but a helluva lot more dangerous. We'd start at the top, five stories up, opening manhole covers on each floor below, hooking up wooden chutes just like in the game of Chutes and Ladders, all the way down to the waiting rail cars below.

The man at the top would unhook the frozen carcass from the overhead railing and drop it on the wooden chute. Thunk! That lamb was followed by another, and another, until a stream of frozen meat was screaming its way through the five floors of industrial freezer.

Every so often, one of the carcasses would get jammed causing huge chunks of frozen meat to fly in all directions. Workers would be ducking for cover. Men were stationed at each junction of the wooden chutes to steer the lamb in the right direction until it hit the bottom. There, another string of men would grab it and toss it into the rail car.

At the end of an exhausting shift, we'd scramble outside, stomping our feet and clasping our hands in an effort to warm ourselves. And what exactly did I learn from my freezing works experience?

I learned that getting up at 5am and spending the next 10 hours in sub-zero temperatures, getting up close and personal with dead sheep, isn't a whole lot of fun.

Time to look for another job. Again.

Five Year Plan

I was young, wild and living on the edge. I had flown home to spend the summer months (June, July and August) in America - remember it was winter in New Zealand as the seasons are reversed.

That's when I applied for a basketball coaching job at Canada Community College. At the time, I was sleeping in a cabin in the woods in Lake Tahoe, Nevada with the brother of one of my ex-wives.

I had to hustle a suit from my boss and then drove all night through a snowstorm to get to the interview in the San Francisco Bay Area.

When one of the interview panel asked me what my five-year plan was, I blanked out. It was like being in a movie when everything goes into slow motion. Trussed up in my borrowed suit, I stared back at the college professor who had asked the question.

I started to laugh, and fairly screamed: 'Five-year plan? Are you kidding me? I don't have a five-year plan! I've got a five-minute plan, buddy. I'm here right now — that's my plan.'

When I stopped ranting, the room was filled with silence or what's often called a pregnant pause. Those who dared to make visual contact no doubt saw the wildness in my eyes.

That was one job I didn't get.

Then I got a job that got me arrested.

Working for the Mob
I've only been arrested one time in my life. I had hooked up with a high school buddy of mine who was a supervisor at the High Sierra Casino in Lake Tahoe, and who got me a job in their sports betting operation. I worked there for the entire summer, gambling and drinking too much.

How could I resist? I worked in a room which housed about a dozen bars. My high school buddy, who was also my immediate boss, kept giving me tokens for free drinks.

The thing that amazed me most about the sports book, as it was known, were the professional gamblers who would casually appear at the window and silently place a briefcase on the counter in one smooth action, popping the latches to reveal stacks of crisp bills in neat rows just like in the movies. Then would follow an avalanche of bets across the board, often more than $100,000 at a crack. With these guys, it's all about mathematics, simple as that.

I once saw the butt of a concealed pistol on one of the regular pros and I asked him if he would actually shoot someone. His expression was lifeless as he responded: 'Whaddaya you think?'

I also learned my mom was absolutely correct when she said money was the dirtiest thing in the world, because after work when I washed my hands, the water would literally run black from all the money I had handled during my shift. I worked that job to the max, pulling double shifts, drinking until the early hours of the morning and taking in any number of great shows.

Drunk and Disorderly

Then one night a coworker and I drove to the state capital of Nevada, Carson City where you can get a great feed of biscuits and gravy for 99 cents at Cactus Jacks. Nevada is home to the 'Bomb!' Nevada is where America used to conduct their nuclear tests. In fact, that test site is known for having the highest concentration of nuclear-detonated weapons in the entire country. Underneath all that serenity of clean open desert air is one of the most tightly controlled States in the Union with more than 80% of the State owned by the Federal Government of the United States of America. So if you're going to pick a place to get arrested for the first time, Nevada is as good a place as any.

We went to the Ormsby House Hotel casino where in the process of having a lot of fun we got so drunk I was thrown out at 3am. I was under the impression that they threw me out for bothering my buddy. I thought that they didn't realise that we were together and it was just some harmless fun; me razzing him.

It never crossed my mind that they tossed me out because I was loud, overbearing and drunk, so I marched right back in through the back entrance to straighten things out.

This time they called the cops and had me arrested. I was still convinced that this was one big misunderstanding and continued to say so through the taking of the mug shots, the recording of my fingerprints and while standing in the holding cell. I honestly believed I could straighten it all out. I was your typical drunk.

All I had to do was explain the circumstances to the judge and everything would be sweet, I thought. The whole matter would surely be dropped.

The day before I was to go to court, I was working the afternoon shift at the High Sierra Casino when the boss of the sports book, a mysterious character from a mafia family in Las Vegas, appeared behind me and whispered in my ear.

'I understand you had a small problem at the Carson hotel.'

I became animated and exclaimed, 'Yeah, and you see it was all a big mistake and...'

'Drop it, pay the fine.' He whispered.

And the way these guys say that kind of thing is exactly the way Tony Soprano of the 'Soprano's' or Marlon Brando in the 'Godfather' would say that kind of thing and you immediately know you're going to do what they say without another word. I paid the fine. It was $250.

I pleaded guilty to being drunk and disorderly and as I had already paid the fine to get out of jail, the judge pounded his gavel to signal that was the end of the matter. This was business as usual, a matter of revenue for the State of Nevada.

Ping

When the summer season ended, I drove my ex-wife's Jeep across the lonely Nevada desert on Highway 50, widely known as the 'loneliest road in America'. I drove through land seemingly untouched by man, except for a few ghost towns and ancient cemeteries, hinting at memories of the Pony Express Trail that had crossed the same desert many years before. Eventually, I passed the Bonneville Salt Flats and arrived in Salt Lake City, Utah, where I slept on the couch that belonged to my ex-wife's boyfriend.

I hung around long enough to take in the sights including their 360 strong Mormon Tabernacle Choir, which since July 15, 1929 has performed a weekly radio broadcast called 'Music and the Spoken Word', the longest running continuous network broadcast in the world.

The Mormon Tabernacle, which seats 8,000 and is made almost entirely of wood - not a nail in the place, with the trusses held together by wooden pegs and rawhide creates astounding acoustics. I had signed up for a tour and at one point the tour guide left us huddled at the back of this massive hall and then strode all the way to the front, which had to be several football fields away. She got up on the stage and dropped a single pin. Without straining, we all clearly heard this distinctive 'ping' as the pin hit the floor - amazing!

Really, I was flabbergasted. So much so that I got up at 5am the next morning and stood in line in the freezing snow to listen to the Mormon Tabernacle Choir and found them to be simply heavenly in every sense of the word.

Porsche
Not surprisingly, my ex-wife's boyfriend wasn't too fond of me sleeping on his couch so I was subtly encouraged to head back to California. As my former wife needed to go to the Bay Area, I offered to drive her back there - using her boyfriend's Porsche.

When we got to California, I continued to use the Porsche - yeah, baby! - and I wasn't looking forward to giving it up. I might be unemployed (again), but I might as well be unemployed in style.

When my ex was ready to return to Salt Lake City, I rang her boyfriend and said I could either put her on a flight home or drive her back in the car. I cunningly anticipated he wouldn't be keen to see me back at his place, taking up space on his couch again, and I was right. She flew home, and I had the use of his Porsche for another month. Bliss. Finally, it was time to give up the Porsche, and decide the next step in my hedonistic lifestyle. Unemployment had its limitations.

Opportunity Knocks

Then out of the blue as it so often happens to me, I got a phone call from an American journalist buddy in New Zealand. He told me I should get my butt back to Auckland because cable television had arrived and they were looking for commentators.

The television network would no doubt need an outrageous loudmouth. I seemed to be suitably qualified.

I flew straight back to New Zealand and wrote to the head of programming at Sky Network, a 'suit' I had never met. They say 'opportunity knocks but once' but in my less-than-humble opinion, that's a crock. Truth is there are all kinds of opportunities trying to kick down the door - the opportunity to be broke, the opportunity to catch a horrendous disease and die an ugly and terrifying death. Those are the kinds of opportunities that can set up camp on your doorstep. They wedge the doorbell down and come sniffing around your windows. Unwelcome opportunities come looking for you.

It's the good ones that actually stay at home. You've got to go knock on their door. Well, I say knock, but it's actually hammer, bite, scratch and claw! I introduced myself to the television executive and told him what a lucky man he was because when it came to sports presenting I was the greatest thing since sliced bread. It was one of my more modest letters. The 'suit' replied with a terse note saying that they 'might get back to me' once they had 'hired a head of sport.' I interpreted his reply like this:

> *Dear John,*
>
> *Fuck you.*
>
> *Love,*
> *The Suit*

He hadn't said 'no.'

To me, that was almost like offering me encouragement.

Elvis

Having a strong belief in persistence and determination as the corner blocks to getting what I wanted, I came up with another plan of attack. Fortunately, as luck would have it when I had arrived back in New Zealand, I'd picked up a job hosting a sports show on the top-rating radio station in the country.

My show was Sports Talk with John Dybvig. I invited one of the entrepreneurs who founded the cable television station onto my radio show as a guest. It's the old ploy of giving someone in an organization that doesn't ordinarily get into the public spotlight some recognition. For instance, if you want to get on the inside of a professional sports team don't ask to see the coach, ask instead to speak with the trainer (usually a forgotten man) and you'll be all but guaranteed to get in. The television executive accepted my invitation and invited me out to his network to look the place over. This would help me get an idea of what they were all about.

Yes! Elvis was in the building. This entrepreneurial suit turned out to be one of those fit, energetic executives. The guy was an enthusiasm bomb. Damn near shook my hand off.

'I'm pleased to meet you, John. I like your radio broadcasting style. You've got enthusiasm. Of course, you're going to work for us aren't you?'

'Well, I've got this letter from your head of programming...'

'Great! Your personality and style are exactly what we think broadcasting is all about.'

'Hmmm, your guy didn't seem too impressed there.'

'Wonderful! It's a question of style, excitement, of involvement! Just the kind of thing you're good at.'

He kept pumping my hand until I was in danger of a nose bleed. He praised me until the synapses in the pleasure center of my brain welded shut. I missed most of the guided tour owing to a lightening trip of my own personal Blue Heaven. Style and enthusiasm, huh. Personality, excitement and involvement, you say? Yes, I like this man. That night, when my new-found friend did his guest spot on my radio show, his new cable network had never sounded better. We talked it up. We told the listeners how great it was going to be. I added 'flatter' to my job-clinching strategy of hammer, bite, scratch and claw.

Peanuts

When the network's head of sport called me in to meet and talk some turkey, it turned out the only turkey in that meeting was me. They should have filmed that session and shown it at business conferences on how not to negotiate a television contract, or any kind of contract for that matter. I might have seen the world but I was so naive when it came to this type of business. I didn't have a clue what I was doing. I had never negotiated a television contract before. And to make matters worse their head of sport was the world's nicest person. He reminded me of actor Jimmy Stewart in It's a Wonderful Life. I waltzed into that meeting with stars in my eyes and visions of pools of money. I sort of expected the red carpet to be rolled right out for me. After all, this was television. Right?

Jimmy started the ball rolling.

'So, John, what sort of fee would you be looking for?'

'Oh, gee, I dunno know. I guess about a small bag of gold.'

'Well, John, I think that's a fair price for you, even though you haven't been in the game all that long.'

I wondered what his definition of 'all that long' was. If he meant a nano-second, he would be right. Jimmy leaned forward, gesturing me to listen carefully.

'You have to understand our budgets,' he said.

I nodded. I tried to look as though I'd done this many times before. No big deal. There followed a careful, twenty-minute explanation of the network's budgetary limitations. I didn't understand a single word he said.

'Oh, well, I guess in that case I'd accept a smaller bag of silver,' I helpfully suggested.

'I'd love to pay that to you, John. I really would. And I bet, if there was another broadcaster out there willing to take you on they'd pay you at least that, but ... '

There followed a careful, thirty-minute explanation of the economies of a limited audience television production. I didn't get it. As my eyes glazed over, and I began to lose the will to live, I wondered when the discussion would turn to my free perks. The clothes I would wear on camera. The company car. The three-Martini lunches. Hey, I had read the gossip columns. I wasn't entirely clueless. I tried another tack. If he was going to treat me like a monkey...

'Maybe I could get by on a large bag of peanuts?'

'A large bag, huh? John, let's try it this way; what's the very least you'd accept?'

Damn!

'Well, I might accept a medium-sized bag but I'm going to have to think about it. I'll need to review my options... '

I looked across the table, hoping he didn't ask what my options were. I had none. Maybe he would respond to thinly-disguised desperation...

'I can't work for nothing!'

There. Take that! See what it's like to come up against a tough negotiator. I walked out in a stupor. I didn't know up from down. What had happened?

I'll tell you what happened. I'd been so unprofessional as to have no idea of my price. I didn't even have a bottom line. Worse, I'd suffered the embarrassment of overpricing myself out of ignorance. But, I learned something that day. I learned you've got to do some homework before you walk into a meeting, any meeting. As I mourned for the loss of the television job I so badly wanted, a friend gave me some great advice.

'Get your pretentious butt down there; knock on the nice man's door and tell him that you'd be glad to work for the industry's standard contract.'

Standard contract? That's how dumb I was. It had never occurred to me there was such a beast.

The Five P's
During my time in the television business I've see so many people walk onto television sets - especially Joe Public - beaming from head to toe dazzled by all the instant attention they're smothered with and the bright lights and then get absolutely slaughtered by the host. Why? They went in unprepared.

I know this is a tired cliché, but nevertheless it's extremely important upon entering meeting rooms, adhere to the Five-P's: Prior Planning Prevents Poor Performance. That's it in a nutshell - spend some time thinking about what you want, not just what your boss or the TV host wants.

For instance when I went on Close Up New Zealand's number one current affairs television programme to discuss my one man campaign to get David Letterman to visit New Zealand I was prepared.

First of all I knew I wasn't going to get a ton of time for this story... it was a light hearted feel good item so when I got to the studios I wasn't surprised when they told me I'd get about 3 minutes. In my mind I had my storyline all mapped out: Why I was doing it, how my wife and family were involved along with my kids' primary school, the Prime Minister John Key and how former All Black captain Buck Shelford fitted in.

The host fired a few questions my way and I neatly and instantly fired back easily weaving in all those components into an entertaining story in my three-minute spot. And the next day I got very positive comments from everyone who had seen me.

Remember in most situations 'attack' is the best defense - have four or five bullet points firmly in your mind - remember television is all about 'sound bites' being long winded is not on - go in prepared!

Lights-camera-action
I ended up hosting Sky Network's first ever live broadcast on March 19, 1990. Television was a completely different world - especially for someone whose recent career had included ducking sheep shit, selling miracle cures and taking money off professional gamblers in Tahoe. One night, I was doing the lead-in for an NFL (National Football League) game being broadcast into New Zealand from the States. I was the only one in the vast studio. The cameras were locked off. The lights cast deep shadows into nothingness. My microphone and earpiece were my only links to the outside world.

'Ground Control to Major Tom.' The director's voice in my ear seemed far, far away.

'Two minutes to air... Hey John, your camera angle's just a fraction off; could you jump up and adjust it?'

I loved that 'jump up'... you don't just 'jump up' from a presentation desk! You unplug all the wires connected to your body and the desk and then gingerly step over them so as not to rip them out. Not for the first time, or for the last, I went through all the drama with the wires and then ran over to re-point the camera at my imaginary self.

'One minute to air... Hey, John, there's a wastepaper basket in the shot. Could you move it, please?'

I unwired once more and hustled over to the bin. I kicked it out of shot, so hard I think it went between the goalposts for the extra point.

'Thirty seconds to air... All that running around has made your head shine, John. There's a powder puff under the desk. Give yourself a dust down.'

With all the unplugging and replugging and running around under hot lights, along with inhaling a dust storm of powder, my throat was bone dry.

'Any chance of getting some water?' I pleaded.

'Love to help you out, John... but we're on air in 5-4-3-2-cue.'

The red light went on.

'Good evening, sports fans,' I gasped, sounding like a lawn-mower choking on a dog bone. Once the show started, you could never be certain what would happen next.

Comment: Being a television presenter is one of those weird jobs. People were always asking me how do you get that kind of job. Honestly, I haven't a clue...basically you just do stuff and then somehow by invitation or dogged perseverance you find yourself sitting behind a presentation desk. Either that or your uncle or father owns the television station. And the thing is - there doesn't seem to be any big deal or skill to being a television presenter. But the truth is not everybody can do it. Appearing to be natural while spouting pre-arranged sentences to a camera lens is more a knack than a skill. It's mostly a matter of talking to the camera without adopting the demeanor of a stunned mackerel or losing your cookies.

O.J. Steals the Show

This is another instance where Homer Simpson and I morph into one as I bumbled my way into another one of life's numerous totally weird situations.

One evening, I was hosting the NBA Championships between the New York Knicks and the Houston Rockets. I was sitting at the presentation desk as the action headed into the second quarter of game four. To my surprise, my director excitedly informed me through my earpiece that we were about to leave the live game and go directly to Los Angeles for a worldwide breaking story. I thought the director's voice sounded a bit peculiar.

Microphones

I always find how one gets into a position to do, what I was about to do, as interesting as the actual headline. Two elements brought me to anchor the news desk at this crucial time:

First up we have the NBA Championships. I was supposed to co-host them with fat boy, but when we showed up together at the studio we were told by our producer/director that only one of us could host the basketball show because they only had one microphone.

Seriously, he said that with a straight face. I was standing there waiting for the punchline, but there wasn't one. This hundred-million-dollar television station only had one microphone for the NBA Championships. It was one of the most unexpected things I've ever had said to me... ever. I was the basketball expert so I got the nod.

The other important element was the Football (soccer) World Cup was on at the same time as the NBA Championships. With soccer being the world's game they used the sports channel to cover it which is where all the station's microphones had ended up bar one and at the same time they used the news channel to show the basketball.

Los Angeles

And that's how I found myself anchoring the news desk at that instant. The picture dramatically switched from a mere basketball game to former all-round nice guy from the Naked Gun series O.J. Simpson hurtling down the freeway, in a white Bronco-holding a gun to his head-with a gaggle of squad cars in hot pursuit!

It took all my willpower not to scream out: "Holy fucking hell!"

One instant the television screen was filled with the frame of the Knicks' seven-foot center Patrick Ewing going head to head with the Rockets 6'11" Nigerian center Akeem Olajiwon. Then we were watching live from a helicopter news crew as they chased O.J. up the freeway. My mind was racing - here was the former athlete who was a household name in the States but mostly known in New Zealand only as the actor from the Naked Gun movie series.

I swallowed hard, held onto my composure on the outside and worked from memory. O.J. was from San Francisco, I explained, and had played football at San Francisco City College before moving on to USC (University of Southern California) where he won the Heisman trophy as a symbol of the nation's greatest collegiate player. I kept talking as I and the audience took in these bizarre images of what looked like the entire police force of Los Angeles chasing this lone vehicle. I continued with my potted biography of the football star who had joined the professional ranks playing for the Buffalo Bills where he continued to set records. I mentioned, of course, that many would recognize him from a series of light-hearted movies starring Leslie Nielson and Priscilla Presley. While O.J. was tearing through L.A. with a Christmas tree of lights following his every move, people were cheering from overhead bridges and from the side of the road. It was as if O.J. was playing a game of football.

'Go, O.J. Go!'

I breathlessly described how O.J. also featured in a series of Hertz commercials with the legendary golfer Arnold Palmer.
'Go, O.J. Go!'

In short, I exhorted, Orenthal James Simpson was an American icon.

'Go, O.J. Go! '

All the while I continued to talk up a storm about O.J. Simpson, football and America. Finally, the chased ended and we watched O.J. sitting in his white Bronco in the driveway of his wealthy estate in Brentwood, threatening to commit suicide. Bizarrely, as I tried to describe what was happening, I saw the small inset box in the bottom right corner of the television screen. It was still showing every move of the NBA championship game. The director decided O.J. had been sitting still too long. The body banging action of the basketball took the main portion of the screen while O.J.'s misery was confined to the tiny panel in the corner where he sat in his matchbox Bronco.

The director switched from basketball to O.J. and back again. The network kept repeating this madness until we eventually settled on a view of O.J.Simpson large as life sitting in his Bronco in his driveway threatening to end his life. We watched and waited. I filled in with random bits of information.

'If you've just tuned in ... blah, blah, blah ...'

Nothing appeared to be happening. It was getting more difficult to fill the silences. The NBA game was slipping away and I suggested to my director that maybe we should switch back to the game.

'John, we're staying with O.J.,' he whispered through my earpiece.

'The game's only got five minutes to go.'

'We're not leaving O.J.'

'How about just a quick update on the game?'

'Listen, John!' my director fairly screamed, 'I'm not going to be the only director in the world to miss O.J. Simpson shooting himself in the head live on worldwide television!'

'Oh.'

Gridiron

Sky TV in the early days was like TV Disneyland where we got to play with a multi-million-dollar toy-box full of tape machines, cameras, microphones and computerized digital effects boxes. It was a giant electronic Lego set for big kids. Sky's biggest production that first year was the Superbowl. Five solid hours of live broadcast. I'd been fronting the NFL broadcasts all season. Our boss called a pre-production meeting to discuss the approach to the show. His first announcement knocked me cross-eyed. Howdy Doody, my co-anchor, would front the show and I would be his sidekick. I must have sat stunned for a while. Then I was on my feet. It was like the scene from The Exorcist when people realize Pazuzu's got control of Linda Blair's vocal chords.

I have no idea what I really said, but I'm sure it was along these lines:

'That's the dumbest fucking thing I've ever heard! Fat Boy here doesn't know shit about American football... He calls it gridiron, for Christ's sake. I'm no expert, but I know enough to front the thing with a real expert. You do it with him and all you're going to get is five hours of how different it is from rugby. It's the biggest event in the American sporting year and you're going to turn it into a quaint curiosity!'

Everybody in the room developed this sudden interest in their feet, and I stood there wondering: 'Who said that?'

Had I actually called him Fat Boy, my other pet name for Howdy Doody? The boss sat still, looking at me for an awful long time. I thought I was a goner for sure. Then he said: 'You know, you're probably right. You front it. Get yourself an expert guest, preferably somebody who's actually played the game.'

Whew! But now I had to come up with the goods after I shot off my big mouth. We were as ready as we could be without knowing exactly what ABC were going to send us over the wire. There was one area where I felt rock solid. Luckily, I discovered someone who had played the game before on a professional level. My expert guest was Ricky Ellison. He had been born in New Zealand but moved to the United States when he was eight. He grew up to be your classic All American. He played his collegiate ball at USC and was then drafted by the San Francisco 49'ers. He played with Joe Montana and Jerry Rice. He not only played with them, he won Superbowl rings with them. I guess you could say I had found myself an expert 'expert.' But, I still had to drive the show.

On the big day we started to receive the signal from America and of course, it was nothing like we rehearsed. The durations of the commercial breaks were all wrong. We were constantly scrambling to cover ourselves. But the show went like a dream. Fronting a television show usually requires split brain activity, as you try to act casual on air, yakking away while listening to a voice giving directions in your ear.

But my director's voice wasn't in my ear. It was right there in my head, as warm and comfortable as my own thoughts. Every time he told me the three-minute break was to be a 60-second one and I had to quickly wrap it up and throw back to the game or that the 30-second one was now going to be five minutes, it felt like my own decision. 'What the heck, I think I'll shoot the breeze with Ricky a bit longer.'

It was the best, most exhilarating ride in the circus, and it was all over way too early. I buzzed for days afterwards. You can definitely get hooked on that stuff. It was like being on one of those reality shows where you get to do the weird and wacky things you've hitherto only dreamed of doing. Only this was for real. I was actually doing this for a living.

Comment: There is a world of difference between being the host of a live television show and being the side kick expert as I was for most of the basketball games we covered. As a side kick you can just relax and wait for the host to fire a few questions your way... no sweat. But as the host you have to drive the entire show... keep it moving along... describe the action... ask your expert questions and throw to commercials. Phew! This Super Bowl was a tough gig for me as this was my first time out of the barn in hosting a major league show. I distinctly remember the opening of the Super Bowl... I ran through the usual, "Good evening and welcome to the 25th Super Bowl between the New York Giants and the Buffalo Bills."

Then and I mean right then the enormity of the occasion hit me like a ton of bricks and I momentarily lost it... I had no idea what to say next... I literally froze... I can't even describe what I was feeling... and right about now anyone who has ever worked in television will just say how in the hell could that happen it's all there on your autocue. Nope! In the early days of Sky we had no autocue... we all worked from memory and remember this was a five hour live show so I had a ton of shit to memorize. My director (aka Jimmy Stewart) the head of sport... that's how big this production was - the head honcho was in charge of it - he instantly sensed that I was in panic mode... so in the calmest voice imaginable in my ear piece he suggested I go into the strengths and weaknesses of each team... and voila, I was off to the races and never looked back. Thank-you!

Comment Two: I asked my director how he knew I was in trouble and he merely replied, "Experience John... experience."

The Game of Life
Something strange happened to me right before I did my first live televised Sunday afternoon sports show. I was sitting at my presentation desk in the studio with the lights down, just before going to air. The silence enveloped me as the buzz of activity ceased and as I was hanging suspended in that moment, two things happened. Firstly, there's a moment in Peter Schaeffer's play 'Equus' where the lead character, this kid finally tells the psychiatrist what he already knew. In the context of the play it hits with a jolt because it's the first time the kid has allowed any honesty at all. Three words: "It was sexy."

The kid's talking about the first time he rode a horse, but I'm talking about every time I'm sitting in a television studio just before going to air. In that silence when the lights go down, and the buzz of everyone else running around frantically has stopped and you're hanging suspended in those moments all to yourself, it's incredibly sexy. Maybe it's having all that technology focused on you. I don't know? And I never really wanted to know. Like a fairy tale, if you know the truth maybe the magic might stop happening. And secondly, suddenly I was struck by how very American I was. How different I was. Surrounded by all these foreigners I suddenly felt naked and exposed. Everything was focused on me and I was about to burst into the living rooms of this nation. And suddenly out of nowhere I had this mini panic attack of self-doubt. Great timing. But isn't life like that? At the most inopportune times we get hit with the fear of failure. What to do? Time was short and I had absolutely nowhere to run so I did what I always do in those situations, I gave myself a pep talk. In my mind I drew a line between myself and the audience. It's nothing more than positive thinking.

But the key is to actually do it. Talk to yourself. Pump yourself up:

"Come on, John, you can do this. Whaddaya they know? They've got no idea what you're on about or what you can do. You've prepared for this, you know what you're doing, so just do it. Have some fun and do your thing. Worry about yourself not them."

This self-belief doesn't just come out of thin air. It's predicated on my philosophy of what I think of the game of life. Life is like theater-in-the-round and that can be very intimidating. Nobody likes to feel like a fool but that's easy to do, so easy because nobody is ever the hero all the time. Like the song says at some time everybody plays the fool. One of the things I try to do is to be less self-conscious and to play the game as hard and as well as I can, and if I make a mistake and look foolish in front of family and friends, so what.

Life is a game of mistakes. Mistakes are accepted, so much so that if you play it without making a mistake you're not normal. You're not trying. You're not pushing yourself. You're not expanding your comfort zone. And as there is no such thing as standing still you are actually going backwards.

So even when you've got a lot of people around watching you closely and even though you may feel like a fool once in a while, relax and feel okay about it, it's all part of the game. After all, whoever learned to walk without falling down? For just as everyone, sooner or later becomes a fool playing the game of life so too do they become a hero, sooner or later.

It all comes down to your 'attitude' no matter how much or how little talent (most people usually sell themselves short) you think you may possess, the one thing you can do in life is 'hustle.' Apply yourself to the task at hand. That's the funny thing about hustling it doesn't require any skill, talent or brains. Hustle and you'd be surprised at just how smart you really are.

The P Word
I've worked for all three national television stations in New Zealand and have had a rip roaring time at all of them in my own unique way. For instance my first job as a basketball commentator was on 5 June 1987 at Madgwick Stadium, Wellington - Saints versus Hawkes Bay. I was the color guy and TVNZ (Television New Zealand) broadcasting icon Peter Williams would be calling the game. During the game one of the Saints players was getting roughed up pretty good so I decided to share this knowledge with the audience at home and inadvertently mentioned urine: "Uh, oh, looks like Gilbert Gordon's getting pissed off," I said.

Suddenly everything was silent. The crackle of voices in the cans stopped dead. Peter lost his casual demeanor and stared at me, horrified. Oowah, John said the P Word. No doubt about it, this was a live broadcast, I'd gone out into the living rooms of the nation with wee-wee on my lips. Suddenly the opportunity to have a one-broadcast television career knocked loudly at the door. On the Monday, Bill McCarthy who was the head of sport at TVNZ called me into his office to tell me that he liked the broadcast. "But, John, you can't say 'piss' on television. Little old ladies in the South Island will be shocked." Oh, Ok. Got it.

Belly Up
And then over at TV3... which is called TV3 because TVNZ has two channels 1 & 2... ha these folks can certainly count. The very first day I started at TV3 the station went belly up. It didn't have the cash to pay its debtors so it was in the hands of the Receiver. I didn't know this when I was having a grand posh lunch meeting with the TV3 producers and director of the new show that I was going to be fronting. We're talking top shelf here Champagne... oysters... the works including a TV3 taxi chit to get home. On the taxi-ride home the driver is listening to the radio when there's a big newsflash TV3 is bankrupt. Then the cab radio sparks up with its own newsflash: Drivers are warned not to take any TV3 taxi chits. Great. I've got about a buck fifty in my pocket and a worthless taxi chit. I actually had to go and knock on my neighbour's door and borrow the money to pay the taxi. Big shot television personality indeed!

Australia
My habit of applying for jobs on impulse had usually paid off, but in Australia it almost got me deported. I had taken a basketball coaching job in Australia and my employers at the South Adelaide Basketball Club had taken care of the immigration paperwork that allowed me to get a work visa. A third of the way through my first season, I noticed an ad in the paper for the position of a Sports Administrator at Flinders University in Adelaide. Without hesitation, I applied and went through an exhaustive interview process and wouldn't you know it, I got the job. I quit my coaching post and took up the position at the university. My previous employers weren't happy about being deserted and alerted the immigration authorities.

The Australian Feds told me I had to leave Australia on my own volition or I would be deported. I couldn't believe they were serious even after the University went in to bat for me, but they were, and I found myself back in New Zealand penniless.

Comment: I remember thinking at the time..."Well, fuck them! I'll just stay and see what happens." But, the head of my department told me that a deportation follows you everywhere and can lead to travel complications down the road. Ah, good point. I left.

White Lab Coat

I was broke so I walked into a joint called The Boss Habit Control Centre and talked myself into a job right on the spot. This place had scam written all over it. I should have known something was up when they asked me to get as much of a cash advance as I could from each sucker - oops, I mean client.

This outfit claimed you could successfully change your life and your future simply by changing your mind. Name a phobia, any phobia and they had a program to fix it. They could even do a Ponce de Leon number on you by slowing down the ageing process. The miracle cure for all this was something called 'Subliminal Cybernetics', or 'Brainwashing' in layman's terms, transmitting messages below the threshold of consciousness. Some companies used to do this kind of thing in movie theatres in the United States in the 1950s. They'd flash up images of deserts that only your subconscious could detect during the ad breaks and all of a sudden you'd be dying of thirst and have to make a trip to the snack stand.

Three decades later, we were peddling the same type of mind tricks. The taped cassettes we sold had a babbling brook soundtrack with the hidden Subliminal Cybernetic message underneath.

I tried to find out what these secret messages were but that was like trying to crack the Colonel's secret recipe of 11 herbs and spices for his Kentucky Fried Chicken.

The beauty of this whole operation was that the only qualifications you appeared to need to be an instant expert was the ability to wear a white lab coat with authority: Paging Dr Dybvig.

I worked at the Boss Centre for three months until one fine Monday morning when I arrived at the office and everything was missing - the people, the furniture and the managing director.

While others were shocked at losing their jobs, I was over it in milliseconds. If I was good at getting jobs, I could be even better at giving them up.

Steel

Sometimes, I would be attracted to go for a job for no other reason than I was not in the least bit qualified to do it. Just to let you know how farcical I could get, on another occasion when I went home to visit my mother I applied for a senior sales position selling steel for a small plant in the San Francisco Bay Area. Steel for Christ's sake! Not that I knew the first thing about steel. I thought if I got a job, it might settle me down. I was looking for an instant foundation to my life, an instant solution that would wipe out a decade of restlessness.

And yes, I sweet talked my way into that position too. When the president of the company called to let me know I had the job I just rolled my eyes, really? I immediately went into panic mode and made up some ridiculous excuse why I couldn't take up the position. Steel salesman, come on get a grip.

Comment: When the president of the company called me with the good news - my immediate thought was... "Man I must be one helluva a persuasive talker" - like the saying goes 'I bet at that time I could sell snow to Eskimos'!?!" I literally knew zero about steel or steel components and yet I had convinced this guy that I could represent his company and sell his steel. Wow! That's amazing and ridiculous at the same time.

Red Sauce

Even when I was a kid I hustled and this one definitely didn't pan out... IN FACT IT GOT ME FIRED! My dad knew the owner of Larry Lorenzo's Pizza restaurant which was in our neighbourhood so he got me a job there when I was 16 washing dishes. So I'm working at this pizza joint and some nights it's a bit slow so one night I've got the kitchen all squared away and I'm standing around twiddling my thumbs... so for some reason - like who really knows what goes on in the mind of a 16-year-old adolescent - I walk into the walk-in ice-box and have a good look around... I noticed several huge pots with red sauce in them but all the pots only have a little bit of sauce in them... so hell I think to myself that's a waste having all these pots in here nearly empty I'll fix that... I'll straighten this situation up... so I grab all the pots and pour all the red sauce into one pot and then I wash all the other pots thinking to myself job well done!

Well... it didn't quite work out that way... Larry Lorenzo goes into the walk-in to get some sauce for one of his dishes and he literally rushes out screaming and clutching his head... "Oh Mamma Mia... non...non...non!"

He then spies me in the back of the kitchen next to all those huge gleaming clean pots and again he's suddenly having another heart attack... he marches up to me and exclaims - "I hadda six different delicious sauces and now I hava all the sauces in one mixed up crazy sauce in one pot..." and he smacks his forehead with the palm of his hand. Larry at this point was actually redder than his red sauces.

All I can say is nobody told me that they were all different sauces... whadda I know about flavors and spices and herbs and all that cooking nonsense... they just looked all red to me...

When I got home my dad told me that Larry Lorenzo had terminated my job. Doh!

Dreams

For all my impulsiveness, I have managed to show great patience with respect to one job. I waited for 53 years to get it. When I was 10, I wanted to be a newspaper delivery boy, mainly because it always looked so cool in the movies and television shows and the kid delivering the papers seem to be having so much fun. Unfortunately I never got the chance to do it as a kid. Flash forward 53 years and my 11-year-old son got a job delivering the local newspaper in our neighborhood. At first, I would trail after him in the car and every so often he'd load up again with papers and carry on. Then he got to the point where he could carry all the papers by himself and he delivered them riding his scooter.

However, when he started high school it all became too much and he told me he didn't have time to do the job anymore. That was fine with me as I'd rather have him concentrating on his school activities. But, instead of cancelling his route I decided to take it over so I became a 63-year-old with a paper route. The money still went into my son's account... but I enjoyed the 30-minute walk around the neighborhood, finally doing a job that gave me some light exercise and the chance to collect my thoughts. I guess it's never too late to fulfill your dreams!

Comment: However I didn't get to do the one thing I really wanted - being a competitive guy I always wanted to see how many papers I could throw over the front yards to land on the porches. But, instead for this route I just placed each paper in the mail boxes out front... boring!

Writing and Ranting

I got my start in the media through newspapers. I was invited to write a weekly basketball column for one of New Zealand's biggest newspapers. I got the column on the basis of being a hot shot American in the sport. New Zealand like the rest of the world has this fickle love/hate relationship with America and Americans. I don't know what it is, our sense of humor, our air of freedom, Disneyland or what, but our point of view on life makes us distinctly different from everyone else roaming the planet.

It's a double-edged sword - on the one hand America to antipodean New Zealand is the big kid on the block. World class. Anything or anyone from America must be the real deal. I evolved into a West Coast version of P.J. O'Rourke and penned my name to any number of zany newspaper columns. I can literally hear my English teachers moaning and turning over in their graves. How can this be? That lunkhead writes for a living. Yes. Yes, I do. But on the flip side of the coin they also have this deep-seated perception that we pilgrims are a bit too crass and vulgar, too rich, too loud, and that we have no sense of ceremony. Hard to argue with that as most of it is true.

Sitting on their Asses
I quickly discovered that writing those columns gave me the opportunity to be my natural sarcastic self. And that I had a natural talent for standing on the toes of New Zealanders.

I didn't speak or write English. I spoke and wrote American. I was blunt, to the point, and took no prisoners. For example: During the 1984 Los Angeles Olympics future world heavyweight champion Evander Holyfield was disqualified for hitting New Zealand boxer Kevin Barry who was constantly holding on to him after the bell. At least that's the way the judges saw it and we all know how corrupt Olympic boxing judges are. Just ask Roy Jones.

Kevin Barry took home the silver medal by default. Holyfield's punch, late or not, had knocked Barry out (actually it knocked him into another universe) and under Olympic rules Barry couldn't fight in the final. All of New Zealand was jumping for joy over this historic win. Me, I felt like puking. Barry didn't belong in the same ring with the class of Holyfield. I gave the country a little zing in my next column pointing out that all of the Kiwi competitors who'd won Olympic medals for New Zealand had done so whilst sitting on their asses: Equestrian, yachting, rowing and even their stalwart boxer Kevin Barry.

Well, that column certainly hit a nerve. I was invited to step outside by any number of patriotic young Kiwis who were keen to put me on my ass. Did that slow me down... hell no, I started my next column with this line: New Zealanders are called 'Kiwis' after their national bird, a flightless nocturnal creature. The Kiwi can't fly, can't see and is nearly extinct. Give me the majestic Eagle any day. Gawd bless America!

Printing

I was the world's most unlikely columnist. When I say I wasn't a writer, I'm not kidding. I couldn't type. My handwriting was so bad I couldn't read it myself. I printed every word, laboriously forming every word with the concentration of a four-year-old who has just discovered crayons. And forget about punctuation; the only punctuation I could handle was the dash. I'd carefully print my first thought, throw in a dash and scrawl out thought number two. My copy looked like a second-grader's composition on 'My Weekend,' minus the stick figures. I can't draw. I sweated over my first column like it was my first newborn. I developed a callous on my finger. My hand curled up into an arthritic claw. Why? Because all of the sweet, clear thoughts I had in my head turned into a big splodge of crap on the page. I was amazed by that. Why was writing so hard?

I finally got my first piece done and ran it by my neighbor. The reason I went to see him was because he was a writer. A professional writer. He actually wrote for a living. And he was a damn nice guy.

I found him in his garden and offered up my two wrinkled pages of childish scrawl linked by dashes. He looked over my scrawl, taking an excruciatingly long time to consider what I'd written. He rubbed his chin and thought some more. As he processed his thinking, I hopped from one foot to the other in anticipation.

Finally, he asked me if I wanted a drink. Huh? New Zealanders have a terrific sense of the occasion (any will do) and there's not a single situation they won't willingly drink to.

'Hell, yes, I want a drink.'

On the Road

He began talking about stream-of-consciousness writers. He told me about Jack Kerouac, Allen Ginsberg and Gregory Corso and all those beat guys. He loaned me an armful of books. He told me the way I wrote was distantly related to their style and I had something I could work on. Hell, I thought all I had to do was scribble a few paragraphs about basketball. 'Keep working on it, John,' he said warmly. 'Get straight to the point, keep it tight and don't ramble. It'll work out.' I'd written two pathetic pages and suddenly my neighbor had me on the road with the 'dharma bums.' Heavy duty motivation, indeed. But that was all I needed; his encouragement was enough to get me started. Besides, I've always felt that good intentions fueled by will-power could become actualities. You just had to want to be a writer badly enough and - presto!

Maybe I should revise my use of the word 'presto'. My writing career didn't happen overnight, but it did happen. When hard slog is the only way forward, pig-headedness can be a useful asset. I slogged. I called on my pig-headed nature. Every week for the next six years, I turned in my ugly, crabbed pages to the sports editor at the newspaper. I was still printing the words by hand, but now I was fairly fast and you could've opened beer bottles on my calloused knuckle. The columns became popular with readers and I got the opportunity to write fifteen-hundred-word feature articles.

It was a big moment. For the first time I felt like I had a modicum of credibility in the media. I had worked hard to get there and I was loving it. So, if I was going to be a proper writer, I would need the tools. After six years, I threw away my pencils and started to wrestle daily with my typewriter. Writing columns had taught me how to share my opinions. It helped that I was never short of an opinion.

Comment: Go ahead and think about that... I was writing columns and fifteen-hundred-word feature articles for national newspapers and yet I printed. For 6 fucking years... only in New Zealand. Once again I'm shaking my head as I write this - the crazy shit I did back in the day. Hmmmmmmmmmmm!

Radio

It seemed a natural step to get into radio. One of the things I love about radio is it's just your voice and your wits making it happen. What you're wearing or how you look have nothing to do with it. You could be stark, bollock naked holding your nuts and nobody would know or care. But, on television you've got to go through the whole make-up thing before you get to do your thing. You usually find Salvador Dali hanging out in the make-up room. They go by any number of names: Gail, Trudy, Diane, but in spirit they're all budding Salvador Dali's.

This is the routine: First you get a sponge down, face cream and powder, they always want a clean canvas. Then they trowel in the skin tone under the eyes, they paint your eyebrows, curl your lashes and gloss the old lips. You usually walk out of make-up looking like Bela Lugosi. Your own mother wouldn't recognize you. And clothes, on TV people believe what you wear as much as what you say. I'm one of those guys who looks rumpled no matter what I'm wearing.

Big Ball News

My radio career began with a basketball comment piece on a show I created called: Big Ball News. This show was all about what was happening in the basketball world in Napier. While coaching in Napier I had to run everything I did by a group of women.

There aren't enough trees in this world to begin to explain how frustrating that was. So one night on my radio spot I just let it all hang out with this burning question: "I don't know, maybe this is the way things are done in New Zealand. Do big business houses make elaborate plans on how to run their business and then ask the janitor to come in and vote on it? I was employed as a professional basketball coach so why bring out an expert in his field, namely me, and then have housewives make the decisions?"

OOOOOOOhhhhh, doggie! That certainly started a bun fight. The station manager loved it. The switchboard lit up like a Christmas tree.

That little blurb taught me the importance of the media and the power of radio in particular. Nothing I said was new to them. I'd said it to their faces often enough. But saying it in public was a whole new ballgame.

Annus Horriblus

The same happened up in Auckland on the city's number one radio station where I had landed a comment spot every week. The mayor had come out in the paper saying she'd be receiving less Japanese dignitaries because so many came to see her and they took up too much of her valuable time.

Well, what can you say, that's the kind of stuff I live on. I did an ongoing bowing gag on my show about how time consuming all that bowing was: They bow and then you bow, which prompts them to bow and of course you've got to bow back so the big question is, when do you stop bowing?

City Hall went berserk! The mayor's office demanded a transcript of the tape and a few days later I received a letter from the mayor herself reminding me that a two-bit foreign scumbag like me could never appreciate the wonderful, virtuous deeds she had pulled off for the city. Two pages' worth, which was longer than my piece. I think she was basically saying, "Kiss my annus horriblus" (a polite way of saying kiss my ugly ass).

Crack A Fat

Ok so one morning I'm driving over to the radio station to record my weekend commentary piece when I see a billboard with a huge picture of a smiling Peter Fatialofa and underneath his picture it says: The Aussies can't crack a Fat.... Peter's nick name was Fats... he played rugby for Auckland and they were about to play Australia so I knew there was a play on words here involving Peter and the Aussies but I'd never heard that expression before so when I got to the radio station I asked the guys in the sports room what that meant...

First off they all started laughing and then they told me that 'cracking a fat' was Aussie slang for getting a boner... a hard-on... and I started laughing as well - very clever I thought... well this was right in my wheelhouse... so I re-did my commentary piece right then and there which involved that billboard message and the various ways sportsmen could crack a fat... it was a ripper and everybody in the sports department were laughing their asses off...

All, that is, save one... the manager of the station, a real straight lace type of guy, heard my recorded piece and marched up to my desk and emphatically declared no way my piece was going to air... I protested that it was on a gigantic billboard in Auckland... but that didn't hold any sway with Mr. Righteous... he just said get writing.

That episode reminded me of the time a publisher in Auckland refused to publish my book Technical Foul because I had a chapter called - Ego Fuck... the Puritans would have been happy with this lot.

My Very Own Show
I wasn't making a lot of friends, but people liked my stuff. Eventually I graduated from my comment pieces to having my own sports show: 'Sports Talk with John Dybvig'.

This was a bit spooky, not only did I have to contend with the mechanics of running a radio show, like working the switchboard, handling the phones, doing the weather round-up and throwing to commercials, but I had to cover sports like rugby, cricket, soccer, netball and rugby league, which were as foreign to me as I was to them. I never set myself up as an expert in any field (except maybe basketball).

I figured my best bet was to be what I was - an interested sports guy. Since the audience was made up of interested sports guys, I just asked the questions that interested me. It seemed to work.

Mother of all Names
One night all hell broke loose as I was just settling in and checking out the panel when one of the stations reporters rushed in and handed me the just released line up for the new All Black team. That may not sound like a big deal but in New Zealand the naming of their national rugby team is akin to Moses trekking down Mount Sinai and releasing the Ten Commandments. The pressure was on this American tin horn. My main problem was the names had been written down hurriedly with a blunt pencil on what looked like soggy toilet paper. Most of the names looked like a snail trail. I chewed them into a list of indecipherable grunts, hiccups and squeaks until I came to the mother of all names to pronounce - Va'aiga Tuigamala. I just sat there and stared at it for a few seconds (an eternity in radio) and finally I just said: "Hey guys, I can't crack this one so I'm just gonna spell it"... and that's what I did. Probably the first time an All Black had his name spelled out on National Radio.

Politics
One day out of the blue as so often happens to me I was offered a job on Radio Live, a talk network to discuss all things American - I didn't have to do an interview or anything really but just show up and the job was mine. Perfect.

I called my show: John Dybvig's Letter from America (of course I stole this from Alistair Cooke). I did occasionally talk about the odd ball things happening in America, but 99 per cent of my show was all about American politics. Now I had the chance to explain the complex layers of the American Government to everyday New Zealanders.

I was educating them but I also learned a lot myself. It was kind of like taking my old civics classes all over again.

I started this show when George W. Bush was starting his second term and on through the Obama years and loved every minute of it.

Even though I wasn't a George Bush fan I respected the office of President of the United States and never dissed George personally or the office. I was a huge fan of Obama but still didn't agree with all his policies... for instance the collateral damage from drone attacks bothered me greatly and I discussed this on my show.

Comment: I'm telling you sometimes I just live in a fog. Sometimes I just don't have a fucking clue as to what's going on. So I get the job at Radio Live and I'm teamed up with Graeme Hill who I had previously worked with at Radio sport for a number of years.

My first day on the job I walk into the station and hook up with Graeme who's sitting in an office talking with some dude. I walk in and yell out in my customary manner: "how you guys doin'... you good!?!" Anyway I take a seat and the other dude doesn't bother to introduce himself which is no big deal and we're all chatting away about this and about that... when I say to the stranger to me in the office: "Hey man, whudaya you do at the station?" He looks at me with a smirk and says - "Well, for one thing I hired you." Yeah, you got it... the guy was the boss... he ran the station. Sometimes I just kill myself.

Comment Zero: Wow... WTF... what's up with a comment zero? Well, I called this comment zero because it's the only comment in the book that comes before the story... all the rest come after the story... but seeing as Trump is such a bewildering topic that I've constantly hemmed and hawed over while writing this book I think the label fits. Originally for this book I had written an entire chapter on Trump... but when I took a step back and looked at it I decided that this chapter was way... way too dark, mean and nasty and it just kept repeating itself as to what a dolt this guy was... kind of like smashing an ant with a sledge hammer over and over... but more importantly it was not in the spirit of my book so I left it out...

But then again that's exactly how I see Trump so whaddya gonna do? So here I am in a conundrum what to do... I mean it would be ridiculous to just ignore him after all I covered him for my show 'Letter from America' on radio for over four years... so instead of an entire chapter I have condensed my thoughts into this piece.

I chose my words and events very carefully I squeezed the words in because there are volumes and volumes of Trump transgressions that you could write about... but I'll leave that to the scholars whom I'm sure will be writing enough books about this period to make a complete set of the Encyclopedia Britannica (wow - you sure don't hear about them anymore - we used to have a complete set in my house when I was a youngster. Instead of going to Google in those days you went to your Encyclopedia Britannica).

Trump is the modern day version of P.T. Barnum the ultimate con artist... a personality bigger than life and sure you'll get a following with that kind of persona... hell Dr. Phil has a following... but I think you'll get the message that I'm not a Trump fan... to me he's the antithesis of what America stands for.

Trump
I really did love doing my show about America because it kept me in touch with my homeland... but I stopped loving it when Trump came on the scene. I never recognized him as the President because to me he was illegitimate, a Benedict Arnold who accepted outside help from the Russians. He cheated. And probably what annoyed me the most was he only spoke to the people who voted for him - the official title of the office is: President of the United States... that's United... the whole shebang... the whole enchilada... not just President of those who voted for you. American democracy was certainly put to the test under this wannabe dictator. Never in the annuals of our history has one individual done so much damage in such a short period of time.

Observations
Ok so here we go my observations from covering Trump and his administration:

First I'd say the overwhelming notion that comes to my mind in labelling Trump in a simple sentence is: He's a pathological lying narcissist. The Washington Post had this guy lying over 30,000 times during his run...Trump's whole philosophy regarding his lies is: Who are you going to believe - ME - or your lying eyes... the frequency, degree and impact of lying in politics are now unprecedented as a result of Trump... which brings me to my major complaint about the main stream media covering Trump... just because he was the President they actually tiptoed around this jerk when he was lying straight out of the gate... the media didn't call him out on his lies for over two years... I mean come on damn it, I'm an adult and I know when some son-of-a-bitch is lying to my face - Trump's lies were the modern day example of The Emperor's New Clothes... the whole world could see right through him it was plain as day he was constantly lying right through his teeth... it was laughable... and yet these journalists... these big shot reporters were just so damn timid... I wanted to scream!!!

Below I'm just gonna highlight some of the most obvious and some of his stupidest lies:

Trump's Whoppers (Lies)

The most telling lie right from the get go: "It didn't rain on my parade" (I couldn't help myself) his inauguration...Yeah Trump kept saying it didn't rain on him during his speech and that it was really sunny... when in actual fact and you can ask all the people with their umbrellas up - it did rain on him during his speech and the sun never came out period... just another stupid lie from a very stupid man... and then there were the vast empty stands and the crowd was sparse indeed... still Trump claimed the largest crowd in history... we had the photos... we had the pictures... everyone saw them... there they were and the crowd just wasn't there... people just didn't show up... the stands were empty... period... that was it... and yet Trump and his Press Secretary Sean Spicer and everyone else in his administration insisted that Trump's inauguration crowd was the biggest in history... it was just so stupid... but little did anyone realise then that 'stupidity' was going to be their calling card for the next four years...

The most dangerous lie: That Coronavirus was under control. 550,000 dead folks and counting attest to the fact it wasn't... Trump and the Republican Party have blood on their hands. So, so many of these folks simply did not have to die.

The most ridiculous lie: Sharpie-gate. Yeah Trump used a sharpie to include the State of Alabama in a hurricane's path when in actual fact it wasn't... to see him on television holding up a map and it's clear that he's used a black sharpie to draw an extra bubble around Alabama was strictly grade school stuff... and he's insisting he's right even when the National Weather service said no Alabama wasn't in the hurricane's path...

The most traditional big lie: Trump looked right down the barrel of the TV cameras and said he didn't know anything about the hush money payment to porn star Stormy Daniels... later check stubs with his signature were found in his lawyers' office made out to Stormy... and that's not to mention that there were also audio tapes of Trump discussing with his lawyer what bank accounts the money should come from...

The crazy uncle lie: Windmill noise causes cancer...nothing more to add to this utter nonsense...

The most hucksterish lie: For whatever problem there was, like National Healthcare, there was a plan that according to Trump was coming in two weeks... and, of course, no plans of any description ever came for any of the problems in two weeks or anytime really...

Stupidest lie: "My father is German, right? Was German, and born in a very wonderful place in Germany."... Trump's father Fred Trump was born in New York City...

His 'I'm winking' lie: I'll release my taxes as soon as the audit is complete. Yeah right....

Trump's most depressing lie: I won the 2020 election... which gets us down to the nitty and the gritty here...

Trump's ultimate lie...

THE BIG LIE

Trump actually said this and yeah people believed him and still believe him to this day and will probably always believe this big lie:

"IF I DON'T WIN THE ELECTION THEN IT WAS RIGGED."

Ok here we go: The FBI, Homeland Security, the United States Election Commission, over 60 Federal and State Judges, United States Attorney General William Barr, the Supreme Court and every State election official both Democratic and Republican all said the election was fair and there was absolutely zero evidence... that's zero evidence of any fraud in the 2020 Presidential election... and yet 8 out of 10 Republican voters think the election was rigged just because Trump kept repeating 'The Big Lie' without any evidence to back up his 'Big Lie' whatsoever. Zero facts to support his Big Lie!!!

So ya just gotta ask the obvious question: What the fuck is up with these people? I guess it's just as simple as Forrest Gump said: "Stupid is as stupid does"... naturally I'm shaking my head and shrugging my shoulders as I write this.

The problem with his outrageous 'Big Lie' is the Republican Party went right along with him so now the country is completely divided... these Republican Congress men and women have absolutely no shame... they are morally bankrupt. In the final analysis when all is said and done Trump doesn't care one shred about America or Americans... all he's ever cared about is himself and all his petty grievances.

Comment: I gotta say here if I was a grown adult in the United States of America today and I believed any of Trump's bullshit lies... well I mean how in the hell could you look in your children's eyes and have any self respect for yourself... when deep in your heart... deep... deep... deep lying somewhere in your sub-conscious on some level you know... you really do know that it's all been one gigantic con.

Narcissism

When I saw this it made me want to vomit!!!

Trump constantly has to have his ego massaged by everyone around him even if it's fake. Early in his term he invited the television cameras into the White House so the entire Nation could witness each member of his cabinet grovel in front of Trump and in glowing lavish praise tell him what a great leader he was... what a tremendous person he was... what character and strength he possessed... and how lucky they were under God to personally serve him and on and on ad nauseam... it was one of the most pathetic displays of total narcissistic bullshit I've ever seen.

The only saving grace was Secretary of Defense General Jim Mattis who had the balls to not talk about Trump and instead said something about the honor of serving the Constitution... and guess what happened... yeah you got it... the general didn't last long before he was booted outta there.

Alternative Facts

Instead of just lying and denying, Trump and his administration came up with Alternative Facts... yeah they said this with a straight face whenever they got caught in an obvious lie... they just made up shit and called it Alternative Facts... which to any rationally thinking person is another name for straight out lies... there is no such thing as an Alternative Fact... in fact just saying that should make you laugh out loud it's so stupid... but these people... the folks who were running the country just kept repeating 'Alternative Facts' with a straight face... a fact is a fact, period, and yet we had to live with Alternative Facts under Trump and his administration...

Death

Trump finally did it... his constant lying that he won the 2020 Presidential race in a landslide lured a young woman from San Diego, California to fly across the United States into Washington, D.C. fully believing in those relentless lies until a Capitol Hill plainclothes police officer shot her dead. 35-year-old Ashli Babbitt was an ardent supporter of Trump, and bought into his false narrative lock stock and barrel - that he lost to Joe Biden because of election fraud...

Trump used his twitter account to summon his base for the "Save America Rally," as he urged them to 'stop the steal' while Congress was going about their lawful duty in certifying Joe Biden's victory at the nation's citadel of freedom... as events unfolded Babbitt was part of a group that was trying to force its way into an area were members of Congress were taking shelter from the mob... who were screaming - "where the fuck are they... where the fuck are they." Finally the moment comes when the mob is forcefully trying to break down the barricaded door... behind that door were several plainclothes Capitol police standing with their guns drawn... the mob were unable to break the door down so instead they smashed the door's windows and that's when Ashli Babbitt made her fatal attempt to climb through - the second that she climbed through that window, she was shot dead. Trump is delusional... his supporters are delusional. This was one of the many headlines the next day:

ASHLI BABBITT, MILITARY VETERAN KILLED INSIDE U.S. CAPITOL, FOLLOWED HER BELIEF IN PRESIDENT TRUMP TO HER DEATH

Comment: People on the Trump side of the equation will say he wasn't to blame... but that is such a lame argument... Ashli Babbitt was there for only one reason and that reason was she firmly believed in Trump's lies that the election was stolen from him... if he hadn't said that repeatedly she wouldn't have been there it's as simple as that... words matter and they matter a whole lot more when you're the President of the United States.

Impeachment
The list of Presidents who have been impeached are as follows: Andrew Johnson (1868), Bill Clinton (1998), Donald Trump (2019) and wait for it... yes Donald Trump (2021)... Trump will go down as the absolute biggest loser of a President ever in the entire history of the United States...

I mean who gets impeached once let alone twice in a single term... hell he'll have a complete page all to himself... when you talk about bad Presidents... Warren G. Harding pops up or James Buchanan or Andrew Johnson... well they've all moved up a rung on the ladder... because Trump is in the hall of fame as the worst President ever all by himself... he's set a record that no one and I repeat no one will ever come close to repeating... he's in a class all by himself as a loser.. an all-time loser... a loser for life...

Breath Of Fresh Air
Wow... it's been several months now with virtually no one having to constantly listen to Trump and it's great... like a breath of fresh air. America is letting out a huge sigh of relief. But, still every now and again Trump lets out with one of his outlandish whoppers (lies)... now he's calling the insurrection on the Nation's Capitol building a gigantic San Francisco summer 'Love Fest' with everybody hugging and kissing the police and the guards and what great relationships they all had... he went on to say and I quote - "It was zero threat, right from the start... it was zero threat." But, here's the thing - there are reams and reams of very explicit video footage of the absolute violence and carnage that happened at the hands of these thugs who stormed the Capitol which went on for several hours as they vandalized and ransacked the building smashing windows and doors and anything else they could get their hands on. And yet Trump's followers will still vote for him and the Republican Party will still back him... it's an absolute tragedy on a Shakespearian scale for American Democracy.

Comment: I'll tell ya what - this entire debacle with Trump and all his lies and bullshit behaviour and all the idiotic Americans who hang on his every lie... the entire mess should be an exhibition in Ripley's Believe It or Not Odditorium... Ripley's Believe It or Not is an American franchise, founded by Robert Ripley, which deals in bizarre events so strange and unusual that people might question the claims... and believe me there's nothing stranger on this planet than Trump and his bizarre caravan of numb nut followers!

Final Comment: So let's all pray that Trump doesn't pull an Arnold Schwarzenegger: I'LL BE BACK!

Pooping Cats

Then one day, the network boss surprised me by asking if I fancied a crack at hosting a talkback show. I turned it down mainly because I hate talkback radio and I never listen to it. A few weeks later, the boss tried again, pointing out I would need to be outspoken, opinionated and never boring which he said suited me to a tee. I thought it through, this time contemplating the mysterious life forces that govern our decisions. I said I would do it. The money would help the family. Deep down, I thought I would be a natural. But my talkback role was a disaster and I hated it. As usual with almost every new job I've undertaken, I hopped into the hot seat with no training and with few clues as to what I was supposed to do. Not a huge problem for me as I was used to winging it. I spent my first show stabbing at buttons on the control board, cutting off callers before they went to air. 'Hey, where did that guy go? We'll be back in a second, folks...'

Then the calls stopped coming up. It took a while before I realised I had been giving out the wrong phone number for the station. Doh! And to top it all off my producer was a lovely young girl, but she was Chinese for crying out loud, and I couldn't understand anything she said. And just to even things up, when I bellowed at her for help in my loud American voice she couldn't understand anything I said. Talk about the Keystone cops.

I sat in the studio, wondering how I managed to land myself in situations as ridiculous as this. It was ironic that I was being paid to talk. Now, I'm a natural talker and I love to do it. This should have been my dream job. But the longer I sat behind the microphone, the less I felt like talking. The following topic was the straw that broke the camel's back: One afternoon before I left for the studio for a four-hour shift my neighbor was bemoaning all the cats in the neighborhood pooping in his garden. So innocently I opened my show with this question: "Hey guys my neighbor wants to know how he can stop the neighborhood cats from using his garden as a giant outdoor toilet?"

Wow, my switchboard immediately lit up brighter than the Eiffel Tower on a clear Parisian night. And that was it, I couldn't stop the flood of calls pouring in for the next four hours listening to people drone on and on and on about pooping cats. At one point I actually declared, "No more calls on this subject." Nobody took any notice of me as the advice for how to stop cats from pooping in your garden kept coming in unabated. One female caller sensed my apathy when calling the station.

'John, it sounds like you don't care about this very important matter?' she ventured.

'You're right. I don't care!'

Had I really said that aloud?

And thus ended my short tenure as a radio talkback host.

Comment: Literally after that show I was pooped out.

Son-of-a-Bitch
I get a call one day from the manager of the radio station I worked at... he wanted to address my swearing during my show. Specifically, he told me that a father had called him to complain that when he was listening to my show with his kids in the car I swore a certain amount of times... guy must have been an accountant he was counting how many times I swore.

My reply to my manager was to tell the son-of-a-bitch to change the channel... problem solved. The manager immediately jumped on attack and told me that that was one of the swear words this guy had counted. I scoffed and told him that calling someone a son-of-a-bitch or a dumb bastard or exclaiming out loud - gawddamnit or saying this shit isn't working was not swearing - I'm an American and that's just part of our lexicon.

Comment: But hey, I'm definitely not the Lone Ranger when it comes to swearing you Kiwis swear like truck drivers too... when I told this to a New Zealand friend he was taken back and exclaimed: "Bullshit!" I rest my case.

It's A Man's World

Having worked in the macho world of sport, I found myself in demand as a guest speaker at the sort of functions where real men ruled, and women usually brought a plate. One year, I was invited to Greymouth, in the South Island of New Zealand, to speak at their West Coast Sportsman of the Year Dinner. Sports(man) being the operative word here: It was one of the most unusual experiences I've ever had as a guest speaker. This was a men-only event, no women allowed even though one of the award nominees was a young female athlete. She wasn't invited. Talk about being misogynist these guys took it to a whole new level.

We assembled inside the high school gym for dinner which was served to us by the women. Then we men walked across the road to the St Columba Hall where jugs of beer and whisky were laid out on the tables, and we commenced to swap lies for several hours.While the women back at the gym cleaned up all the dirty dinner dishes and got dessert ready.

At the conclusion of the evening, the men all walked back across the road to be served dessert by the women. After dessert we men stood around drinking coffee while the women cleaned up after us and did the dessert dishes. I just stood there taking in this 1950's scene of the dutiful housewives reality show and really couldn't believe my eyes. Amazing really.

Rubber Chicken

Because I was constantly right in the public's faces big time with my own national newspaper column... radio show... television show... and with me barnstorming around the countryside swearing at any referee going I kept getting deluged with speaking requests. After dinner speaking was an entirely new gig for me but it was a lot of fun... I got paid and I got to meet a lot of New Zealanders.

I've been to Invercargill where it gets cold and where you can shake hands with penguins. I've been to Dunedin (cold there too), Timaru, Oamaru, Twizel (a dying town), Geraldine, Fairley, Lake Lyndon (I got lost there), Hasst (nothing there but a petrol station and a pub), Queenstown, the Milford Sounds (beautiful!), Arthur's Pass, Reefton (went down a coal mine there), Greymouth (they tried to drown me in beer there), Christchurch (won my first national championship there), Nelson (won my first Countrywide league game there), Wellington (my favorite fans there are transvestites), Porirua (never lost a game there), Hutt Valley (beat the New Zealand national team there), Dannevirke (good public toilets), Palmerston North (ordered from the stadium there), Wanganui (lived on a Marae there), New Plymouth (banned for life there), Napier (too many stories to tell there), Hastings, Hamilton, Gisborne (ate a lot of potatoes there), Tauranga, Rotorua (won $500 bucks and had a good hot soak there), Cambridge, Otahuhu (worked in the freezing works there), Auckland (beat Stan Hill and lost to big Stan there), Dargarville, Whangarei, Kaitaia, and Cape Reinga and a lot more places in between.

Here is just a sampling of the places I've spoken to:

Southland Basketball Association annual awards dinner. Ascot Park Motor Hotel. 150 men and women.

Hurley's Grand Hotel, Wanganui. The Wanganui Track and Cycle Club's annual dinner. 150 people, men and women. Dick Quax is also speaking. Before I talk someone raffles off a cartoon showing caricatures of Quax and Dybvig and it's labelled Up the Establishment. It goes for $1000.

Wakatipu Sports Club, Queenstown. It's their annual Sportsman of the year dinner. 135 men and women. Cricketer Warren Lees is also on the bill. He and I had a day of jet-boating and river rafting, compliments of the club.

Tamatea Motor Inn, Napier, Gannett Club luncheon, 125 businessmen attending. I'm introduced by the MC: "I'm sure you've heard of our guest speaker, he says, You may have read about him in the newspaper or heard him on radio or seen him on television where you rushed quickly to turn down the volume (laughter), he's wild, unpredictable, but entertaining, because unlike most of us, he's a man who speaks his mind."

Upper Hutt Sportsman of the Year dinner. The Governor-General, Sir David Beattie, and Lady Beattie are in attendance with 200 others. TVNZ sports commentator Peter Williams is compere and other guest speakers include cricketer John Morrison.

Equipage Sports Club. Tamaki Yacht Club, Auckland. 250 businessmen, among them major sponsors of sport in New Zealand.

And so it went. I considered myself a very lucky guy to be paid to travel around this fabulous country and just speak my mind. My talks were based around a form of entertainment... I usually did my Mr. Shout basketball routine... and sometimes I'd just throw out some weird shit like this – "before we get started, a couple of thoughts. The bathtub was invented in 1850, but the telephone wasn't invented until 1875. The next time you're lying in a nice relaxing way in your bathtub and the phone rings, remember that if you were taking that bath in 1850 you would have to wait 25 years to hear that phone ring... which got me what I was after a lot of puzzled looks and then I'd say, "Remember one man's telephone is another man's number" which always got me my laughs.

The other thing about being a guest speaker was you just never knew what was going to happen on the night... for instance I had more than a few guys come up to me and tell me they thought I was an asshole... and I'd always reply, "Well it's good to have an opinion."

Then in Christchurch one night at an after-dinner speech I was giving New Zealand's America's Cup effort a zing... New Zealand had challenged Dennis Conner for the Cup again, only this time they showed up in San Diego with a huge vessel, about five times the normal size of the usual America's Cup yacht. They expected Conner to follow suit with a normal boat but ya gotta laugh, Dennis Conner accepted their challenge, only he came out with a catamaran. David and Goliath in reverse. Naturally New Zealand didn't stand a snowball in hell's chance against the quick wispy catamaran. The New Zealand media went apeshit over this mismatch and the apparent skullduggery of Dirty Den. I decided to join the fray with this little ditty:

Blub, blub, blub

Here comes little old New Zealand in their big old tub.
While swoooooooooosh

There goes Conner - quick as a cat

And as Porky Pig so aptly put it

"Th-Th-Th-Th-Th-Th-Th-Th-That's all folks!"

Not the greatest line in the world, but when you're the lone solider behind enemy lines it has a tendency to stand out. Somebody threw a chair at me... helluva good throw as I had to actually scramble out of the way as it whizzed past me.

Then when I was speaking at St. Pat's High School in Wellington when I was finished I had a woman charge up to me in a furious state exclaiming that that was the most misogynist talk that she had ever heard and at almost the same time the Priest came up to me and enthusiastically exclaimed what a great talk I did... go figure.

But, the weirdest shit always happened at rugby clubs... oh what a surprise. This happened twice in the same year... at two different rugby clubs where I was the guest speaker the president of the club would introduce me to a group of young women and just nakedly announce to them right in front of me that "John could use a fuck tonight so if anyone was inclined..." I don't get easily surprised or rattled but literally: what the fuck!!!... I would quickly say, "I'm good, thanks ladies".

And of course there were plenty of jokes... I'll leave you with one of my favorites:

Question: How do you become an international long distance runner?
Answer: Sit on the toilet until your Dick Quax!

Comment One: I'm laughing out loud right now!!! I can't help it... simple shit like that just cracks me up. The day I first heard this joke I saw Quax running in my neighbourhood along the waterfront in Mission Bay so I jumped up and ran out the door and excitedly told him his joke... the look of disbelief on his face was brilliant... listen mate he said - "I've heard that joke a million and one times". Personally I thought it was very cool to have a joke named after you... to me it's a testament to what a great runner Dick was. On a side note: I used to run in Cornwall Park and one day I bumped into John Walker and Dick Quax who told me they were going for a casual jog and I was welcome to join them. I knew John and Dick having done some after-dinner speaking with both of them. Cool, I thought, two world class runners and a plodder (me). It may have been a casual jog to these world champions but to me it was like an all-out sprint. And the thing is they really were very casual in their movements it looked so effortless on their part - like they were just gliding over the ground while I was grunting and straining every muscle in my body to barely keep up... eventually I slowed up to a casual crawl huffing and puffing and told the boys to carry on and I'd catch up with them in about a week - that's how fast these guys were moving.

Comment: Dick Quax died of cancer in Auckland on May 28th 2018, aged 70.

Comment Two: Of course like all things I just charged into public speaking not having a clue as to what I was doing. When I started to get more and more requests I decided that I needed to up my game so I went to see one of New Zealand's doyen's of the speaking circuit Phil Gifford or as he was more commonly known in those days - Loosehead Len. Phil was very gracious with his time and gave me some great advice on how to deliver an after dinner address: He told me that you had to be funny and entertaining but just as important was to leave the audience with some substance of who you are as a person. And then we spent some time organising my thoughts into a coherent pattern... so thanks Phil.

Comment Three: It's called the Rubber Chicken circuit because that's usually what you get for dinner because it's cheap.

Grizz

My penchant for controversy made me easy fodder for any journalist in search of a headline. I got a call from the editor of Rugby News, the country's biggest sports publication. He asked if I would like to write an opinion piece on the selection of the next All Black coach.

'I don't know if you know anything about rugby,' he ventured.

As if that would stop me.

'No problem, buddy. I don't need to know anything to have an opinion,' I assured him.

Two guys were going for the job, and they had divided public opinion and support. Aucklander John Hart was a corporate type, a thinker who talked about strategy and goal-setting and setting benchmarks. His rival was Alex Wyllie, a Christchurch-born farmer whose nickname was Grizz and who was known for being hard-nosed and physically solid. How important is rugby in New Zealand? Rugby is New Zealand's national game and is taken so seriously that when their national team known as the All Blacks (they play in all black uniforms) lose it's reported in the news with all the gravity of Plato announcing the death of Socrates.

Left Nut

Rugby players are the absolute toughest athletes in the known universe. Compared to rugby, every other macho sport is like kissing your sister. I know, I know. America's NFL is tough and brutal but I doubt any player in that league - even the legendary fiercely unrelenting Dick Butkus - would have done what undefeated All Black captain Buck Shelford did as a matter of course. As a player, Buck was one tough son-of-a-bitch... you wanna know how tough? In one game against France he had his left testicle ripped right out of his scrotum... Owwwwww! Did Buck faint? Nah! Was he carried off the field on a stretcher? Nah! With blood gushing from his mouth - because he had also lost four teeth - he took his team into the dressing room for a half-time team talk. While he addressed his players, he calmly told the physio to put his ball back in its sack and stitch it up. His players hung on every word, their eyes fixed on Buck's mouth and not once veering to the medic's needle and thread. It kinda sheds new light on that old expression, 'I'd give my left nut for...'

NASA

Rugby's tough image starts with the uniform. With American football, the uniform is all about state of the art technology. When fully dressed for a game an American football player looks like he's wearing a NASA spacesuit and is about to go for a walk on the moon.

When a rugby player is ready to play there's no helmet, no jumbo shoulder pads, no elbow pads, no hip pads, no thigh pads, no knee pads - just skin and bone. Rugby players go to war naked. Fully dressed for a game of rugby - rugby players look like they're going down to the beach to play touch football.

Barbed Wire

By far the strangest sports event I have ever seen was a rugby contest between the Maori All Blacks and the South African Springboks in 1981. At the time, most of the world was boycotting South African sporting teams and governments were boycotting the whole of South Africa for its inhuman treatment of blacks.

New Zealand's government had decided it shouldn't interfere with people's rights to play sport and they refused to stop the rugby-mad South Africans from touring. New Zealand found itself engaged in a civil war. On the one side, the rugby purists argued that sport and politics don't mix. On the opposite side of the fence were the protesters who argued that by engaging in sport, especially a sport like rugby which was so important to both countries, New Zealand was in essence supporting apartheid. Both sides were grimly determined - one to see the games go ahead, the other to see the tour brought to an end.

The Maori All Blacks versus the South African Springboks game was held in Napier, a serene setting for a cauldron of passion. I lived out by the airport and on the day of the game I watched in fascination as seven planes landed in succession and out marched hundreds and hundreds of men in full riot gear. The streets leading to the stadium were barricaded with huge metal garbage dumpsters manned by security guards. Everybody going to the game was given a full body search at the stadium, and I mean full.

But more surprises were in store inside the stadium. The entire field was ringed by a ten-foot-high razor barbed wire fence. I had never seen anything like it and I fully don't ever expect to see it again. It was like a giant cage-fighting arena, more like a scene from the 1981 movie Victory starring Sylvester Stallone, Michael Caine and Pele about prisoners in a WWII camp about to play the Nazi guards in a game of soccer. Outside the fence, the riot police I had seen earlier at the airport, stood an arm's length apart around the entire field.

They faced the crowd, not the pitch. They weren't smiling.

Comment: I'm a sports guy thru and thru but sports was the last thing on my mind that day. I went to that game because I knew it was going to be an extraordinary event. Politics surrounded and consumed this contest - I went for the real life drama of the occasion and it certainly didn't disappoint.

Bombs Away
In the final international game of that tour, one protester took to the air, flying a small Cessna plane above Auckland's Eden Park and dropping flour bombs onto the pitch, hitting a few of the players. At another match, at Hamilton, demonstrators invaded the pitch, refused to leave and forced the cancellation of the game. The stand-off between those involved in the 1981 Springbok tour divided families and ended friendships. Some All Blacks refused to play while the wife of another player lay down on a freeway, trying to halt the team bus her husband was on.

Who said New Zealanders were a passionless people?

Comment: That tour had everything: riots, marches, fields ringed with barbed wire, protesters with cracked heads pouring blood in the streets and riot police everywhere in full riot gear...and yes even flour bombs dropped from a plane onto the field of play. That, my friends, was no simple rugby tour - it was a display of wills... ideals... and life itself.

Back to Grizz
I explain all this about rugby, and the part it plays in the lives of the New Zealand people, so you'll understand why I should never have agreed to write my column about the relative merits of John Hart and Alex Wyllie. I should have left well enough alone. I wrote what I thought was a beautifully-worded, well thought-out and logical piece explaining why the innovative thinker would be far better for the future of the game. I argued that a has-been tough-nut called Grizz should be left to roam with the other dinosaurs. In reality, I really knew next to nothing about this guy, but had heard he had a reputation for being something of a knuckle-headed caveman.

Naturally, my American sarcastic side rose to the surface as I added this flippant off-the-cuff comment to the bottom of my piece:

'PS: Please don't hit me, Grizz.'

For the life of me, I still can't explain why I wrote that line. Like so many things in my life, I just did it without thinking. The magazine hit the streets and in the days following, I received a variety of feedback ranging from 'well done' to 'why don't you stick to what you know?' Someone gave me the standard 'go home, Yank' advice but one Auckland truck driver honked his horn and gave me the 'thumbs up' as I walked down Queen Street. My flirtation with rugby punditry had been brief, well paid and was now over. Or so I thought.

Death wears a Mustache

Later in the year, I received an invitation to address one of the most famous rugby clubs in the country. One of its players, a young man I had coached at basketball in Napier, led me to believe that speaking to members of the Shirley Rugby Club in Christchurch would be a prestigious event and something of an honor for me.

He failed to mention that also on the guest list was one of Canterbury's most famous sons, a certain player who had captained Canterbury, led the All Blacks and was now its new coach.

When I got to the function, I stood in the haze of cigarette smoke so common in bars and clubs back then, and shared a few beers with the locals. We were making small talk and I felt quite at home. When suddenly the clubhouse doors burst open and, seemingly, all eyes turned towards the giant frame silhouetted in the door frame. A thousand people focused their stares in dewy anticipation at the legend universally known as Grizz. In silence, and what I interpreted as deathly anticipation, a thousand set of eyes then swung back to me.

My beer seemed to have gone flat.

It was my first view of Alex Wyllie in the flesh and it was unnerving.

I'm no lightweight but here was a mountain of a man, with muscles in places where normal people don't even have places.

Faint Buzz

Thankfully, the club was so packed we didn't have to share the same space and no one insisted we hook up for an introduction. The dinner was ready and the guests took their seats. Eventually, it was time for me to speak. It all seemed to go smoothly. The audience was attentive, laughed in most of the right places and I sat down to a round of enthusiastic applause. Mission accomplished.

That's when I detected a faint buzz, an electricity in the air. The Master of Ceremonies rose to his feet and announced that the current All Black coach, a certain Mr. Wyllie, would like to say a few words. The man mountain started to make his way from the back of the club towards the podium. As his massive feet pounded the floor, the building was filled by a tsunami of wild clapping, loud cheers, shrill whistles, the stomping of feet and a chorus of grunting. The grunting made me especially nervous.

Grizz, or Mr Wyllie as I now thought of him, was ready to speak. He looked across his alcohol-filled kingdom with steely eyes above an impressive Zapata moustache and a hawk-curved nose. He looked to me like a pasty white version of Odd Job, the villain from the classic James Bond movie, Goldfinger - he had massive forearms, a barrel chest, and an expression that would remain the same whether he was laughing or frowning. And just like Odd Job, he had too much body squeezed into his skin for a man of his height. My sphincter muscles began doing funny things.

Grizz cleared his throat and slowly turned his squat head to look at me sitting along the head table. In a voice that could crumble concrete blocks, he rumbled, 'Don't worry, Dybvig, I won't hit you...'

My relief was palpable and I must have looked appreciative.

But I could hear the jibes from the mob in front of me.

'Thatta boy, Grizz. You tell the big Yank a thing or two.'

Then with a cobra stare, Wyllie finished his statement.

'...because shit splatters!'

A cacophony of wild hooting swept through the room again. I felt distinctly queasy. With the formal proceedings completed, I was escorted to the bar for a few drinks. I couldn't escape. I felt my hosts were toying with me like a cat with a mouse before it moved in for the kill. I found myself before a semi-circle of huge blokes, rugby blokes, the kind of blokes with strips of skin missing and ears that looked like they had been minced and stuck to the sides of their square heads.

Oddjob appeared in front of me. He poked one of his fingers, a small redwood that had been grafted onto his hand, into the center of my chest. I was convinced I was about to part company with my sternum.

'Whattaya know about rugby, Yank?' he bellowed.

I recall having a flash of pride that he had even read my article. After all, who cares what an American thinks about rugby? But I knew I would have to answer his question. I could see his arm twitching.

'Not as much as you,' I barked back, making sure I locked my eyes onto his. We stood toe to toe, eyeing each other like a couple of high school punks.

'Drink whisky?' he finally barked.

'You betcha,' I grunted back.

Somehow, I had passed the New Zealand test of manhood. The final exam involved a bottle of Johnny Walker.

The Russians Are Coming
Then the Russians came to town. That's the Russian National Basketball team. They were a high powered international team who continually toured the world.

They were in town to play a local American all-star squad in preparation for the 1988 Seoul Olympics. We (Howdy Doody/Fat Boy and me) were there in the stadium, calling the shots live. A couple of days before the game I happened to glance at the Russians' line up.

Whoa! I did a double take. That can't be right. It must be a printer's mistake. Who in their right mind would put letters together like that? I quickly discovered that the Russians would. They had names as big as their players - like Tkachenko, Tikhonenko, Jukanenko, Marchulenis and worse. I couldn't pronounce those names in a day let alone on the end of a fast break. I took a little alcohol on the off chance it might stimulate the language center in my brain or stop my heart from doing all that wimpy pitty pat stuff. No such luck. I had a whack at Tikonenko and damn near swallowed my tongue. Then I had a brainwave, I'd go up to the Language department at Auckland University. They could give me the phonetic pronunciations of the names. Bad move. Take my advice. If you only want to know an itty bitty little bit about something, don't ask an expert, especially when they're in the mood to be helpful.

Einstein

Experts know so much stuff they can't believe you'd be happy with just a tiny morsel. The genius I spoke to wasn't just helpful, he was downright magnanimous. He looked the part - he had a combination of that wild hair in the style of Albert Einstein and actor Christopher Lloyd in Back to the Future. This nerd not only gave me the phonic spellings, but also a short course in the Slavonic group of Indo-European languages. He led me through some of the trickier uses of the glottal stop and introduced me to diphthongs.

Diphthongs! Einstein showed me his epiglottis. He told me things about the lips, tongue and palate that no God-fearing English speaker ought to hear. He got all the way to the history of the Cyrillic Alphabet before I passed out. I eventually escaped with the phonetic codes and did my absolute best to forget the hideous knowledge with which he cursed me. But old shock hair chanted one sinister phrase I couldn't shake:

'The Triumvirate of Palate, Teeth and Tongue.'

Once you've got that baby stuck in your head, you can't say diddly-poop without being aware of your tongue in relation to your teeth and the roof of your mouth. And once you start thinking about your tongue, you're in big ass trouble speech wise. Before I met my overly friendly foreign language expert, I could at least pronounce Volkov. Now when I tried, I scoped onto the Big Three and my tongue just shot out of my mouth like a hungry dog through a butcher-shop door.

Volkov came out Vlap.

Lurch

The Russians were a huge draw card and the stadium was packed to the rafters. Their main attraction was their 7' 4", three-hundred-fifty-pound center Vladimir Tkachenko. He was the spitting image of Lurch from the Addams Family, only bigger. This monster had the biggest juttingest jaw I ever saw. The all-time Clutch Cargo jaw of the world. He'd be under the hoop at his end and his jaw would be way over half court waiting for the fast break. It looked like he had the Rock of Gibraltar under his nose. Tkachenko's jaw must have outweighed his entire team.

I was still having trouble talking. I could buzz my vocal chords, but my tongue had become accustomed to years of working without supervision, and all this concentration was confusing it. To take my mind off my tongue I was having a cup of coffee. The floor manager for the broadcast was trying to get my attention. My co-commentator, Fat Boy, slammed one of his meaty elbows into my side giving me a nudge (into the next row). His nudge spilled my little Styrofoam cup of coffee all over my list of phonic spellings and obliterated half the team. I got one hell of a fright and forgot to concentrate on not thinking about my tongue. My tongue seized the moment and regained its independence.

'Oh shit!' it blurted out, relishing its freedom.

All in all, things were looking up. At least I could speak. I heard the floor manager count us down to the broadcast: '3-2-1-cue.'

It was a great game. The Russians spent the night kicking butt and taking names.

Their own Slavonic Indo-European John Henrys flowed fully formed from my lips. I suddenly got the insane urge to recite a Boris Pasternak poem. Luckily for the audience I didn't know one. After the game, I asked Fat Boy if he thought, you know, that I might have been acting kind of weird before the show? 'Well,' he mused with a chuckle, 'maybe for somebody else, but not for you.'

Accent Coach
Despite four decades living in New Zealand, I've never learned to speak New Zinglish. I don't have 'mates', I have 'buddies'. I don't say 'gidday', I ask 'how ya doing?' If anything my American accent is stronger now than ever. And it's earning me a living.

Since the 1990s, New Zealand has become a much-used location for shooting American movies and television shows and commercials.

The country has rivers, mountains, rain forests, volcanoes and towns big and small - locations can be transformed to look like vintage England or the Moon.

The vegetation has doubled for Vietnamese jungles and farm paddocks have been turned into homes for hobbits.

These advantages of nature, and a workforce unrestricted by union rules, have encouraged producers to shoot a growing number of projects there. New Zealanders joke that every street has at least one resident who has featured as an extra in Hercules, Xena or at least one of Sir Peter Jackson's Lord of the Rings trilogy. People in small towns have queued to audition to become hobbits.

All of this has put a premium on anyone who can talk with an American accent and even more so, anyone who can coach someone to speak with an American accent.

That's how I became an American accent coach.

The Song

It's all about cadence; the song of speech. Cadence is made up of pace, rhythm and inflection in a combination, which becomes peculiar to native speakers. Cadence is the Tango in Latin America, the Limbo of the Caribbean or the Twang of America. It turns out I have some talent for getting foreigners to learn the Twang of America. I can make them sound just like us. This is no mean feat in a country where they call a two-by-four a four-by-two, and they think their ass is an arse.

I can make Russell Crowe sound like John Wayne ('Gawd willin' and the river don't rise, Pilgrim.') How do you teach someone to master an accent? For starters, it involves more than just your voice. One must cross the great cultural divide, which cuts both ways, because this ornery, cussed un-American little outpost is not a smaller, cuter, stranger, quieter version of the US of A. Different cultures, different strokes for different folks - when I walk onto a film set, as the American accent coach, most producers and directors haven't a clue about what I do. This was clearly evident when I started working with New Zealand acting icon Rena Owen (star of Once Were Warriors), on the movie When Love Comes Along. Rena has a rather distinctive voice and the producer was in a panic that I'd change it.

I explained to them that the first rule of getting an American accent was it had to be your voice, your natural voice. If you pinch your voice and start talking like a cartoon character on helium then that's exactly how you'll come across on film, and really how many times are you asked to speak like Bugs Bunny?

Feel

Americans are stereotypically loud and full of energy; we get fired up! Kiwis often think Americans have 'egos bigger than Texas' and we should be embarrassed about it, whereas New Zealanders have taken to heart that best of British traditions of not showing emotion about anything. It's all so very wet and snobbish.

Learning the American accent is not hard. What's difficult is getting the 'feel' of the American sound so you come across as a genuine American on film. The bottom line is: the better you act, the better your accent will be. An accent is not just about your voice but your whole being; how you hold yourself, how you move, your behavior and your attitude. To be blunt, that means if you're English, the first thing you've got to do is bend over and pull the carrot out from your ass. I always get confused looks from English actors when I tell them that and then quickly explain that I just want them to loosen up. Don't be so stiff; go with the flow, brother; feel the groove. Most of the time the confused looks continue. It's hilarious.

Disney Dad

Working on the Disney Channel film, You Wish, the job was proving to be difficult because one actor thought he was doing Shakespeare. But once I thoroughly and firmly explained to him that he was in actual fact playing the part of a 'nerdy Disney dad', and all that that entailed - namely that his character was on the receiving end of most of the jokes in the movie - his behaviour changed and his accent came together beautifully.

Comment: I gotta say I really enjoyed working with this actor: We were both on the same wave length when it came to the finer things in life. When he wasn't on set we'd both sit in front of his camper-van drinking peppermint tea and smoking a very nice cigar. Beautiful way to while away the time.

Habits

So many actors and non-actors alike mistakenly assume that to do an American accent all you have to do is roll your 'R's'. In a word - No! Picking up an American accent is dropping some of your habits and picking up on some of ours for instance. Don't add an extra letter R to the end of words. Kiwis do this all the time. They say 'Coke a Colar, Madonner, I have an idear, Americar ...' At the other extreme, don't drop the letter R from words. Classic Kiwisms include 'I remembuh, what's the mattuh, or I'm going to the pictuhs.'

Pronounce the R's. Let them breathe. Don't roll them: 'I remember... what's the matter... I'm going to the pictures.' Another way to get the American sound is to substitute D's for T's, not always but a lot of the time. For instance, matter becomes madder ('hey, what's the madder?') Better becomes bedder, butter is budder and the classic party becomes 'Let's Par-d-y!' And then it comes down to how we pronounce certain words. 'Been' is pronounced 'bean' in New Zealand ('where have you bean?') Americans pronounce it 'bin' as in trash bin ('where have you bin?')

Double D Cup

Much of my work as an accent coach is done off the set. This is an area where I find actors wanting at times - the precious darlings find it difficult to put in the hard yards.

They expect me to somehow magically give them my accent, but that's definitely not how it works. I instruct, the actor practices, and then I help the actor make adjustments to refine his or her accent.

One of the funniest experiences I had on set as an accent coach came about during the filming of Atomic Twister starring Sharon Lawrence (NYPD Blue) and Corbin Bernstein (LA Law).

After we shot one scene the director bellowed out 'Electric' several times to one of New Zealand's leading actresses. She was pumped! I saw her chest swell to at least a forty-eight Double D Cup. This diva was under the assumption that the director was describing her performance.

It fell to me to inform her that he was merely instructing her on the correct pronunciation of the word 'electric'.

Wow, did she deflate in a big hurry. Whooooooosh!

Then I had to trot over to the director and correct him on his pronunciation. He was a Canadian and, yes, there's an enormous difference between how we sound.

Charlie Chan

Sometimes you can get thrown a curve-ball and it pays not to take yourself too seriously. Mine came when I was asked to voice coach a journalist friend of mine. He was a highly-intelligent noted Chinese New Zealander lured by the offer to appear as a Chinese Warlord in an episode of Xena. I set about coaching his accent with my usual gusto and attention to detail. By the time I was finished with him you would have sworn he had eaten peanut butter and jelly sandwiches all his life on Wisteria Lane. In this case, however, what the director wanted was a cartoon character. Yeah, he wanted my man to speak in that comical Chinese-American accent 'rat dey roost to roo in dose' old Charlie Chan movies, kind of like a human Scooby-Do! My journalist buddy had too much class to do that. He stuck with his day job.

Comment: I gotta say racist or not I really loved those old Charlie Chan movies when I was a kid. The original actor playing Chan was actually a South Korean... the next guy was a Swedish actor Warner Oland. And then came American actor Sidney Toler. And finally, another American actor Roland Winters. Really not an Asian in sight.

Gawd Bless America

Generally speaking, the American accent required Down Under is a flat No-where's-ville accent. When I'm teaching an American accent class, I ask my actors to stand in front of the camera looking straight down the barrel and thinking of apple pie... mom... hot dogs and the American flag. I then ask them to purr, in dewy sincerity, 'Gawd Bless America.'

It's amazing the number of actors who choke on those very words. They have this idea that 'things American' are a bit crass, vulgar, plastic and over-the-top, when compared to the English way of doing things, and they just can't bring themselves to say it with meaning, if they can say it at all. Their behavior on film gives them away every time. I just point to it and say, 'So, you want to be an actor, well act then, it's not just about your voice, it's about your behavior - living truthfully under imaginary circumstances - and nobody gives a flying fuck what your politics are.'

Comment: I had this problem once on a $2-million-dollar American television commercial shoot with a hot young New Zealand actor who all of a sudden, right in the middle of filming, found it beneath his dignity to be a pushy over-the-top crass American. Puhleeeease! I looked at him like the total numb-nuts he was and pointed out the blinking obvious. He knew this was an ad for America when he auditioned for it. These are the sort of times you'd just like to knock some sense into these silly buggers with a short sharp biff.

Huh

On the set of Power Rangers I had an actor ask me in all seriousness how to say an American 'huh' in a way that would emote all the years of emotional struggle his character had had with his brother.

I gave him my best quizzical look, hoping it conveyed the message 'you can't be serious, dude.' I turned to walk away and mumbled, 'Huh?'

Nice and Easy

The best advice I give actors is to slow down. This is really important. Slow Down! Slowing down allows the actor to lengthen his vowels and consonants which allows them the time and space to say the words in the correct cadence.

When an actor first starts to do the American accent, the tendency is to rush... to speed through the dialogue because they're uncomfortable. New Zealanders talk much faster than Americans and they clip their words - they cut them off like they're falling off a cliff. Kiwis talk down to their chest while Americans tend to speak out as if they are announcing their thoughts. Every accent has a peculiar trait, something to hang your hat on. In American speech, it's an inherent laziness. That doesn't mean that you talk s-l-o-w l-i-k-e t-h-i-s. Slowing down just means the actor is letting the words and sentences have their own life; letting them breathe, not choking them to death out of fear.

Comment: Kiwis talk so fast they can squeeze an entire sentence into a single word... which means an American audience is never going to understand them. Slow Down! Let each word have a life of its own - let them breathe.

The Beat

The American sound primarily comes from the back of the tongue just before it drops into the throat. And our inflexions tend to come down at the end of sentences. I'm constantly reminding my New Zealand actors that American scripts are written in American cadence so they need to learn their script in their American accent; quietly, flat, rote with no emotion. This gives their body a chance to get familiar with the cadence of the writing, the American beats, letting them soak in, getting real comfortable with the language before they start to add the mustard. If the accent is coming out of your behaviour that will help to automatically put you on the right cadence track.

Comment: Whenever I land a role down here that is written by a New Zealander the first thing I notice is - some of the beats and the cadence is ass backwards. I wouldn't talk like that and it does throw you off. Every country has its own way of expressing itself.

Hints

And finally just some obvious hints: speak American until you speak American.

It's necessary for the accent to be of second nature so that the actor may concentrate on acting rather than speech - an accent is most often a subtle thing. Don't let it overshadow everything else you're doing as an actor.

Take your accent on the road - to the grocery store, the bank, the post office, gas station.

Using an accent is all about confidence and the way to get confident is to put in the hard yards.

As American Idol judge Randy Jackson would exclaim: 'Yo dawg, check it out.'

Get your game face on, your swagger down, your behavior right and your attitude right along with your voice and you can talk American with anyone.

Comment One: I had no interest in becoming an American accent coach... zero... nada... nope... didn't want any part of it. But, for whatever reasons sometimes you just have to go against the tide. I was kind of forced into this job simply because there wasn't anybody else around to do it.

I started out when the Hercules and Xena shows hit these shores. Actors would call me up to help them go over their scripts. Which I did making the obvious corrections here and there. But at that stage I really didn't have a plan. Soon I was getting swamped not only with American television shows... but TV commercials... and movies... the Disney Channel... HBO. I needed a plan... a foundation that I could give the actors something to work on.

I hooked up with my Australian producer friend who knew a ton about linguistics and together we whipped up a ten-page booklet on how to quickly develop an American accent.

Comment Two: Just in case anybody out there is interested here are the four general rules for the American accent:

1. It's got to be your natural voice. You can't put on an American accent. Don't become a cartoon character.
2. Lengthen your vowels. Don't pinch them off. Let each word and sentence breathe.
3. Slow down. Slowing down will allow you to lengthen your vowels.
4. You've got to have a P.O.V. Point of view. When adopting another accent a lot of actors suddenly stop acting because they're concentrating so hard on the accent. Which means the audience will be listening to a talking head and won't be engaged in what you're doing.

Remember this - the better you act the better your accent will be.

Comment Three: Fortunately, today the place is crawling with American accent coaches so I only get the occasional job now which is just fine with me.

CHAPTER FIVE

How to Survive as a Sports Jock with Attitude
How a nice boy from California almost freezes to death in Montana, kicks off a college game riot and gets banned from basketball.

Sacked

It is what it is. I was trapped. Leopards don't change their spots. The ending was already written. Yeah, that's right; I was cornered by every cliché in sport. I had nowhere to run. I had retired from professional coaching twenty-five years ago but I found myself coaching my son's elementary school basketball team. We were playing a private school team that should have creamed us, but with a minute left in the game, we were up.

Here's the backstory that makes us being in this situation so dramatic: This was a junior high team made up of players from year 7 and 8. But, for this game the first of the season I only had year 7 players because the entire year 8 class (all my studs) were away for their camp week. I only had six players and one of my starters was a kid from Paraguay who had never played basketball before and didn't speak English.

Also that day the year 7 class including me had spent the entire day at one of New Zealand's wildest West Coast beaches with a team of lifeguards learning about the dangers of riptides and how to handle yourself if you got caught in one. We spent the entire day in a very rough ocean so everyone was dead tired before we even got to the first jump ball. I was going into that game hoping we would just survive.

Not only did we survive we had inched ahead in the dying moments of the game. Sensing victory, the adrenaline soared through me - I went more ballistic than usual, charging up and down the sideline, screaming and pointing at my guys to play defense. I only mention that I was screaming at the top of my lungs because New Zealand coaches practice the Marcel Marceau method of coaching... they all just sit there like bumps on a log saying nothing. Dead silence.

No matter what the kids are doing there's absolutely no coaching taking place. So I kind of stood out in this regard and besides I was the only loud American in the joint. I ended up beside the other coach's bench. He looks up and snarls at me to stop yelling at my kids (that's my kids, not his). I stood there looking at him. It was one of those situations where it takes a second or two for you to comprehend what the guy actually meant - he was accusing me of verbally abusing my kids by yelling at them when in fact I was doing the exact opposite. I was giving them my energy and encouragement to hang in there on defense and to keep hustling when I knew they were dead tired. I stood there looking down at this dude who was dressed in rugby gear (typical for New Zealand no matter what the sport is) bemused for a couple of seconds and then I just casually told him to "go fuck yourself asshole-you coach your own goddamn team and I'll coach my team." And then I went right back to coaching my team at the top of my lungs. And that's how I got fired by a primary school. But, hey, we won the game... helluva victory!

Comment One: I just want to say here that if some guy in any situation whether in a public setting or in private told me to go fuck myself I'd just automatically yell right back at him to go fuck himself. Yeah, I know not very grown-up of me but that's simply my DNA make-up and I can't change it at this late date. But one thing I would never ever do in a million years... hell it wouldn't even cross my mind... is to go and whine to another adult that some guy yelled at me. That's what this other punk did... he cried to his school principal that he got his feelings hurt because the other coach (me) yelled at him... so his principal called mine and the whole thing was blown up beyond all proportion. What is it with today's metrosexuals (young men), grow a pair.

Comment Two: When it comes to gutter language I'm right in there with the best of them. That's not a brag - that's just how it is. When I was down in Christchurch one year for the finals of the domestic basketball championships as a television commentator I got into a stoush with some Australian midget security guard. The guy tried to force me into going another way when I was actually just following the way everybody else was going. This guy knew who I was and he decided he was going to make a power play on me.

We went nose to nose verbally blasting one another: 'Fuck you!" "No fuck you!!" "Fuck you asshole!!!" "Go fuck yourself!!!!" "No, you go fuck yourself!" That was the entire make-up of our conversation - two Neanderthals going toe to toe with nothing but - 'Fuck You' as our weapons of choice! And we were loud with me being really loud and very aggressive.

The funny bit here is there was a preliminary game playing before the main event which is where I was going at the time and we were right next to one of the corporate boxes with all the big-wigs sipping Champagne while we were just a few feet away verbally attacking one another. One of these chaps in the corporate box was former All White Captain and soccer legend Steve Sumner (who sadly passed away from prostate cancer in 2017). I knew Sumner from sharing a motel room on our days on the charity trail raising funds for the children's Ronald McDonald Cancer House. My battle with this security guard is going full throttle in this very open public arena when Sumner jumps up out of his seat and runs over to break us up and calm the situation down...Sumner exclaimed, "Okay that's it boys lets walk away this is no place for that kind of language" and as I turned to leave he leaned in and whispered to me, "But I love your aggression John!"

Attila the Hun

Along the way, I've continued to veer in and out of professional sport, sometimes as a bad-ass coach, but often as an anchor for television and radio shows about everything from pro wrestling to horse racing. Did I mention that I won a Coach of the Year Award and got a two-year ban at the same time? Or that one place barred me from entering its city limits with a basketball ever again? No?

Well, time I explained. There comes a time when a person has to take a break from boredom and monotony and allow his animal instinct to run free. For me that time is called 'basketball'. On the court I turn into Attila the Hun. I scream and shake and kick chairs. And I yell, but you've probably already figured that out. I hate referees who aren't doing their job ... I gotta get my foot up the ass of players who aren't doing their jobs ... I get in the face of lippy spectators who need to be addressed and told to shut the fuck up!
At times like that, I'm loud, aggressive and hostile. I never back down from a good fight. That's because when I'm on the court I reign supreme. I have purpose and I shake rattle and roll! I'm there to motivate people - to WIN the game.

Teenage Basketball Slut

The funny thing is when I lived in the States I didn't have this inane urge to be a media slut. I was a lot more one dimensional. I was just a struggling assistant basketball coach trying to establish a career. I was a basketball slut. Basketball and basketball alone ruled my universe. I was born and raised in California. I grew up in the San Francisco Bay area during the sixties. Need I say more?

The Grateful Dead, Jimmy Hendrix, Janis Joplin, Jim Morrison and The Doors, the explosion of the drug culture and Mario Savio challenging the then Governor of California, Ronald Reagan about the freedom of speech at the University of California at Berkeley. Student demonstrations, the Vietnam protests, the Kent State murders and Armstrong walking on the Moon. Those were exciting times! Yeah, I'll tell you how excited I was: When Armstrong was creating history; I fell asleep. I was pumping gas at a Chevron station on the El Camino Real (the Kings Highway) about thirty miles south of San Francisco. Normally this road is bumper to bumper, but on that particular afternoon - July 20th 1969 - you could have landed a plane on it and not hit a thing. So I made myself real comfy in the overstuffed armchair, in the small grimy office and was soon fast asleep. Ultimately I was jostled by a customer who was shouting: "Armstrong did it! Armstrong did it! Armstrong just walked on the moon!"

"Huh. What?" I mumbled wiping the huge pool of drool from the corner of my mouth.

Yeah, exciting times.

Social Angst

I lived in the same apartment complex as Associate Professor Angela Davis (she sported one of the all-time great Afro hairstyles of the day).

At the time she was under investigation by the FBI for a raft of dubious deeds (a gun she owned was used to shoot a Superior Court judge) but her worst crime was being a Communist while teaching at Cal Berkeley. Reds under the beds. Ronald Reagan's obsession.

I even went to hear Professor Harry Edwards speak. He being the black social conscience of the time influencing sprinters John Carlos and Tommy Smith to raise their black gloved fists in defiance on the victory dais during the 1968 Olympics. I distinctly remember two things when I went to hear Edwards speak: Firstly, he's a big man 6'5" and his mere presence when he walks into a room screams attention he was a very imposing figure and secondly Edwards had a fierce debate with a Native American Indian in the back of the room over who had the most grievances against the establishment with neither of them backing down. Fascinating live theatre.

I grew up first hand in this whirlwind of social angst, but it all sorta just slipped by without me really noticing, like watching a baseball game at Candlestick Park slowly getting fogged out. My entire world revolved around hoops. I knew where I was heading in life from the age of fourteen. Everything I did was predicated on being a basketball coach. I went through high school and college not necessarily to get an education but to play roundball and to eventually coach it one day. I had fast tracked my way through the education process with the sole purpose of being a basketball coach. Nothing else mattered.

Every institution of higher learning I enrolled in I graduated from. Graduating from high school at the age of 17, I went to De Anza College where I earned my Associate of Arts degree in Liberal Arts in two years, and then transferred to Stanislaus State University where I got my BA in Physical Education with a minor in American Colonial History. From there, I went straight to San Jose State University where I achieved my Master's Degree, Lifetime Secondary and Community College teaching credentials, all by the age of 22.

Comment: I wasn't an Einstein in the classroom, but I was smart enough to get the results I wanted. I knew how to play the system.

Mr. Most

On the other hand, as a player on the court, I was not a gifted athlete. Michael Jordan and I didn't come from the same gene pool. The only time I ever held any records was at De Anza, a two-year California community college. I enrolled there in 1967, the day it opened its doors for the first time and became a member of the initial De Anza College basketball team. The entire enrollment at the college in those days was just under 2,000 pupils. Today, the enrollment tops 45,000 students. The coach in those early years must have had halitosis or something because nobody returned the next year except me. That made me the school's very first two-year player. And that's why for a brief stint I held every basketball record at the college.

The record book looked like this:

Most points scored in De Anza history: me.
Most rebounds: me.
Most games played: me.
Most assists: me.
Most everything: me.
Mr Most: John T. Dybvig (1967 - 1969)

I guess that also made me the worst two-year player they had in '69, but let's not overdo the memories...

Perfect Record

I had a ton of fun being involved in the game. Basketball got me through school; it got me interesting jobs and it took me around the world. In fact, basketball in a roundabout way got me my only high school honor. I never wanted to miss school because I was always playing so in four years I racked up a perfect attendance record. Not a single day missing. When I graduated, I received a certificate at the ceremonies. I didn't even know it was coming. My reaction was, 'Huh?'

Comment: I was actually kind of embarrassed by getting that certificate - I thought it was kind of a sissy thing to get an award for - which just goes to show what a macho lunkhead I was in those days.

Harriet Took

Generally speaking I skated through high school pretty well unscathed .I always managed to be one step ahead of the posse... except when it came to Harriet... she was my year 11 English teacher... she was a frail little old lady about 65 years old... and no match for an immature 16 year old kid... I made her life hell for no other reason than I could... for instance when she wanted to show the class a movie I would volunteer to run the projector...

Of course I knew nothing about how to run a projector so soon there were yards and yards of film flying everywhere in the classroom... everyone in the class was laughing their asses off while poor old Harriet was running around in a panic trying to gather all the miles of errant film... ahhhh the hi-jinks of an adolescent... I kept this routine of mayhem up until one day... I was talking a mile a minute to one of my friends as we left Mrs Took's class and suddenly I found myself smashed against the wall right outside her classroom... the football coach who looked exactly like those pictures you saw in National Geographic of Cro-Magnon man had grabbed me by the front of my shirt and swung me around into that wall... he was right in my face and I mean right there big time... our noses were touching... that's in the very uncomfortable zone... he snarled:

Cro-Magnon Man: I understand you're giving Harriet a hard time....
Me - scared kid: Uh... yeah... I guess so...
Cro-Magnon Man: Knock it off...
Me - scared Kid: Uh... Ok...
Cro-Magnon Man: Do we have an understanding... (he grips me harder and pulls me even closer - I can hardly breathe)
Me - scared Kid: Yes sir!

And that was it he released his grip on me and walked away without another word... end of story... end of the matter... no conferences... no red tape... no nothing... the facts of the case were pretty simple... I was being an asshole in the classroom of a frail old lady... the football coach an old fashioned kind of guy had heard about it and handled the matter in the quickest and most efficient way possible.

317

Comment: Wow... try handling a problem kid that way in today's world and find out how quickly you get a lawyers summons... me I never gave it a seconds thought... I knew I was being a jerk and got what I deserved... in today's world nobody and I mean nobody accepts any responsibility for their actions even if they're completely in the wrong... it's always the other guy's fault.

38 Special

When I was in high school the big thing to do late on a Friday night was to toilet paper someone's house... we'd get bags and bags of toilet paper and just throw them unleashing long streams of toilet paper back and forth across the entire roof of the house... it always looked awesome... we'd even do the trees and garden shrubbery...

Then one day we got the bright idea that it would be super cool to toilet paper the inside of a house... we picked our victim one of the guards who played with us on our senior basketball team... and when I say victim I mean that in a nice way because it was a mark of pride if you got your house toilet papered... you were one of the cool people... whatever that means...

Anyway we got into this guy's house late one night and toilet papered the crap out of it... the kitchen... the dining room... the front room.... all covered in streams of toilet paper... I remember we were all virtually jumping out of our skins fearful that we'd wake up his dad... but we never did we all got out of there without making a peep...

The next day we were all so full of ourselves having pulled off this massive stunt... the guy knew that I was in on this gag and he told me that his dad wanted to see me... of course I knew his dad because I saw and talked to him all the time at our games...

I went over to his house thinking that I would have to apologise but instead he quietly had me follow him upstairs to his bed room and I'm thinking what the hell is this...

We walked over to his night table next to his bed... there he pulled open the drawer and right there as big as life lay a 38 special...

I can remember just staring at it... I'd never seen a gun up that close before... he just said: "Something to think about..."

Things could have gone tragically wrong that night... I've never forgotten that lesson.

Comment: Then one night it was my turn to have my house turned into a gigantic toilet paper factory. One morning we woke up to find our house and garden wrapped in streams of paper tissue. Naturally I was delighted. My father was furious. You have to remember that he grew up in the depression when you didn't waste anything and malarkey of this nature wasn't tolerated, period. He didn't think of it as performance art but more like performance vandalism. He called the cops and demanded they take immediate action. When they arrived, he called me into the front room and told me to give the cops the names of the culprits. I just stood there and laughed. The cops couldn't help themselves either, and found the incident highly amusing as they excused themselves to attend to more pressing matters. The only one who didn't find it funny was my dad... God bless him.

What Party
On another occasion my friend Jeff London and I pulled another trick on the same guy... this guy was always hinting that it'd be cool if we threw him a birthday party... so Jeff and I did...

We called a whole bunch of our high school friends on his birthday and told them that we were throwing a surprise birthday party for Dave...

We told half the crowd that it was going to be a casual bar-b-cue affair and then we told the other half that it was a formal dress affair...

Then on the night Jeff and I parked at the end of the block with a clear view of Dave's house and we watched as people started arriving with some in shorts and some in dress clothes and even one guy in a tuxedo...

The twist here was there was no party... Jeff and I made the whole thing up...

Dave and his parents were just as baffled as were the party guests as they slowly walked back to their cars swearing that they got a party invite...

Jeff and I thought we were the funniest guys on the planet that night.

George Trapp

I had some hell-raising times playing college ball. In my first year at De Anza, we were a very young green team and finished fourth in the league. However, the first three teams were caught cheating so we got to go to the State Championships in Los Angeles. Our first round opponents were Pasadena City College, coached by the infamous Jerry 'Tark the Shark' Tarkanian. Jerry's team featured two future pro players - 6'9" George Trapp and 6'10" Sam Robinson. And yes, it seemed that every other player on that team was a skyscraper. They had a simply awesome team; so much so Sports Illustrated carried a story on our game and quoted our coach as saying: 'I just hope they don't kill us.'

Tark's Machine, as the team was labeled by the press, was entirely made up of big muscular black studs from the city who played their game in the stratosphere, way above the rim. Our team was composed of white guys who could barely jump.

As the crowd settled into their seats, we went on court for our preparations. We were warming up when, suddenly, all hell broke loose. Pasadena's monster men exploded onto the hardwood to the beat of an all drum band. They put on a dazzling show, propelling themselves time and again miles above the basket, slamming the ball with enormous force on the way down. The whole building seemed to shake with each slam dunk. This was purely magical for me, a white suburban kid who rarely had any contact with blacks in any shape or form. We stopped our puny acrobatics and stood there transfixed, mouths agape and ooohing and awwwwing along with the crowd. Our coach wasn't impressed. He stomped onto the court and scolded us like naughty school kids caught with our hands in the cookie jar. Killjoy!

George Trapp's opening shot summed up the entire game. It was a fifteen-foot baseline jumper. He towered over me by about a mile, but I was enthusiastic. I was all over him like a bad rash; he was mine; I owned him; I had him locked down. The shot was nothing but net. I honestly don't think George even knew I was there.

On his follow-through, his elbow came crashing into my forehead like a runaway elevator car plummeting from the 105th floor. I saw stars. The ref whistled a foul on me. We didn't win.

Comment: Playing college basketball really did open up another whole world to me. I was a suburban white kid who had little to no exposure to the black world. Now I was suddenly experiencing another culture... another way of life. I just met it head on. I remember the time we played Compton College in a Christmas tournament down in Los Angeles. The Compton boys were some very tough dudes... but that didn't bother me I went right after them and traded blow for blow. We beat them by a point which was a huge win for us... in the locker room my coach was ribbing the guy I was guarding - a very muscular 6'5" man child... my coach said to this guy, "You were beating my guy up pretty good out there" meaning me...but I felt very good with the guy's reply, he simply said, "Your guy can handle himself, he gave as good as he got."

Road Trip

I graduated from De Anza and moved to Modesto, California where another George had made an impression. Modesto was the setting for George Lucas' movie American Graffiti. I was still pursuing my hoop dream. The attraction for me was Stanislaus State, my next basketball port of call. The basketball program there didn't quite match the movie budget. We'd drive all the way to Los Angeles, play, grab a quick bite to eat and then drive straight back to the school. Our road trips were 24-hour-open, all-night affairs. Thousand-mile car rides (drive-a-thons) with a basketball game thrown in.

Comment: Those were long, long exhausting trips and on the way home I was always scared shitless that we'd be a headline in the paper the next day: Stanislaus State van driver falls asleep, kills basketball squad. While everyone else was in a deep sleep I always stayed wide awake to keep the driver company... and to keep him awake!

Uncle Sam

My most memorable game at Stanislaus was against the United States Army team.

Before the game, our coach told us that the Army coach, Hal Fisher, would like a quiet word with us. We're all like "what the fuck!" First and only time in my entire career that the opposing coach came into our locker room before the game even started. Hal calmly addressed us: "My boys are playing for spots on the U.S. Army team. That means they make the squad and their army career consists of touring the world shooting baskets. They miss the cut and, well, their career quickly changes to touring the world, peeling spuds and dodging bullets."

We all looked at each other, somewhat somberly.

"Gentlemen, prepare yourselves for a very physical game."

The word 'physical' was woefully inadequate for the onslaught that took place. It was all-out war. Hamburger Hill, Battle of the Bulge, Gettysburg - call it what you like. Every inch of the court became a battlefield. You couldn't move an inch without getting an elbow, a knee or just completely body checked. This game was more brutal than an ice hockey game. I had bruises on my bruises on my bruises.

I began my career at Stanislaus playing guard, but an injury to our center meant that once again I was battling the Goliaths under the basket, at 6'3" I considered myself taller than average, but as a collegiate basketball center I was a midget. Being a midget center meant that I had to come up with something unique to get my shot off over the skyscrapers towering above me. I came up with the 'sudden-no-look-slam-hook.' But, the Army's center was another 6'9" giant destined for the pro's, Darnell "Dr. Dunk" Hillman. This gazelle was a nose bleeder, a sky walker, a light bulb changer... the man could fly. He once snatched a $100 bill off the top of the backboard as part of a bet - and pocketed it before landing. And oh yeah, he won the NBA's inaugural dunk contest beating Dr. J and Kareem Abdul Jabbar in the process. Naturally that didn't bother this naive, suburban white kid; I went right at him. As I unleashed my deadly guided missile - my soon-to-be-legendary sudden-no-look-slam-hook - Darnell blasted into the air with so much power he actually out-jumped my shot and the ball became wedged in his armpit.

The referee called goaltending. 'Yes!' I screamed. I got cocky. Unfortunately for some fan sitting in the sixteenth row, my next sudden-no-look-slam-hook left a deep imprint of Spalding on his face. It was all downhill from there; the Army boys opened up a big 'ole can of whup-ass and whupped our asses.

Godzilla

When my playing days ended, I finally fulfilled my destiny and moved to the sidelines. Fast and furious would be the only way to describe my coaching career. I had finished my formal education to become a struggling assistant basketball coach. Granted, I already had the personality of Godzilla smashing Tokyo. But who's asking? After a game at Gonzaga University one night, I was so enraged I kicked the door to the referees' room right off its hinges, much to their astonishment and mine as they sat wide-eyed watching the door crash to the floor.

Accidental Riot

My coaching career launched with a hiss and a roar: I almost froze to death at one school and started a riot at another. The riot wasn't my fault, I swear. I was working at Santa Clara University and our arch rivals USF (University of San Francisco) were the number one ranked team in the United States. They had four players from their team go on to the pro ranks. The best was their seven-foot center Bill Cartwright who later played with Michael Jordan and the world champion Chicago Bulls. We had our own weapons, including the rugged Kurt Rambis, who later starred with Kareem Abdul Jabbar and Magic Johnson on several Los Angeles Laker NBA championship teams.

The game was an absolute barn burner. It went bucket for bucket inside an immense cauldron of noise. Everyone was wound up as tight as a drum as the game dwindled down to the final six seconds. Kurt Rambis was shooting a free throw, with us ahead by one. Naturally, he missed. Seven-foot Cartwright gobbled up the errant shot and fired a great outlet pass to a streaking Chubby Cox, who frantically tore down the sideline and burped up a 40--foot 'Hail Mary' at the buzzer. Nothing but net! The stadium erupted into pandemonium.

I looked around as the scene dissolved into a swirl of events in slow motion: USF jumping for joy; our players with downward drawn sunken faces; the coaches striding towards each other with outstretched hands. It had turned into a nightmare for us. The crushing weight of a near-great upset had been so cruelly snatched away at the last possible moment. Ouch. Double ouch. Out of this unfolding landscape I saw the referees gliding toward their locker room. Simultaneously, I sensed a flinch from one of our assistant coaches. Instinctively, I knew he was going after them. With cat-like reflexes I threw myself between our man and the refs. Thus we have another Homer Simpson moment.

Unfortunately, my peace-making move was mistaken for the first blow in what was to be an almighty brawl encompassing the whole stadium (the players and most of the crowd). The refs immediately counter-attacked. One whipped his arms around me in a great big bear hug...
Picked me up...
Dug his head into my chest... and in a great adrenaline rush he drove me into the corner of the hallway that led to the men's locker room.

While this crazed man was smashing the back of my skull into the wall it seemed that the entire crowd instantly got sucked into that particular small corner of the court. All pulling, grabbing, twisting and shouting; and all this happened in less than a heartbeat. Total mayhem. I couldn't move a muscle - wrapped in a bear hug - pinned and crushed by the weight of the mob. A single voice cut through all the screaming: 'Don't hit him, John!' It was my boss. Under the circumstances I found this quite amusing. No problem.

Later I filed a police report. Just in case. After all it was all just a big 'misunderstanding'. Right? Right.

Comment: A few weeks later I ran into that referee when my JV team played the preliminary game at Sacramento State. I was walking out of the locker room and he was walking in - we paused when we saw each other and he immediately stuck out his hand to shake mine and said, "no hard feelings". And of course there wasn't because it wasn't personal it was just part and parcel of a very exciting game packed with a ton of emotion.

The Ice Age

Not long after the Santa Clara Riot, I found myself driving to Spokane, Washington, to become the head assistant basketball coach at Gonzaga University. Gonzaga is famous for being the home of crooner Bing Crosby, and some exceptionally good professional sports stars including Utah Jazz basketball great John Stockton. He was just this little stick of a kid at Gonzaga Prep then. I'm talking dinky here, folks - heck, in those days the ball bounced him up the court. I used to eat huge ham sandwiches and drink schooners of beer at his father's tavern, Jack & Dan's, right across from the school. John was always in the joint helping out (good kid) and I gotta confess not once did I ever look at him and think, 'NBA legend'. I had never heard of Spokane or Gonzaga (it sounded like a venereal disease to me), nor did I have the foggiest notion where they were located when I accepted the position. It simply didn't matter. They could have been on Mars for all I cared. I was moving up the basketball coaching ladder.

I hit town sporting a California tan and sunglasses. Instead, I should have worn a snowsuit, a Himalayan snowsuit. The place was one gigantic ice block - 26 degrees below. This was definitely not life as I knew it. I was your typical Californian-living-in-the-snow-for-the-first-time-in-his-life. I just ignored my surroundings. I pretended the snow and ice didn't exist. I walked around in my normal clothes, shivering with every step. One day, I was putting some gas in my car, dressed in jeans and a T-shirt. It was a beautiful day, sunny with clear blue skies, but what did I know? The attendant shuffled out, swathed in a Grizzly Adams-style bear coat, the type with a mountain of fur around the collar of the hood. I looked at him and quipped: 'Yeah, I guess it's a little cold.' The grease jockey looked me over for the green tin horn that I was and informed me it was 15 below.

During the winter unknown to me the outdoor faucet - or tap as I learned to call it when I moved to live Down Under - had developed a tiny drip, spreading a trickle of water in my garage. Big deal, right? What harm would a little drip cause? Well, that trickle turned into a shallow puddle, which evolved into a small pond, which eventually froze solid.

As Spring approached I was sipping coffee in my kitchen one morning when I heard this almighty wrenching sound followed by a loud crash. I rushed outside in a light breezy shirt to investigate. As the weather had turned warmer, the ice had turned into a slow-moving glacier and had ripped the immense garage door right off its hinges.

Comment: I remember standing there looking at the wreckage shivering and thinking - "man, I'm really out of my element here".

Rednecks
Even when we left on road trips, the elements seemed to track me down. We had travelled to Montana for a double-header against the University of Montana in Missoula and Montana State in Bozeman. On that cold Arctic weekend in Big Sky country I almost became a permanent member of the ice age. On the first night we had checked into our Holiday Inn and drove over to Montana University for shooting practice at their stadium Adams Field House. When we finished around 10pm, the head coach (who was a running nut) sent the players back in the van. He looked at me and casually said, 'Let's jog back.' I questioned the logic of running in what seemed to me to be outer Siberia (it was 25 below). He assured me it wasn't a problem, and for this Boy Scout it wasn't. He was wrapped in a hat, gloves, thermal underwear and enough Arctic gear to the point where I thought I was jogging with the Michelin Tire man. Me? All I had on was a skimpy T-shirt, a pair of thin cotton sweatpants with nothing beneath (not even underwear) and tennis shoes (no socks - California style). He gave me that 'don't be a wimp' look so I shot back, 'Sure. Why not? Let's go.'

What a dumb move.

We stepped out of that nice warm, cozy stadium into the outer limits. The night was extremely still; eerie; like it had a life of its own. When it's that many degrees below zero, it takes the cold a while to sneak up on you. But, when it does get there, you know it. I felt this body-hugging ice-suit encasing me in my own sweat. It got to the point where I almost froze in mid-stride. And to top it off, we got lost.

Finally, around midnight, we stumbled into a small café to ask for directions; the Michelin Tire man and his naked sidekick, Stupid Boy. When we burst in, the waitress swung around with a pot of hot coffee in her hand, looked directly at us, dropped her jaw and halted in her tracks. All the customers looked and stared. Some old codger was lifting a cup to his lips and I swear even the steam from his hot coffee stopped rising. I usually love freaking people out like that, but I was way too cold to enjoy their shock. I was in shock.

Somebody eventually came to their senses and we got our directions and trudged off, crunching the snow. I don't know if I was hallucinating or not but I was starting to feel a direct kinship with Alaska's Iditarod huskies. And then I saw it: the elixir of life. I have never ever been so excited to see the yellow and pink neon glow of a Holiday Inn sign. Once inside the warmth of my room, I felt nauseous. My balls had completely disappeared - somewhere up near my Adam's apple, I think. The university's trainer marched into my room, called me a stupid jackass and then applied hot towels to my lower regions in an effort to coax my missing marbles back home. Aaaaahhh!

Comment One: I had just got my balls settled down when all hell broke loose. On road trips we let the captain handle team curfew. For this trip our captain set the time for everybody to be back in the hotel at midnight. One of our freshman players came in at 12:30 a half hour late. Our captain was waiting for him in the lobby...when he walked in our captain knocked him out cold with one punch.

The hotel manager was pounding on our head coach's door. Naturally all the players were now up and the rumors were flying about what happened. Our head coach sent everybody back to their rooms. He called me to his room and we discussed what we were going to do about it in the morning. Then abruptly he changed his mind... he said nope we need to tackle this problem right now... so I called everybody on the team into our room and we had a team meeting. Our head coach asked our captain why he hit the freshman player. Our captain explained, "he's a freshman coach... this is a business trip and he has to learn right from the start to tend to business."

Next we asked our freshman player why he was late he explained, "I just met up with a high school friend who's going to school here and I lost track of the time."

Our head coach then said "ok here's the situation": To our captain he said "I like your logic but you over stepped the punishment part so I'm fining you one day's pay." To our freshman he said "our captain is right this is a business trip and you need to pay more attention to what you do on these trips... our goal being to win the games... so I'm fining you two day's pay." We then asked the team if they thought that was fair and they all agreed that it was fair. And that settled the matter so the next day nothing was hanging over the team.

Comment Two: That incident and how our head coach handled the matter right on the spot was a great lesson for me and I've never forgotten it... don't let situations fester when you can deal with them right on the spot... get the air cleared and then you can move on.

42 Below

The next day, when we flew into Bozeman for our game against Montana State it was still 42 below and blowing. Nothing was normal here, not even the basketball stadium. Montana State is the home of the NCAA Rodeo. The Marlboro Man would ride very tall in Bozeman. The basketball court sits elevated in an enormous rodeo ring, two feet above the dust and dirt and the cow poop. Anchored to the end of the court were mammoth Brahma Bull shoots. The parking lot was full: 7,000 pickup trucks, all with gun racks. The stands were packed with 10,000 cowboys wearing cowboy boots and cowboy hats with one bulging cheek. I have never ever in my life contemplated chewing tobacco, but in that setting I felt like it that night. I remember during warm-ups looking at the packed stadium and thinking "man, you've gotta be some kind of basketball nutter to come out in 42 below weather."

Comment: We lost badly in Missoula. Mainly because our black players got intimidated by all the racial abuse yelled at them throughout the game. Our head coach did warn our players that in Montana the only black thing that people saw there was the road leading out of town. In other words, don't expect a lot of warm cuddles.

The Big Sky league consisted of all white toast States: Washington, Arizona, Idaho, Montana and Utah. The entire league only had 20 black players in it and at Gonzaga we had half that total... we had ten black players on our roster. So, yes, whenever we traveled we took a lot of crap and racial abuse hurled in our direction. Welcome to America! But we played a blinder of a game that night in Bozeman and spanked the opposition good. I remember being so proud of how the guys rebounded from the night before and they weren't going to be intimidated any longer.

After the game I never even contemplated jogging anywhere - I rode back to the hotel with the team along with our running nut of a head coach with the car heater cranked up full!

On the Trail
American cowboys ride the Santa Fe trail; American basketball coaches ride the recruitment trail. Cowboys ride horses; basketball coaches ride cars and airplanes. Cowboys round up stray beef they can turn into food; basketball coaches round up stray beef they can turn into players. East and West they roam, North and South they drive and fly ... into big cities and out to small country towns ... over great mountains, the Rockies or perhaps the High Sierras. It's all in search of finding a player with 'the right stuff.'

Having 'the right stuff' means the player has been worth an investment of time and money in return for more games won than lost and, who knows, maybe even a championship. As a recruiter for Gonzaga, I'd fly to places like Boone, Iowa; small places where regional tournaments were held, where I'd spend a few days talking to kids and coaches and watching games. Then I might fly to Colorado or Arizona or Texas to meet more people, do more talking, and from there, somewhere else. Sometimes I'd get a lead on a kid while I was on the trail which broke me away from my scheduled itinerary. I would head off to meet another stranger. It would feel like I was off on a blind date.

Without doubt, the strangest place I went was Casper, Wyoming, on Thanksgiving Day. I flew in on a pitch black night so I saw nothing of the town as I checked into the local Radisson Hotel.

The next morning, I threw open the curtains and shrieked at the top of my lungs... oh, my gawd! I was sure I'd been abducted by aliens and transported to another planet during the night. It was the most barren landscape I'd ever seen... not a tree in sight. It looked as if the earth had been scorched. Instead of green foliage the landscape was covered by what seemed like thousands of mechanical oil rigs. The kind that look like giant metal grasshoppers. No matter which direction you looked, these man-made giant bugs constantly pumped their bounty from the earth. The view reminded me of Orson Wells' famous radio broadcast of 'War of the Worlds' in which our planet had been invaded by Martians.

Golden Penis
And, of course, you meet all kinds of people on the trail. One of the fathers of a great kid who played for us was an oil worker in Ventura, California, and I'll never forget him. He wore a small gold pierced earring shaped like a man's genitals... an intricately designed penis with two little golden balls. Strange, I thought at the time, but my philosophy about people was to accept them for how I found them, not how they might appear... especially if they had a kid who could play the game.

How Ya Goin'
Recruiting is, of course, a matter of introducing yourself. You have to do it all the time. You can't be shy and be a good recruiter, you have to force yourself onto people. Day-in, day-out, I was constantly introducing myself and talking about my university, the basketball program there and the head coach.

'Hi! How ya doin'? (shake hands). My name is John Dybvig. I'm the assistant basketball coach from Gonzaga University in Spokane, Washington, on the West Coast. Yeah, we play in the West Coast Athletic Conference. Yeah, we play in San Francisco and Los Angeles. Yeah, we have no football at our university so basketball is the major sport. Yeah, Spokane is a beautiful city and Washington is a great State. Yeah, our head coach is a great coach and a dynamic guy. Yeah, we take good care of our players.'

Eventually I would take a name and address and go onto the next guy.

'Hi! How ya doin'? (shake hands). My name is John Dybvig. I'm the assistant basketball coach from Gonzaga University in Spokane, Washington, on the West Coast...'

Once, I introduced myself so many times, I found myself standing in front of a telephone pole at the end of the day, saying 'Hi! How ya doin'...?'

Comment: The whole idea of recruiting is to establish a relationship with the player. You intently follow their progress during the year... calling them... visiting their school... their home... chatting with their friends... their girlfriends. Ya gotta go the whole nine yards. Which if you really want to think about it can be a bit creepy... you're a grown man constantly kissing the ass of some 17-year-old punk.

Paging

One trick recruiters use to capture public attention is to walk over to the public address announcer in the stadium during a game and tell them that so-and-so is wanted on the telephone - would they please page the guy. But the name they give him is their own. They then hustle back to their seat, and wait for their name to be paged over the loudspeaker. When the announcement is made, the recruiter struts majestically out of the door in a way that identifies them with the paged name. It's like setting up your own introduction.

'Paging Mr John Dybvig from Gonzaga University. There's a call for Mr John Dybvig from Gonzaga University in the lobby.'

It's like free advertising. Oops, excuse me, I must go get my page.

Comment: I know you're thinking that that's bullshit. But, no, I actually pulled this stunt at the California State basketball championship being held at the Oakland Coliseum. Coaches do all kinds of crazy shit to hook up with potential recruits. When we were recruiting Kurt Rambis who went on to have a 14 year pro career in the NBA, our head coach and his assistant took empty suitcases to the airport on the pretext that they were flying somewhere just so they could bump into Rambis at the airport who they knew was coming home from another recruiting trip.

Chicken Salad

'You can't make chicken salad out of chicken shit.' Meaning? You can't build a good basketball program unless you have good players to build it with. That's why coaches take to the trail in search of players to make their salad palatable, if not gourmet. In America a coach's job rests on his success on the court, and his success on the court depends on his success on the Trail.

Happy Trails

I liked recruiting in the summer the best. Summertime was always more relaxed for me, but not for everyone. I was sitting in a gym in Los Angeles in my Bermuda shorts and t-shirt one hot sunny day with a young recruiter from Brigham Young University (Mormon) who was dressed in slacks and a white shirt open at the collar. Suddenly, he looked at his watch, stood up and put on his clip-on tie.
'What's up?' I asked.
He replied he had to go out to the airport to pick up his head coach.
'What's with the tie?' I asked.
He shrugged and said it was their dress code: long pants, collared shirt and a tie at all times.
I thought to myself: "Glad I'm not a Mormon as sweat trickled down my forehead.

I guess we all end up doing something we don't want to do. And I had come round to realising that recruiting was nothing more than ass-kissing. Anybody associated with a good player in some way got their ass kissed. Forget the glamour of pro sport. It begins - and sometimes ends - on the Kiss-Ass Trail. One day, I decided to get off the trail. I stood in front of the mirror and said, 'Hi, how ya doin'? My name is John Dybvig and I'm no longer the assistant coach at Gonzaga University. I no longer kiss asses for a living.'

Napier

Though I had played and coached basketball through my 20s, and had remained fit, I'd put on a few extra pounds. To get back into shape, I'd been going back to the gym at De Anza College to work out. That's where I met the son of a coach from the old days, a guy who had become New Zealand's national director of coaching.

This kid told me his old man had heard I was back in town and wanted to see me. After my workout, I went over to his place and he offered me a job coaching basketball in New Zealand. I was intrigued. During my playing days, there were always tales of guys playing and coaching in foreign countries and it always sounded mysterious and super cool - kind of like joining the Foreign Legion.

Being at a loose end... a very loose end... I'd agreed within minutes to go to New Zealand and become the director of coaching at some place called Napier.

Instant Excitement

I packed an amazing amount of excitement into the few years I coached in New Zealand. I'm banned for life in one town. I had the referees' association refuse to referee any game I coached in Auckland city. I had a bus driver refuse to drive my team to our games. I prompted a score bench to walk out during a televised game. One year the New Zealand Basketball Federation tried to suspend me right in the middle of the season so I took them to the high court (and won). I had to appear in front of numerous tribunals... and finally I was totally banned from the game for two years.

Somehow, amidst that lot, and when the officials can't have been looking, I was voted the Coach of the Year one season. I also wrote New Zealand's first basketball book, appropriately titled Technical Foul. And followed that up with a complete coaching manual appropriately titled: John Dybvig on Basketball.

I know it sounds like I caused a storm in New Zealand but let's remember the people who live here get excited about watching cricket and eating cucumber sandwiches. I sometimes felt that trying to coach basketball in New Zealand was like trying to sell birth control pills at the Vatican. At least for me. So, where did it all go wrong?

Old Geezer

The town that banned me for life, New Plymouth, did so because I took my team off the court five minutes into a championship final. Ha! They weren't expecting that.

The night before the final, an old local basketball geezer told me the local referees would foul out my big American import in the first five minutes. I thought he was full of hot air right up until they did exactly that, and when I tried to talk to them about the situation they started firing technical fouls on me. I tried to explain to them that I was the captain of the team and was allowed to ask questions. That approach didn't deter them for one second as they continued to fire technical fouls on me like an out of control popcorn machine.

So, we left. When the moment arrived to make a decision I didn't have to think, I moved instinctively. I dragged my team off the court and ordered them into the team bus. As we drove home from New Plymouth, we listened to a radio report on the affair. The guy reporting on the game was nearly hysterical; you would have thought he was describing the D-Day landings, not a game of basketball. He kept referring to the American import who fouled out in record time as 'The Big American' and to me as 'The Small American'. The Big American did this and then the Small American did that... blah... blah... blah!

'The Big American' was 6' 8" and I, 'The Small American', was 6' 3". That was the first and only time I think anyone has described me as 'small'.

Comment: I remember I didn't really think too much of the life ban, but they sure as hell did. A few years later a coaching friend of mine added my name to his team list when playing in a tournament in New Plymouth. The score bench upon seeing my name immediately marched over to him and said in no uncertain terms that my name couldn't be on his team list otherwise they would forfeit all their games. Wow - hold a grudge why don't you!

The Fat Ref

The referees' association of Auckland refused to work my games because of the way I described one of their refs. Blessed with an expansive and well-practiced range of cuss words, I had plenty of insults to choose from. In the end, I dared to tell him he was 'fat'.
Now, this wasn't exactly a major revelation - he would have made George Foreman look skinny.

I'd made the comment that the guy was too fat to referee at top level. My view was if a ref couldn't keep up with the game, he shouldn't be allowed to referee. If players are too fat - guess what - they don't make the squad. Why should referees be any different? Once again I didn't really take this threat seriously until I found myself coaching my team in the finals of the city championships from the second row of the stands. A championship we won... yeah baby!

Comment: This whole situation seemed ludicrous to me... there I am sitting right behind the team bench in the second row and it's obvious that I'm coaching the team. The games we play both on and off the court.

Moron

The incident that led to the score bench walking out on me was a misunderstanding. Honest. During a nationally televised game, I sent one of my players over to the subs bench and while he was waiting to go into the game, the scorekeeper was giving him a hard time... talking shit to him. So, I charged over and shouted:

'Hey, moron, keep, your trap shut! And just do your job.'

The guy burst into tears and walked out at half-time. The entire score bench followed him, walking out to show their support for him. I had to scramble like hell to organize a new score bench right on the spot. And I was left thinking, 'what is it with these people? Are they all anal retentive?' In my mind, the guy was a moron, jackass, smartass... whatever, he was giving my player a lot of gyp, and as a coach I'm very protective of my players I don't stand for any of that bullshit. But, the upshot here is: The guy was a moron! The guy really was a moron!

How the hell was I supposed to know that?

Which prompted the New Zealand Basketball Federation into ordering me to go to their lawyer's office and apologize to this guy. I walked in and exclaimed to the lawyer as the scorekeeper was standing next to him: "Hey man, if I had known the guy really was a moron, of course I wouldn't have called him a 'moron'."

The Feds lawyer just gave me a withering look. Diplomacy is not my strong suit. Like I've said, Homer and I are one.

Cabs

The bus driver incident was just plain ridiculous. Even as I'm writing this and thinking back on that episode I'm dumbfounded. I was coaching the New Zealand National Women's basketball team in the Commonwealth Games where we'd made it to the semi-finals against England. The night before our big game, I was putting the team through an extensive workout of what we had to do to beat England. Not a lot of physical stuff rather mental preparation and shooting. I was right in the middle of explaining something when I found a white-haired old fart tugging on my arm, saying it was time to go.

'We're not finished yet,' I objected.

'It's six o'clock,' he retorted.

'We'll get a cab back,' I parried.

'No, I'm your assigned driver we need to go now,' he thrusted.

'Get lost!' Now in glorious full rebuttal.

The driver was like a dog with a bone - he just wouldn't let go. He kept pestering me until, finally, I decided I'd had enough. I turned and carefully put things in perspective for him at a volume even his hearing aid would cope with: 'Get the FUCK out of my gym before I FUCKING kill you!'

That got his attention. He left. I got the team back to the hotel, without a problem.

The next day, the driver refused to take us to our game. Big deal; we took cabs.

For some reason, the New Zealand Basketball Federation thought this was a big deal and fired me from my national coaching position when the tournament finished.

I didn't even argue. The whole issue seemed silly to me.

Comment: And that was half the problem... the basketball Federation took everything so seriously like every little thing was a matter of life and death. Whereas most of the time I just found it amusing and really never took them or their outrage seriously... which pissed them off even more.

Banned

Before long, I was living a dual life in New Zealand - half of it was developing a media profile, the other was as a basketball gun-for-hire. I had landed a nice comfortable job working in radio in a small provincial town. No pressure. Then I got a call out of the blue that changed all of that. The basketball team I originally came to New Zealand to coach was in trouble. It was mid-season and they hadn't won a game. To top it off, one of their American imports had knocked out their current Kiwi coach in the locker room during his half time talk, giving ironic meaning to the term 'a cross-cultural-exchange.'

This was the kind of challenge I couldn't resist. So now I'm coaching this ragamuffin group and we're playing the top team that hadn't lost a game all year on their home court and here we are a team that hadn't won a game all year. Hmmm ... what to do? This is looking like it's gonna be a slaughter.

15 seconds

During the pre-game warm-ups, I was mulling over my options and decided to pull a stunt used in heavyweight boxing. They do it all the time in boxing - when the challenger comes out to the ring, the champ makes him wait. He makes the challenger sweat and wins the psychological battle at the start.

I didn't spend any time pre-planning my attack. I put practically no thought into it at all... I just thought of it while sitting on the bench, watching my team warm up whilst waiting for the other team to come onto the court. I believe one of my strengths is making decisions under pressure. Yeah, some of my ideas are outside the square but they work. In this case, it worked the way it was supposed to work. But it also got me kicked out of the sport.

What happened was I took my team back to the locker room and decided we weren't coming back out until tip-off. It was a mind game, a ploy to have the other team wonder where we were and what was going to happen. I wanted them thinking about us, and not about their own game. While we waited, we could hear the crowd getting worked up. The officials were calling us onto the court through the closed doors, clearly anxious about the situation. Still, I held my guys back and told them to wait. Meanwhile the officials kept calling us through the locked doors to come out. We held our ground. As the officials got more and more frustrated they were now actually pounding on the closed and locked locker room doors demanding that we come out. I could hear the sell-out crowd going bonkers! The tension was sky high both outside the locker room and definitely inside... my guys were wide-eyed and pumped for action. I warned them that when they eventually started the game, it was likely the refs would award a technical foul against us, or I could even be ordered off the court. You just never knew with these clowns.

Finally, at last, we burst onto the court and the crowd went nuts screaming and throwing shit onto the court. My plan had worked the fans into a frenzy, creating an electric atmosphere for a game that was supposed to be a walkover for our rivals. But the officials had other ideas. The timekeepers had a stopwatch on us and they declared we had breached the rules of the competition by being 15 seconds late for the game.

Yes, 15 measly seconds. It was the quarter of a minute that cost us that game and ultimately finished my basketball career. The officials ordered us to forfeit that match, causing mayhem in the stadium. Causing even more mayhem for the stadium manager who had to refund a full house... ouch! My opposing coach told me later our actions had indeed psyched his team - the very thing I was trying to achieve - but I would never find out whether it was enough to earn us the win.

Comment One: The New Zealand Basketball Federation tried to immediately ban me from coaching (I did have to coach two games from the stands).

I hired a lawyer and took them to the High Court in Christchurch and won a stay of execution but only until the end of the season where, even in the presence of my lawyer, they hung me out to dry. I found myself at another basketball trial in front of a judge no less and mobs of lawyers. I felt I was at basketball's equivalent of the Salem Witch Trials and the odds of getting off ranged from slim to none, and 'slim' was out of town. Way out of town.

Comment Two: I don't know what it is down here at the end of the world... but they love to have trials in any sport going. Rugby and rugby league players are always fronting up to a tribunal with their lawyers for any number of violations on the field...mostly for cheap shots during tackles. And oh yeah for one American who swears loudly! Basically that's really all I ever did: I was very loud... I was very foreign... and I swore... big fucking deal right!?!

High Court Judge
But, before that trial we had to play in the end of season promotion/relegation series where I was allowed to coach via a decree from a high court judge (which cost me about 4 thousand bucks). Anybody will tell you - the guy on the street corner will tell you - that playing First Division in any sport, in any country in the world, is a hell of a lot better than playing Second Division. The pressure from the sponsors was really on us. And on me because for starters my team consisted of only seven players, one of whom was deaf. He was the only one who asked decent questions at practice, though it was a little time consuming as he had to write down all his questions and I had to write my answers back to him: He couldn't hear, but he could read very, very well.

We lost our opening game by a couple of points to the top Second division team not a great start. The next morning (10:00am) we had to play the other Division One team in the series. This was a team that had previously demolished us - by more than twenty-five points - both times we'd met. Things weren't exactly looking rosy... we lose this game and we're out!

Tough Season Coach
But, I knew from experience that morning games are an altogether different creature.

For starters, nobody would be there. The stadium would be empty...
And everybody's 'body rhythms' are a bit strange in the morning.

I insisted my team get to the stadium the next day, bright and early,
an hour before the game. I wanted them to get a good healthy warm
up and get comfortable with being in the gym at that hour of the day.
We got there so early we had to go next door to get the caretaker to
come and open up the gym. And just like I thought the gym was
cold, drafty and very empty.

The other team came straggling in at five minutes to tip-off. They
appeared cocky, indifferent and disinterested. This pissed me off no
end. They gave us no respect. They knew they were gonna kick our
ass once again. And that would be the finish for us! Welcome back
to Second Division which usually meant the loss of sponsorships and
a real struggle to stay afloat. Adding insult to injury, one of their
players shuffled over and shook my hand, offering me his
condolences on a tough season. In effect he was telling me to my
face that I was gonna lose this game - big time! Before the game had
even started! Now, I was ropeable! I was way beyond pissed! I was
livid!

The Chair
I called my captain over and told him to get the team into the locker
room. He started to protest about the shortage of time. I cut him off
and hissed: 'Now!' Inside the locker room, it was deathly quiet... I
walked up to every player and eyeballed them in the face before I
said a thing. Quietly - but with enormous intensity (I was shaking) - I
told them that some son-of-a-bitch from the other team had come
over to shake my hand before the game. That this team was showing
us absolutely zero respect...

And then I picked up a chair and told them in no uncertain terms that
if I didn't see the other team on the floor in the first five minutes that
I was going to take this chair...

And I was gonna run out onto the court ... and SMACK THEM
AROUND WITH IT!

And when I say THEM, I meant MY TEAM!

I wasn't kidding. And they knew it. So in this case I had a genuine and instant fear as my motivational tool. It wasn't planned... It happened off the other team's behavior.

Flying Fists
The first five minutes of that game was pure hell for the other team. My guys were so jacked up they literally threw themselves into their opposition. The game at this point far more resembled ice hockey than basketball. In my mind's eye, I can still see one particular play where their center went up for a rebound and one of my players went with him but instead of fighting for the ball he simply smacked him in the side of the head as hard as he could. And the amazing thing was we created all this mayhem with such confidence and bravado that the referees didn't call any fouls. The other team were completely dazed and shell shocked.

At this point I called a time out and told my team it was time to cut out the obvious physical stuff and to concentrate on playing basketball. I knew that if we continued in the vain that we were going we'd never finish the game. The other team never regained their composure as they kept looking for punches that never came.

It's funny how things work out in certain games.... maybe we were destined to win that game no matter what... because for that particular game I had developed a special out of bounds play for my best three point shooting guard. And I told him that he had to shoot the ball no matter what, I didn't care if his defender was right on top of him and blocked the shot, he had to shoot the ball, otherwise if he didn't I was gonna take him out of the game. The kid made 5 out of 8 three point bombs on that play alone. We hung in there and beat them by three points. It never would have happened if that other player hadn't come over. In this case, instant motivation won the day as we beat the other Division Two side that night and survived to fight another day in the First Division.

Comment: This little incident right after the game finished might have had something to do with the two-year ban from the sport I received at yet another one of my trials.

The gym was packed with all the New Zealand Basketball Federation officials sitting right in the middle of the stands all peacocking in their bright blue official basketball blazers. These guys were old and decrepit and looked exactly like all those old non-smiling Russian officials you used to see in Red Square in front of the Kremlin in their black overcoats watching their military parades. Not a lot of jovial banter going on with this group. When the game finished we were all jumping for joy and then right in the middle of our celebrations I marched out to the middle of the court pointed to the old farts giving them the finger and bellowed:

"Hey, assholes... Fuck You!"

This busted up the crowd who were all laughing themselves silly, hooting and hollering at the officials: "Fuck you...Fuck you..." which caused all the Federation officials to turned a deep crimson red. Like I've said plenty of times before diplomacy is definitely not my strong suit. But, I knew these jerks were hoping like hell that we would lose and be out of the first division so they wouldn't have to deal with me any longer. But, in the end they dealt with me one more time at the trial and I was out. But, in an ironic twist Television New Zealand hired me during my suspension to call the televised games the following year... ha! They just couldn't get rid of me.

Lloyd Daniels
I wasn't the only American in the country having problems, with former pro Lloyd Daniels making a brief appearance. He stayed just long enough to spit on a referee on his way back to the airport. Lloyd should have stayed. New Zealand would have just given him a smack on the hand for bad manners. Instead he went home and walked into three bullets over a drug deal gone sour in New York.

Comment: But, the amazing thing is the next time I saw Lloyd he was on ESPN playing point guard for the Los Angeles Lakers. That's a helluva transition: New Zealand spit... New York three bullets... Los Angeles Lakers starting point guard. Go figure?

Dan Wright
Another import, Dan Wright, lifted bad behavior to a new level.

Dan Wright came from the City of Angels (Los Angeles - Compton), but he was not one of them; just before he split from Down Under he robbed a gas station. Not the smartest move in the world. First of all New Zealand is white toast territory, there were at the time only a few black American basketball imports in the entire country and only one who matched the gas station attendant's description of his assailant.

I got a call from the police asking me if I knew of any black Americans who fitted the description of 'Fat Albert.' Doh! Again I'm not making that up - that's exactly what the cops asked me.But from there things got even dumber. Wright decided to play in an All-Star basketball game against the touring National Russian side before he flew home the next day and guess what? Yeah, the gas station attendant he strong-armed and robbed was sitting in the stands watching the game. When the announcer introduced Dan Wright to the crowd this guy jumped up and started screaming hysterically and pointing his finger:

"That's him... that's him... that's the guy who robbed me!"

Wright was immediately arrested and deported from New Zealand.

Lamont Robinson
But my favorite import singing the blues was Lamont Robinson. This guy was a real work of art. What he was on nobody will ever know. Lamont was a six-foot-four-inch shooting guard out of Lamar University. He had a great resume: He was drafted by the Cleveland Cavaliers and was a whisker from making the team. Robinson went on to play for the Harlem Globetrotters. Mr. Robinson was a stud. The man could play.

So naturally the locals who brought him out couldn't believe their luck in landing such a gifted athlete. They should have been suspicious. Basically when their Lamont Robinson hit the court he couldn't walk and chew gum at the same time. Their guy was a dud! Their guy definitely could not play. What gives? As the fake Lamont kept fumbling up and down from one end of the court to the other the coach of this team did a little detective work and got hold of the fake Lamont Robinson's resume.

What gives was there were two "Lamont Robinsons" and the one who could play wasn't within a zillion miles of New Zealand. The one who couldn't play, the one in New Zealand was from Sacramento, California and apparently he and his agent thought that the good country folk of New Zealand would think all blacks looked the same and attempted to pull off a sting by sending in the resume of the real Lamont Robinson. Believe it or not it never occurred to them that for this sting to work the fake Robinson had to be able to play the game at least a fraction better than a paraplegic pygmy.

So the coach brought the fake Robinson into his office sat him down and presented the two different Lamont Robinson resumes. The coach sat there looking at the two resumes and then looked at the fake Lamont Robinson sitting in front of him. Lamont looked down at the two resumes and then looked up at the coach sitting in front of him and exclaimed:

"Ok, ya got me."

Comment: The story broke and went worldwide, featuring in USA Today in the States. I absolutely loved it. The balls of that guy!

Michael Jordan
Naturally, I decided to run a piece on the television sports show I was hosting at the time. In the introduction to my show I told my viewers I had a special guest on the show: Michael Jordan. Yes, the Michael Jordan of the Chicago Bulls was going to be my guest in the studio later in the show.

I did a piece about the Lamont Robinson scam and announced Michael Jordan would be with us right after the commercial break. When we returned, I was sitting in the studio with a friend of mine in dark sunglasses.

'You're Michael Jordan?' I asked straight-faced.

'Yes, I am.' My friend nodded in agreement.

'Michael Jordan, the pro basketball player?'

'That's right.'

'Michael Jordan is six foot six and black.'

'Correct.'

'But, you're five foot ten and white.'

My friend hesitated for a second, whipped off his sunglasses and exclaimed:

'Ok, ya got me.'

Comment: That piece was Da Bomb; everybody in the country loved it and we got a ton of requests to show it again and again.

Toughest League in the World

The toughest league I ever played in albeit briefly was one of my own creation. It took place in the Dalgety's Wool Shed. I worked there one summer, pressing wool, and naturally I started a basketball league during lunchtime. We had a full hour for lunch and I easily got bored. I mean, how long does it take to eat a couple of sandwiches? So I organized a basketball team and we challenged another warehouse to a game. Word spread and before you knew it all the warehouses wanted in. I organized a league and it was all on.

This was streetball at its roughest and crudest. The court was the shed's cement floor. Nobody wore Nike's in this league. The choice of footwear was steel-toed work boots. And finesse didn't hold much weight in this league as a good straight jab or a powerful uppercut was way more important than a killer crossover. We'd find an open space in the warehouse amongst the stacked up bales of wool and hoist two wooden pallets with rings nailed to them up ten feet on forklifts.

We always drew a good crowd and the games were entertaining in more ways than one. For instance, it just wasn't advisable to drive the lane for a lay-up. I saw more split skulls smashing into the steel shafts of the forklifts from a full on, forearm shove from the defender than I care to remember.

Nothing these guys did was subtle. And it didn't pay to dribble the ball too close to the sidelines either as stray fists flew out of the crowd, smacking the dribbler in the side of the head or an errant boot was stuck out tripping him up. And you could guarantee at least 337 fights per game.

But, we did have our funny moments. One time one of the guys on my team had an open lane to the basket so I yelled:

'Drive!'

'Drive!'

This monster of a man, covered in tattoos and with more metal in his body parts than a dozen heavy metal bands combined, looked at me, shrugged his shoulders and grunted: 'Drive what?' I think he expected me to throw him a set of car keys.

During another game, a guy who resembled Lurch from television's Addams Family threw the ball at the basket with such force it ricocheted off the backboard, hitting another player who was going in for the rebound. It smashed him square in the face, almost knocking him out.

I couldn't help being my sarcastic self and quipped, 'Nice touch.'

The other Neanderthal guarding him bellowed, 'But, I never touched him!'

Comment: But this league proved a point to me that I already knew. Namely that everyone no matter your age... gender... or skill level... everyone loves throwing a ball through a hoop. Most of these guys were the shits at the game but they played with plenty of gusto and it didn't really matter what skill level they were at.

You Talking To Me

I don't know why, but from the second I started coaching basketball in New Zealand it was ME versus THEM. I never intentionally went about looking for a fight, it was just there of its own natural accord. The locals found me loud, never short of a word and I was foreign. From my point of view, I was bitterly disappointed in their 'she'll be right' attitude towards the game. I figured they just didn't give a shit and I did. When I coached my very first game in New Zealand it really shook people up. I whacked the chair next to me when a call didn't go our way and the damn chair splintered into a thousand pieces (had to be a really cheap chair). The hall erupted. And that was it: in a single play I became the controversial American basketball coach for life. I didn't think I was controversial. I thought quite the opposite in that I thought New Zealand was controversial because life in a small island nation stuck in the middle of nowhere can become pretty boring. People have nothing to talk about because nothing much happens, so they make things up. They make up controversy in order to make their lives a little less boring. So the way I looked at it I wasn't really controversial at all, I was just a victim of New Zealand's boredom. Well, that's my slant on it.

Comment One: Ok here's the deal. The conflict between me and New Zealand germinated way... way before I even got here, please let me explain: Yes, I'm a total nutter, nutjob, maniac when it comes to basketball. When I landed in Napier it was like Godzilla invading Tokyo. I just ripped the shit out of the place! Just to give you a small picture of the lengths I would go to for the game let's talk about my Bozeman, Montana scouting trip:

It's dead in the middle of winter snowing like crazy and blowing even harder. It's also dead in the middle of the Big Sky league competition. We've got an upcoming game against Montana State in Bozeman, Montana. We don't yet have a scouting report on Montana State. So I climb into my 1968 green Volkswagen at 5:30am on a very cold morning and drive a total of some 500 miles to scout a single game of basketball. That trip took me over three mountain ranges with elevations upwards of 5 to 6,000 feet. When I got to the Montana State campus that night right before the game I noticed that all the cars in the parking lot had their engines plugged into a heating outlet. It was 42 below zero and, like I said, blowing hard.

After the game surprise... surprise, my car wouldn't start... not only wouldn't it start but usually when you turned the key if the battery's flat it will make a clicking sound - my key turning produced no sound whatsoever. The car was a total goner. Frozen solid. I'm standing there wondering what to do next when this Grizzly Adams type guy - mountain of a man with a full beard and a wild mop of long hair wearing one of those enormous fur lined coats popped up out of nowhere and bellowed that I was a dumb fuck - he had spied my California license plates on my car. At that point I couldn't really argue with him as I was totally unprepared to be out in this kind of weather period. He pulled a chain out of his truck and wrapped one end around my bumper and the other end around his bumper and commenced to drag my car around the by now empty parking lot until it warmed up enough to be jump started. I thanked him immensely and he told me to get the fuck out of there and don't fucking stop (a real charmer). It's around midnight now and one would assume that I was going to do the sensible thing and drive into town and check into a motel... but oh no not me, not Mr. Numb Nuts. I drove straight back to Spokane in the dead of night in 42 below weather.

On the way back my car suddenly started making this unbelievably loud siren type noise and then just as suddenly there was a huge bang and then silence. Shit like that in the middle of the night on a completely deserted highway can really give you the jitters. I stopped and got out to have a look. It turned out to be my odometer freezing to the point that it just literally exploded.

Then from out of nowhere a Montana State trooper pulled over in his cruiser to ask me what the hell I was doing out in the middle of nowhere in this kind of weather? I just explained to him that I was on my way back from scouting the game in Bozeman and was heading back to Spokane, Washington. I don't have the words to describe the look on this guy's face. Before I got back on the road he asked me if I had a candle in the car? I said no, why? He explained to me that if my car broke down in the sub-zero temperatures a lit candle would provide enough heat in the car to keep me from freezing to death. Of course I told him no that I didn't have a candle, but he never offered me one (which is kinda weird - why ask in the first place) so I got back in my car and drove off.

I finally arrived home the next day around 6am in the morning where it was only 26 below zero - absolutely balmy. Now that's one helluva of a 24 hour scouting trip. But I didn't think anything of it... that's just the kind of stuff I did.

Comment Two: Was that unusual for me... hell no! I once drove all the way from San Francisco to Phoenix, Arizona (16 straight hours) to watch a high school basketball tournament. Basketball for me was not just a sport, it was a way of life - my life. So hey, you take that kind of intensity coupled with the enormous amount of urgency I put towards the game of basketball and of course there was going to be some fireworks, to put it mildly, when I landed in sleepy little old New Zealand. They weren't ready for me - and I certainly wasn't ready for them. As George would say in Seinfeld: "We lived in colliding worlds".

Comment Three: Was I still basketball crazy when I landed in New Zealand? You betcha! Like I've said I'm a competitor to the max and all I cared about was winning. I realized with the team I had in Napier we were a bit undersized for the league we were playing in so I actually gave up my job to bring in another American import. I brought in a 6'8" shooting forward and gave him my job... which meant that I had to really scramble to make ends meet... but we were a much more competitive team. And that's all I really cared about.

Comment Four: The crazy lives on: When we were forced to play in that promotion/relegation tournament at the end of the season I went the extra mile to give us a chance to win. I covered all the bases. I know money speaks a special language all of its own so when we got to the tournament site and had our first practice in the gym I lined up all my players in front of me on the baseline. Then I walked up to each kiwi player and gave them a one hundred dollar bill (remember these guys were amateurs and didn't get paid so that was a lot of money to them)... I gave my two American imports each five one hundred dollar bills. And I told them to hold it and feel it and take a good look at it... then I collected them all.

I told the guys we win and stay up in the first division I'll give you back the money. That was my personal money... all the money I had. But I just wanted to win so badly and keep the small town of Napier in the first division that I was going to do everything I could do to give us an edge. As I've said earlier we did win and we stayed in the First Division - I left broke but very... very happy!

Re-Entry

I had a lot of weird things happen to me during my time in Napier. And this little episode says a lot about life in New Zealand. While I was in Napier I was selected as one of the coaches for the National women's team to tour Taiwan. Because I was a foreigner I had to go to the immigration office and get a re-entry visa stamped into my American passport so I could get back into the country. No big deal. Except it seems even the simplest things turn out to be a big deal for me one way or the other. Doh!

Believe it or not this happened on the same day as the historic first re-entry of the Space Shuttle Columbia - April 14, 1981. The phrase "Re-Entry" was everywhere in the news that day. I walked into the immigration office and the lady behind the counter quietly said, "Can I help you?"

"Yes, yes you can," I boomed! "I've got a ticket on the next space shuttle and I need a re-entry visa," I proudly proclaimed.

This immigration official who looked like Morticia from the Adams Family gave me the coldest, stoniest look I've ever seen... she didn't crack one facial muscle.

She looked straight through me.

It was like she had sucked every ounce of life from the room.

She turned and walked away.

Comment: This gal was staunch... she wouldn't help me period. I actually had to wait until another clerk came in... I know it wasn't the world's greatest joke... but come on.

The Streak

Even with all the battles I fought, I loved coaching basketball in New Zealand. It was like barnstorming across America in the 1950s. And I got to play again. I was a player coach. There were two reasons that an oldish white guy who couldn't jump could still play the game in New Zealand.

First, the standard of play was just a wee bit beyond James Naismith's first basketball class of 1891. Second, there weren't any black players in the country. The game was played below the ring so, quite literally, white men didn't have to jump.

The club I coached involved three teams: the senior men, the senior women and the junior men and we'd drive all over the country to play, and tradition dictated that anyone who fouled out of a game on the road had to streak on the way home; women included!

The funniest streaking episode involving my club wasn't a streak at all. It involved all of my players stark naked in the middle of the road, on their hands and knees, formed into a human pyramid of bare asses. A pyramid moonshot! I'd never seen anything quite like it before, or since.

Ray Stevens

I had never streaked before so when I fouled out of a game, everyone was waiting for the old man to do it. I told them to keep their pants on (pun intended) and that I'd get around to it sooner or later. The right time would come and I had to remind them that although I wasn't an expert on streaking I imagined it was a lot like basketball... Ball bouncing has to be done with a sense of timing.

We left the gym and climbed into our vans to head home. Along the way, we stopped for some food in a small village. While everyone else sat around eating their fish and chips, I walked down the street a few blocks, stepped into some bushes and took off all my clothes, bar my sneakers.

I hesitated for a second and then streaked up the main street of the town, waving as I flew past my startled players.

Everyone loved it, including a couple of American tourists: 'Lookathim... Lookathim...'

Steven Adams

I suppose it would be remiss of me being a basketball guy and all, not to make some remarks on New Zealand's top NBA (National Basketball Association) player. I'm going to keep this as short and sharp as the mercurial rise was of a barefoot kid running wild in Rotorua to becoming a multi-millionaire sneaker streaking demon in the bright lights of the NBA. And it all seemed to happen in the snap of a finger!

Right from the beginning Adams was a big gawky kid who had no idea of how to play the game. But if you looked at him - his size- his physical tools - his ability to move up and down the court even if he looked like an ungainly duck all arms and legs going in all directions - you just knew this kid had potential to be something special. Kenny McFadden saw this and convinced Steven to move to Wellington so he could attend Kenny's 6:00am morning basketball clinics... that was his first step on the road to stardom. Steven Adams next period defies explanation - he went to Scots College in Wellington and played on their basketball team... played a few games for the Saints club in the National Basketball League... then it was off to America where he attended Notre Dame Preparatory School and played one season for their team... next he landed at the University of Pittsburgh where he played a single season. In all those short stints at each institution he made no impact... no headlines as the next phenom. So what happens next? Everyone expected him to mature and develop his skills by returning to the University of Pittsburgh... but then to the astonishment of practically everyone he and his manager Kenny McFadden decided to enter him into the NBA draft and viola he is the number one draft pick for the Oklahoma City Thunder being the 12th pick overall... if that's not a movie in the making I don't know what is!

So at this point ya gotta be asking the questions - Why? - How did this kid from the sticks rise so fast? Well, there are a few reasons: Number one is Steven Adams is a big unit standing 7 feet tall and there's an old cliché in the basketball world that states: You can't coach height...

Steven also has a great pair of hands and an even greater set of wheels... for all his size and strength this kid can really motor up and down the court and he has no problem wrapping his huge mitts around the ball...

Next in line would be his mentor former Saints player and coach Kenny McFadden (an outstanding player in his own right) who got Adams to move to Wellington so he could go to his coaching sessions at 6am every morning - and Adams showed up every morning which brings me to probably his greatest asset... Steven Adams has an outstanding work ethic... this kid flat out works at his craft... works to improve his skills... as a young man he got up at dawn and went to Kenny's early morning workouts day in and day out to learn the basic rudiments... the fundamentals of the game which involves repeating basic body skill techniques over and over and over... the key to success in any sport is repetition... repetition... repetition... and that takes a ton of dedication and desire to improve yourself - not every young buck has that quality... it wasn't luck that he ended up where he's ended up... sure he had the tools to be something special but without his dedication and determination to get better he would have been just another tall kid with tons of potential but going nowhere... Steven Adams saw his opportunity and grabbed it with both hands - good on him.

Comment: So now New Zealand's got a genuine world class basketball stud... an NBA stud... so everyone in the New Zealand basketball world is salivating in anticipation as to what big Steven Adams is going to bring to the table for the national team The Tall Blacks. Looking at the New Zealand national basketball team they have a really fine group of international players... but they're mostly guards and swingmen... what they lack to be really competitive on the international stage is the Aircraft Carrier - the big man in the middle... well one would think then enter New Zealand's number one NBA stud Steven Adams to fill that role... but the irony here is... even when this little dot in the South West Pacific finally gets an NBA stud he refuses to play for the national squad...what the fuck...why? Who the hell knows... only Steven Adams knows the answer to that question... life is strange and don't let anybody tell you otherwise...

Time Out
The following section details me coaching my ten-year-old son's primary school basketball team. And yes you would be correct in assuming it didn't always go smoothly

Coaching demon
NEWS FLASH: Not every kid wants to play sport just for fun. There are plenty of kids who want to win... badly want to win.

Some want to be pushed hard and are prepared to work so they can excel. They want someone who'll tap their potential and get the best out of them. So why punish the kids who desperately want to win by giving in to adults who think it's wrong to encourage the idea of winning and losing.

I've coached at a variety of levels from showing gawky high school teenagers how to shoot a ball, to seasoned professionals and a lot in between.

My approach to coaching has always been the same. I've been hard-nosed, I'll tell it straight and no, I don't take prisoners.

Along the way, it's got me into trouble - I've started riots, been kicked out of the odd game (or is it a hundred games?), been banned and acquired a reputation for being the crazy man of basketball.

So, that's why I politely declined when the administrator at my son's elementary school asked me if I would coach the school basketball team.

It's why I turned down the offer when I was asked for the second and third time... and warned:

'Honestly, you do not, under any circumstances, want to see my "coaching demon" unleashed in a competitive environment at this level.'

Sam

I thought I had been fairly clear and that would be the end of the matter. But with the passage of time, when my son Sam turned 10, he and his school buddies desperately needed a real coach. By 'real', I mean a coach that did more than the moms and teachers who had supposedly 'coached' the kids before. They had supervised the kids, not coached them. These raw, talented boys had been playing grade school basketball for three years but had learned little. And they lost every single game... they never won or were even close to winning. They were losing interest, becoming bored and some were ready to give up the game. In one game they lost 66 to 4... and no I'm not making that up. I watched that game and cringed throughout the entire embarrassing experience as the mother coach just sat there and said nothing... did nothing as these bewildered kids were getting slaughtered. That's definitely not good for your emotional well-being.

Winning

On my very first day of practice I asked the kids: "What do you want... what's your goal?" And without any hesitation they all exclaimed that they wanted to win. And I could see it in their faces they just wanted to win some damn games. They were tired of being losers all the time.

Adults

I took the plunge. Despite my misgivings, and warnings to the school, I decided to give them the coach I thought they deserved - someone who would help them achieve their potential.

I learned plenty from the experience. And top of my list of learnings was realizing that some adults needed to grow up. The main problem I had coaching at this level was with other adults (school administrators, parents and league officials) who treated my kids like babies. These grown-ups tiptoed around the kids, as if on eggshells, afraid that actual demands might be put on them and they would have to measure up.

Newsflash

But, hey, here's another newsflash: kids aren't dumb; they crave strong, decisive leadership. In fact, they thrive on it.

I stuck to my philosophies of coaching and, yes, I was demanding of them. Did I lose any kids? Yes. The ones who weren't able to commit with passion dropped out. That's life - you can't please everyone. I don't want to please everyone.

The Game

Coaching these 10-year-olds was one of the toughest assignments of my coaching career.

Having never been properly coached, the players were not only extremely limited in the skill department, they didn't even know the basic rudiments of the game... they had no clue as to how to actually play the game. They didn't even know how to take the ball out of bounds. Teaching kids how to play a game is such a simple concept it's often overlooked by most coaches... structured games are a completely different animal to the loose games kids play on the playground.

Games with a strict code of rules, a score keeper and a clock are a whole new experience for children being introduced to competitive sport. For instance, when my son was playing soccer, they'd have a two-hour practice every week and yet when I went to their first game, their goalie was trying to head the ball away when the other team took shots at the goal because he didn't know that he could use his hands. Yeah, I know, hard to believe, but true.

My job was to mold my group of 10-year-olds into a competitive team with one 45-minute practice a week. I saw all this as a great challenge. I didn't take the bull by the horns - I grabbed its testicles, jumped on its back and rode it all the way to practice. And the first thing I did was to double the practices to two a week. Einstein in action... ha.

The Game Plan

It makes no difference whether I'm coaching kids or seasoned pro's - I've always had a game plan.

Here's how I went about turning around a bunch of kids who couldn't win:

<u>Newton's Third Law of Motion:</u> One of the most important things to teach kids is how to stop themselves under control. Two-foot stops. A basketball court is really a small space, so to be able to run and come to a controlled stop is essential. And when you think about it, it's only logical that to be able to control a rubber ball one needs to be in control of oneself.

So, my first coaching lesson involved no balls. I told the kids to put all the balls to one side. This is where Sir Isaac Newton's third law of motion comes into play because the first thing the kids did was to fire the balls off the court towards the far wall. The balls hit the wall and came bouncing back onto the court. I explained to the boys Newton's third law of motion: For every action there's an equal and opposite reaction... hence if you roll a rubber ball against a wall it'll come right back at you. I hear you ask what does Sir Isaac Newton's Third Law of Motion have to do with learning basketball skills? Not much really but it's interesting and life is interesting if you make it that way. In the early days of practice, I repeated this phrase so often you could ask any of my players about Newton's third law of motion and they'd tell you. I decided not to place too much emphasis on defense... I know... I know defense wins games... but when you're young, you want to have fun.

<u>Scoring:</u> And what's the most enjoyable aspect of basketball? Right; tossing the ball through the hoop. Remember, I had a limited time to be effective so in the early stages, we concentrated on the correct fundamentals of shooting the ball. And besides, no matter how good your defense is, at some point you've got to score to win games. One of the problems with young coaches is they are too keen to impress everybody (other adults, to be more accurate) with how much they know. So they tend to throw way too much material at their young charges too quickly. They march relentlessly through one drill after another which looks impressive. But kids need time and repetition to learn new skills.

<u>Raw Talent:</u> Here's what I had to work with: I had one Asian kid who was a pretty good ball handler; my own kid who knew how to shoot the ball; one very tall player from Nigeria who couldn't drop the ball in the ocean if he was standing on the Queen Mary; and a bunch of keen, green kids with zero skills.

First, I explained to them the proper names for the basketball court (every game has its own language).

The Basics: I talked to them about the court in practical terms, a player's concept of what he has to work with. A basketball court is 94 feet long and 50 feet wide. There are two 'rings'; one at each end of the court. They are attached to rectangular boards called 'backboards' and are ten feet high. These rings are also called baskets, buckets, hoops and the hole. There are two sidelines, simply called 'sidelines'. The two end lines are called 'baselines'. At each end of the court is an area called the 'key' (it looks like an old fashioned key hole for skeleton keys). The key consists of two-lane lines and a free throw line. There are three 'circles' on a basketball court, one at either end attached to the top of the keys, and one in the center of the court (this is where we have jump balls). The line running through the center circle is called the 'half-court line'.

Now, that's not difficult, is it? But young players need to start with those basics.

Home Base: Next, I talked about how a player's style and size will help determine where he'll position himself on the court. The two guards, what we call the 'back-court', usually operate in the area from the lane lines extended up and away from the basket because their size enables them to dribble and handle the ball better. Forwards are usually taller and therefore better rebounders and operate in the area from free throw line extended wide down around the basket area.

The center or post player is usually the biggest member of the team and usually the best rebounder so he will position himself down low near the basket on either side of the key.

This is most important to give the kids a sense of where they belong on the court (home base) and gives your team instant floor balance. I also assigned a certain player to always take the ball out of bounds. This gives the players a sense of purpose and they don't have to guess what they should be doing so they have a lot more confidence in what they're trying to do

With inexperienced players, you limit their choices... the idea is to put them into situations where they can have success and not to leave it too chance.

Take the 'she'll be right' attitude with youngsters and all you get is one big mess. I taught them the mechanics of what to do during a game - what to do in certain game situations, where to line up on the floor for both offensive and defensive situations, such as when we or the other team were shooting free throws (how to line up on the key) or what to do on out of bounds situations. Once we got that sorted, and, believe me, I repeated these game basics more than once. In fact, I'd give them pop quizzes during practice which the kids loved and taught them to think on their feet.

<u>Eye on the Target:</u> Right from the get go, I taught them the fundamentals of shooting. I would line them up about a foot and a half from the basket and they'd have to execute the basics of shooting the ball, hitting the square on the backboard five times in a row and then the next player would do the same. You'd be surprised how often the ball goes into the basket if you shoot the ball off that little square. We did this religiously at every practice in the beginning until they got into the habit of putting the ball into the basket. Success breeds success. Was this boring? Yes! But it needed to be done if we were to have any chance of reaching our goal of winning games.

<u>Sir Isaac Newton Again:</u> I need to point out here that lay-ups are not an easy shot. Most people think making a lay-up is a simple process because you're so close to the basket, but this is a misconception especially for youngsters just starting out. First of all, you shoot a lay-up with the same shooting fundamentals you use with a fifteen-foot jump shot but here's the difference; with a lay-up it's all about timing and rhythm on the move.

The kid has to dribble the ball towards the basket and at a certain point he has to stop dribbling, take off on one foot and change his forward momentum to one of jumping up (read Newton's second law of motion - changing the direction of your inertia) as this allows for a soft shot.

While doing that, he has to gather the ball in two hands to his chest area and as he's rising up towards the basket, he has to extend his arms and move his hands into the shooting position while lifting his head to look at his target. Then, and only then, he softly shoots the ball against the backboard.

All this requires excellent self-control. Releasing the ball, while jumping high and at speed, is difficult for most adults, let alone a 10-year-old kid. Inexperienced players will launch the ball with the velocity of a bullet train, sending it ricocheting off the backboard back to half-court. These kids just didn't get Newton's Second Law of Motion.

To solve this problem, I went back to our initial drill and instructed the players who couldn't do a proper lay-up to come to a two-foot stop in the games, even if they were completely ahead of the pack, and to shoot the ball off the square (like we did in our drills).

Voila! Suddenly, kids who couldn't have scored a bucket in a thousand attempts could see how it was done, and they were sinking them.

The key is to constantly evaluate the kid's talent and see what they're doing in the game. If you can get them into the best possible situation for them to succeed, they'll get the idea and will master the required skill.

Big Man: Not afraid to look for ways for the team to win, I decided my big guy was going to be critical. I put in a ton of time teaching him how to post up, catch the ball and turn and face the basket, again shooting the ball off the square behind the basket on the backboard. I worked with him on this over and over and then a lot more (like before school on the outdoor baskets).

This kid was certainly tall but no one had ever taught him the fundamentals of low post play. He was a quick learner and became an effective basketball player (in his final year at the school he was the Most Valuable Player at the National Under 13 Championships).

And now we had a big guy who could sink baskets, we spent a lot of time working on how to pass the ball into him - lob passes, bounce passes, baseline hook passes. It's not rocket science; you work to your strengths.

The Moment
And as with most teams, even a team of 10 year olds, we had a defining moment. We were going to play one of the top teams, one they had never beaten and I asked my big man, my stud if he was fired up to play? His response floored me. 'Maybe,' he barely mumbled.

I called the rest of the team over for a quick meeting and relayed to them what I was just told. I barked (loudly and directly) that this type of attitude was totally unacceptable and if they weren't fully committed they could forget about it. 'I'm 62-years-old, guys, and I don't really need this crap, and I'm definitely not kissing any 10-year-old's ass!' Looking directly at my big man I exclaimed, "If the best you can do is 'maybe' then don't show up."

Well, we played a blinder, edging the other team by three points. The big guy showed up big time and played one helluva game.

I was beaming when the other coach wandered around, looking completely befuddled after the game, because he thought it was going to be business as usual when playing us. He expected they'd win without breaking a sweat. It was one of our better games all year and from there we really gelled as a team.

The Demon Never Sleeps
Was it easy?
No!
My staunch and unrelenting attitude caused some problems.
Was I a good boy?
Not always.

In the grand final of the winter competition, a father from the other team we were playing was throwing a few verbal blasts my way when I suddenly spun around looked directly at him and forcefully gave him the one-finger salute.

He got the message, became embarrassed and immediately sat down.

Was I proud of that?
No.
Was it a good role model example for my son and the other kids?
No.
Did I feel bad about?
 Not really. That's me, that's my personality in a competitive situation. If I get challenged I answer back, hard.

Did I explain the rights and wrongs of this to my team?

You betcha. I told them that in a heated situation if they can remain calm then they'd be better off for it. The thing is you can't shield your offspring entirely from the evils and disappointments of the world. I'm the first to admit - I'm not perfect.

Did I get called into the Headmaster's office?
Yes.
Did I need that at 62 years of age?
No.
He wanted an explanation.
Did I lie?
No.
I told him that another dad got a little heated and I solved the situation without saying a word.

I did something for those kids that seldom gets done in today's PC world.

I was honest with them.

Studs
The point for me was I turned those boys into competitors and witnessed first-hand how their self-confidence soared. When they walked into the stadium they held their heads high because they knew they were good... they knew it would take a damn good team to beat them.

To me in that stage of their development that was just as important if not more so than any grade they got in a classroom. I clearly saw this growth in their confidence and belief in themselves but the school's principal and the teachers just didn't get it. This not only amazed me it frustrated the hell out of me... emotional growth at this stage in a kid's life is so important and these lunkheads at the school were oblivious to it.

Listening

Once the word got out that there was an honest basketball program I had more kids wanting to join our team than I could handle. The beautiful thing with that group of kids is every one of them took a journey with me and developed like they never had before both on and off the court. I too took a journey of my own. On the way to the winter championship game my son said, 'Dad, win or lose, could you find some good things to say to the team?'

I listened; I listened real hard because these were heartfelt words from my boy, a 10-year-old kid and there's a fine balance between pushing them to succeed and leeching all the fun out of the game. When Sam spoke to me about his concern for his team mates I felt really good that we had the kind of relationship that he felt comfortable in telling me that and that he was concerned for them.

Rebounding Mom

Were there funny moments? plenty, but this one will always stick out in my mind. One morning at practice I had divided the team into groups at several baskets doing a rebounding drill.

We've all heard how some mothers will go to any lengths to ensure that their little darling will succeed.

Well, this particular mother, God bless her, took the cake. I looked over at one of the rebounding stations and this mom was actually in amongst the kids herself rebounding the hell out of the ball and giving the ball to her son.

I laughed, walking over to her, and politely explained that, no, she couldn't do the work for her son. He had to do this drill all by himself.

Comment One: Twenty-five years after I retired from coaching I discovered that, once a competitor... always a competitor. Case in point: I'm an old man now coaching a bunch of ten-year-old kids. This should have been a breeze a walk in the park. I mean how tough could it be? This wasn't a highly competitive league as most of the teams had their mothers as their coach. But, I just couldn't help myself - my competitive DNA took over. I scouted every team... I took notes... I knew who their best players were and what their strengths were and what their weak points were and how we were going to stop them. And I can guarantee you that nobody else in the league was doing what I was doing!

As a coaching mentor of mine had told me many years before it doesn't matter if you're coaching at the highest levels or down in a dog league just make sure you're the top dog!

Basically I took a group of kids who had no idea of what they were doing on the basketball court, who had never won and turned them into a competitive unit. They won 19 games and lost only two games all year. And, yes, that was our goal; to win games and we succeeded and I'll take that any day of the week, thank you, and I make no apologies for wanting to teach kids that winning is a helluva lot better than losing.

I also taught them life lessons along the way, and we had lots of laughs.

But, in the end instead of being the loveable grandpa type coach everyone else (including school administrators) wanted, I was my usual self - a fire-breathing dragon - granted, an old fart fire-breathing dragon, but still one with enough puff to rile anyone in my path and so with my reputation as the Loud American, and my side line antics, complaints were laid and the school felt it had its good name to protect, and that was way more important than whether I was developing the young players on my team.

My conscience was clear. I had, after all, warned the school of what would happen if my 'coaching demon' was unleashed.

Comment Two: Ten years down the track I still bump into the kids on that team who are all young men now and they all say the same thing: They call me coach, and exclaim what a great time they had being on that team.

Competitor versus Participant

I'm a competitor, not a participant. Most people think of themselves as competitors but, in reality, they're just participants. They just take up space.

A competitor is someone who doesn't like to lose. It doesn't matter how nice you are, if you like to lose you're not a competitor. Competitors do not accept losing with a smile - with a handshake, maybe. But never with a smile, and once in a while with a tear.

In my philosophy, there are three areas that make up being a competitor.

Point One
The first area is mental toughness.

How tough are you when the going gets rough? Everybody loves riding in the wagon when it's going down hill ... But what about pushing it uphill?

We all have our personal problems - wife, family, kids, love affairs, getting stuck in traffic, money worries ... Do you take all that extra baggage with you when you've got a job to do or do you put it aside and get on with the task at hand? Because it's not like a faucet that you turn on and off. Day in and day out, how tough are you mentally?

Point Two
The second area is what I like to call game day.

I'll use sports here to illustrate, but it could be any situation.

Imagine, you are out on the field and things just aren't going your way. You're getting bum calls from the ref. You're getting stepped on and knocked down and bruised. The ebb and flow of the game, or situation, just isn't going your way.

And then BANG! Suddenly, right in front of you, there's a chance to compete one-on-one. Head-to-head. But you let it slip away... You say I'll get it next time... I'll be ready on the next play... Bullshit! A competitor competes. Yes, competes! Every time. On every play.

No, you don't always win. Yes, sometimes the other guy will beat you!

In whatever field you are in - whether it's acting, sports or sales... you might get 10 opportunities a day... or in a game... or, yes, maybe just in one lifetime...

Say, you only choose to 'compete' on just half of them. Say, you win three of that half. Now you have won three out of five. Except it's not really three out of five, is it? It's three out of 10!

Even with a 50/50 chance you could have brought that average up to five out of 10 but only if you had chosen to compete on all 10 of the opportunities presented to you!

How many games are won by the narrowest of margins? How many contracts are signed to the guy who did just that little extra bit of work?

Imagine if every guy in your team or your company decided to compete on all TEN opportunities that were presented to him...
Go ahead... imagine! The book can wait... Imagine!

Point Three
The third area I focus on is philosophy.

You can choose to play as an object in the game... a body... moving and doing things as best as you can which is to say you are a simple participant.

Or you can add another dimension to what you do.

Become more than just a body in motion by thinking about what you're doing as you do it. A person who thinks about what they're doing and has a philosophy about why they're doing it is more than a simple participant they are a player and only as a player can they become a creative force. And creative forces are competitors who make things happen. I made things happen!

The Spider's Web
And finally this is my ode to all the basketball junkies in the world: When you struggle through a season... the highs... the lows... the emotions... the trust... the good times and the bad times... the sweat... the strain and the aspirations... the accomplishments... getting there and not getting there... the crying and the laughter... the anticipation... the loyalty and the let downs... the hours and hours of practice and planning... dreams and frustrations... sudden joy and exaltation and the equally sudden sadness and despair... these are feelings that build up between teammates during the course of a season and like all good things they take time to develop and they become like a spider's web that holds a group of people together however fine it may be.

The person who sits next to you in the locker room has gone through the whole scene with you from the beginning to the end and the people you sweat with throughout a season or a career you never forget. It's a special feeling all of its own that only belongs to those who go through it together.

Part Two

JENNIFER

CHAPTER SIX

How to Survive Falling in Love on the 3rd Strike

After leaving a trail of broken relationships, and suffering a midlife breakdown, Dybvig unexpectedly finds salvation and true love.

Rock Bottom

I was living in the New Zealand version of the Addams Family home all on my own. The house was a rambling, five-bedroom Victorian mansion. There was a huge fireplace in the living room and another in the kitchen. There was a sun room with beautiful lead-lined windows and doors. I had a ton of firewood in the driveway with which I built an enormous fire every night. I had that place so hot the timbers in the ceiling cracked like whips.

One night I was eating another gourmet meal, half a loaf of toast and four fried eggs (sunny side up) smothered in a mountain of baked beans. Suddenly the room started to spin. I was getting these hot and cold flashes and I was sweating a river, then bam I hit the floor. My gut felt like it was in a vice slowly tightening. I spent about an hour on my knees, too scared to move, just locked into this agony in my gut. It started to ease and then, bam it hits me again. After another hour, the pain vanished. What the heck was that? I decided to ignore it. I didn't even think about it. I left it laying there on the floor of my memory like a discarded pair of pants and sort of snuck away like nothing had happened. Bad move.

Bile

Two weeks later it happened again. Well, I can take a hint. I called my doctor. "Gallstones," he replied sternly. I went and had a scan, no doubt about it, gallstones. Turns out everyone has a small pear-shaped sac of bile just under their liver, except, instead of mine being full of bile I've got a rock garden.

"We'll have to operate," said my doctor in grave 'doctor tones'. Fear can really sharpen the mind. I don't know exactly where the information came from, but I became this instantaneous expert on gallstones. I told my doctor about ultrasound and lasers and all sorts of painless ways they've got for dissolving gallstones these days.

My doctor was a stubborn guy and declared that an operation was the only thing. Apparently, my rocks were spread far and wide. I ignored him. What do doctors know?

I went about my business. Who needs a bile reservoir anyway?

Comment: I was acting like one of those characters in day time soaps who ignore the obvious causing the audience at home to scream at the television berating their stupidity.

Rhinoceros

The last attack was a doozy. I'd just finished hosting my NFL show at the Sky television network and had stopped off at the Golden Horse for combination fried rice and a dozen deep fried wontons. Then it was home for a hot soak in the tub, before hitting the sack, the good life.

Three a.m. and I wake with a rhinoceros horning into my ribs. I'm projectile vomiting all the way to the far wall. I'm not at all well.

I called my doctor, and he said he'd come over and see me before he did his hospital rounds at six in the morning. I hung up and staggered back to bed.

Suddenly my stomach was trying to throw up some huge internal organ. I crawled back to the phone. I'm like Sergeant Rock jaw wounded in no man's land, crawling through barbed wire.

And I was concentrating like crazy so that I could find the right words to impress my doctor regarding the gravity of the situation: "Death is trying to break down my door, get the fuck over here, bring drugs, now!"

Home

I was the absolute worst patient they had ever seen at Auckland Hospital. My doctor had shot a bucket of morphine into my thigh, but fear had generated a bathtub of adrenaline to counteract it. I kept getting out of bed, and they kept putting me back in. I'd pass out long enough for them to relax, then struggle back to consciousness and wander the corridors looking for an escape route.

The chief surgeon turned up at my bedside with his juvenile posse of young doctors just like in 'Grey's Anatomy'. They all stood around me discussing my bag of rocks like I wasn't there and then just assumed that I was going under the knife. This irritated me no end: "Forget it. What knife? Who are you? I don't even know you."

They all looked at the chief surgeon, who bemusedly shook his head and left. Later the Ward Sister (nurse) came over and sternly told me I'd been summoned to the chief's office. This guy was huge, he reminded me of Burl Ives playing Kris Kringle with his full white beard in Miracle on 34th Street with a scalpel. He told me that I couldn't avoid the inevitable. The attacks were triggered by fried foods and would only get worse (uh oh - there go the fried wontons). He described the operation: They'd slice (nice comforting terminology) from the middle of my stomach clear around to my back. I pushed my line of ultra laser or whatever and he squashed that. Apparently, some boulders had found their way into my intestines. This scared the hell out of me so I told him I'd have to think it over and left. I went back to the ward and was getting my things together when I was ambushed by the Sister (nurse).

"Where are you going?"

"I'm outta here, lady."

"Oh, no, you're not."

"Oh, yeah. You wanna bet?"

Great. Now I'm contemplating beating up a nurse.

Ok Already
I finally came to my senses and agreed to the operation like I'm doing them a big favor. I made one stipulation. I recorded my NFL (National Football League) show every Tuesday night and I had to fit the operation in between that. They laughed. But I was deadly serious. I was going to do that show even if it killed me.

The night before Dr. Shaw was going to slice me in half for real I woke up in the wee small hours... I was feeling alone and vulnerable.

Nobody knew I was in the hospital.

I hadn't even told my boss at the television station as I knew he'd get someone to replace me for my show and that's a definite 'no no' in 'show business', never, and I repeat never ever give anyone a shot at your gig.

I hadn't even called my mother in California.

Nope, this was just between me and Burl. But my situation also got me thinking: "How in the hell did I get into a position where I was so completely alone in the world?" Nobody even came to visit me... that's sad.

Drifting

It's like the 'homeless people' you step over them every day in some cities and wonder how did they allow themselves to get into that position in the first place?' What went wrong? Where did they step off the path? Believe me it's not that hard it's gradual...a step here... a step there... a broken relationship... moving away from family and friends... job instability... a bit too much booze... constantly being on the move with no real fixed abode... all adds up to inching that much closer to the side of the path and the next thing you know you're in 'no-man's land' sleeping under a bridge (I once slept in a friend's office for a time) or lying in a hospital bed all alone. I went through jobs and relationships like a hot knife through butter, with reckless abandon. And I was always on the move.

I travelled throughout the world hopping from one position to another, I flew over to Sydney, Australia and worked in a café in Kings Cross (their red light district). I was carefree and loose, exceedingly loose, I was working as a barista and part-time security guard hitting the nightclubs after every shift, not a care in the world.

I definitely wasn't paying attention. My 'timing and rhythm' was all out of whack and I just didn't see it. From Sydney I suddenly jetted back to New Zealand and took up a post as a journalist, wrote and published a basketball manual (I wrote a 125-page outline for this book a few months earlier in my mother's kitchen when I was in the San Francisco Bay Area) while sleeping on the couch of a friend and then just as suddenly I took off to Australia again, this time landing in Adelaide to coach a basketball team for the South Adelaide Basketball Club. Live that kind of life-style for a decade and even though you're working high-profile jobs you're walking on quicksand. There simply isn't any foundation underneath you.

So, it really wasn't that surprising that I found myself fitfully awake with my brain in overdrive all alone in a foreign hospital in a foreign country in the wee small hours before a surgeon who was the spitting image of Burl Ives was going to slice me in half. And it's just weird how the craziest stuff just pops into your head: I couldn't get rock singer Bobby "Splish-Splash" Darin out of my head. In my 'minds-eye' I could clearly see him talking to chat show host Mike Douglas in the States about his impending heart surgery. Both men cracked jokes about it as the funniest topic in the world that afternoon.

Bobby Darin didn't make it...

Comment: The security job in Sydney was wild to say the least. The head of security for the apartment complex was the guy I was flatting with hence my part-time position. We'd go on patrol during the night to roust the 'Rent' boys (gay guys) and prostitutes from plying their trade outside the building.

We also had to patrol the underground parking lots wearing plastic gloves so we could pick up the cum filled tissues the prostitutes in the area used to wipe their mouths after giving one of their customers a blow job and then they'd just tossed them on the ground. Yuck! We also had to keep alert as we'd occasionally come across a junkie shooting up. Like I said wild times.

Andy Warhol

I had asked my own doctor just how complicated an operation it was? Mr. 'Everybody would be famous for fifteen minutes' Andy Warhol died from complications after gallbladder surgery. He shrugged his shoulders and exhaled, "Every time you opened someone up, there's always a certain amount of risk."

Great, way to make a guy feel good.

"Gee, thanks, Doc." I had to have the timing down just right if I was going to make my show. I checked into the hospital on Wednesday. The anesthetist dropped by and asked me if I wanted to stay partially awake and observe the proceedings?

"Are you kidding? I want the full dose. I want a double dose. Get a grip!"

When the time came I was wheeled into the theater and I could see the crew, all standing around in their green smocks and hair nets. Burl came bursting through the doors like actor Vince Edwards used to do in the opening shot of his show Ben Casey.

He was looking deadly serious and was wearing the regulation gear except for one bit of flash; he's got a bright red bandanna tied over his head. The last thought I could nail down before going bye byes was, "Oh, my god. I'm gonna have a freakin' extra from 'Pirates of the Caribbean' rummaging through my belly for rocks."

I didn't wake up until Friday morning. I had twenty-five metal clips holding the entire right side of my body together, and they'd piped me into the city's water reticulation scheme. Every single bodily orifice had a tube stuck in it, plus they'd drilled a couple of extra holes. I had an oxygen tube jammed into each nostril, liquid food was dripping into a hole in my arm, and pain killer leaking into two holes in my back. And to top it off, a plastic pipe from what looks like a plug hole in my stomach oozing blood, glop and some greenish slime into a jar by the bed.

Knifed

A bunch of Samoan kids were in the ward visiting one of their hip-hop friends. One of them recognised me from my sports shows and came over, "What happened to you, coach?" I popped my smock and showed him the scar. A big angry red slash. "Foo," he whistled, "Somebody finally caught up with you, eh?" He was convinced I'd been stabbed.

There were only four days to go to my NFL show and I was determined to make it. The Doc and Sisters just nodded their heads in amusement, "Let's see how you progress," they'd smile. Turns out my 'progress' was to be measured by the movement of my bowels. I hadn't eaten in a week. On Sunday I farted, significant move. It hurt like hell. On Monday they gave me breakfast and later that morning I managed a weak miniscule little poop, about what a Hamster would do. Yes! Success! Finally, and after much pestering from me, the hospital staff were too tired to argue with me any longer. They told me I could go back to my grand but empty house.

Of course there was no one to pick me up from the hospital. I ordered a taxi and an orderly wheeled me to its door. It took ages and a huge amount of effort to bend my body into the cab, but eventually I managed it. I returned to the solitude of my home. I had 36 hours to recuperate if I was to make it back to work on time. I wondered how I was going to feed myself. There was next to nothing to eat in the house and, anyway, I certainly wasn't up to cooking. I would have to go out for food.

The house was at the bottom of a very steep hill and I ventured outside, in my baggy convalescence clothes, wondering if I'd make it to the top. I couldn't bend or even lean forward so I quickly conceded that normal walking was next to impossible. With a bit of experimentation, I realized I could climb the hill backwards. In pain, I forced my toes against the ground, pushing backwards with all my strength to slowly reverse my body up the hill. Sweating and in pain, I finally made it to the KFC on the corner where I bought a dinner of whipped mash potatoes and gravy.

The next day, I turned up at Sky walking like a 90-year-old. As I entered the studio, no one seemed to notice my discomfort. One of the production crew came over.

'Hey, John, where've you been all week? We've been trying to call you.'

'Let me tell you about my operation,' I offered.

He raised his hand to stop me.

'Yeah. Right. Love to hear about it sometime. Gotta go.'

Comment: I remember when I was in Burl's office and he was discussing how he was going to operate my immediate thought was, "I've got absolutely zero money... I can't afford this operation." So, I asked him point blank, "Hey man, how much is this gonna cost...? I haven't got any savings I can't afford this."

His reply floored me, "Nothing."

I think I just blurted out, "Bullshit!" But he insisted that all the costs were covered by the government. I just couldn't wrap my head around that - it was my first experience with socialized medicine.

Mr Staunch
When it came to relationships, I had always used my masculinity to mask my emotions. I built a wall around myself and hid behind it.
In fact, my personal relationships were a minefield of disasters with two broken marriages by the time I was 30.

I married my first wife, Denile, when we were fresh out of our teens. She was my high school sweetheart and we started dating in our senior year.

I went to university to study physical education (i.e. to become a basketball coach) and to get my teaching qualifications. We married in my senior year there, in a service at a Lutheran church across the road from our high school.

My mother-in-law was a beautiful person in every way full of love and kindness. She was also a devout follower of the religion Christian Science. I really didn't know anything about this religion - in fact I had never even heard of it before so I asked Denile about its foundations and beliefs. One of the things she told me about this religion just floored me... namely that Christian Science believers didn't believe in surgery. They called in people to pray for you.

This caused a problem early in our marriage when Denile became sick and didn't say enough to make me aware. Eventually, her appendix burst and I rushed her to the hospital where the doctors told me she needed an immediate operation. Despite her protests, I signed the papers authorising the doctors to treat her.

I found it hard to believe that any religion could encourage people to deny themselves the wonders of modern medicine, and the family's beliefs eventually cost Denile's mother her life when she refused treatment for a clot in her leg. It travelled to her brain and killed her.

Mr. Stupid
While I studied for my Master's Degree, Denile and I struggled through like many young couples.

I pumped gas at the weekends and cleared lunchtime tables at my father's restaurant during the week. It kept us busy and we didn't have to focus on the marriage.

I applied to join the Peace Corps and Graduate School and was going for whichever one came through first.

Graduate School won. With my Master's Degree in Physical Education, I was offered a position at De Anza College, teaching phys ed and being the assistant basketball coach.

And while I buried myself in the challenges of this work, our marriage started to unravel. I guess we weren't talking on any meaningful level and to say I was brash, reckless and extremely selfish back then would be an understatement.

Within a few years, we were divorced. Looking back, Denile was my first real girlfriend and I think we did what was expected of us. I had no idea about the responsibilities of marriage, or of how to look after someone else.

When we were preparing to get married, I remember our family priest asking the standard question: 'Where do you see yourself in five years?'

I rattled off my response: 'When I graduate, I'll get a job; we'll buy a house and have a couple of children.'

Of course, I never discussed any of that with Denile before I said it, nor did we discuss it later.

Basically I was too immature to sustain any sort of meaningful relationship.

Second Time Around
On the rebound, I married again and the results were exactly the same. My decision to marry for the second time typified the way I thought in those days. Or rather it typified the way I failed to think at all - just dive in without too much thought.

It came about when I landed the coaching job at Gonzaga University and I just assumed my girlfriend, Kathleen, would move with me to Spokane, Washington.

She had other ideas and wouldn't make the move unless we were married first. I remember being shocked at this development but that shows how little credence I gave to the thoughts and feelings of others.

Nonetheless, we got married and threw our junk into a U-Haul and drove 1,600 miles to Spokane, Washington, where we bought a house and started an entirely new life with little forethought and even less discussion.

When my dad died, and I tossed in my coaching position to move back to California, I did so without consulting anyone, including Kathleen.

Looking back, I can't believe how brazen I was, how stupid I acted. But I didn't know any better. It never occurred to me I should discuss things that affected both of us. I always acted out of self-interest.

I was Mr Staunch because that's how I thought a man was supposed to behave.

When I left the States to move Down Under, Kathleen and I were still married. She came with me but became sick and needed to return several times to the States for treatment.

On one of those trips home, she decided not to come back to New Zealand and she divorced me.

My second marriage had lasted less than five years and I still hadn't learned the importance of communication.

If I needed proof, it came when I learned only after the divorce that Kathleen's mother was actually a New Zealander, having been born in the Chatham Islands. Hard to believe that I didn't even know my mother-in-law was a Kiwi, but it shows how self-absorbed I was.

Dante's Inferno
Amazingly, I almost married again on the rebound from the rebound. I went the whole nine yards with her because that's what I did back then. I fell into relationships without putting any real thought into them.

I aimlessly drifted from one entanglement to another.

One particularly messy relationship pretty much summed up my interactions with women.

Little did I know that I was about to enter Dante's Inferno.

This young woman was a writer and aficionado of the theatre, she was strong willed and fiery and bent to no one. She was French-Samoan. As George exclaimed in an episode of Seinfeld, we lived in "Colliding Worlds."

Something wasn't quite right. We were both moody and selfish and drawn to each other's darker aspects. It was a fatal attraction and deep down I knew this and yet I couldn't stop myself. I don't do drugs but I was definitely addicted to this Polynesian beauty.

Taking an apartment in the city we worked as flunkeys in a restaurant. It was dream stuff.

The jobs were just interruptions - real life was our apartment and bedroom. We indulged ourselves in mainline, overdose emotions there. A couple of passion junkies racing home for another fix.

At first the emotion was all on the upside of the scale. Love, sex, kindness. But soon enough we needed to spice it from the downside. Anger, sex, hurt.

We decided to split. Chronic withdrawal. All kinds of shit would remind me of her; half-empty wine bottles; a book page with its corner folded down; the cool underside of a pillow.

Ugly Mating Ritual
The separation didn't last. We got hooked again. Living apart, but conducting a guerrilla love affair. We'd whip each other into screaming, angry, emotional ecstasy and pay it off with love making. We'd stay away from each other for weeks and then one would turn up at the other's door in the middle of the night. Search and destroy missions. I told her I hated her and bought her a diamond ring. She told me she loved me and sold it.

It was getting dangerous. You never knew what was real and what was a tactic. My life had refined down to two speeds: hysterical, high-pitched emotion; or dreary melancholy. Mentally, I carried around a weight, a miserable, grey, fuzzy ball of funk.

Finally, I called it off. I wouldn't answer her calls. I stayed away from home. Cold turkey. She stopped calling and took up with another dreamer.

We didn't see each other for a couple of months. Then one night I was working a basketball game for television in Auckland and there she was sitting in the Champagne and paté zone. She was with her new beau, a hulking 6'8" monster.

All the cold turkey had been for nothing. She called me a bastard and a shithead. I called her a bitch and an asshole.

Her new love interest didn't like it at all. He grabbed me by the shoulders and started to push. I grabbed him by his shoulders and shoved back.

Tables and chairs and wheels of Brie and Champagne buckets hit the floor.

We locked arms and bulled each other all over the place like a couple of rutting stags. Cleared a big circle. She waltzed around us, trying to get a shot at me with her handbag, screaming insults. She found a cup of hot coffee and threw it in my face. Ugly mating ritual.

The security guards arrived and broke it up and escorted them from the building. I still had a commentating job to do.

Freedom
On my way home after the game it just suddenly hit me: The cold, gray, weight I had been carrying around had gone. Just lifted up and out of me. Like I'd been through an exorcism. The two-tone life I'd been living was over. I wasn't angry and I wasn't miserable: I was clear.

The next day a friend of mine called to see if I was okay. I told him I felt great! Like a prisoner who'd served his hard time, a lifer given a reprieve. I'd just walked out of jail and the sun was shining.

Jennifer

After my last episode in the 'love stakes' I had decided that enough was enough and I'd just cool it for a while. I'd give the love game a rest. I lived on my own for about five years just minding my own business. I was comfortable in my own skin.

'The truth is I like my own company best if the truth is to be known' that's a line from my favorite New Zealand song: ('For Today' by the Netherworld Dancing Toys).

Then the unexpected happened.

I met Jennifer through a good bunch of friends, mostly from my place of employment at the Sky Television Network.

Some of them thought it was time they played Cupid and invited me to a barbecue, arranging a blind date for me with their friend Jennifer, a woman who, by all accounts, was smart, attractive and single. She was in business, travelling the world and importing textiles and fashion accessories.
Was I nervous?

Are you kidding? Is the Pope Catholic, do bears shit in the woods!?! Of course I was nervous. I was completely off the scale.

I found myself the lone American in a backyard full of quiet conservative New Zealanders, trying to make small talk to this most attractive female. She was curvy in all the right places with great legs and a wonderful head of thick luscious hair. But it was her smile and the twinkle in her bluest of blue eyes that knocked me out. As my nerves took over, I went from Mr. Relaxed Guy to Fully-Qualified Buffoon.

I was the embodiment of all the worst things you hear about Americans abroad. I was loud, obnoxious, overbearing and told the crudest jokes to the point that everyone, including Jennifer my blind date, decided they had pressing engagements elsewhere. The only idiotic American thing I didn't do was to wear loud plaid Bermuda shorts, and that was only because I didn't have any. Instead I wore a ridiculously over-the-top floral Hawaiian shirt.

The Joke
So here it is, this is the joke that was the icebreaker. The deal breaker which created an instant stampede for the exit as one of the women at the table suddenly looked at her watch and exclaimed: "Oh, look at the time, we have to get home for the baby sitter." In my loud booming voice I entertained all these strangers with this little gem:

One day this guy gets up and goes down to have breakfast when his wife sees him she says: "Honey, you look bad!" And he says, "but I feel good." He leaves the house and walks down to the bus stop where a complete stranger exclaims: Wow, you're looking baaaaad!" Shocked, the guy pleads, "But I feel good." When he gets to work his secretary says: "whoa, whoa, whoa you look bad." With this the guy fairly shouts: "But, I feel gooooood." So, when he walks into his office he mutters to himself, "I've gotta find out what the hell's going on here" so he grabs a dictionary flipping through several pages until he comes upon: "Looking bad - feeling good"

You're a CUNT!

Comment One: Come on! I mean really!?! What the hell was I thinking there... obviously not much. I told that joke to a table of complete strangers in mixed company... what an idiot!

Comment Two: That joke was an absolute winner when I was on the speaking circuit at rugby clubs. And I always made the guy a referee... a local ref which always and I mean always brought the house down on the punchline. Like the guy said: There's a time and place for everything.

Blind Date Number Two

Was I the least bit concerned about my social ineptitude? Nope, not on your life. I never even gave it a second's thought. I went straight back to my bachelor pad and continued to crash through life like a Neanderthal on speed.

Several weeks later, I received another call inviting me to dinner as my friends persisted in their attempt to set me up. When I arrived at the restaurant, I discovered a second blind date had been arranged. She was ready to join the group that included my previous blind date, Jennifer.

For once, I didn't say a word. I just went with the flow. As the meal progressed, I found I was hitting it off just fine with the new gal, but by the end of the evening I had become mesmerized by my original blind date, Jennifer.

By the end of that evening, we were together.

I couldn't for the life of me tell you how or why it happened. It just happened. One of those mysteries of life you can never seem to properly explain.

Just Moving My Bag

Jennifer and I started dating and we got along like a house on fire.

Early in our relationship, I discovered Jennifer's wicked sense of style and humor.

And one simple move changed my entire life forever.

One hot humid night, the air was thick enough to cut with a knife. Lying in bed, my scrotum was sticking to the inside of my leg as I tried to get comfortable for a good night's sleep. I pinched it with two fingers and peeled it from between my legs.

Yeah, I know that sounds gross. I apologize for giving you this amount of detail but it's hard to tell the story otherwise.

Frankly, there are times when your sack sticks to your leg and it needs to be moved. The beautiful woman lying next to me murmured: 'What are you doing?'

'Just moving my bag,' I casually responded, not wanting to be overly graphic.

Five minutes later, she slipped out of bed and just as casually picked up her handbag and moved it across the room. She slipped back into bed without a word.

Smiling in my sleepy stupor, I immediately felt a connection with this wonderful woman.

I hardly knew her, but in that instant I realised she was special. And I knew that she had me right then and there. Helluva move.

The Jerk
As our relationship grew, I still managed to jeopardize it through my own stupidity. I could have won awards for being a jerk.

Instead, I had been nominated for Best Supporting Actor in a Drama, for my part in the television series Fallout.

This, and my ongoing work as a television and radio presenter with my own newspaper column, meant I was enjoying my time in the public spotlight and my image as a man about town. It was easy to let it go to my head.

The newspaper I wrote for wanted to include me in a feature about New Zealand's most eligible bachelors. Would I want to be included? 'Sure,' I said without a moment's hesitation, 'count me in.'

It never occurred to me what the impact might be on Jennifer, her family and friends.

The story came out with headlines blazing 'New Zealand's Hunky Eligible Bachelors' with photographs of the smiling hunks, including me. All the other guys in the story either said they had a girlfriend or were living with someone, but not me.

Oh no, I boldly stated I was twice-divorced. It got worse as I revealed myself to be a tidy house keeper (they had a picture of me with a vacuum cleaner that I had borrowed) and loved to cook. My comments made me sound like a big cuddly teddy bear living on my own - so come and get me, girls!

So much for being a media darling.

Jennifer's friends blasted me for being a selfish pig, pointing out that I had treated her as if she was invisible, as if she didn't even exist in my life.

The truth was that Jennifer had been a rock for me when I'd been sick with viral meningitis; cooking meals and helping me get back on my feet. And this was how I'd repaid her.

At first, I dismissed Jennifer's friends and their criticism, blaming their ignorance of the media and how it all works.

Over time, I changed my view.

In my eagerness to enjoy my small piece of fame, I had forgotten that nothing matters more than those close to you. The media works to its own agenda and really doesn't give a hoot about the person in the news, or their family.

Since then, I've always put those I love first.

Fiji

Jennifer taught me I needed to learn to love myself so that I would be receptive to the love of others. One night over dinner she tentatively announced she had something to say.

She was apprehensive. I was apprehensive. It was one of those classic awkward moments where we just looked at each other waiting for something to happen.

Finally it came out that she had booked us a Fijian holiday. I was flabbergasted, not knowing what to say and finally I was flattered that she would do such a thing.

That Fijian trip became an important step in our relationship. You know what they say about travelling with someone - you really find out about the person behind the person. And the couple.

We found out alright. We simply hit it off big time

However, the trip turned out to be a blast in more ways than one. When it was time to leave, we had to drive across the main island from Suva to Nadi where we were going to stay at an inexpensive hotel near the airport before our flight home the next day. Unfortunately for me, I got a bad case of Delhi Belly and my sphincter was in clench mode for the entire trip across the island.

Finally it got to the point where something had to give.

I gasped through gritted teeth that we had to stop.

Now!

I mean, NOW!

RIGHT NOW!

We swerved to the side of the road in a burst of flying gravel and dust as I launched myself from the car and scurried behind some exotic bushes.

I was in the process of tugging down my pants when Jennifer started screaming for me to stop.

I glanced over my shoulder and there, sitting on the veranda of a house, was a large Fijian family slowly fanning themselves as they smiled and waved to me.

Who said I couldn't draw a crowd?

My unexpected audience gave me renewed resolve and I nodded back, calling out 'Bula', Fijian for hello. I mumbled some lame excuse about checking out their native fauna before I hurriedly wobbled back to the car.

The Lobby
The sweat was running down my head and body and my inner boiler room was making those deep gurgling sounds that can mean only one thing - trouble, the worst kind of trouble.

And then the gods of fortune smiled on us as we spotted a sign, pointing to the Sheraton.

Step on it, I urged Jennifer.

We screamed into the reception area of this five-star hotel. I emerged from the vehicle with my face a mask of forced restraint. The bellhop took one look and without a word he pointed to the nearest restrooms.

I gingerly scooted like an overgrown penguin towards relief. Within seconds of my arrival in the toilet I cleared the joint. People ran screaming in search of clean air, clutching their throats and mopping their weeping eyes.

Okay, that last bit might be something of an exaggeration but we actor types sometimes let our imaginations run crazy. Butt (pun intended) after all that commotion, I felt much better so we decided to have lunch.

Ports o' Call
Dining at the Sheraton in Fiji is like, well, like dining in paradise. In fact my all-time favorite restaurant in the world is Ports o' Call with its authentic decor of a 1930s cruise ship at the Sheraton Fiji.

It's hushed and elegant with burly Fijian waiters in white starched jackets singing as they bring your meal to your table. When every plate is set down, the waiters whisk away their silver cloche coverings at the same precise time, and in deep rumbling voices they simultaneously chant, 'Enjoy'.

It's so lovely and simple and old fashioned that it brings tears to my eyes just thinking about it.

We had the most amazing crêpe there one night. The Fijian gentleman who prepared our crêpe in his black tuxedo was pure entertainment. He looked like one of those elderly trumpet players leading the march in New Orleans to 'Oh when the Saints come marching in."

He told stories as he peeled an orange in one long continuous peel, he did a little dance as he poured the brandy down the peel and lit it as it burst into a dazzling bluish flame. He bowed as he folded the crêpes with a flourish and set them before us.

Chef Anthony Bourdain, author of Kitchen Confidential, once wrote: 'Context and memory play powerful roles in all truly great meals in one's life.' I couldn't agree more.

They could serve me a hotdog on a stick at Ports o' Call and it would still be the best meal in the world to me because the only time I've eaten there is with the love of my life.

Down Market
After lunch at the Sheraton, we went down-market big time when we checked into our hotel near the airport. Cheesy describes it best. Everything about it was cheap and plastic and tired looking.

We entered our room which was no bigger than a shoe box. I'm not kidding; the table was a small shelf sticking out from the wall beside two stools. The bathroom door opened right into the living room, giving us a full view of the toilet.

My stomach started to rumble again.

Jennifer took in the situation, turned and gave me one of her looks that says far more than mere words. We booked into the Sheraton.

And once again I knew.

I intuitively knew that this woman was something special.

Comment: The Sheraton resort on Denarau island is just so magical and fun that Jennifer and I spent our stay there taking it all in in one day: we swam, we hit the jacuzzi, played pitch and putt golf, walked amongst the most beautiful gardens, drank the most amazing cocktails right on the beach, ate dinner under the stars, took the Bula bus around to several other resorts on the island and finally came back to the Sheraton for a nightcap at one of their boutique bars. We hit the sack at 2:00am and had to get up at 4:00am to catch our flight home. Amazing... amazing amount of experiences squeezed into a single day. And I knew... again we were just beginning our relationship... but I knew that one day Jennifer and I would get married right there on that beach at the resort.

Bonding
Without immediately realizing it, we bonded together in Fiji and it wasn't because we filled our days with overly fantastic things, just the opposite really.

We spent most of our time lazing around our condominium, reading, eating fruit and taking dips in the sea, which came up to a few steps outside our door.

One day we decided to go snorkeling. A local Fijian took us out to sea in his small dinghy and, without warning, there it was - a tiny spit of whiter than white sand, seemingly afloat in the middle of the ocean. The Fijian cut the motor and ran his boat onto this tiny slip of sand and we jumped out.

It was such a glorious feeling to be the only ones on that spot, with the water so crystal clear then spreading into aqua-green then aqua-blue and finally into a dazzling brilliant deep blue.

Wow! And the snorkeling was absolutely out of this world. The best.

Separate Ways
Jennifer and I spent time getting to know each other, and you know it's working when you can be with someone and you don't have to constantly fill the silences with needless chatter about nothing. You can let the moments just be.

I discovered what a warm, generous and caring person she was.

It came as something of a jolt to both of us when we landed back in New Zealand and went our separate ways, and to our separate homes.

It no longer seemed right to be apart and we tentatively broached the subject of living together.

I was still nervous about making the 'big move'. I wanted to think this thing through - that was a new experience for me, given my record of recklessly diving into situations.

We made the decision to move in together.

Jennifer and I had forged an easy relationship that existed without any judgments or preconceived notions of what it should be. I had finally matured to the point that it mattered to me what she thought and how she was feeling.

When we talked, Jennifer had my undivided attention. In fact, she was the sole focus of my attention.

I was no longer looking for better opportunities.

Jennifer was my opportunity.

Thick Accent

I wanted Jennifer to meet my family back in California. When I told them I was bringing her halfway round the world to meet them, they realized she must be something special.

Soon after our arrival in San Francisco, my 15-year-old niece blurted out that Jennifer was really nice but had a very 'thick accent'.

'Oh,' Jennifer responded with a smile.

Teenagers, what can you do?

But a few days later, Jennifer pulled me aside and quietly asked why my family were always leaning towards her, staring at her so intently.

'They're not staring sweetheart, they're listening.'
'What do you mean?'
'They don't understand you.'
'What?'
'Yeah, they can't follow what you're talking about.'
'Don't be ridiculous! I speak perfectly clear English.'
'Maybe to your ear, darling, but not to theirs,' I chuckled.

The funny thing about accents is everybody thinks they're fine and it's the other guy who sounds weird.

My American friends insisted that when we went out to restaurants, Jennifer should order for everyone.

They loved listening to her accent and everyone got a huge kick out of the confused looks on the waiter's face.

Hamburger Heaven

While we were in the States I wanted Jennifer to get an up close and personal glimpse of my American culture. Of course, I took her only to the best places. So, there we were, standing at the Jack-in-the-Box counter, ordering lunch.

Jennifer hadn't yet come to grips with the term 'fast food'. She was intently studying the menu on the wall like there was no tomorrow. To slow things down further, she was asking the counter guy pointed questions about how the food was prepared.

I was standing a bit to the side, watching this intriguing clash of cultures when finally, in total exasperation, a hulking construction worker directly behind in the line loomed over her.

'Alright, already!' he boomed. 'Come on, lady, what're ya doin', memorizing the menu?'

Jennifer may be a bit on the short side (she is 5'5"), but for her, propriety and manners are all important.

She slowly turned, looked up into the face of this Goliath and gave just the hint of a raised eyebrow. "I'm terribly sorry, but it's my turn. Please do wait for your turn, thank you,' she said in her delightfully clipped and cultured New Zealand accent.

The big guy was dumbfounded.

Jennifer might have been a long way from home but she didn't hesitate to stick up for herself. She liked milk in her coffee - real milk, that is, not the milk creamer that comes in small plastic containers in American restaurants. When she ordered coffee, she would request a small glass of real milk from the waiter - a simple enough matter but one that would frequently turn into a lengthy negotiation to rival an international peace treaty.

One time, my brother Bob was finishing his meal when the waiter picked up his plate, forcing him to stab the last bite of his sausage in mid-flight. He didn't mind but that was not good enough for Jennifer who slapped the hand of the startled waiter.

'He's not finished. Please set the plate back down,' she admonished him. The rest of us were busting up.

Of course, I didn't escape her fast food wrath either. My all-time favorite burger is Burger King's Double Beef Whopper.

One day, I was halfway through a freshly made, big juicy Whopper with traces of mayonnaise, ketchup and tomato juice running down my chin. She gave me 'The Look'.

'What?'

She summed up the entire California culinary experience in a single sentence.

'It's all about 'Hamburger' here, isn't it?'

'You betcha,' I chomped.

Tush

Thankfully, Jennifer wasn't a total snob when it came to Californian food and she became hooked big time on Cadillac margaritas, Buffalo wings and deep-fried mozzarella sticks.

Weight Watchers anyone?

And just as the Dybvig family had delighted in the quirks of Jennifer's Kiwi accent, she was exposed to the vagaries of my homeland's particular way of putting things.

We had boarded a Southwest Airlines flight headed for Los Angeles, and were standing in the aisle trying to untangle ourselves from all the junk one collects while travelling, when an urgent announcement came over the public address system: 'Please get your tush in the cush so we can push.'

With her beautiful face scrunched up in confusion, Jennifer turned and asked, 'Pardon?'

I laughed and played the role of interpreter.

'Honey, they want you to sit down quickly so we can get the heck out of here.'

The trip to California was a success, with my family accepting Jennifer and seeing how happy we were together.

But my teenage niece was being cautious. She told her mother, my sister, that she thought Jennifer was really nice, and she hoped that Uncle John wouldn't screw up this time.

It's the Little Things
When Jennifer went to Sydney on business I tagged along to keep her company. Between her business appointments, Jennifer and I took in the city.

We ate fresh shrimp and drank beer at Pyrmont Bay, and we drank wine and watched the world stroll by at Cockle Bay.

Waiting in line at Circular Quay to catch the Manly ferry, we enthused over two of the best Kransky sausages we've ever eaten. On Oxford Street, we discovered The Balkan Seafood restaurant.

One evening, at a café nestled between the Opera House and the Sydney Harbor Bridge, we slurped down oyster shooters, sipped Champagne and munched on French fries.

It was one of the most magical nights of our lives.

As corny as it sounds, when you're in love with someone, it's those intimate and often unplanned moments that stay with you forever.

There was not another living soul I'd rather hang out with than Jennifer.

I started to discover pleasure in the simplest of activities. We had found a beach wall that runs along Kalakaua Avenue, in Waikiki, and turned it into one of our favorite hangout spots. We would buy bottled margaritas from the ABC Store and just watch the human parade as it passed by.

Comment: On another occasion when I tagged along with Jennifer on another business trip this time to Melbourne we had a very interesting encounter with a sales woman.

We were in Melbourne right before racings biggest day in the Southern Hemisphere -The Melbourne Cup. Jennifer and I were in Myer's department store in downtown Melbourne. We were in the hat section... with these hats going from the $800 hundred to $1000...dollar range.

Jennifer was trying on some hats as I looked on... the sales gal wandered over and somewhat greeted us... it was obvious that she didn't think we were really in the market for such expensive hats... I guess she thought that because I was dressed in my usual splendour in faded Levi's with a few rips here and there and a t-shirt.

Anyway Jennifer was buying these hats for work (they were paying for them)... so Jennifer selects one that she likes and says we'll have that one... and then she selects another and another... all told Jennifer purchased four rather expensive hats and by now this sales gal is literally jumping over the moon... she's actually talking to me saying how generous I am and of course I'm playing up to this with... "Yeah, it's only money"

Mr. Big Shot... ha... finally Jennifer picks up a beautiful green number and tries it on... the sales woman is now acting like that sales woman in the movie 'Pretty Woman' who really sucks up to Julia Roberts... so suddenly she's sucking up big time to Jennifer... she exclaims: "You look beautiful in that hat... simply stunning - it matches your eyes... don't you agree sir?"

I looked at Jennifer and then at the sales woman and remarked, "Yeah Jennifer does look stunning in that hat - but unless I've been sleeping with another woman my wife has blue eyes." Oops... awkward. Like the wicked witch of the East in the Wizard of Oz when she gets a bucket of water thrown on her that sales woman just melted right on the spot.

The Knife
I continued to learn from her.

My spell at acting school was about to end and I asked Jennifer to come along for our graduation night. It was a special occasion and Jennifer baked a cake to mark it. We arrived at the class, laughing and chatting.

The instructor, a good friend of mine, turned to Jennifer and brutally told her to leave the class.

Dumbfounded, she left the room, taking the cake with her.

When the class was over, I went outside to look for Jennifer, hoping she'd be waiting.

She had gone but the cake remained on the table outside the classroom. Protruding from the center of the cake, and no doubt inserted with a great deal of anger, was a large butcher's knife.

My friend the instructor was shocked and couldn't understand why Jennifer had responded in such a fashion.

I shook my head and explained.

'Man, I don't talk to her like that, what makes you think you can?'

He tried to justify his rudeness by saying he didn't allow non-actors in the class.

'You just don't get it do you?' I said with a degree of frustration.

I tried to explain that he had treated her like she was an extra chair in the room, and that he didn't give her the common courtesy of explaining his position. Instead he had arrogantly dismissed her.

As I tried to explain, it struck me that not too long before, I would have been oblivious to the situation. I was growing.

Mrs Sherlock Holmes

I quickly learned I couldn't fool Jennifer. One way or another, she would find me out.

We often decided to go on diets and we have pretty much tried the lot - we've tried the Liver Cleansing diet, the Atkins, South Beach, Weight Watchers, Jenny Craig. You name it and we've done it.

One time we were doing one of those extreme diets, the type where you've got to guzzle gallons of water with lemon juice and cayenne pepper in it to cleanse the body.

I was going through extreme withdrawals and needed a fix, not ordinary food, but some good old fashioned junk food, something with a kick.

Late in the day, I finally succumbed to a large bag of sour cream and chives potato chips. They were so good I didn't even chew them. Like a starving dog, I just wolfed them down whole. I felt guilty (for about a second), but I wasn't going to beat myself up over it.

That night we were in bed reading when Jennifer twitched her nose, not unlike actress Elizabeth Montgomery used to do in the television series Bewitched.

I had forgotten Jennifer's peculiarly well-honed sense of smell.

'What's that smell?' she asked.

'What smell? I don't smell anything,' I said, wondering where the conversation was heading. I couldn't smell anything unusual.

'I smell something,' Jennifer insisted.

'Beats me.'

'It smells like garlic.'

Oops. Maybe I did know where this was going. But I had left no evidence of the ill-gotten potato chips, had I?

Jennifer's attention immediately shifted to my armpit.

Sniffing it carefully, she declared: 'The pores in your arm reek of garlic.'

'What?'

Actor or no actor, it was becoming difficult to feign ignorance.

'Don't play dumb with me.' Jennifer looked me full in the eyes. 'You've been eating sour cream and chives potato chips haven't you?'

You could have floored me. I was so impressed, I immediately confessed.

'Wow, that's amazing, sweetie! If you ever lose your job, you can always get work out at the airport as a sniffer dog.'

Ding How
Together, we were hard to beat. We both shared the same appetite for life - and Chinese food. One night we went to Ding How, in central Auckland, determined to have a slap up feed.

I had always had a huge appetite but Jennifer could match me. We ordered $88 of food, so much that the waiter would let us order no more, convinced we would not be able to cope.

When we polished off this fine meal, the chefs came out from the kitchen and gave us a hardy round of applause at our table.

Loopy

Talk about doing everything together. Jennifer and I both had impacted wisdom teeth so we booked into the oral surgeon's together. We sat holding hands after the surgery with swollen faces and loopy grins from the painkillers. The surgeon gave us a discount because we came in together.

Laughter

As I neared the end of my fifth decade on this planet, I had spent five years getting to know and appreciate Jennifer. I was still trying to know and appreciate the person I was becoming.

Despite my reckless and troubled past, I knew I had found true love. I was never more aware of it than in the morning, when Jennifer would wake and start the day with a laugh. It's a great laugh and that sparkle of good humor carried me throughout the day.

Until that time, my life could have skewed in any direction. I could have stayed stubborn and single, and I could easily have stepped off the path to be one of those lost souls sleeping on the side of the road with lots of potential but with nowhere to go.

Committed

I sensed I was at the turning point in my life.

I sensed the timing was right for me to have faith in the new me, and that maybe this was my last chance. So I grabbed my chance and asked Jennifer to marry me.

I committed myself one hundred per cent. In acting terms, I let the stone hit the bottom.

My entire life changed for the better from the moment I committed myself to Jennifer.

We were just so much in sync.

We got married in Fiji with family and fifty of our friends, not too far from one of my favorite 'restrooms' in the world.

The wedding could not have been more perfect. Half of the wedding party arrived at Auckland's international airport several days before the big day and we all flew together to Fiji, drinking Champagne and laughing.

There, we swam, sailed, played golf and tennis, and naturally drank an amazing array of lavish cocktails every night. Every day we greeted more and more of our friends and relations as they arrived at the resort.

We watched from our balcony as the Fijians laughed and giggled away the days while they wove and plaited fern leaves into a wedding altar on the beach where the ceremony was to take place.

Everything was peaceful, easy and fun.

No phones, no television, no tensions.

We exchanged vows as the sun was setting in the distance, surrounded by swaying palms, watched by our friends and family, and a gathering of tourists from the hotel who stopped for a peek.

It was a scene we have relived many times since, as we return to Fiji every year, taking that familiar 20-minute drive from Nadi Airport and checking into the same hotel on Denarau Island.

Oops
While our wedding day went so perfectly, I typically managed to give the wrong impression at a party we held in Auckland for all the friends who couldn't celebrate with us in Fiji.

Again, my grasp of Kiwi colloquialisms got me into trouble.

The room was buzzing with successive generations of the family I'd married into and their friends.

About a hundred Kiwis settled down to listen to the only American in the room. I started out well, and the crowd was with me, with everyone nodding and smiling.

Then it turned ugly. The smiles faded into frowns. Suddenly the room got quiet.

Wud-I-say?

All I had said was that when I met Jennifer I really 'lucked out'. Nothing beats the cold muted stare of a hundred New Zealanders - I wrapped up my speech and sat down.

My new wife had tears in her eyes from laughing when she whispered in my ear that 'lucked out' in this part of the world meant that you'd run out of luck.

'You gave them the impression that you were stuck with me,' she chuckled.

Timing

Looking back, I thank God I had the sense not to walk past Jennifer on my way to one of the numerous summits in life we men are always trying to conquer.

Some people play life's game as if the world was about to end at any moment and that just throws their timing completely to the wind, which is exactly how I raced through life before I met Jennifer.

I've had a chance to fulfil a lot of my boyhood dreams down here at the end of the planet and have met and worked with a host of fascinating people, but I know in the end it all would have meant squat if I hadn't met and married Jennifer.

CHAPTER SEVEN

How to Survive Being a New Dad at Fifty
Wild Man Dybvig discovers his softer side when he becomes a father and house-husband in his fifties.

The New Age Dad
One night I was a guest at a book launch and was excusing myself early to look after my little one when some knucklehead with a testosterone overload peered at me with a look of skepticism.

'You're not one of those New Age dads who changes nappies are you?' he inquired.

'I am,' I proudly replied with a grin.

One of the benefits of being a 50-something dad was that I didn't have to act cool. Nor did I give a hoot about having food and snot stains on my clothes. I wore them like a badge of honor.

I loved being a dad.

Comment: Here's something that happens in New Zealand during every school year... and it starts in earnest on the radio... what are you going to do with the kids during school holidays... oh horrors the kids your kids are going to be home for the next two weeks... how in the world are you going to cope... you poor thing... will you survive... and on and on it goes... and no I'm not exaggerating about this topic...

In fact when there's just a few days left they keep announcing this on the radio... ok parents... ok mum... only three more days of school holiday left... then all the radio jocks go crazy exclaiming... yeah... only one day to go... congratulations parents you've survived another school holiday... every school holiday the moaning and groaning starts...

Personally I love school holidays... they're never long enough for me... take your kids to the museum... the movies... go for a hike... a bike ride... a picnic... put a puzzle together... get an ice cream cone... walk along the beach... the possibilities are endless if you want them to be... but social media and the news and particularly radio drone on and on about what a chore it is to have your kids around... well if you think that then don't have kids in the first place.

Change
For most of my life It had all been about me.

Then I met Jennifer, fell in love and as I entered my fifth decade, I became a dad and a house husband at our home in Auckland, New Zealand.

Only a few years before, I used to stumble out of bed, make my way to the fridge to grab an old slice of cold pizza for breakfast, make strong coffee to combat a hangover and would then muddle my way through a newspaper. If I completed all that before noon, well, I was way ahead of schedule.

With two infants in the house, my routine had drastically changed. At 5.30am, I would get up to make warm milk for Lily and Sam. Then I'd make coffee and walk up our long driveway to get the paper.

By the time I got back to the house, Jennifer would be up. We'd share a kiss as she was getting out of the shower and I was getting ready for mine. Then my job was to get breakfast for the kids, make sure they were cleaned and dressed. Jennifer and I would kiss again as she headed out the door for work.

I would get out the vacuum cleaner to clean up the thousand crumbs that every child leaves behind. Kids can change your behaviour in so many ways. I never used to own a vacuum cleaner, but as a house husband, I quickly turned into a vacuum cleaning nutter. I became obsessed, and I get the vacuum cleaner out at even the slightest hint of a crumb about to hit the floor. Since then, I've burned out half a dozen cleaners.

With floors clean and children fed, it was time to head to the park for some fresh air.

And it was still only 8.45am.

Sam

Life had never been so good. I had turned 50. The world was about to celebrate the Millennium. I was finding work as an actor. And there was Jennifer, the love of my life, to make my life complete. Or almost complete.

Then one day out of the blue my lovely wife told me that we were preggers. My first child was on its way!

During Jennifer's pregnancy I was with her every step of the way, holding her hand so much you would have thought we were glued together.

Every doctor's visit, every ultrasound, even to the fertility clinic when they threw a mini-javelin disguised as a needle straight through the centre of her swollen stomach doing an amniocentesis test.

As the American anchor on radio and television sports shows in New Zealand, I had become famous for being loud and talkative. But watching that needle go into Jennifer's stomach left me stone cold quiet.

The round of visits to doctors and clinics was an excellent ego check for me and no doubt other males who go through the process - for all intents and purposes, you become invisible to every doctor or nurse. They only have eyes for the pregnant woman.

Comment: The doctor doing the amniocentesis test did remark on how quiet I was. He exclaimed, "I never thought I'd see the day when John Dybvig sat there like a monk totally speechless."

Kid's Bowling Ball

Jennifer and I had planned to celebrate the turn of the Millennium in Las Vegas, wallowing in the glitz and bright lights. With a baby on the way, we dumped those plans, choosing to see in the noughties beneath the drizzle of an overcast night on a nearly deserted St Heliers beach in Auckland.

Sam was 15 days overdue and showing absolutely zero signs of coming out when we got a panicked call from our doctor telling us we needed to get to the hospital like NOW. Apparently, Sam was growing bigger than Texas and showed no signs of slowing down. The strangest thing about potentially having a King-Kong-sized baby was every doctor in the hospital felt it was their professional duty to have a feel. I certainly can't confirm this but I got the distinct impression that they had an office pool going around guessing how big he really was. They were lined up in the hall way taking numbers. It seemed every time I turned around there was another strange doctor with his arm half-way up Jennifer's legs. As the intensity of Jennifer's labor increased, she began to push and grunt, focusing on the baby that was now ready to emerge.

During Jennifer's delivery we had that classic emotive scene that's in every movie showing a woman giving birth. In the final stages of her labour Jennifer was tired and sweating with the effort of pushing and grunting and plainly had had enough. She pushed. She grunted. She pushed. We both grunted.

The sweat ran off her tired face as she put all her remaining energy into the last stages. She pushed once more.

The veins in her neck stood out as she held her breath and gathered strength for yet one more push.

She pushed. And pushed. I held my breath and inwardly pushed too. We held hands and pushed together.

Jennifer was close to tears, totally exhausted by her efforts. I could almost hear her heart beat as no one moved or said anything. Then suddenly from out of nowhere the phone in the room rang!

Now that's a very strange sound in the heat of delivering a baby, an intrusion at a sacred moment. We ignored it. The grunting and straining continued. It rang again. It seemed louder this time, more annoying. We ignored it again, I mean whaddaya gonna do?

"Hello, ah uh nooooh I don't really have the time to do a quick survey on what's the world's best pizza. I've got my hands full at the moment."

And then nothing but deafening silence. A silence that screams with the tension of a woman giving birth, which puts you in a very weird space because we were all kind of waiting, expecting it to ring again?

This throws you into a kind of split brain activity, half of your attention is focused on Jennifer, and the other half is leaning towards the phone, very weird. Jennifer is close to tears now and totally exhausted from the final assault of pushing Sam out, when the shrill jingle of the phone simply exploded throughout the room one more time.

Everybody in the room jumped and turned to look in the direction of the phone at precisely the same instant, even the doctor waiting to catch Sam.

We looked like a musical number from The Rocky Horror Picture Show.

And it would have been funny except... they say that hell hath no fury like a woman scorned. That may well be true, but I now know that hell has a little bit more fury when a woman is in the final stages of a long labour and the phone rings one too many times.

On that last ring I witnessed another side to my lovely sweet gentle wife as she morphed into Linda Blair from the 'Exorcist' and in that famous low gravely husky voice that would have made any professional wrestler green with envy, she slowly rotated her head towards the phone and erupted,

"RIP THAT FUCKING PHONE OUT OF THE WALL!!!"
It was a very truthful moment, a beautiful moment of raw energy let loose. Tom Cruise and his Scientology buddies with all their 'silence is golden' during delivery baloney would have thrown a hissy-fit. But, as it turned out Sam wasn't the world's biggest baby. He popped out as a kid's bowling ball coming in at just under ten pounds which Jennifer thought was big enough thank-you.

Comment: I can think of nothing that matches the strain... the pressure...the absolute concentration... and then that so... so... soooooo beautiful moment when your child emerges into the world... the emotion of that moment is beyond words.

Hurricane
When Jennifer was pregnant we told all our friends and family that having children wasn't going to change our life style.

I honestly believed it wouldn't. I was under the firm impression that we'd just fit them into "OUR" lifestyle. They gave us knowing smiles and left the room to laugh themselves silly.

Children didn't change our life style, they absolutely destroyed it. No more drinks after work, no rushing to catch the cheap movie. We felt like we were on house detention the first six months. My friends would call me in the evening exclaiming: "The beers in the box and the game is on the tube - come on over!"

And I'd fire right back, "The kids are in the tub and dinner's on the stove - that's my game brother." We quickly found out that when you have kids, you invite the forces of chaos into your life. Nothing is normal anymore and fitting them into your desired lifestyle just doesn't cut any mustard with them.

You can no more schedule kids than you can schedule your way through a hurricane, when the wind blows, you go.

Comment: I suppose like most parents I just had no idea... I mean come on I was fifty and had already been through a ton of life's ups and downs and adventures... surely having a baby wasn't going to be that tough... like I said I simply had no idea. Raising a kid is not easy with both parents in command... now I have a lot of empathy for single parents.

Oysters and Bathwater
My life is intricately more complicated now and I play a heck of a lot less golf, but it's also so much more enriched. People always ask me if being an older parent made me a smarter parent? "Hell No!" I always roared back. Age has nothing to do with it when it's the first one out of the barn.

When it came time to give the little man his first bath - forget about it. The plastic tub had to be filled with warm water at just the right temperature, along with an enormous stack of fresh towels, oil, moisturizer, powder and other vials and tubes all elaborately laid out on the dining room table. We had so much stuff stacked on the table I couldn't find my baby. And right in the middle of Sam's first bath, a very good friend dropped over with Champagne, oysters, beautiful blue vein cheese and lovely Mediterranean olives, and laid out this exquisite feast around Sam in his tub.

Another perk of being an older parent - your friends have the knowledge and bank account to bring over the good stuff. I slurped down an oyster and gulped a bit of bubbly while Sam, slippery as an oiled eel did his own gulping on some bath water as he went under. Trying to combine the two events didn't work out and it suddenly dawned on us that our lives had taken on different priorities.

Comment One: The very first day we brought Sam home we made our first rookie mistake: Sam slept for a solid eight hours. This worried us so much we woke him up. Big mistake. Huge! He didn't sleep for the next two years and neither did we.

Comment Two: Things change in your life when you have kids that you would never have imagined before... Jennifer and I are big on chilling out in a café with a nice cup of coffee... we absolutely love it... this is one of our go to things to do... to just sit together chill out and chat about things... and then it happened... bang just like that... when Sam got to be about two and half or three we finally came to the conclusion that we had to stop going to coffee shops... it just wasn't worth the effort any more... why you ask... because it was simply too much damn trouble trying to relax with a cup of coffee and a fresh muffin while also trying to corral a wild mustang... oops no I meant our child the lovely Sam as he ran wild throughout the shop causing so much mayhem and chaos that the words 'relax' and 'café' no longer went together. We actually stopped going to cafes for a couple of years.

Swallow Damnit

There are times when you can actually be too smart for your own britches: When Sam was about two and a half I had to give him some medicine which I had just purchased in St. Heliers village. I had a brilliant plan to get him to take it.

I took him to a lovely cafe right on the oceanfront and ordered some French fries in the hopes of bribing him into taking his medicine while I relaxed with a nice flat white. Sam, flat out refused. He wasn't swallowing anything. I calmly tried to reason with him. No go. He wouldn't budge. At this point I'm getting a bit hot under the collar. Sam is still refusing and crying and blowing snot bubbles, but I'm not backing off. I got stubborn and dug in, we're not going anywhere until the young man swallows.

Somewhere about now I'm yelling and beside myself when I feel a tap on my shoulder, it's the waiter who quietly informs me that this was a restaurant. In the acting world this is a perfect example of the 'pinch and ouch'. The waiter was the pinch to my ouch - I immediately exploded with purple rage at high volume that I was perfectly well aware that we were in a gawd damn restaurant. In the end, defeated and with my tail between my legs, I took Sam home and called the Chemist (pharmacist) who patiently explained that I could easily just put the medicine into some juice. Doh!

Liverpool Kiss

I know you don't get an instruction manual when your kid pops out but there is something I think hospitals could do and that's to hand out a warning slip. For all the warm fuzzy words they have to describe a baby - like cuddly, soft, silky and smooth as a baby's bottom - you'd think they'd have a word for the baby version of the Liverpool Kiss. Babies do it all the time. Since the wee munchkins are way too wobbly to maintain an erect posture in your arms, they're constantly flopping about. And just when you're cooing and clucking and feeling very contented with yourself, they suddenly raise themselves as high as they can, rear back and then flop their tiny hard heads with all the force of a crashing meteorite straight into your face.

Hurts like hell! The 'baby head butt' would rival anything Zindine Zadane (French soccer star who was red-carded for head butting an Italian opponent in the 2006 World Cup) could produce.

Nipples

It's been said many times that men and women's brains are wired differently. Being a new parent gave me plenty of chances to realize how differently.

Like most males, I suppose, I'd never given much thought to the actual mechanics of breast feeding. To me, it seemed to be one of the most natural acts in the world as the woman presented her breast to the child, and the kid's eyes would light up. End of story.

But as I was finding out, real life was never as simple. For many moms, including Jennifer, breastfeeding requires a bit of technique and whatever help modern medicine can deliver.

In the early days of Sam's life, Jennifer was struggling with cracked nipples. They had developed cracks and had started to bleed. She was extremely sore, grumpy and frustrated. She was in agony and couldn't feed Sam.

So one night at 10pm, I set off to find whatever relief was on offer at our local urgent pharmacy. I presented my dilemma to the rumpled middle-aged guy behind the counter and he produced two models of a contraption called a breast pump. He showed me both types, explaining that as far as he could tell the only difference between them was the price and I could save myself a few bucks by taking the cheap one.

On cue, his wife poked her head between the curtains separating the store from their private quarters. The look on her face told me everything I needed to know. I bought the more expensive breast pump; the one that actually worked, the one that put a smile on Jennifer's face. Some things you should never take a chance on...

Comment: Whenever I think back about that episode it always brings a smile to my face - two clowns who didn't have a clue as to what they were doing and like most men we were going to go with the cheaper model and save a couple of bucks... which brings me to that tired old cliché but so very true in this case: You get what you pay for.

Rubik's Cube

I soon found out that getting a little baby dressed is no easy task. It took about a month to master the best way to dress young Sam. It was as tricky as trying to line up all the colors on a Rubik's Cube, getting all his tweeny-weeny limp limbs to go into all the appropriate openings.

Ouch!

Here's a task I just hated. Jennifer wouldn't do it - she made me be the bad guy. My task was to hold our kids down for their first inoculations at the doctor's surgery. They would laugh and coo as I held them safe and snug, until the sudden jab of the needle made them pause for that micro-second before the realization hits them and they start screaming blue bloody murder. The instant look of betrayal in their wee faces staring directly back at you is haunting.

Comment: I always thought they were thinking, "What the fuck man... how could you let that bastard in the white coat do that to me?"

Big Bird

To say I was a nervous and over-protective parent would be an understatement. When Sam was about six months old, I was feeding him his bottle of pumped breast milk and talking on the phone to my older sister Nancy who lives in San Diego.

Suddenly a wild bird with an extremely long beak flew into the house through the open French doors. I went ballistic, screaming to my sister that I had to go. I bundled up Sam in my arms and made a mad dash past this beastly bird to find sanctuary in our bedroom.

Later, I relayed this frightening story to Jennifer with grave concern and feeling slightly heroic about my efforts to protect our new born. Jennifer's response was to fall about with laughter, explaining the bird was a harmless kingfisher.

Comment: Yeah right, it may have been a harmless bird... but it still had a beak that looked about 3 miles long to me.

Snot Frenzy

I was quickly learning that our child would always come first, no matter what the circumstance. There was nothing I wouldn't do to protect him or to try to take away his pain.

This was put to the test when we took baby Sam on a trip, and he was clearly in severe discomfort as we boarded our flight. His sinuses were blocked with mucous and it was obviously going to hurt when the flight took off and rapidly gained altitude.

The pain in his ears would be terrible. I desperately wondered what I could do to save him this pain. I had read about this technique somewhere so I gently put my mouth over my son's nose and carefully sucked out the mucous.

Jennifer just about fainted. I guess my conversion to New Age fatherhood had its limits.

Comment: I didn't see what the big deal was...after all what's a little snot compared to the mountains of shit one must handle while changing countless nappies... I mean come on our little guy could shit so much that it came gushing out the back of his nappy right up his back side... that's a helluva an effort... and one helluva mess to clean up.

Lunch

When you don't start having a family till you are 50, it can create a sense of urgency - and Jennifer and I were soon doing our best to provide Sam with a playmate. It didn't take long before Jennifer was pregnant again, and this time we thought we would be well prepared after our experience with Sam.

We should have known better.

Like Sam, our second baby was running late. We decided to call in to see the doctor for a quick check-up on our way to an Italian restaurant where Jennifer had booked us in for lunch.

The doctor's routine check revealed our baby was laying sideways, a position that could be potentially dangerous if the baby decided to arrive without warning and we couldn't get to the hospital in time. He suggested we should go straight to the hospital. When we arrived there, Jennifer handed over the doctor's notes to the hospital receptionist and politely explained that we wouldn't be staying long as we had a booking for lunch.

Within minutes, a nurse was leading us to a private room while Jennifer explained once more that we had a lunch date awaiting us.

And Jennifer continued to believe we would be ploughing into spaghetti and tomato sauce, even as the nurse helped her in to bed and strapped a plastic identity band around her wrist.

It was only when someone brought in the plastic lunch tray that Jennifer finally accepted we weren't going anywhere.

We burst into a fit of giggling, full of excitement.

Comment: I gotta say we men can be such Neanderthals when it comes to the actual act of producing children... and vain and a whole bunch of other things... when we decided to have a second child because Jennifer was right in her busiest period for her work with travel she gave me a two week window for this to happen... yeah the pressure was on... well in my mind it was... and then when she informed me that she indeed was pregnant... I instantly started pumping the air and shouted out - "Yeah baby!" Like I was a stud horse... I was Da Man... service completed... yeah ok calm down.

Baby Whisperer

Lily was overdue, having set up a hammock in Jennifer's womb, and was lying sideways quite comfortably thank you - we had to enlist the help of a 'Baby Whisperer' to get her ready for delivery. This doctor came in with some kind of mystic calming aurora surrounding him and spoke in whispers urging our wee little girl to get a move on so she could greet the world.

After a marathon session of hocus-pocus, which involved stroking, massaging and cajoling, our newly found family witchdoctor slowly turned to face the expectant crowd of doctors, nurses, midwives, consultants, and every other Tom, Dick and Harry who had crammed into our tiny room to watch this unusual procedure, I swear he morphed into Robert Redford and his boyish shit-eating grin when he solemnly announced, "Houston we are ready to launch," with just the hint of a smirk.

And like your typical American (old or not) I leapt up into the air pumping my fist screaming, "Yeah, baby! Way to go Doc!"

All the staid reserved New Zealanders looked at me as if I was an alien. An old alien. However the most amazing thing about this episode was because this witch doctor with the magic fingers worked out of another hospital - our hospital charged him to park in their parking lot. Talk about no perks. So on principle he refused and parked on the street. Every two hours he and I would duck out to move our cars so they wouldn't be towed. New Zealand hospital boards are so tight they'd have charged Moses a road tax when he parted the Red Sea.

Comment: I know that last bit sounds crazy - but I'm not making that up... the doc and I really did duck out every two hours to move our cars. To this day that still amazes me - what a juxtaposition on life... on the one hand you've got the miracle of birth occurring and at the same time you're worried about a tow truck. Life is indeed strange.

Competitor

We had all the resources we needed for Lily's birth because it was May 13 and the hospital was not busy thanks to the superstitious mothers who had cancelled their Caesarean births. But while we had access to the hospital's team, our own carefully-selected delivery team, with the exception of our Irish midwife, couldn't get to the hospital in time at short notice.

It proved to be a difficult birth.

Twice the doctor had to reach inside Jennifer to prick our little girl's scalp to get some blood tests.

Every time they stabbed her I was going nuts inside.

I felt so helpless and I just about lost it when they had to harpoon her with a cable attached to a monitor to keep track of her vital signs.

The atmosphere in the room was extremely tense.

The lead doctor was a small and determined Iranian woman and I quickly learned that doctors can be just as competitive as anyone I'd faced in sport or across a movie set.

When it was suggested we could get our own delivery specialist there for the final stage, the doctor fairly hissed under her breath, 'Feel free, but this is my delivery. He can watch.'

Eventually, the monitor sprang to life with bells and blinking lights signaling that Lily was now in real distress.

Jennifer was pushing with all the strength she could harness and I watched in awe as this wee slip of a doctor went into action.

'This baby needs to come out now,' she declared.

She literally reached inside and pulled Lily into the world.

Learning to Worry
Somehow, after years of living the bachelor lifestyle with no responsibilities, I had been blessed with a beautiful wife, son and now a daughter.

By comparison with our introduction to parenthood, it was amazing how much easier having a second child seemed. When Sam arrived, Jennifer and I were flustered and life was so hectic in those first few weeks. We had been the classic anxious parents. The first time we had left Sam to be babysat by Jennifer's parents, we didn't even make it out of the neighborhood before we rang to check if he was okay.

Now, like magic, we were able to cope with our second baby much better.

We felt like veterans in the child game. We did things with Lily that we would never have contemplated with Sam.

We decided to fly to Fiji for Christmas when Lily was barely seven months old. Of course, there comes a point where over-confidence becomes as much a problem as being over-cautious.

More experienced and confident, yes. Smarter, no.

The temperatures in Fiji at Christmas can quickly go through the 40s and it's not the ideal environment for a tiny baby.

Fever

But from the moment we arrived in Fiji, Lily was a hit with the locals. At Nadi Airport, a laughing Fijian woman plucked Lily from my arms, smothering her in kisses and walking her in circles of delight.

We went to Castaway Island where a line of burly men stood knee deep in the crystal clear sea, ready to bring passengers and luggage from the boat to the shore.

They picked up Lily, strapped in her buggy, and passed her high above their heads as she giggled away.

My heart was in my mouth the whole time, inwardly urging the men not to drop our precious little bundle.

We welcomed the New Year on Castaway Island, sipping Champagne and eating pizza while we looked across the whitest of white sand beaches under an azure sky.

Life was fantastic.

Then Lily came down with a dreadful fever.

Back at the Sheraton on Denarau, we took her to the resort's doctor in Nadi. He told us she'd be fine, though we suspected he wasn't keen to recommend any line of action that would take our business away from the resort. We weren't happy with that diagnosis so we took Lily to a private doctor who told us to put her in a cold bath. We tried that but Lily just wasn't getting any better. We had one of those package tickets that we couldn't change even though we desperately wanted by now to get Lily home.

Lily's temperature wouldn't budge and when it was suggested we take her to a hospital in Nadi, Jennifer decided to take control.

'I want to take her home now,' she insisted.

After a series of calls to Air New Zealand, we found a sympathetic supervisor who booked us on the next plane out.

Comment: That is the only time I was happy to be leaving Fiji.

Mama Bird

When we got back to Auckland, our doctor said Lily had caught some type of tropical bug and it took two more weeks before she fought it off and our lives returned to normal.

I guess no parent ever gets used to their child being ill. But having reached my fifties before becoming a parent, it was an experience I struggled with.

When Lily was two, she caught one of those hacking coughs that can absolutely shake you to the core.

This was especially worrisome for us because she had all the body mass of a cotton bud, so when she coughed her entire frame shook violently. Her coughing went on for most of the night until she completely wore herself out.

We were beside ourselves.

We had been giving her some medicine but Lily always spat it out, refusing to swallow it. Nothing we tried worked. Finally, I took her back to our doctor who told me I was going to have to play the mother bird role.

This meant I had to hold Lily down like a professional wrestler, forcing open her mouth and sticking a dropper filled with medicine down her throat until she was gagging and turning purple. Then I would squeeze the dropper, shooting the medicine straight down her throat. It worked, but I dreaded giving her the medicine.

It was an emotional workout for me every time.

A few years before, I'd tumbled through life with barely a worry. Now I was learning how to cope with worry about those I loved.

Father and Daughter
I don't know exactly what it is or how to describe it but my relationship with Lily is different to my relationship with Sam.

I love both of them to pieces but I also feel more protective of my little girl.

Lily has always been able to put a smile on my face, and often in the strangest of circumstances. When she was three, we flew back to San Francisco to attend my niece's wedding, in which Lily and Sam were involved.

As an added bonus on the same trip, I was to be inducted into my high school's Hall of Fame, largely for my basketball exploits there and appearing in Peter Jackson's movie King Kong. The school was right into all that rah-rah stuff, with a squillion pep rallies, cheerleaders, song-girls and marching bands.

I loved it and I was really looking forward to having my New Zealand family check out my American over-the-top school spirit. It hadn't changed one iota since I had left 40 years before.

The entire student body were in the gym, screaming and cheering, and they had huge posters with King Kong and my name on them. The school band was blasting out noisy brass band tunes.

Wow, it brought back so many memories.

Full of pride, I asked Lily what she thought of it all, hoping and expecting she'd be as excited as me.

She placed her hands over her ears and looked wistfully at me. 'Too loud, Daddy,' she said. Oh.

Comment: I remember being very disappointed when Lily said that... mostly I think because I was so excited... but later thinking about it of course I was pumped I had a whole history of the school behind me... but to a three year old damn right it was too gawddamn noisey... what with a couple of thousand kids literally screaming their heads off and a bold brass band tooting for all it was worth in a small high school gymnasium...

Like the saying goes - put yourself in the other guy's shoes even if they are just a wee three-year-old girl.

Pooh Bear
After the wedding and my Hall of Fame induction, we flew to Los Angeles and took the kids to Disneyland. I was particularly excited about this as I had grown up going to Disneyland almost every year. I also knew the park had a Winnie-the-Pooh Land and that my little girl doted on Pooh Bear.

I took Lily's hand and led her towards Winnie-the-Pooh Land, giving her a big build-up as to what she was about to see.

Suddenly, she wrenched her hand free and turned to walk away.

'Sweetie, don't you want to see Pooh Bear?' I asked.

Apparently not. Lily had caught sight of the actor dressed up as Winnie.

'Too big,' Lily lamented.

I was crestfallen.

Since then, Lily has developed a disdain for costumes.

I understand.

After reading Stephen King's novel IT, I developed a phobia of clowns, as weird as that sounds, and I know how easy it is to feel spooked.

I'm so spooked by clowns that I had to unfriend a buddy of mine on Facebook because he had a picture of a clown on his page and I knew it was there so I had to eliminate it.

Lily once turned down an invitation to a friend's birthday party at a place called Chipmunks where the kids would be entertained by a guy dressed as a giant chipmunk.

She's avoided going to Breakers basketball games because they have a guy dressed in some kind of bird outfit.

Racing Clown

And one year she pulled out of her race at kids' athletics because she had spotted a clown in full uniform on the far side of the field. She was a good runner and I tried to persuade her that the clown was a long way away and she could win a ribbon.

She gave me her cutest little girl frown and we left the track without a ribbon but together, a child with a mind of her own and a dad who'll always try to understand.

I just accept that she can be different.

For instance, at the end of every school term, Sam and I go down to our local sushi shop. It's a tradition we've developed. But Lily has always refused to set foot in the place. Apparently, she was scared of the guy who ran the joint who looked like a Japanese Buddha. He did but just for the record the guy was one of the nicest guys I've ever met.

Instead, I would park the car directly outside and Lily would happily sit in it. Sam and I would tuck into sushi and Lily would wave to us through the window.

Comment: That's one of the things I love about both Sam and Lily... we have always encouraged them from an early age to have their own opinions and not to just go along with the crowd. And I can definitely say that both of them are independent as hell... at times going against my wishes... which is fine you can't have it both ways.

Brother and Sister
While Sam and Lily are quite different in many ways, I take a huge amount of pleasure seeing them together and knowing they are there for each other.

I once found a story that Lily wrote about Sam when she was seven years old.

She didn't show the story around; I just found it among her things.

Story about my brother.
My brother has lovely blond and brown hair. He loves listening to music on his iPod. Absolutely loves Christmas and always wears shorts. A bit tanned on his arm. Likes staying up late. His favorite colour is green. Doesn't like going to sleep and loves watching TV. He loves me. He is called Sam Dybvig.

Comment: The pride I felt when reading that letter - I just thought, wow that's so very cool.

Bastard

Sometimes, I see parts of me in Lily.

Another time, when Lily was four, I asked her what she was thinking. She replied she didn't have any thoughts in her head because she was too young.

While Sam is a lot quieter than me, it's Lily who can sometimes hit the decibel ratings.

One day I was looking for a parking space in St Heliers when a driver nipped in front of me and took the empty spot.

'Bastard took our parking space, Lil,' I said.

When we got home, Lily loudly and proudly announced to Jennifer, 'Some bastard took our parking spot.'

Comment: When Lily blurted out my bastard comment I was kind of pumped that we were on the same page... that's right sweetie I thought that bastard did take our parking spot... however Jennifer was less impressed giving me a look that screamed: Oh that's great you're teaching our four year old to swear... doh!

Hide and Seek

Somehow a daughter can keep any dad grounded, even at an early age. When Lily was two and a half, we had just started playing a game of hide and seek around our home.

The phone rang. It was my older brother, Bob, calling from the States and making his first call to me in the 30 years I had lived in New Zealand.

He was ringing to let me know our mother had passed away.

I was stunned and devastated.

Though she was 83 and had been suffering from a host of health problems, I had only just been talking to her on the phone, and she seemed lively and positive.

We were planning a trip to the States for my niece's wedding in three months' time, giving her the chance to meet Lily for the first time.

I had so badly wanted to take my lovely Lily and introduce her to her grandmother.

I had always thought of my mother in a loving fond way. She had always been there for me, my brother and sisters, making dinner, packing our lunches and taking us shopping for school clothes.

We had even worked together in long ago summers, when she found work for herself as a waitress and for me as a busboy. I had always felt a close connection to her.

When the words ran out with my brother, I hung up the phone and sat down, crying like a baby. I let it all pour out.

My beautiful little girl watched and looked to interrupt my sobs.

'Daddy, when you're through crying, can we play hide and seek?'

What can you do? It puts it all into perspective.

We live. We die. We live.

Comment: All I can say is there was a ton of emotion packed into that game of hide and seek... one I will always remember.

The House Husband
I had taken on the most important job of my life - that of house husband. This was no job taken on a whim, with me sweet talking my way past an interviewer.

You've heard of the expression: Don't assume because you'll only make an Ass out of U and Me. Well, that's exactly what I did when Sam was born. I just assumed that Jennifer would quit her job and stay home to look after our child and I would in turn be the family breadwinner. How 50's thinking can you get. When I made this announcement Jennifer just looked at me with a blank face and announced right back that she had no intention of quitting her job as a director of the family company. A job that carried with it great responsibility and travel around the world. Oh, I replied. I guess that leaves the job of looking after Sam to me. Okay. Jennifer and I agreed that she should resume her career as soon as possible. It was a no-brainer, really, because I admire Jennifer's business skills and knew it made sense that she continued her work with the family firm. I would become a full-time dad, ensuring the children had a stable and happy upbringing.

Not every segment of New Zealand society responded as positively as me when they learned of my new role.

When I went to my father-in-law's golf club to pick up a load of firewood, I approached the two elderly gents in charge. When I identified myself, one smugly chortled to the other, 'He's the housekeeper.'

Comment: Once again comments like that just didn't faze me... I'm definitely an Alpha male... but I really loved looking after the little guy.

Dirty Clothes
My daily routines offered new challenges and becoming a house husband led me to develop the most unusual of skills - laundry, for instance.

One day I found myself in conversation with a local friend who had been forced to stay at home for a few months after an operation. He thought he would help his wife by hanging out the laundry but apparently his washing line style was all wrong and his wife would re-hang it when she got home. He was at a loss to understand the logic of this and took solace from the news that my wife was always giving me grief about putting in towels with the shirts.

The problem with me and washing machines was usually one of space. Whenever I peered into the machine, it never looked full so I would keep filling it with towels. Besides, if you have a full machine, you would use less powder and save time.

I put this theory to the test one day, putting a lime green table cloth in with the clothes. To my surprise, the clothes emerged with a lime green hue. Some of the shirts looked really cool, in my opinion, but Jennifer was not impressed. In my defense, I did ask how the heck was I supposed to know the table cloth was going to run - maybe I was raised on another planet or just missed that lesson...

Comment: I'm much better now... but it still bothers the hell out of me to run the washing machine when it's not full. Ahhhhhh the simple frustrations of life.

Catching Flies
I've had a lot of fun chasing flies around the house, as Sam and I tried to capture them as food for his pet frog.

During summer, finding flies for the frog is easy but during the winter we've had to be more cunning, leaving strips of bacon on the deck to attract a few hardy insects that have survived the cold.

You should see the faces of guests when we spot a stray fly in the house and rush to corner it.
We were having lunch in the dead of winter when I spotted an errant fly and almost caught it with my tongue. That was a conversation stopper as the mouths of those around the table fell open.

Then there is Fred, the family's guinea pig, who needs to be watered and fed with a slice or two of cucumber or some fresh carrots
As I enter and leave our garden many times a day, I always call out in my booming voice: 'Freddieeeeeee!' He jumps up from his snooze and calls back with his own trademark squeak, his nose pressed to the side of the cage in anticipation of a run in the yard or a chunk of apple.

Comment: The thing with the frog and the flies was it became a competitive game to me... so every time I saw a fly and it didn't matter where I saw it I immediately thought - yeah you're mine... I actually became obsessed with the damn things... yeah I know that sounds crazy but you know me I'm just a competitive nutter.

Early Challenges

Naturally, as the kids grew up, they would want their friends around. At kindergarten, these are known as play dates. One day, the mother of a friend of Sam's asked me if she could bring her youngster to our place for a play date. Of course I said yes, but then I wondered what Jennifer would think of me having these young spunky mothers round to our place. That's the insecurity of an old man on display right there. Jennifer just laughed. On the other hand some of the mothers of Lily's friends seemed reluctant to have their children over to the house of a big ugly bald American. You just can't win for losing.

Comment: I distinctly remember standing in the school yard waiting to pick up the kids from Primary school and being the Lone Ranger. I stood by myself as groups of moms and other dads were all over the place yacking a mile a minute. Not me, I was the lone American.

The Boogieman

Every day had its challenges. For Sam, one early challenge was getting him a haircut. The problem started when he was about six months old and he was ready for his first haircut.

In keeping with the status of this significant event, I took him to the barber's shop I've used myself for 25 years. It's one of those old fashioned macho establishments where you can sit back, take your time and bullshit all you want about politics and sport.

Sam was sitting on my lap, wide-eyed and taking in everything around him. One of the older barbers decided it would be fun to sneak up on Sam, give him a boogieman laugh and snap his scissors in front of his face. I guess my barbers weren't used to having babies around. Sam went ballistic, trying desperately to scramble out of the chair. He's had an issue with haircuts ever since. In fact, one hairdresser asked us not to bring him back.

Over the years, I'd been thrown out of many a game of basketball. Now Sam had earned his first ejection at the age of six months - I guess that's the Dybvig way.

Comment: The funny thing about the hairdresser thinking it best if Sam didn't come back happened after we left her shop: I was livid while carrying Sam to the car.

When I set him in his car seat I discovered he still had one of the hair dresser's toys. I was so mad that I grabbed the toy and smashed it to smithereens on the sidewalk (very grown-up of me).

When we got home and I told Jennifer that it was a no go... Sam piped up and smugly told his mother, "Mom, dad broke a toy... and it wasn't even ours." The important things from a child's perspective... ha!

The Russian
Jennifer decided to try taking Sam to our local hairdresser. She returned frazzled and covered with juvenile slime and a son still with unkempt hair. She demanded that I take him for a second attempt, which I did. The shop was owned by a no-nonsense Russian woman who greeted us with stern silence. I plopped Sam into the hairdressing chair and he responded with his favorite trick of squealing from the bottom of his lungs and blowing bubbles of snot.

The Russian woman gave me a cold stare, and I stared right back.

'He's in your chair,' I pointed out. 'Do what ya gotta do.'

She firmly grasped him, scolding him in Russian for being a naughty boy. Somehow, her incomprehensible ranting confused him long enough for her to cut his hair.

As I paid the bill, the woman leaned forward, indicating I should listen carefully.

'You tell your wife to stay home, she no understand. You a man, you understand!' Gawd, I laughed and couldn't wait to get home to tell Jennifer that she just 'no understand'.

Comment: And you bet I told Jennifer what the Russian gal said and then laughed my ass off with her reaction... all I can say here is Jennifer was not impressed!

The True Meaning of Fear

A friend told me that it's only when you have children you learn the true meaning of fear. I never gave it a second thought until I had children of my own. Only then did I understand the truism that until you have kids of your own, you'll never understand.

When Sam was three, we went shopping in a vast store. We had wandered deep into the building, between the many lines of shelves and stock displays. I stopped to read some product information and became engrossed. Suddenly, something didn't seem right. Something had triggered my parental alarm. I stopped reading and looked around. I was alone.

Where was Sam?

I tracked back to the last aisle we'd walked down.

No Sam.

I quickly walked to the next and still no sign.

My feeling of unease was quickly turning to panic. I ran past the end of several more aisles, searching for my son and seeing nothing.

I felt fear. Real fear.

I recalled the story of the woman who lost her child in the Toys R Us store in San Francisco. The staff had immediately locked all doors to the store and found the missing girl with some creep dying her hair in one of the restrooms. That was the moment I panicked big time.

I felt the icy ripple of fear spreading through my body. It was as if I was sinking.

I sprinted to the front of the store, screaming as loud as I could: 'Lock the doors. My little boy is missing, he's three years old, blond hair, blue eyes, lock all the doors!'

People didn't know what to do. Unlike in some countries, random kidnappings are not a big problem in New Zealand and no one seemed ready to help. Clearly, some of the people thought I was mad and avoided making eye contact with me.

Those people were right.

I was mad, mad with fear.

It was fear like I'd never experienced before.

All I wanted was my little boy.

I was still bellowing Sam's name and running back and forth when a security guard rushed up to me with Sam in his arms.

My sense of relief was so great I didn't even take my little guy from the guard; instead I encased both of them in a huge bear hug with tears streaming down my face.

I learned that Sam had found a toy bike and had ridden a couple of miles to the far side of the store. That episode taught me to anticipate every possible risk and danger that could beset one of my kids, and to take as many precautions as possible. For instance, whenever I go to pay for gas at the service station, I won't leave the keys in the car. The fear of losing my children makes me more aware of how much I treasure them. Whenever I'm out with them, I feel proud to be their dad and I know it must show.

Comment: Thinking back to that episode up to that point in my life I had never experienced anything remotely close to the absolute panic that gripped me like an iron vise and wouldn't let go.

Lucky Me

And being an-older-parent I get this all the time. One day I was in Wellington the capital of New Zealand sitting on an airport baggage carousel while Sam and Lily were giggling themselves silly using me as their personal jungle gym. I looked up and saw an immaculately dressed older woman with snow-white hair looking our way with a twinkle in her eye.

She leaned down and whispered, "You've got beautiful grandchildren."

I nodded back immediately. "Yes, they are beautiful." I hesitated just a moment never breaking our connection and then with the world's widest grin I leaned over to her and proudly announced, "And they're mine!"

She paused and studied me with a measured gaze and then with a gentle sigh of resignation exhaled, "Well, lucky you."

Yes! Yes, I am.

Mr Grumpy v Stroppy Mom

One side effect of growing older is becoming a grump. Turning into a grumpy old man is not so bad, but turning into a grumpy old parent is something else.

When Sam started primary school, we quickly got into the habit of walking together for the seven or eight blocks it took to get from home to school. It usually took less than 10 minutes and it gave us enough time to talk and have a laugh or two.

Then I was asked to join the school's 'Walking Bus', an arrangement that required parents and children to march to school together in a tightly-choreographed phalanx.

I politely declined.

I saw no logical reason to officially sign up to do something that we were already doing, and didn't need to change. But the PTA (Parent Teachers Association) wanted to formalize the simple activity of walking to school and gentle pressure was put on parents to conform. Sometimes we get involved whether we want to or not.

Eventually, Sam and I unofficially joined the 'Walking Bus', on which we were considered to be 'casual walkers', because my son's classroom buddy was on it and his mother was the 'Conductor'.

Every morning, we'd scamper up our driveway and join the large group of parents and kids walking to school. It turned out to be easy, low-key and quite a pleasant experience.

After about a year, our official 'Conductor' abruptly quit.

I asked her why and she told me the PTA were always hassling her to attend meetings to report on the 'Walking Bus', but with two children and a husband, she didn't have time to get to meetings. It was simpler for her to quit her role.

The 'Walking Bus' continued but it was never the same. We had several different 'Conductors' and the fun went out of it.

Another year on, we had another passenger for the 'Walking Bus' as Lily started school.

We also had a new 'Conductor'. I think of her as Stroppy Mom for reasons that will become obvious.

She was a large mother and brought with her a larger German Shepherd dog that she had to continually pull along by his lead.

Our new 'Conductor' would insist that the parents and kids walk in a tight group. Sometimes the dog would stop for a pee and Stroppy Mom would halt the 'Walking Bus'.

She expected the kids to stop and start to order, and I mean order. Kids are not robots and don't naturally tend to march to order.

And not all kids feel comfortable being around large dogs.

Lily was only five and was nervous when the dog came close baring its teeth, sniffing her face and drooling from its mouth. I was there to hold her hand, though I privately thought our 'Conductor' might have been wiser to leave the dog at home. But no big deal.

I should have known that trouble was on its way.

Barking Mad

One morning, Stroppy Mom and her snarling beast came marching towards our drive. My son spotted his buddy and we quickly joined him. The four of us put on a spurt so we were a few paces ahead of the group, away from the dog that Lily didn't like and wasn't comfortable around.

Stroppy Mom didn't like this.

She called out for Sam's friend to drop back to the main group because he was officially signed up with the 'Walking Bus' (unlike the 'casual walkers' from the Dybvig family).

The young boy and the Dybvigs ignored the woman and kept walking ahead of the group.

She kept barking orders.

Her dog kept barking.

We kept ignoring her.

Finally, Stroppy Mom rushed forward to catch up with us and screeched that our son's friend must walk with the group.

I told her that I was a parent - an older parent at that - and we were just fine strolling as we were. We kept walking.

She wasn't happy.

'I'm responsible,' she said, alluding to her formal designation as 'Conductor'.

I assured her that I would take responsibility for the kids walking with me.

No, she insisted. She was the assigned 'Conductor'.

Drawing on the benefits of a college education, and almost six decades of worldly experience, I told her to piss off. Not the most elegant of rebuttals, I concede, but it seemed to fit the moment.

In no time we arrived at the corner crosswalk to the school and were soon joined by the rest of the group.

We were all standing on the corner waiting for the light to change so I asked, 'What's the problem? We're all here...'

Stroppy Mom immediately started to squawk that she was responsible for ensuring we kept to rules for health and safety.

I shook my head and told her she was paying more attention to her damn dog than the kids.

'Look, lady, you're the safety problem!'

This sparked her into overdrive, declaring, 'Oh I know all about you.'

This was starting to be fun. I was like a dog with a bone now.

'Oh yeah, whaddaya know? Come on, spill the beans, might be interesting to find out all about me.'

By now, another mother rushed forward and told me not to yell in front of the children.

I told her I wasn't yelling and that I was just talking loudly in my normal voice. I told her to get a life; the kids weren't going to melt.

That afternoon, when it was time to collect the kids from school, the headmaster marched up to me and demanded to know why I had been yelling at the mothers.

How do you explain? And where do you start?

Walking to school isn't exactly the most complicated activity but some people seem intent on making it so. The 'Walking Bus' had managed to operate for a couple of years without a problem. The arrival of one new bossy bitch, and a dog, had changed everything.

The 'Walking Bus' idea fizzled out soon after my grumpy exchange with Stroppy Mom, and I didn't see her or the dog again.

Comment: But I was left wondering why I always managed to end up being The Bad Guy.

Listening to Kids

Recalling my own childhood, and the lack of communication with my dad, I was determined to try to listen to my kids, and to have meaningful conversations with them whenever I could.

When Sam started school, he also started going to the Bible classes there. They had been learning about the crucifixion and Sam explained to me in no uncertain terms that Jesus got snagged on a tree.

I said, chuckling, "Yeah, that's one way of looking at it."

Later that week, I picked up Sam in my Jeep and had the most unusual of conversations with him. He began telling me about a girl in his class who spoke Burmese and was from Downing Sindrum, which I assumed was the name of the Burmese town she came from. He said she took a while to speak and be understood by the other kids.

Seeing this as an opportunity to converse with my son, I launched into an explanation about world politics and how there had been a revolution in Burma so it was now called Myanmar, though some people continued to call it Burma and the country was really ruled by one of the world's toughest military juntas, and every once in a while the country's monks would march in protest but they were always brutally put down.

I paused for breath and checked that young Sam was taking all this in. He looked nonplussed.

It wasn't till much later when I replayed the conversation in my head. Downing Sindrum. I realized that Sam had meant Down Syndrome. The little girl must have Down Syndrome.

I chuckled to myself, marveling at how easily I manage to make any situation more complicated than it really needs to be.

Comment: The interesting thing here is that Sam was being given Bible lessons in a public school without the parents' knowledge or consent. I have absolutely no problem with this but this would never have happened in America where everyone is so over the top anal about religion. In fact when Sam was three we sent him to a Baptist day care center mainly because I thought he should get the opportunity to play with other little kids. My father-in-law questioned the fact that the day care center was of Baptist origin. I just told him I wasn't overly concerned with who prayed for my son.

Go with The Flow
The older I get, the more I learn from my relationship with my children and about myself and the relationship with my own father. It's not always easy to realize which parts of our behaviour are inherited or result from the habits we learned from our parents.

Remembering my father's strict views, I have always been anxious that I don't impose myself on our kids in the same way.

I want my children to learn to think for themselves and be tolerant of others' views. I've always enjoyed debating anything with anyone, and I have no problems talking to the Mormons or the Seventh Day Adventists or the Jehovah's Witnesses who knock on our door. Jennifer always clears out when I settle in for a robust discussion.

If Sam is there, I encourage him to take part which can be difficult for a youngster. But I explain to him that he doesn't have to agree with what someone else tells him, he can make up his own mind about these matters.

I encourage him to show some tolerance to others, even if you think what the other guy is saying is a load of crap. Everyone is entitled to their opinion as long as they don't force it on you.

The Mormons
I've had a few brief encounters with the Mormons. When I was thirteen I signed up to the Mormon Church so I could play in their softball league in Modesto, California. That night two Mormon Elders dropped by the house... their visit was brief... it was like they were in a revolving door... they walked in announced who they were and my dad just immediately turned them around and marched them right back out the front door... my Mormon membership and softball career was just as short.

In New Zealand one year the Women's national basketball tournament was being held in Hamilton... Temple View is a nearby suburb... this is where the only Mormon Temple in the South Pacific is located... one of my players had an aunt who lived in Temple View and she kindly let me and my team stay there for the week of the tournament... well one bloke in a house with 12 women didn't sit all that well with the Mormon Elders... they came to visit... which cracked me up because they were a posse of little old wizened guys all dressed in black... I assured them that all would be fine and there wasn't going to be any hanky panky.

And then during the basketball season we had several games in the Church College stadium and every time we went there this same posse of little old men dressed in black would visit me before the game and gently remind me of where I was... the point being everyone knew how volatile I could get during a game and with Mormonism being such a family oriented religion there were always a ton of families in the stands... I always assured them that I knew exactly where I was and that I would do my best to respect the Lord.

Comment: To get a different view of the Mormon religion than I got from those wizened little old men read 'Under the Banner of Heaven: A Story of Violent Faith' by John Krakauer... this is a story about the origin and evolution of The Church of Jesus Christ of Latter-day Saints, and a modern double murder committed in the name of God by brothers Ron and Dan Lafferty, who subscribed to a fundamentalist version of Mormonism. Excellent book... I highly recommend it.

Nuts

As a dad, I try to give good advice to the kids. But my track record isn't that great when I look back at some of the decisions I've made in my own life. But I try my best, with varying results.

When Sam was seven, he came home from school saying a kid was bugging him and pestering him all the time. My solution was straightforward enough - I told Sam to tell the kid to stop it or he would kick him square in the nuts.

It's the only time Sam has ever been sent to the headmaster's office. But, the kid did stop bothering him.

Lily knows better than to take my advice without thinking it through. When she was seven, she was also on the receiving end of a girl who was annoying her.

Recalling my previous advice to Sam, I thought a non-violent approach might be better, so I suggested to Lily that she might tell this little girl to 'piss off'.

'Dad,' she admonished, with a look of horror, 'we're not allowed to say that at school.'

Sensible girl. She must get it from her mother...

Comment: Yeah... yeah... I know that being so straight forward in today's world is not how it's done... but that's just me... I'm an old fashioned kind of guy who calls a spade a spade... and I still think that getting straight to the heart of the matter is a better way to go than dancing all around it with touchy... feely language that never really addresses the issue...

Case in point: At my children's primary school as is normal there was this one kid who was a jerk... a little smart aleck who was always giving the other kids a hard time... well this one time he picked on the wrong kid because this little whipper snapper just turned around and punched him straight in the face... and yeah the bully never bothered him again...

But as is usual with schools today they thought this one punch was akin to the Battle of the Bulge and addressed it accordingly with grave conferences and meetings and bringing in the parents and school councilors for an endless session of pow wows... and naturally nobody came out and said that the bully actually got what he deserved... but in the end I was absolutely delighted with the dad of the kid who threw the punch... this dad told me that he was as Happy as Larry that his kid stood his ground... and you could tell that he was one proud dad that his kid was no push over... in fact he told me that he was taking his kid out to dinner to celebrate...

Having experienced both my kids going through the school system this is the thing you've got to remember about schools... they are never concerned about the children if anything goes wrong... oh no... their first concern is always to protect their own asses... every school writes reams and reams of flowery language about their strict policy that bullying will not be tolerated in their school... but that's all it is - a lot of mumbo jumbo bullshit because in reality when push comes to shove school administrators do absolutely nothing because they're too afraid to stick their neck out in case they offend someone by actually getting to the truth.

Father and Son

When I found out my father had died from a heart attack while pushing a full wheelbarrow of wet cement, I couldn't believe that he'd been dumb enough to be doing something like that when he knew he had a dodgy ticker.

He had incredibly high blood pressure and lugging wet cement was the last thing he should have been doing. He was 57 when he died.

When I was in my fifties, I discovered I had heart problems of a different kind. My blood pressure was too low because my heart wasn't pumping enough blood through my system.

After hearing the diagnosis from a heart specialist, I stopped off at the supermarket where my Jeep stalled, the victim of a low battery. My response?

I jumped out and tried to push start it by myself in the blazing hot sun, sweating and wheezing like an 80-year-old.

Like father, like son.

Comment: Once I got home I did realize how incredibly stupid I had been. Although I was going to be even stupider in the not too distant future. I was in Guangzhou, China on a business trip with my wife Jennifer. My first clue that something wasn't quite right took place in the hotel massage parlor where Jennifer and I were getting a foot message. We had walked so much my legs had swollen to the point it looked like I had elephantiasis. The Chinese gal giving me my foot message kept poking her finger deep into my puffy leg and then would launch into hysterics and laugh herself silly while all the others in the room would look over and just bust up.

I just thought the long plane flight along with all the walking we did had puffed up my legs.

When we got home I continued to do my neighbourhood paper route. Then one day as I was walking up a slight incline I just stopped dead in my tracks... couldn't take another step and my mouth had that watery feeling like I was going to vomit.

I stopped and just stood there and about five minutes later I could resume my walking. I just brushed this off like I normally do with anything that concerns my body like not taking notice of anything unusual will automatically fix it.

This occurred on a Friday... that night was Jennifer's big turning fifty party.

We partied hard dancing the night away. Later that night I had this terrible chest pain and I still didn't get it.

Sunday night I had another huge pain in my chest so I thought I would go see my doctor the next day. When I explained what my symptoms were I wasn't even half-way finished when he immediately sent me to see my heart specialist.

My heart specialist said I needed an immediate angiogram... like right this minute.

He went in and discovered that both the main arteries to my heart were 99 per cent blocked.

Then on the screen he showed me what looked like a little bubble gum bubble and he said that is what we call a 'widow maker'... that bursts and you're dead. period.

So there ya go I was running around all over China and back here in New Zealand and I could have dropped dead at any second from a massive heart attack.

The signs were all there and I failed miserably at reading them.

In the end I was just one lucky son-of-a-bitch!

Dogs

When it came to coaching my son's soccer team I quickly discovered why I prefer dogs: When Sam turned five I volunteered to coach his soccer team. I was really looking forward to coaching my little guy and all his little buddies, after all it looked like so much fun when Steve Martin did it in 'The Parent Trap' movies - but I never really totally enjoyed the experience because my genetic DNA spells: "COMPETITOR" loud and clear, meaning that every Saturday I had to constantly police myself to keep that competitive streak under control.

The thing is when you're dealing with younger kids it all comes down to cats and dogs. Kids are like cats. They do what they want to do when they want to do it.

My first year as a weekend soccer coach to a team of five year olds was interesting to say the least - they used to just stop playing right in the middle of the game and hug each other.

The first time this happened, the competitive beast in me wanted to snarl and scream, "Stop that right now, there's no hugging during the game!"

But, as a parent it just doesn't get any cuter than that. Kids are here and there and everywhere but you never really know where they're at or where they're coming from, which is usually nowhere at all.

On a coaching level I prefer dogs. Dogs are somewhere. They are always coming from somewhere and going somewhere and they obey commands.

Comment: Coaching at that level had all kinds of challenges... we had one kid who was so nervous about going onto the field that his dad actually held his hand the whole time while the kid was running up and down playing the game... hilarious and touching at the same time.

Pedal to the Metal
But, that doesn't mean you can't teach kids the fundamentals of sport, being an ex-basketball coach means my boy can dribble a basketball with either hand and he knows the correct fundamentals of how to shoot. When Sam was just eight years old playing in his elementary school competition he executed a killer cross-over to blow by two defenders and scored a basket. I can tell you that I was one proud father sitting up in the stands - I was happy to see him score but hey the cross-over dribble at such a young age had me glowing.

Town Sheriff
I sometimes look at Sam and wonder how much he takes after me.

How much of my personality has he inherited?

Have I passed on some of my baggage to him?

He's certainly more sensitive than me, but he's also picked up some of my American sarcasm. One day we were driving to school and we saw one of Sam's schoolmates walking to school in his uniform but wearing tennis shoes. The school rules insist the students wear black shoes, with school socks pulled up.

I started to slow the car so I could give the kid a little shot.

Sam showed his sensitive side.

'Come on, Dad. Don't say anything,'

I yelled through the window to the kid: 'Hey, buddy, what's with the tennis shoes?'

The startled kid looked up, confused.

I drove off, sensing that Sam didn't approve.

'What are you, Dad?' he asked. 'The town sheriff?'

I busted up.

Pirates

One of the great pleasures of having children is that they provide a wonderful excuse for an adult to indulge in the shenanigans of childhood.

When Sam was three, he loved pirates. So, when we went to Castaway Island in Fiji for Christmas, I told him we'd dig for buried treasure.

In the afternoon, while Sam was napping, I travelled to the far side of the island and buried a small pirate treasure chest filled with Fijian coins and a pirate sword, marking the spot with some pieces of drift wood in the sign of an X.

When Sam woke, he put on his pirate outfit and we set off on our grand adventure. What a lovely feeling it was, walking with my boy along that deserted beach watching his excitement grow. We hiked over some rocks and there it was, that hallowed X. Sam squealed with delight and dug furiously, soon discovering the chest and sword.

The expression on his face brought tears to my eyes.

We sat and discussed all the possibilities about how that treasure and sword came to be buried at that spot. I don't know who had more fun, Sam or his dad.

Part Three

WISDOM

What I've Learned

So, with many of my crazy lives already lived, it's time to reflect on a life that is less crazy now that I've found love with Jennifer and my children.

All the same, there is much I have learned...

I've learned that I was a late bloomer - never was it more blindingly evident than when I received a card in the mail from an old high school classmate, proudly announcing the graduation of her two sons from university. I replied with hearty congratulations on a job well done and just as proudly announced the enrolment of Sam at kindergarten.

I've learned never to surrender my dreams, no matter how tough life gets or how many times they seemed impossible. I always kept them alive. I don't let the opinions of others affect what I do in life. I won't be influenced by the negativity of others. You know what I mean, people without imaginations are always saying things like 'that can't be done' or 'I don't think that's a good idea' or 'I don't know about that' or 'that's embarrassing, that might make you look foolish'.

I've learned that not everyone understands my ability to live to excess. When I went to work for Gonzaga University, I told them I liked nothing more than to talk to fellow basketball coaches, to help me learn more about the game. As part of my deal, they gave me an 'unlimited phone account'. Rarely a day went by without me calling a coach in America, Europe or Australia. It wasn't long before the financial controller called me into his office to tell me I had overspent my unlimited account!

I've learned to dare to change. I started my life again at 42 when I realised it was heading in the wrong direction. I learned it was never too late to change.

I've learned to take people as I find them. In return, I love it when I'm accepted for what, and who, I am. I was once invited to speak to the movers and shakers from multinational computer giants, IBM. Their conference was at Auckland's Sheraton Hotel and I pulled up outside the front doors in a dilapidated wreck of a car that I started with a screwdriver.

The doorman, in top hat and full posh hotel regalia, opened my door, inviting me to step out so my car could be valet parked. I waved the screwdriver and was about to explain my predicament. The doorman simply said, 'I understand.' And by his manner and the tone of his voice, I knew straight away he really did understand and there would be no problem. I just thought to myself - that's very cool.

I've learned to appreciate the value of outstanding teachers. Nothing beats your 10-year-old son coming home from school declaring that reading is way better than watching television.

I've learned to hustle. It's about attitude, and not selling yourself short. Don't worry about whether you have the talent, brains or ability, just get out there and ask for your opportunity. You'll be surprised how smart you turn out to be.

I've learned to encourage my kids not to worry about failing. By the time we reach adulthood, we are conditioned to see failure as a major crisis, whereas children should see failure as a way to learn. I encourage Sam and Lily to believe that the most important thing is to try, and if they don't succeed at first, it's no big deal.

I've learned that there are few objects more powerful than a television camera. At the 2000 Sydney Olympics, I had the rare opportunity to interview 80-year-old Sir Edmund Hillary at the famous Sydney Opera House.

On the same trip, I bumped into former Australian Prime Minister Bob Hawke and we chatted for some time. I climbed Sydney's Harbor Bridge, enjoyed a free aerial view of Sydney in a small seaplane and was treated to a gourmet meal beside the city's harbor.

Did I land all these goodies by being a deserving guy with a persuasive nature? No way. Most doors open to anyone with a crew and a camera.

I've learned not to live with regrets. When my father died, no one from our family spoke at his funeral. We let an undertaker who never knew him speak about his life.

I felt it was wrong and wanted to get up and say something on his behalf. But I hesitated, which was so unlike me, and the moment passed. I always regretted it. When my mother passed on, I made sure I stood and spoke about her life. I felt I had put something right.

I've learned that some parents just don't get what's really important. One morning I watched my children's primary school headmaster addressing the kids. He carefully told the assembled young students how important manners were and when speaking to an adult they should look them in the eye. The mother standing next to me started to walk away.

'I wonder if he'll ever say anything of importance,' she said, with a look of flippant disregard.

I've learned to knock. I once barged into the make-up room at TV3 and caught then Prime Minister Helen Clark half-naked getting dressed. I hastily apologised and excused myself.

I've learned to be more relaxed about stuff. For instance, I love taking my kids with me to work - that means they've come along with me to auditions, television appearances and for radio shows.

It's a wonderful reflection of life in New Zealand that with few exceptions, they are welcomed and accepted in a natural way. It's also helped the kids build confidence and feel at ease in an adult world.

I learned at 50 there's no better feeling in the world than to smile at your wee one and have that smile beamed right back at you.

I've learned to be more aware of what's happening around me, especially when it concerns my children and their lives. I try to make it a point of asking them about their day, what happened at school and about their problems and conflicts. I try to listen to their stories. I try not to get so wrapped up in myself - which is something I can still do, make no mistake. But I try to pull myself back because I want to be a more rounded person, more than ever before. It's an evolving process.

I've learned that if all you've got is yelling and screaming, you won't last. To be honest, I think I knew that all along. If you can teach people skills and techniques and respect for what you're doing, you've got something people want.

I've learned that gentle persistence can pay off. Ever since our kids were young, I've tried to tempt them with American soft drinks that I love. But they simply hate A&W Root Beer and find another favorite of mine, Dr Pepper, disgusting. But I've got them into Crème Soda which at least means we can share a drink together.

I've learned that when it comes down to a conversation between yourself and your wife, it doesn't matter who is right and who is wrong.

It counts for squat. Letting go of your fixed position is what it's all about.

I've learned that doing a good job can be stronger than any form of legal contract. When I took my first basketball job in New Zealand, I refused to sign a contract, saying if at any stage they didn't like what I was doing, they could let me go. In fact, I didn't sign a contract with any sports club I worked for, nor did I sign any paperwork for Sky, Television New Zealand or TV3. When TV3 was taken over by new owners, I was working on three of their shows. In the shake-up that followed the takeover, I was called into a senior executive's office.

'John,' he said, 'we can't seem to find your contract.'

I explained the situation and saw the light go on behind his eyes. I realised right away it wouldn't be long before I would be gone. I do have to put a caveat in here: I did all this cavalier not signing contracts stuff when I was on my own, when I was a completely wild boy who literally didn't give a shit about rules and contracts and all kinds of other important stuff. But, now having a family to look after please show me a contract before I do anything. Thank-you.

I've learned that nothing will beat the memories you can create simply by spending time with your loved ones. I'd always loved boogie boarding and the whole experience of being in the sea, with its salty taste and being in the sun and sand. The thrill of the ride as you catch the wave and drop down to scoot towards the shore is exhilarating.

But no matter how many times I had enjoyed a day's boarding it would never match the first day I took Lily out on the water at Long Beach in Russell. To watch the delight on a child's face as they finally master that tricky first connection with the wave is hard to beat.

And all it costs is time. And love.

I've learned that some things can't be explained, no matter how hard you try. After my mother passed away, I was given a beautiful framed chalk drawing of her when she was a young waitress. When I got home to New Zealand I hung it in pride of place in our front hallway.

Exactly one year from the day she died, that picture fell off the wall. And it hasn't budged since.

I've learned that there are forces out there that we're not aware of... period! Eons ago when I was working for my high school buddy Rick Korte at the High Sierra Casino in Lake Tahoe he borrowed $200 bucks from me to make a payment on his car. No big deal. I gave him the money and didn't really expect to get it back. I didn't.

Moving forward 15 years and I'm living in New Zealand and have totally lost any contact with Rick. Then one night I have this explicit dream of Rick Korte it's one of those dreams where you'd swear that the two of you were talking and running around doing stuff. This dream was so vivid and clear in my mind the next morning I told my wife Jennifer all about it. That very same afternoon I get a letter in the mail from Rick Korte with a check for $200 dollars in it. Explain that.

I've learned to never be surprised by anything: One year this guy in Fiji tried to hustle Jennifer and myself into buying a fake gold necklace. He and I and Jennifer found ourselves in a booth in a bar (his hangout) where I had bought a round of beers for everyone. We ended up in that booth because naturally I just struck up a conversation with this complete stranger much to the chagrin of Jennifer.

Finally when we finished our beers and I told him in no uncertain terms that we weren't in the market for his gold necklaces I went up to the cash register to pay for the beers. This guy follows me up there and get this: He actually asks me for a tip. Yeah, that's right the guy wants me to tip him for trying to hustle us. My immediate thought was one of being flabbergasted...the gall of the guy... the nerve... what the hell.... I look at him in utter disbelief and exclaim, "why should I tip you - I bought the beers!"

He calmly replies that he worked hard in trying to hustle me... that was his reasoning he actually confessed that he was hustling us. Amazing really. So we're standing there and I really want to tell him to go fuck himself but then I look over at the joint's bouncer a 6'9" towering piece of granite disguised as a human being standing in the doorway who is giving me the death stare so I offer the guy a measly $5 bucks which I'm thinking there's no way in hell he's going to accept that but he happily does.

I still can't believe the guy took a measly five bucks. I'm still shaking my head as I type this... the world is definitely a strange place.

I've learned that once your mother closes down a topic of conversation... that's it... discussion of said topic is closed period. Case in point: When I turned 18, I had to sign up for the draft in the American military. To do that, I had to take my original birth certificate to the local draft board. You can imagine my surprise when my mom gave me my birth certificate and it listed my name as John Thomas Brown.

My mother had been married to a sailor by the name of Brown and he apparently was my real father when she hooked up with the man I had always considered to be my real father, Donald Dybvig.

Despite my change of name, I remained curious about my lineage. My older brother and older sister both looked alike, with the same nose and facial features. But my younger sister and I didn't share their features - we both had the same large Norwegian hook nose as we saw on our 'father', Donald Dybvig. After checking the date I was born and when my mother hooked up with Donald Dybvig, I suspected he might be my true father after all.

In the late 1940's, when they were together but not married, society frowned on couples who 'lived in sin' so maybe they had taken the safe route and given me the surname on my mother's wedding certificate.

Late in my mother's life, I decided to try to settle the mystery once and for all. Jennifer and I had flown to the States for my mom's 80th birthday and we took her for a drive around our old neighbourhood.

As we reminisced about the days of my childhood, I put the question to her directly: "Mom, is Donald Dybvig my real father?" I asked.

My mother thought for a second and then looked me full in the eye. "I've always been a good girl," she said.

And that was all she ever said on the subject. The file was closed and will remain that way.

I've learned that I'll always be a goofy West Coast American no matter where I am. I was living in a little square box of a place in Napier. It was in the middle of a sprawling suburban housing sub-division and to say I found it depressing is an understatement.

So I arranged for trailer-loads of pure white sand to be brought to the house and I turned my living room into my own beach. It was beautiful, especially when I added coconuts, suntan oil, jandals and a small bucket and spade. The finishing touch was one of my dazzlingly bright Hawaiian shirts which I hung on the back wall.

I learned a valuable lesson while working on one of New Zealand's local soaps in one of my first acting roles - namely that physical contact with female actors should be discussed prior to shooting.

I was playing a con man with a spunky assistant. In our first scene I was supposed to meet her in a café. At the last minute, I decided to improvise. I came in, slid behind her and gave her a quick peck on the cheek. All hell broke loose! She shrieked and whipped her head back and forth several times, giving our noses a chance to get better acquainted. The director yelled: "John, John, what are you doing?" He got up out of his chair and hurried onto the set, frantically looking through his script. "There's no kissing in this scene!"

"Oh." I thought I was trying to be artistic, but everybody else thought I was just a sleezeball.

I've learned that all you have to do to be an instant expert on anything is to put a patch on the pocket of a blue blazer.

One year I was asked to be the color guy for television's coverage of the Auckland Summer Racing Carnival. They gave me a nice pair of slacks to wear, white shirt and tie and a beautiful blue blazer with a snazzy patch on the pocket which boldly stated: TV3 Racing above a picture of a race horse.

There was only one slight problem. I knew one end of a horse from the other, and that was about the limit of my knowledge.

But the general public didn't know that did they - all they saw was the official-looking patch on my breast pocket declaring me to be a horse racing guy. Supposedly a guy with some inside knowledge. I can't tell you how many people came sniffing around thinking I might give them some tips. I'd be standing there in front of a horse and someone would casually sidle up to me and say, "beautiful looking animal." And I'd look at the horse standing there and just agree with them, "yeah good looking horse." And that's all I would ever say. People walked away disappointed.

I've learned that not everyone thinks Disneyland is cool. The first year the kids show Power Rangers starting filming in New Zealand I was their American accent coach for their young cast of New Zealand and Australian actors. The very first day we were sitting around the conference table about to do a read thru of the first episode's script. Before that started as everyone was getting settled in the young actors were discussing the show Fear Factor where one of the challenges is to eat disgusting stuff when one of kids asked the question: "Would you eat shit on that show?" The executive producer of Power Rangers who was sitting right next to me said, "I eat shit everyday - I work for Disney."

I've learned that no matter how hard you try, many people like to put you in whatever pigeon hole makes them feel comfortable.

I remember going to my first Christmas bash at my acting agent's place and an actor couldn't hide his surprise.

'What are you doing here? You're a sports guy.' Clearly, anyone who had coached basketball could not become an actor.

I've learned that no matter how long I live in New Zealand, I'll still try every so often to open the passenger's door of the car when I want to drive.

I've learned that dogs know best: I was walking my dog in an industrial area when we came upon a bowl of water sitting on the grass verge outside a garden warehouse. It was an extremely hot day. My dog was thirsty so when he spied the bowl of water he went over to it for a nice noisy slurp.

Suddenly some guy came storming out of the warehouse screaming, "Hey, stop that dog - that's a birdbath bowl. I stood there looking at the guy in bemusement and fired back, "Hey man you can't be serious... a bowl of water on the ground is a dog bowl to a dog... a birdbath bowl sits up on a pedestal. Get a grip."

I've learned to keep things in perspective: President Bill Clinton said that one of the lessons he learned early in his Presidency was to compartmentalise. In other words the job was so vast with so many problem areas that he had to push aside the myriad of obstacles in his way each day and concentrate on the task at hand. Give your all to the moment then move on to the next don't let the complexity of your position freeze you into accomplishing nothing.

My late mother was like that she was a fighter all the way. Late in life after her husband my father passed she totally reinvented herself while having to declare bankruptcy which was pretty damn tough at her age, but did that stop her? Hell no! She immediately went out and fanangled her way into purchasing a lovely mobile home and carried on. I greatly admired her tenacity and her determination to not let little problems like having no money stop her from getting what she wanted. The other thing she did during this period was to become a salesperson for one of those national companies that sell what they advertise as miracle cleaning products. When I visited her one year I discovered that all of her closets were stuffed full of said products. I asked her if she sold anything and her answer floored me.

Oh no she said... she wasn't interested in selling anything... rather she enjoyed going to the conventions they held... she went to Las Vegas... New Orleans and even South Korea... amazing really. But, the point is she was enjoying life... traveling... meeting new people... and talking... gawd she loved to talk. I went with her to one of the local conventions and there I heard this story and I've always kind of kept it in the back of my mind.

The Monk & The Strawberry
We all worry way too much. Money, career, wife, girlfriend, boyfriend, pimples, fat, thin, wobbly, thinning hair, no hair, too much hair, asking a girl for a date, college entrance exams, am I cool?, diet, exercise, what car to buy.

Then parenthood throws in a whole new set of worries: Are we good parents, braces for the kids' teeth, what school to send them to, prom night, kids and drugs, kids and alcohol, kids driving! The list is endless and in a lot of cases pointless.

The next time you get caught in a 'worry wobble' just think of the 'Monk and the Strawberry'.

In the middle of a dense jungle sits a Buddhist Monk. He's praying. The monk is in silent meditation totally immersed in the moment until he senses something - the slightest movement - that movement turns out to be a huge Bengal Tiger on his haunches slowly creeping up stalking him. The Monk hesitates for the briefest of seconds before leaping to his feet and tearing through the jungle, putting all of his new found faith into his pumping legs as he's running for his life with the Bengal Tiger in hot pursuit. The Monk is running for all he's worth but the Bengal Tiger is rapidly gaining on him with every bound. Suddenly without warning the jungle ends. The Monk screeches to a shuddering halt, before him is a thousand-foot cliff. The Monk frantically looks everywhere for an escape route when he spies a vine dangling over the cliff, falling to the valley floor below.

Just as the Tiger leaps the Monk leaps, throwing caution to the wind he flies over the cliff scrambling wildly to grab that vine. Holding on for dear life the Monk looks up and nearly loses his head as the Bengal Tiger stretches over the cliff and takes a long swipe at his intended prey. Quickly arching back the Monk instinctively starts to scuttle down the vine. Half way down the vine the Monk looks back up in fear as the frustrated Tiger is staring down at him roaring his head off. The Monk gathers himself and then looks down and screams in renewed terror - for at the bottom of the vine waiting for him circles another Bengal Tiger roaring his head off in anticipation. The Monk is stuck, he's clutching the vine with nowhere to go.

The Monk is pondering his situation when suddenly a very large jungle rat leaps out of a crevice in the face of the cliff and immediately begins gnawing on the vine. What a pickle he's in now. The sweat is readily pouring off his worried face. What to do? The Monk looks up at the Bengal Tiger bellowing from above.

The Monk looks down to the Bengal Tiger virtually licking his lips below. And finally the Monk looks over at the jungle rat busily gnawing his way through the vine. In the midst of all this the Monk notices a single ripe plump strawberry growing out of the side of the cliff, within his reach. The Monk gazes intently at this strawberry. Finally he plucks it and bites into it and delights at the pleasure of the sweet nectar as it runs down the sides of his mouth. And the Monk enjoys that strawberry.

The moral of this tale is simple:

Too often we spend all our time worrying about everything that has happened to us in our past (the tiger at the top of the cliff). And too often we spend too much time worrying about what might happen to us in the future (the tiger at the bottom of the cliff). Or, worst of all, we spend too much time worrying about the nibbling, nagging worries of each and every day (the rat). And when a true strawberry in our life comes along, we forget to pluck it, eat it, and most of all... ENJOY it! Problems in the past (Bengal Tiger at the top of the cliff) and problems in your future (Bengal Tiger at the bottom of the cliff) will always be there. Don't let worrying about them prevent you from enjoying what you're doing...

Right now!

Finally
Homer's Odyssey Idiocy truly belongs to all of us: I've learned that I can spend my life travelling to the farthest corners of the planet, searching for life's thrills and a pot of gold, but true happiness sits right beside me. There's no better feeling in the world than to pick up your wee ones and have them stroke your shoulder absent-mindedly because they feel safe and snug in your arms. Every day I wake up to the family I love. My wife's family lives just up the road. We're in this life together. I found my soul mate and a life I thought had passed me by.

What more could I ask for? I have all I need.

John Dybvig

Epilogue

Tidy Guy

I've got bladder cancer. A lot of people have cancer of one type or another. It's sad, it's tragic, it's a lot of things, but it's not unusual. The only interesting thing about my cancer at least to me is how I discovered it.

I'm not a clean freak type of guy. I'm more of a tidy guy. Sometimes I'm extra fastidious, orderly, I like my 'ducks in a row' so shoot me, everybody's got their little quirks mine is straightening crooked pictures hanging on the wall even when they're not in my own home. My wife Jennifer likes to recount the first time she visited my flat in Mission Bay. She opened one of the cupboards to discover that I had several packets of dried peas standing lined up in neat order at the back of the cupboard. They stood out because otherwise the cupboard was empty. I remember lining these packets up the very first day I moved into the flat. The packets weren't even mine, they came with the flat. I opened the cupboard and there they were lying scattered about.

Without giving it too much thought I just gathered them up and neatly lined them up against the back of the cupboard. Neat and orderly. Like I said I like a world that's squared away. I lived in that flat for four years, the packets were still lined up when I left.

Then one day I have a moment that changes my life forever. September 21st 2016 early afternoon blue skies and the sun is shining brightly and I'm running a little behind for a few appointments in town.

I dash out of the house in dress slacks, button-down long sleeve shirt and highly polished dress shoes. I hurry up to my car in the driveway open the door and am just about to slide in... when? When what?

I have a moment that literally changes my life. Why that moment and why that moment at that particular time is the big question here.

Why? Why... in the world did I do what I did. I had absolutely no reason to do this but something... some mysterious force propelled me to do it. I paused for the briefest of seconds and looked up. It felt like someone or something was telling me to look up. I looked up at the hedge that stands about thirty feet above our driveway.

This is about the time you have to ask yourself the question: Why do we do these random acts - is it blind luck or do you believe it's more complex than that?

I looked up and saw a nice orderly shaped hedge except for a few errant twigs sticking out here and there. I hesitated and stood there for a second squinting at those rebellious twigs ruining the perfect shape of my hedge.

Being the nut job that I am I sprang into action. I could have trimmed those sticky out bits later when I got back or the next day for that matter. There was no rush. But, I'm an orderly type of guy. I was annoyed that the hedge wasn't even. So I quickly shut the car door, hustled into the garage, got my ladder out, extended it to its full height, retrieved my weed whip, got my 25 foot extension cord out, unraveled it, plugged one end of it into the wall socket in the garage, plugged the other end into the weed whip and commenced to climb.

Why? What drove me?

Do you believe in Angels looking over you?

Suddenly I'm standing on my ladder high in the air with my arms above my head holding an outstretched unwieldy weed whip trying to clip some messy twigs.

My mind is not on the job at hand, instead it's on those errands I'm supposed to be doing. I lost my balance. And plummeted straight down onto the main beam of the wooden trellis over the garage.

I'm not a small guy. I'm 6' 3" weighing in at around the 230, 240 mark. I landed with a massive thump instantly sucking all the wind from me. I was stunned and could barely breathe.

Fortunately because I had my arms outstretched above my head when I came down I instinctively hooked my arm over the beam as I bounced off of it thus preventing me from smashing my head into the pavement below.

I hung there like a monkey with my one arm draped over the beam entangled in my weed whip cord dazed and trying to breathe. Finally I was able to grab the beam and lower myself down to the ground.

But, something wasn't quite right. I still couldn't breathe. I tried to man it out by slowly walking around, but my rib cage was killing me.

My wife Jennifer took me to the Emergency room at the hospital. I was given a CT scan. They wanted to check to see if maybe the fall had done some damage to my liver. Instead they found that I had cracked a couple of ribs and oh yeah they discovered a small tumour in my bladder. I had to go through the whole nine yards of having a biopsy and consultation with a surgeon. The news wasn't good. Turns out it was top shelf invasive bladder cancer. I had no symptoms. I felt great. My doctor told me that bladder cancer is known as the silent killer because generally speaking when you've discovered that you've got it, it's already too late. I found mine early by falling off that ladder. That fall saved my life.

So, was it just blind luck, dumb luck... what?

Maybe... just maybe it was someone looking after me?

Thank you Lord!

Acknowledgments

Wow... this is a tough one. Lots and lots of people have helped me get to this point with this book. But the most important people are my family: My wife Jennifer is one tough cookie. And yet on the flip-side she's as tender and loving a person as you would ever want to meet. She supports me one hundred percent and then some and yet she takes no guff from me. Definitely keeps me on my toes... so thank you sweetie!

My children... and I gotta say I love writing that... my children... are a daily inspiration. I love their enthusiasm and energy. They too take no guff from me and have their own opinions on any topic you care to discuss...which also keeps me on my toes. So thanks guys... good job!

But I do need to especially mention someone outside my family: I met this joker 20 years ago in Ante-natal class and we've kept in touch ever since. So a special thanks goes out to Gavin McCardle who I can honestly say without his input getting this book in print would not have happened... not in a million years. And just like me Gavin is a family man so he's had his lovely wife Felicity and his son Chris and his daughter Anna carefully go over this manuscript to make it the best book it can possibly be so a huge thank-you to the entire McCardle family. And the really cool thing here is I can give Gavin as much guff as I want although I don't, we usually just talk about stuff... politics... our kids... the world... ha! Thanks big guy.